REVIEW OF TECHNOLOGIES AND DISRUPTIVE BUSINESS STRATEGIES

This book thoroughly analyses how technology and business strategy interact, providing practical advice for overcoming innovation's obstacles. An essential read for anyone hoping to influence change in the growing fields of innovation and technologies.

—***Carolyn Strong*, Professor,**
Cardiff Business School, Cardiff University,
Wales, UK

A seminal work that bridges the gap between theoretical exploration and practical application in the realm of technological disruption and innovation that will potentially transform the market and marketing research in the near future. I am pleased to recommended it for academics and practitioners alike in the service industry.

—***Metin Kozak*, Professor,**
Kadir Has University,
Turkey

This book masterfully navigates the complexities of disruptive technologies and their impact on business strategies. It is an essential read for those looking to understand the future of business in the digital age.

—***JP Verma*, Sr. Director and Head,**
Quantitative Finance, Trepp, Inc,
New York, United States

Through its insightful analysis and forward-thinking perspectives, 'Review of Technologies and Disruptive Business Strategies' offers a comprehensive exploration of the digital transformation landscape. An invaluable resource for strategists and innovators.

—***Mohita G Sharma*, Professor,**
Indian Institute of Management,
Shirmour, India

REVIEW OF MANAGEMENT LITERATURE

Series Editor: Sudhir Rana

Review of Management Literature is a multidisciplinary series presenting unique and groundbreaking literature reviews and examinations of new and emerging trends in research across the management discipline and beyond.

Examining broad disciplinary areas including new research developments in fields including Marketing, Operations Management, Finance, International Business, and HRM, as well as well as more focused studies on the big data and gamification in management literature, the series also explores practical research guidance with titles examining methodologies for conducting literature reviews in management domain.

Supported by a highly reputable editorial board from across the globe, the series will be an essential research resource to access and interpret cutting-edge global developments from across the management discipline.

VOLUMES IN THIS SERIES

Exploring the Latest Trends in Management Literature – Edited by Sudhir Rana, with Sakshi and Jagroop Singh

Advancing Methodologies for Conducting Literature Reviews in Management – Edited by Sudhir Rana with Jagroop Singh and Sakshi

EDITORIAL BOARD

EDITORIAL ADVISORY BOARD

Avinash K. Shrivastava
International Management Institute, India

Ekta Singhal
Lal Bahadur Shastri Institute of Management, India

Peter Stokes
Leicester Castle Business School, De Montfort University, UK

Huam Hon Tat
Putra Business School, UPM, Malaysia

Anand S. Upadhyay
College of Banking and Financial Studies, Oman

Justin Zuopeng Zhang
University of North Florida, USA

REVIEW OF MANAGEMENT LITERATURE VOLUME 3

REVIEW OF TECHNOLOGIES AND DISRUPTIVE BUSINESS STRATEGIES

EDITED BY

RAHUL PRATAP SINGH KAURAV
FORE School of Management, India

AND

VINAYTOSH MISHRA
Gulf Medical University, UAE

emerald PUBLISHING

United Kingdom – North America – Japan
India – Malaysia – China

Emerald Publishing Limited
Emerald Publishing, Floor 5, Northspring, 21-23 Wellington Street, Leeds LS1 4DL

First edition 2024

British Library Cataloguing in Publication Data
A catalogue record for this book is available from the British Library

ISBN: 978-1-83797-457-3 (Print)
ISBN: 978-1-83797-456-6 (Online)
ISBN: 978-1-83797-458-0 (Epub)

ISSN: 2754-5865 (Series)

Printed and bound by CPI Group (UK) Ltd, Croydon, CR0 4YY

CONTENTS

LIST OF FIGURES AND TABLES

Figures

Tables

ABOUT THE EDITORS

Rahul Pratap Singh Kaurav, an Associate Professor at FORE School of Management, New Delhi, specializes in Marketing Management and Analytics, emphasizing both teaching and research. With expertise in quantitative and qualitative research tools, he has contributed significantly to academic journals across various rankings. His global academic footprint extends to adjunct roles at the University of Liverpool, BITS-Pilani, and Taylor's University, Malaysia, underscoring his commitment to syllabus development and research efficacy.

Vinaytosh Mishra is the Director of Thumbay Institute for AI in Healthcare, Gulf Medical University, Ajman, UAE. He is also an Associate Professor (Healthcare Management, Digital Health and Health Analytics) with the College of Healthcare Management and Economics, Gulf Medical University, Ajman, UAE. He is a Post Doc Fellow in AI in Healthcare from the University of Arizona, USA, and a Post Doc Fellow in Ethical AI in Healthcare from the University of Ben Gurion, Israel. He has a PhD in Decision Science and Engineering (Healthcare Management) and a Bachelor of Technology in Electronics Engineering from the Indian Institute of Technology (BHU), India. Dr Mishra has over 19 years of experience in industries such as Information Technology, Manufacturing, Finance, Healthcare, and Education. He has one Australian and One German Patent in AI in Healthcare. He has more than 50 publications in journals of international repute.

ABOUT THE CONTRIBUTORS

Goknur Arzu Akyuz, Associate Professor in Logistics Management Department, University of Turkish Aeronautical Association (THK University). She has received her Bs degree from the Industrial Engineering Department, Middle East Technical University (METU). She has 12 years of experience in production planning and control and Enterprise Resources Planning (ERP) in different projects and sectors. She also holds an MSc degree in Computer Engineering and a PhD degree in MODES (Modeling and Design of Engineering Systems) from Atilim University. Her research interests include production planning and control, enterprise resources planning, and web-based supply chain management.

Dursun Balkan, Associate Professor in Industrial Engineering Department, University of Turkish Aeronautical Association (THK University). He has received his BSc, MSc, and PhD degrees in Industrial Engineering Department, Gazi University. He worked at National Productivity Center and Ministry of Science, Industry and Technology as Productivity Specialist. In 2017, he became an Institution Representative of the Ministry of Science, Industry and Technology at State Information Coordination Center of Presidency of the Republic of Turkey. He has offered various courses and consultancy services to public and private enterprises at different levels and participated in seminars and workshops at international organizations. His research interests include service systems management, productivity measurement and analysis, performance management, and facilities planning.

Shagun Chib did her PhD from the School of Business, Shri Mata Vaishno Devi University, Katra, India. She has published several research articles in various journals, e.g., *Children and Youth Services Review*, *Academy of Marketing Studies Journal*, Digital Creativity, etc. Her research interests include religious products, consumer psychology, and influencing marketing.

Manoj Kumar Dash is an Associate Professor in the Department of Management Studies at ABV-Indian Institute of Information Technology & Management, Gwalior (MP), since June 2023. He has a distinguished academic background, having earned MA, MPhil, and PhD degrees in Economics, along with an MBA in Marketing from Berhampur University, Odisha. His association with ABV IIITM Gwalior began on March 31, 2010. Possessing over 21 years of extensive teaching and research experience, Dr Dash is recognized for his expertise in Econometrics, Marketing Analytics, Consumer Decision-Making Styles, Entrepreneurship, and Innovation Management. He guided seven research scholars and awarded their PhD degrees, and he has completed six funded projects sponsored by ICSSR, MP School of Governance, State Open University Odisha, and MHRD, with an ongoing project funded by MSME.

Rahela Farooqi, a Professor at Department of Management Studies, Jamia Millia Islamia, New Delhi, with 25+ years of experience, brings subject expertise in Services Marketing, Retail Management, and E-marketing. She is also the Honorary Director of University Placement Cell at JMI for over 2 years. With a PhD in Management and an MBA from Aligarh Muslim University, she has numerous publications in refereed international and national journals published by Emerald, Sage, Springer, etc. Her paper presentations in international and national conferences span across India, Denmark, Germany, Malaysia, and Thailand covering prestigious institutions including IITs, IIMs, and MDI. Her remarkable contributions include a UGC-sponsored research project, editing management books, organizing workshops and conferences, guiding 20 doctoral students, and conducting extensive faculty development programs.

Sheereen Fauzel is an Associate Professor at the University of Mauritius. Having completed a PhD in Development Economics from the University of Mauritius, her areas of expertise are International and Development Economics, Tourism Economics, and related areas. She has participated in a number of international conferences. She has published extensively and been involved in a number of consultancy projects with Ministries, public institutions, and international organizations.

Surabhi Gore is an Assistant Professor in the Department of Bachelor of Business Administration (Travel and Tourism) at Rosary College of Commerce and Arts, Navelim, Goa, since 2012. She has 15 years of teaching and 4 years of industry experience. She has a doctorate in Management Studies from Goa University, Goa, India. Her research interests are tourism, strategy, planning and marketing, transport, services marketing, and customer relationship management. She has published research papers in national and international, indexed multidisciplinary and tourism journals.

Piyush Gupta is a Faculty in the area of Operations Management. He has done a PhD from the Indian Institute of Management (IIM) Ranchi and a postgraduation in MTech from the Indian Institute of Technology (IIT) Dhanbad in Industrial Engineering & Management. He has more than four years of teaching and research experience. He has published many high-quality papers in top journals such as *Information Technology & People*, *International Journal of Retail & Distribution Management*, *International Journal of Productivity & Performance Management*, to name a few. His research interests include service operations, behavioral operations research, process analysis and improvement. He has been involved in doing inter-disciplinary research as well. He is also serving as an Associate Editor in Emerald Publishing Journal.

Pooja Jain, Associate Professor in the area of Finance and Accounting at Amity Business School, Amity University, Gwalior, Madhya Pradesh. She actively focuses on research work. Some research work has been published in Scopus Listed Journals and reputed peer-reviewed journals. Till now, around 32 papers have been published in national and international publications, and some are in conference proceedings. Apart from research papers, she has written chapters in a reputed book which has been published in IGI Global, Routledge, and Taylor & Francis. She has also edited one book in the area of Finance. Her research interests include behavioral finance, financial management, and financial market, and her teaching interests include financial accounting and reporting, cost and management accounting, auditing, financial management, financial markets and services, project management, and behavioral finance.

Sahil Singh Jasrotia is currently working as an Assistant Professor at the International Management Institute, Kolkata, India. His research work has been published in prestigious journals such as the *International Journal of Retail and Distributions Management*, *Journal of Quality Assurance in Hospitality & Tourism*, *Society and Business Review*, *Asia Pacific Management Review*, etc. Throughout his academic career, Dr Sahil has displayed a dedication to research, teaching, and collaboration, making significant contributions to the field of Marketing, particularly in the areas of channel choice behavior, product adoption, digital payments, and corporate governance.

Sumi Jha is an Associate Dean and a Professor at the Indian Institute of Management Mumbai in India. She has published in international journals such as the *Journal of Business Research*, *European Management Journal*, *Benchmarking*, *Gender in Management*, *Global Business Review*, *Industrial and Commercial Training*, *International Journal of Commerce and Management*, *International Journal of Entrepreneurship and Small Business*, and *International Journal of Ethics and Systems*, among others.

Priya Jindal is currently working as an Associate Professor at Chitkara Business School, Chitkara University, Punjab, India, and holds a Master's degree in commerce and economics. She earned her doctorate in Management. She has contributed more than 17 years in teaching. She supervised four PhD research scholars and two MPhil candidates. There are numerous research papers to her credit in leading journals; among them, seven research papers have been published in Scopus Indexed Journal. Her areas of research included banking, finance, and insurance. She has filed more than 21 patents and two copyrights. She is the editor of three books under IGI Global and Nova Science publications, and the books got indexed in Scopus.

Manoj Kumar Kamila is currently pursuing a Fellow Program in Management from Jaipuria Institute of Management, Indore, India. His research primarily focuses on ethics in marketing and corporate governance, with his work being published in esteemed publishers like Elsevier, Emerald Insight, Springer Nature, Sage, Taylor & Francis, and Inderscience, among others. Manoj has actively participated in several national and international conferences, and one of the research presentations also got the best paper award at "Third International

Conference on E-Business Technologies" – EBT2023, University of Belgrade, Serbia in 2023.

Anoop Kumar, a management doctoral scholar of Amity Business School, Amity University Madhya Pradesh. He has completed his Master of Business Administration from Sikkim Manipal University. His research interests include social entrepreneurship, entrepreneurial intentions, digital payment systems, the hospitality and tourism industry, organizational culture, and organizational effectiveness. One of his book chapters is accepted and under publication in a reputed book series by Routledge. He is passionate about learning new research tools to improve his qualitative and quantitative analytical skills in the academic domain.

Yonghao Liu is a young researcher at the College of Management, Sichuan Agricultural University (SAU). Her research interest focuses on artificial intelligence in healthcare. She is the leader of the Innovation Training Planning Project of Sichuan University Students "The effective empowerment of artificial intelligence in rural Healthcare supply" and the SAU-supported research project "The factors influencing the acceptance of artificial intelligence-assisted rural Healthcare."

Shashi Jeevita Matadeen is a Senior Lecturer at the University of Mauritius in the Faculty of Law and Management since 2016. She delivers lectures both at undergraduate and postgraduate levels in finance, investment, and derivatives modules. She has successfully completed the CFA program since 2014 and is a CFA charter holder. She also holds a PhD in Finance since 2016. Her research interests include economic development, financial development, investment, and stock markets. She has also been involved in a few research projects at national and international level, including one funded by the IDRC.

Smriti Mishra, Architect and Urban Planner, is currently working as an Associate Professor in the Department of Architecture and Planning, Birla Institute of Technology, Mesra, Ranchi, India, and heading the department. She specializes in the field of urban and regional planning and has research interests in perception studies, tourism heritage management, vulnerability of peri-urban areas, vernacular architecture, indigenous planning, and energy conservation and has few publications in her records.

Vivek Mishra is a Faculty in the area of Marketing. Having completed a PhD from KIIT School of Management, KIIT D/U Bhubaneswar, he has more than 6 years of teaching and research experience coupled with over 9 years of industry exposure, in sales and business development. He has published impactful research papers in journals of national and international repute. His area of research interests falls in brand management and Generation Z consumer behavior research.

Yu Mu is an Associate Professor at College of Management, Sichuan Agricultural University. She received two PhD degrees, respectively, in Science, Business, and Innovation from Vrije Universiteit Amsterdam, the Netherlands, and in

Business Administration from Donghua University, China. Her research interests include service innovation and artificial intelligence. Her work appears in journals including *Annals of Tourism Research* and *The Service Industries Journal.*

Aditi Nag, Architect and Urban Planner, pursuing a PhD in the Department of Architecture and Planning, Birla Institute of Technology, Mesra, Ranchi, India. She has done research in the field of urban and rural planning and has a few publications in her record, specializing in the field of heritage planning and tourism management. She is the first to have been awarded the DST Inspire Fellowship in the field of Architecture and Planning by the Ministry of Science and Technology, Govt. of India.

Sumit Narula is the Director of the Amity School of Communication at Amity University Gurgaon, Haryana, India. He is working extensively in the area of catching Fake/Predatory/Cloned journals and Fraud/Misleading Impact Factors in academics and got copyrights and also developed an App named "Amity Quality Journal Checker" at the Google Play Store and IOS Platforms. He has also started a famous WhatsApp channel named Bharat Journal Checking/ Verification to help all from this dual menace.

Amarnath Padhi is an Assistant Professor at School of Management Studies, NIST University in India, completed his PhD in Strategic Human Resource Development from Fakir Mohan University, Balasore. He specializes in Strategic HRM, Strategic HRD, Knowledge Management, and HR Analytics. He actively contributes to national and international conferences and reputable journals. Additionally, he reviews papers for Scopus indexed journals and is affiliated with esteemed associations like ISTD, ISTE, and NHRD, where he works toward advancing HR practices and promoting academic exchange.

Gayatri Panda is an Assistant Professor at School of Management Studies, NIST University in India, completed his PhD in competency-based training from KIIT University, Bhubaneswar. She specializes in training and development, performance management, and compensation management. She actively contributes to national and international conferences and reputable journals. She has published various articles in national and international journals.

Anil Singh Parihar, Associate Professor at Department of Management, Manipal University Jaipur. He has more than 15 years of teaching experience in the field of economics and management. A total of two PhDs have been awarded under his supervision. His research interests include consumer behavior, the hospitality and tourism industry, artificial intelligence, entrepreneurial intentions, and organizational culture. He has contributed to the academic domain through around 20 of his multidisciplinary research works and various book chapters which have been published in various peer-reviewed high-indexed journals. He had conducted eight workshops on research methodology in both physical and online modes. He is an avid learner of advanced research analytics software tools and efficiently passes his knowledge to the scholars pursuing PhD under his supervision.

Maria Prokofieva is a Senior Lecturer at Victoria University and a lead Data Scientist at the Mitchell Institute for Policy Development. With over 15 years of research and industry experience, Maria focuses on the real-world impact of AI and disruptive technologies, emphasizing innovation and policy implications to shape future-ready enterprises. For the past three years, she has led a software development group aiming to translate research into practical applications for business transformation and the integration of AI into business strategies. Maria is a top publishing author and a technology evangelist in her area of expertise.

Dhruv Sabharwal is the Head of Department and an Associate Professor Sharda School of Media Film & Entertainment Sharda University Greater Noida. PhD in Advertising from Amity University. He has published various articles in national and international journals. Published three books on advertising and public relations.

Anshuman Adarsh Sahu is a research enthusiast at Birla Global University, India. He is pursuing Bachelor of Business Administration (BBA) with a Marketing specialization.

Anjali Singh is a Research Fellow at the Indian Institute of Management Mumbai in India. She has published in international journals such as the *Journal of Business Research*, *European Management Journal*, *International Journal of Productivity and Performance Management*, *Foresight*, and the *International Journal of Information and Communication Technology Education*.

Verena Tandrayen-Ragoobur is an Associate Professor in Economics at the University of Mauritius. She is currently the Dean of the Faculty of Social Sciences and Humanities. Her research areas focus on international and development economics. She works on social protection, social policies, labor market, trade, climate change, gender, and poverty. She is currently heading the Pole of Applied Socio-Economic Research and Analysis at the University of Mauritius (http://www.uom.ac.mu/research/asera/). She is also the cochair of the WTO Chairs Program at the University. She has been involved in various research projects internationally and locally and has published extensively in various peer-reviewed journals.

Mohammad Zaid is a Research Scholar currently pursuing his PhD in Marketing from Jamia Millia Islamia. His research interests include marketing technologies like Internet of Things (IoT), artificial intelligence, etc., advertising, and consumer behavior. As he continues his academic pursuits, he is passionate about learning and expanding his research expertise that is well-supported by his real-world experience as a Research Analyst. Besides his scholarly endeavors, he is an avid reader and loves to spend time with nature. Zaid with his astute observations and profound understanding of the human journey enriches the quality of life for himself and everyone around.

PREFACE

In this era of rapid technological advancement and digital transformation, understanding the multifaceted impact of disruptive innovations becomes crucial for both academics and practitioners alike. This edited volume, comprising 13 chapters, offers a comprehensive exploration of the intersection between disruptive technologies, market transformation, and strategic business practices. Each chapter contributes a unique perspective, meticulously researched, and presented by leading academics and researchers from diverse backgrounds.

The book is structured into five sections, each focusing on a different aspect of technological disruptions and innovations. The first section lays the groundwork by examining the effects of disruptive innovations on market transformation, while the second section delves into the evolving landscape of digital and artificial intelligence in services and marketing. The third section offers insights into sector-specific technological disruptions, highlighting case studies and practical applications. The fourth section shifts the focus to strategic perspectives in business and technology, exploring the dynamics of leadership and collaboration in the face of technological change. Finally, the fifth section provides an overview of smart technologies and services, suggesting directions for future research and implementation.

TABLE OF CONTRIBUTIONS

Chapter	Title	Key Contribution
1	Change Management in the Adoption of Disruptive Innovation: A Critical Review	Explores the critical role of change management in the successful adoption of disruptive innovations.
2	A Systematic Review of the Hospitality and Tourism Industry through the Lens of Disruptive Innovations	Analyzes the impact of disruptive technologies on the hospitality and tourism industry.
3	Digital Enigma: Understanding Ethical Dilemmas in Design and Marketing	Investigates the ethical challenges in digital design and marketing strategies.

(Continued)

(Continued)

Chapter	Title	Key Contribution
4	A Bibliometric Analysis and Visualization of Medical Artificial Intelligence Research	Presents an analysis of trends and developments in medical AI research.
5	Metaverse Marketing: A Guide to Reaching the Next Generation of Consumers	Discusses strategies for engaging consumers in the emerging digital landscape of the metaverse.
6	A Review of Self-Service Technology Adoption in the Tourism and Hospitality Industry	Examines the adoption and implications of self-service technologies in tourism and hospitality.
7	Sustainable Competitive Advantage in Heritage Tourism: Leveraging Cultural Legacy in a Data-Driven World	Explores strategies for leveraging cultural heritage for competitive advantage in tourism.
8	Transformative Influence of Disruptive Innovations on Markets and Business Performance	Analyzes the transformative impact of disruptive innovations on business strategies and market performance.
9	A Literature Survey of Technological Disruptions in the Service Sector	Provides a comprehensive survey of technological disruptions in the service sector.
10	Navigating Strategic Leadership: Unraveling the Dynamics of Technological Innovation in Organizations	Explores the role of strategic leadership in navigating technological innovation.
11	Collaborative Arrangements in Developing Successful Business Strategies: Literature Review	Investigates the importance of collaborative strategies in business success.
12	A Literature Review on Smart Technologies in Service Systems: How Should We Work on in the Future?	Offers insights into the role of smart technologies in service systems and future directions.
13	Exploring the Internet of Things-Marketing Connection: A Bibliometric Review and Directions for Future Research	Analyzes the connection between IoT and marketing, suggesting areas for future research.

This volume aims to equip readers with a nuanced understanding of how disruptive technologies are reshaping industries, challenging existing business models, and creating new opportunities for innovation and growth. It encourages a multidisciplinary approach to studying and leveraging technological disruptions, emphasizing the importance of adaptability, strategic foresight, and collaboration in the digital age.

This book, *Review of Technologies and Disruptive Business Strategies*, encapsulates a vast array of perspectives on the intersection of technology and business, making it an indispensable resource for scholars, academicians, and practitioners alike. Its comprehensive exploration of the literature offers a deep dive into the transformative effects of technological innovations on business practices, providing readers with the insights needed to navigate the complexities of the modern business landscape. This collection is poised to serve as a foundational text for anyone seeking to understand or contribute to the evolving discourse on technological disruption and business strategy.

***

LEVERAGING DISRUPTIVE TECHNOLOGIES AND STRATEGIES FOR COMPETITIVE ADVANTAGE

Vinaytosh Mishra[a] and Rahul Pratap Singh Kaurav[b]

[a]*Gulf Medical University, UAE*
[b]*FORE School of Management, India*

ABSTRACT

The recent pandemic has witnessed increased digitalization. The supply chain disruptions have forced businesses to adopt innovative business strategies that were not prevalent in previous years. This chapter elaborates on how integrating disruptive technologies such as artificial intelligence (AI), blockchain, and the Internet of Things (IoT) into business strategies is essential for modern organizations. It emphasizes creating and capturing value through business model innovation, highlighting the significance of developing a value proposition differentiating an enterprise in the market. This involves rethinking and redesigning how organizations create customer value, leveraging these technologies to enhance efficiency, customer experience, and competitive advantage. This chapter advocates for a proactive approach to technology adoption, stressing the importance of agility, innovation, and a forward-thinking leadership mindset in capitalizing on the opportunities presented by technological advancements.

Keywords: Dynamics capabilities; business model innovation; disruptive technologies; disruptive business strategies; technology integration

1. INTRODUCTION

In an era marked by rapid technological evolution, the deliberation exploring the critical intersection between disruptive technologies and business strategies within management practices has become imperative. Disruptive technologies are innovations that significantly alter how businesses, industries, or markets operate.

Review of Technologies and Disruptive Business Strategies
Review of Management Literature, Volume 3, 1–16

Published under exclusive licence by Emerald Publishing Limited
ISSN: 2754-5865/doi:10.1108/S2754-586520240000003001

These technologies can potentially displace established technologies, shake up the industry, or create new ones. They are characterized by their ability to offer better functionality, convenience, or other benefits at a lower cost, which can lead to rapid adoption and transformation of current practices or economic structures (Bongomin et al., 2020).

1.1 Understanding Disruptive Technologies

Disruptive technologies are not just improvements or enhancements of existing technologies; they are innovations that cause a paradigm shift. They often start by catering to a niche market or need but eventually grow to dominate or significantly alter the existing market landscape, leading to the obsolescence of older technologies or methods. Key characteristics of disruptive technologies include (Abdel-Basset et al., 2021).

- *Innovativeness:* They bring something novel to the market, including new business models, products, or services that have not been seen before.
- *Accessibility:* They tend to make products or services more accessible and affordable to a broad segment of the population, which was previously excluded due to cost or complexity.
- *Market Transformation:* Disruptive technologies can potentially change the way markets or industries operate, often leading to new standards and practices.
- *Displacement of Established Technologies*: Over time, these technologies can displace established technologies, making them obsolete. This displacement can happen quickly or over a more extended period, depending on various factors, including the technology's adoption rate and the existing market structure.
- *Creation of New Value Networks:* They often create new markets and value networks, leading to the reconfiguration of existing industries or the emergence of new ones.

Understanding and identifying disruptive technologies is crucial for businesses and policymakers to stay ahead of trends, invest wisely, and adapt to changes that could impact their operations or sectors (Taeihagh et al., 2021). Adopting or adapting to disruptive technologies can provide significant competitive advantages, open new markets, and lead to substantial economic benefits (Bongomin et al., 2020).

1.2 Understanding Disruptive Business Strategies

Disruptive business strategies refer to approaches and methodologies that fundamentally alter the competitive dynamics of industries or markets (Olabode et al., 2022). Organizations typically employ these strategies to introduce innovations that disrupt existing market structures, displace established market leaders, or create entirely new markets. Disruptive strategies are not just about technology; they encompass new business models, processes, and ways of delivering value to customers that significantly impact how an industry operates. Disruptive business strategies require visionary leadership, a willingness to take risks, and a deep understanding of market needs and trends. While these strategies can offer significant rewards, including rapid growth and market leadership, they also carry risks, as they often challenge established market norms and provoke strong responses from existing competitors (Abu-Rumman, 2021).

Here are several key aspects and examples of disruptive business strategies, some of which are listed below:

- Innovative Business Models: Companies employ innovative business models that challenge the status quo, offering products or services in a way that is not only different but often more efficient, cost-effective, or accessible than traditional methods (Shakeel et al., 2020)
- Market Re-segmentation: Identifying underserved or overlooked market segments and targeting them with tailored products or services. This strategy often involves offering simpler, more affordable solutions that appeal to customers who do not need or cannot afford the full-featured offerings of the incumbents (Sincharoenkul, 2022).
- Cost Structure Innovation: Radically changing the cost structure of delivering a product or service, allowing for lower prices or different pricing models that can attract a broader customer base. This could involve automation to reduce labor costs, outsourcing to take advantage of lower cost resources, or innovative supply chain management (Lestari et al., 2020).
- Value Network Redefinition: Changing how a company delivers value to its customers, often by leveraging digital platforms to create direct relationships with end users, bypassing traditional intermediaries (Martín et al., 2022).
- Sustainability and Social Impact: Developing business strategies that address environmental concerns, social issues, or both can disrupt industries by appealing to the growing segment of consumers who prioritize sustainability and ethical considerations in their purchasing decisions (Hanaysha et al., 2020).

This special issue delves into how organizations can adapt to and leverage emerging technologies – such as artificial intelligence (AI), blockchain, and the Internet of Things (IoT) – to foster innovation, enhance competitive advantage, and drive sustainable growth. The issue further emphasizes the importance of agile strategic planning, the role of visionary leadership, and the necessity for a culture that embraces change. By highlighting successful case studies and offering practical frameworks, the discussion underlines that the effective integration of disruptive technologies into business strategies is not merely an option but a necessity for thriving in the contemporary business landscape.

2. DYNAMIC CAPABILITIES

Dynamic capabilities refer to an organization's ability to integrate, build, and reconfigure internal and external competencies to address rapidly changing environments (Kurtmollaiev, 2020). This concept is rooted in the fields of strategic management and organizational theory. It emphasizes the need for companies to adapt, innovate, and renew their resources and processes to maintain competitive advantage in dynamic markets (Mishra & Sharma, 2022; Wang & Ahmed, 2007). Dynamic capabilities can be understood through three primary activities:

(1) *Sensing and Shaping Opportunities and Threats:* The ability to identify, evaluate, and seize business opportunities in the environment, including technological changes, market trends, and shifts in consumer preferences. This also involves recognizing potential threats and adapting strategies accordingly.
(2) *Seizing Opportunities:* Once opportunities are identified, the organization must mobilize resources to capture these opportunities. This involves investing in new technologies, launching new products or services, entering new markets, or enhancing existing offerings.
(3) *Reconfiguring:* Organizations must continuously reconfigure their asset base and structure to adapt to changing environments. This includes modifying processes, restructuring organizational models, and developing or enhancing new capabilities.

Dynamic capabilities are critical for sustaining competitive advantage, especially in industries characterized by rapid technological change and high levels of uncertainty. They allow firms to be more agile, innovative, and responsive to changes, ensuring long-term success and viability.

3. BUSINESS MODEL INNOVATION

Business model innovation involves rethinking your company's approach to creating, delivering, and capturing value. It's a broad concept encompassing changes in products or services, processes, market segments, and revenue streams (Vaska et al., 2021). A key aspect of business model innovation is the value proposition, the unique mix of products, services, and benefits a company offers its customers (Keiningham et al., 2020; Sahni & Kaurav, 2023). Here's how business model innovation can impact value proposition creation and capture:

3.1 Value Proposition Creation

- Customer Needs and Segmentation: Business model innovation often starts with a deep understanding of customer needs, including unmet or underserved needs. Innovating your business model can involve creating new value propositions that more accurately or completely meet these needs.
- Differentiation: By innovating the business model, companies can differentiate their value proposition from competitors. This could involve offering unique products or services, leveraging technology in new ways, or reimagining the customer experience.

- Leveraging Technology: The use of new technologies can enable companies to create value propositions that were previously impossible. For example, digital platforms can connect users and providers in a two-sided market, creating value for both groups.

3.2 Value Capture

- Revenue Models: Business model innovation often includes rethinking how the company makes money. This could involve introducing new revenue streams such as subscriptions, freemium models, or dynamic pricing strategies.
- Efficiency and Scalability: Innovations in the business model can lead to more efficient operations and greater scalability. For example, moving to a digital service delivery model can reduce costs and enable the business to scale more rapidly.
- Strategic Partnerships: Forming new partnerships or ecosystems can be a way to capture value through innovation in a business model. Organizations can offer a more comprehensive value proposition by collaborating with other companies or entering new markets.
- Customer Relationships and Engagement: Innovating the business model can also involve new ways of engaging customers, such as through personalized services or community-building activities. This can enhance customer loyalty and increase lifetime value.

Thus, we can say that business model innovation related to value proposition creation and capture is about finding new ways to serve customers and monetize the value provided. It requires a deep understanding of customer needs, market dynamics, and the potential of technology, combined with a willingness to experiment and adapt.

Fig. 1 depicts a conceptual framework for disruptive innovation through digital technology.

The conceptual framework given in the Fig. 1 outlines a three-phase process:

(1) *Exploration Phase:* This initial phase is where organizations or entities sense opportunities or threats, seize them by investing resources, and reconfigure their assets to adapt to the changes, leveraging dynamic capabilities.
(2) *Expansion Phase:* In this phase, the innovation gains momentum as the value proposition, creation, and capture mechanisms are refined. This often involves business model innovation, where digital technology is used to develop new ways of delivering value to customers and capturing revenue.
(3) *Reinforcement Phase:* The final phase solidifies the disruptive innovation. The value propositions become well-established, and the business models are reinforced to sustain the competitive advantage obtained through the innovation.

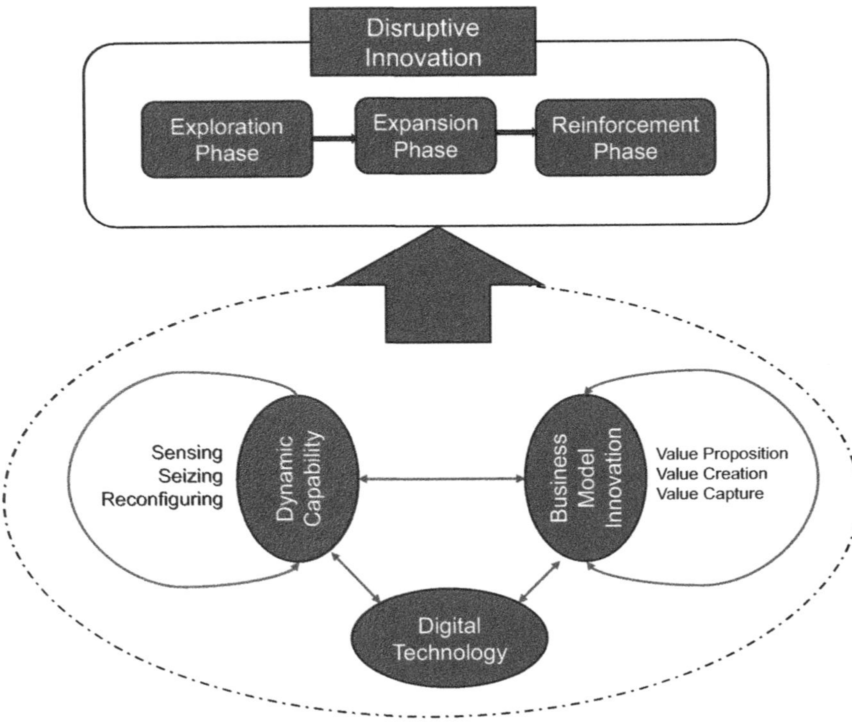

Fig. 1. Conceptual Framework for Disruptive Innovation. *Source:* Author's compilation.

The conceptual framework also highlights the interplay between dynamic capabilities (sensing, seizing, and reconfiguring) and business model innovation (value proposition, value creation, and value capture), suggesting that digital technology is the driving force that connects these elements. This framework suggests that successfully navigating through these phases can help organizations disrupt their industries effectively with digital technology. Next, we discuss five handpicked disruptive technologies and five disruptive business strategies.

4. KEY DISRUPTIVE TECHNOLOGIES

Digital transformation, disruptive technologies, and disruptive business strategies are reshaping industries and altering the competitive landscape at an unprecedented pace (Mishra & Sharma, 2022). Digital transformation refers to integrating digital technology into all business areas, fundamentally changing how it operates and delivers value to customers (Vial, 2021). It's not just about upgrading your IT infrastructure; it's a strategic overhaul that requires rethinking old business models, processes, and customer interactions and considering digital possibilities. At its core, digital transformation is driven by the need to meet changing consumer expectations and to adapt to a digital economy where agility, innovation, and speed are paramount (Shrivastava, 2017).

Key technologies are at the forefront of driving digital transformation and disruption include but are not limited to:

- *AI and Machine Learning (ML):* AI and ML are enabling businesses to predict customer behavior, automate decision-making, and personalize customer experiences at scale (Wu et al., 2021). Holmström (2022) provides a framework in their seminal work, which organizations can utilize to assess AI readiness. Mishra et al. (2015) highlight the importance of ML in risk predictions of chronic diseases such as diabetes. AI can help healthcare professionals deliver precision care, reducing the risk and wastage in healthcare delivery (Johnson et al., 2021).
- *Blockchain Technology (BT):* BT has proven useful in removing business inefficiency (Kant, 2021). This technology offers a secure and transparent way to conduct transactions, impacting industries from finance to supply chain management (Pal et al., 2021). The adoption of blockchain builds trust in supply chains and reduces the cash-to-cash cycle. Blockchain is also important in implementing smart and secure business contracts (Macrinici et al., 2018). Recent literature discusses blockchain use cases in applications such as vaccine passports and the management of counterfeit drugs in pharmaceutical supply chains (Dua et al., 2022; Kaurav et al., 2020; Mishra, 2022; Thakuriya et al., 2023).
- *Internet of Things (IoT):* IoT represents a transformative wave in the digital revolution, embedding intelligence into everyday objects to facilitate seamless interaction between the physical and digital worlds (Sankar et al., 2020). By augmenting physical processes with sensors and network connectivity, IoT allows for the collection and exchange of data across a vast array of items – from home appliances to industrial machinery, creating an interconnected ecosystem that enhances efficiency, enables new services, and improves the quality of life (Mishra & Madakam, 2022). This technology has paved the way for smart homes, intelligent transportation systems, and enhanced healthcare solutions, promising a future where real-time information and automation can significantly influence how we live, work, and interact with our environment (Mishra & Rana, 2023).
- *Cloud Computing:* Cloud computing represents a paradigm shift in how technology is consumed and managed. It offers scalable and flexible IT resources over the internet, available anytime from anywhere (Sunyaev & Sunyaev, 2020). It enables businesses to access immense computing power, storage, and applications as services without upfront investment in expensive physical infrastructure. With its ability to foster innovation, agility, and resilience, cloud computing has become a cornerstone of digital transformation strategies across

industries, reshaping how organizations operate and deliver value to their customers (Oke et al., 2023).

- *5G Technologies:* 5G technology represents the fifth generation of mobile network technology, succeeding the 4G networks that currently facilitate our smartphones' connectivity (Dogra et al., 2020). It promises to revolutionize digital communications by offering significantly faster data download and upload speeds, reduced latency, and more reliable connections (Taboada & Shee, 2021). This leap in technology is not just about speedier internet browsing or quicker download times; it's set to transform a wide array of sectors, including autonomous driving, smart cities, telemedicine, and IoT, enabling devices to communicate with each other more efficiently than ever before.

The technology discussed in the article is interlinked and can be depicted as a honeycomb structure in Fig. 2. The successful utilization of the interplay of these technologies helps an organization harness the full potential of these disruptive technologies.

5. KEY DISRUPTIVE BUSINESS STRATEGIES

Disruption isn't just about technology; it's also about how businesses leverage new technologies to create innovative business models and strategies that

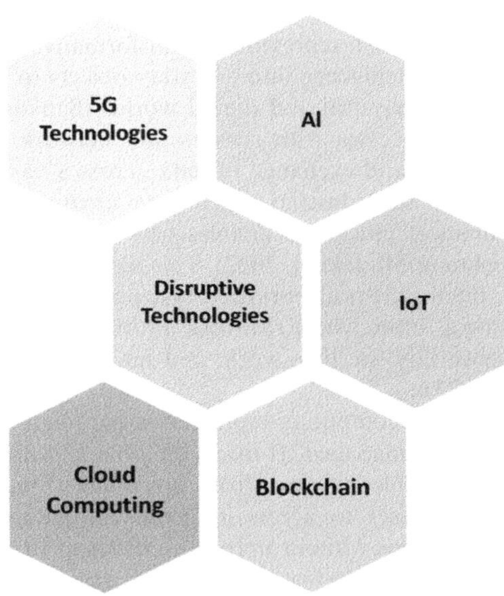

Fig. 2. Key Disruptive Technologies for Competitive Advantage. *Source:* Author's compilation.

challenge the status quo. Thus, technologies are mean and not destinations in themselves. Disruptive business strategies often focus on the following:

- *Customer Centricity*: Putting the customer at the center of the business model, using data to drive better insights into customer needs and deliver personalized experiences (Fader, 2020). Implementing digital technologies can further extend the benefits of traditional business strategies. Mishra and Sharma (2024) in their chapter discuss how digital lean augments the gain from lean methodologies in health care.
- *Agility and Innovation*: Embracing a culture of innovation that encourages experimentation and rapid iteration to respond quickly to market changes (Yildiz & Aykanat, 2021). Digital technologies provide end-to-end supply chain visibility and minimize the risk of supply chain disruption (Roy, 2021). Technologies such as digital twins and simulators make it easy to prototype and test the market beforehand, thus providing distinct advantages over traditional marketing strategies (Lim et al., 2021).
- *Platform Models:* Platform models represent a transformative business strategy that leverages digital technologies to facilitate interactions between two or more distinct but interdependent groups of users, typically consumers and producers or service providers ((Rahman & Thelen, 2019). Unlike traditional linear business models, which directly control and deliver products or services, platform models create value by enabling direct exchanges and fostering network effects that enhance value as more participants join (Täuscher & Laudien, 2018). This approach underpins the success of many tech giants, including Amazon, Uber, and Airbnb, which have disrupted established markets by providing scalable and efficient marketplaces. Recently, the international company Philips developed AI Manager, an innovative marketplace for AI applications in health care. These platforms streamline transactions and leverage data to optimize user experiences, match supply with demand more effectively, and innovate continuously.
- *Subscription/Service-as-a-Model (SaaM):* SaaM is a business paradigm that prioritizes the delivery of services over the sale of physical products, reflecting a shift toward valuing ongoing customer engagement and satisfaction (Kindström, 2010). Moving away from product-based sales to subscription or service-based models provides ongoing value to customers and creates predictable revenue streams. SaaM can be seen across various industries, from IT and cloud computing services, such as Software as a Service (SaaS), Platform as a Service (PaaS), and Infrastructure as a Service (IaaS) to more traditional sectors like transportation, health care, and education, which are increasingly adopting service-oriented approaches.
- *Remote Work and Digital Nomadism:* Accelerated by technology and the COVID-19 pandemic, businesses that support or are built around remote work disrupt traditional office-based work models (Aroles et al., 2020). Companies offering coworking spaces, remote work technologies, and services tailored to digital nomads are at the forefront of this shift (Hannonen, 2020).

Digital nomadism has become a significant trend, reshaping the concept of work and lifestyle in the digital age. An excellent example is the rise of platforms like Nomad List, which serves the digital nomad community by providing essential information and resources to facilitate a mobile lifestyle.

The disruptive business strategies highlighted in this section represent just a selection of the many innovative approaches transforming industries today. While numerous other examples are beyond those mentioned here, the strategies discussed are particularly noteworthy and merit exploration in this issue. The five disruptive strategies discussed in the section are summarized as illustrated in Fig. 3.

Thus, we can summarize those disruptive technologies – AI and ML, BT, IoT, cloud computing, and 5G technologies – are influencing disruptive business strategies like customer centricity, agility and innovation, platform models, subscription/SaaM, and remote work, and digital nomadism. These technologies enable organizations to predict customer behavior, automate decision-making, secure transactions, and enhance connectivity and data exchange. In turn, these capabilities support innovative business models focusing on personalization, flexibility, direct exchanges between users, and a shift toward service-based models and remote work arrangements, reshaping industries, and competitive landscapes.

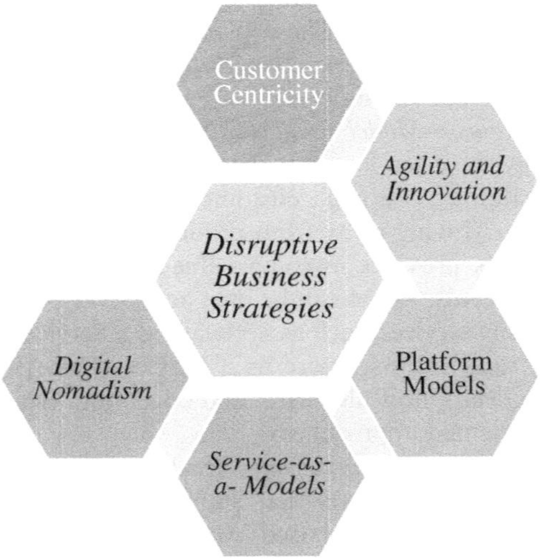

Fig. 3. Key Disruptive Business Strategies for Competitive Advantage. *Source:* Author's compilation.

6. CONTRIBUTION OF THIS VOLUME

This edited volume delves into the multifaceted impact of disruptive innovations and technological advancements across various industries and sectors. It offers an in-depth exploration of strategies, challenges, and opportunities presented by digital transformations, AI, and smart technologies, fostering a comprehensive understanding of their implications for market dynamics, organizational change, and strategic leadership. Through a series of meticulously researched chapters, the book provides valuable insights into navigating the complexities of the evolving digital landscape, emphasizing the importance of adaptability, strategic foresight, and collaborative efforts in achieving sustainable growth and competitiveness.

Section 1: Disruptive Innovations and Market Transformation

Chapter 2: Change Management in the Adoption of Disruptive Innovation: A Critical Review

This chapter delves into the critical role of change management in adopting disruptive innovations, presenting a review by Panda, Padhi, and Dash. It emphasizes organizations' need to cultivate an innovation-supportive culture, highlighting strategies for managing change effectively to embrace disruptive technologies.

Chapter 3: A Systematic Review of the Hospitality and Tourism Industry through the Lens of Disruptive Innovations

Kumar, Parihar, and Jain systematically review how disruptive innovations are reshaping the hospitality and tourism industry. This chapter provides insights into the challenges and opportunities of technological advancements, emphasizing the need for adaptive strategies within the sector.

Section 2: Evolving Digital and AI Landscape in Services and Marketing

Chapter 4: Digital Enigma: Understanding Ethical Dilemmas in Design and Marketing

Kamila, Jasrotia, and Chib explore the ethical dilemmas in digital design and marketing. This chapter sheds light on the complexities of navigating ethical considerations in an increasingly digital world, proposing frameworks for ethical decision-making.

Chapter 5: A Bibliometric Analysis and Visualization of Medical AI Research

Liu and Mu present a bibliometric analysis of medical AI research, offering insights into the evolution and trends within the field. This chapter visualizes the growth of AI in health care, underlining its impact on medical research and practice.

Chapter 6: Metaverse Marketing: A Guide to Reaching the Next Generation of Consumers

Gupta, Mishra, and Sahu explore the emerging concept of metaverse marketing, highlighting its potential to revolutionize consumer engagement. This chapter discusses strategies for brands to navigate this new digital landscape effectively.

Section 3: Sector-Specific Technological Disruptions

Chapter 7: A Review of Self-Service Technology Adoption in the Tourism and Hospitality Industry

Gore examines the adoption of self-service technologies in the tourism and hospitality industry, analyzing the benefits and challenges. This chapter discusses the implications for service delivery and customer experience.

Chapter 8: Sustainable Competitive Advantage in Heritage Tourism: Leveraging Cultural Legacy in a Data-Driven World

Nag and Mishra focus on how heritage tourism can achieve a sustainable competitive advantage by leveraging cultural legacy and integrating data-driven strategies to enhance visitor experience and preserve cultural heritage.

Chapter 9: Transformative Influence of Disruptive Innovations on Markets and Business Performance

Narula and Sabharwal discuss the transformative impact of disruptive innovations on markets and business performance. This chapter examines case studies and strategies for businesses to adapt and thrive in changing markets.

Chapter 10: A Literature Survey of Technological Disruptions in the Service Sector

Fauzel, Tandrayen-Ragoobur, and Matadeen provide a comprehensive survey of technological disruptions in the services sector, offering insights into the challenges and opportunities for service organizations.

Section 4: Strategic Perspectives in Business and Technology

Chapter 11: Navigating Strategic Leadership: Unraveling the Dynamics of Technological Innovation in Organizations

Singh and Jha explore the dynamics of technological innovation in organizations from a strategic leadership perspective. This chapter discusses the roles and challenges of leaders in fostering innovation and guiding their organizations through technological changes.

Chapter 12: Collaborative Arrangements in Developing Successful Business Strategies: Literature Review

Prokofieva examines the role of collaborative arrangements in developing successful business strategies, highlighting the importance of partnerships and alliances in achieving strategic objectives and innovation.

Section 5: Overview of Smart Technologies and Services

Chapter 13: A Literature Review on Smart Technologies in Service Systems: How Should We Work on in Future?

Akyuz and Balkan review the current state of smart technologies in service systems, proposing future research directions. This chapter emphasizes the potential of smart technologies to transform service delivery and customer experience.

Chapter 14: Exploring the Internet of Things-Marketing Connection: A Bibliometric Review and Directions for Future Research

Zaid and Farooqi conducted a bibliometric review on the IoT and its connection to marketing, exploring future research directions. This chapter discusses the implications of IoT for marketing strategies and consumer engagement.

7. CONCLUSION

The recent pandemic has accelerated the process of digital transformation across industries, highlighting the fragility of traditional business models in the face of unexpected global disruptions. Integrating disruptive technologies such as AI, blockchain, and the IoT into business strategies has become more than just a trend; it is now necessary for organizations aiming to thrive in the modern business landscape. This elaboration aims to dissect the critical aspects of incorporating these technologies into business strategies, focusing on innovation, value creation, and achieving a competitive advantage.

AI transforms business operations and customer interactions by enabling data-driven decision-making, automating routine tasks, and personalizing customer experiences. For instance, AI can analyze customer data to predict buying behavior, allowing companies to tailor their marketing strategies effectively. Moreover, AI-driven process automation can lead to significant cost savings and efficiency improvements. Similarly, blockchain offers unparalleled advantages in terms of transparency, security, and traceability of transactions. Its application extends beyond cryptocurrency to supply chain management, where it can help mitigate disruptions by providing real-time visibility into supply chain operations. This technology can also foster trust among stakeholders by ensuring data integrity across business networks. Another technology, IoT, connects physical objects to the internet, enabling data collection and exchange. IoT can enhance operational efficiency, improve safety, and create new revenue streams in a business context. For example, IoT devices can monitor equipment health to predict failures before they occur, reducing downtime and maintenance costs.

Similar to technologies, this chapter includes a discussion on business model innovation. Integrating disruptive technologies necessitates a rethink of the traditional business models to focus on creating and capturing value in novel ways. This involves developing a unique value proposition that sets an enterprise apart from its competitors. Organizations must redesign how they create customer value, leveraging AI, blockchain, and IoT to enhance efficiency, enrich the customer experience, and solidify their competitive position.

The essence of integrating these technologies lies in their ability to offer customized and enhanced experiences to customers. Businesses can understand and anticipate customer needs by utilizing data analytics and IoT, providing timely and relevant solutions. Blockchain's transparency can also add value to customers' increasing concern about ethical and sustainable business practices. To capture value from these technological investments, businesses must develop strategies aligning with their objectives and market positioning. This might include adopting a subscription model, leveraging data as a service, or creating new products and services enabled by these technologies. Adopting a proactive approach to technology adoption is crucial. This requires agility, innovation, and a forward-thinking leadership mindset. Organizations must be willing to experiment with new business models and be prepared to pivot based on market feedback and technological evolution. The ability to rapidly adapt to changes and capitalize on technological advancements can give businesses a significant competitive edge.

Thus, this chapter highlights that integrating AI, blockchain, and IoT into business strategies is not merely about adopting new technologies but about reimagining how businesses operate and compete in the digital era. By creating and capturing value through business model innovation, organizations can enhance their resilience against disruptions, improve customer satisfaction, and secure a competitive advantage. It underscores the critical role of agility, innovation, and leadership in navigating the complexities of the digital landscape.

Our aspiration with this volume is to spark a sense of curiosity and inquiry within our readers about the transformative technologies and innovative business strategies that are redefining the contours of the business world in the aftermath of the COVID-19 pandemic. Through an extensive literature review, we aim to lay the groundwork for ongoing dialogue and serve as a foundational resource for further scholarly exploration. We encourage you to delve deeper into the following pages, embarking on a journey of discovery that extends beyond the surface of these critical and timely topics.

REFERENCES

Abdel-Basset, M., Chang, V., & Nabeeh, N. A. (2021). An intelligent framework using disruptive technologies for COVID-19 analysis. *Technological Forecasting and Social Change*, *163*, 120431.

Abu-Rumman, A. (2021). Transformational leadership and human capital within the disruptive business environment of academia. *World Journal on Educational Technology: Current Issues*, *13*(2), 178–187.

Aroles, J., Granter, E., & de Vaujany, F. X. (2020). 'Becoming mainstream': The professionalization and corporatization of digital nomadism. *New Technology, Work and Employment*, *35*(1), 114–129.

Bongomin, O., Gilibrays Ocen, G., Oyondi Nganyi, E., Musinguzi, A., & Omara, T. (2020). Exponential disruptive technologies and the required skills of industry 4.0. *Journal of Engineering*, *2020*, 1–17.

Dogra, A., Jha, R. K., & Jain, S. (2020). A survey on beyond 5G network with the advent of 6G: Architecture and emerging technologies. *IEEE Access*, *9*, 67512–67547.

Dua, S., Sharma, M. G., Mishra, V., & Kulkarni, S. D. (2022). Modelling perceived risk in blockchain-enabled supply chain utilizing fuzzy-AHP. *Journal of Global Operations and Strategic Sourcing*, *16*(1), 161–177.

Fader, P. (2020). *Customer centricity: Focus on the right customers for strategic advantage*. University of Pennsylvania Press.

Hanaysha, J. R., Al-Shaikh, M. E., Joghee, S., & Alzoubi, H. M. (2022). Impact of innovation capabilities on business sustainability in small and medium enterprises. *FIIB Business Review*, *11*(1), 67–78.

Hannonen, O. (2020). In search of a digital nomad: Defining the phenomenon. *Information Technology & Tourism*, *22*, 335–353.

Holmström, J. (2022). From AI to digital transformation: The AI readiness framework. *Business Horizons*, *65*(3), 329–339.

Johnson, K. B., Wei, W. Q., Weeraratne, D., Frisse, M. E., Misulis, K., Rhee, K., Zhao, J., & Snowdon, J. L. (2021). Precision medicine, AI, and the future of personalized health care. *Clinical and Translational Science*, *14*(1), 86–93.

Kant, N. (2021). Blockchain: A strategic resource to attain and sustain competitive advantage. *International Journal of Innovation Science*, *13*(4), 520–538.

Kaurav, R. P. S., Baber, R., & Rajput, S. (2020). Technology-driven tourism and hospitality industry as a tool for economic development: A bibliometric analysis. In *The Emerald Handbook of ICT in Tourism and Hospitality* (pp. 469–486). Emerald Publishing Limited.

Keiningham, T., Aksoy, L., Bruce, H. L., Cadet, F., Clennell, N., Hodgkinson, I. R., & Kearney, T. (2020). Customer experience-driven business model innovation. *Journal of Business Research*, *116*, 431–440.

Kindström, D. (2010). Towards a service-based business model – Key aspects for future competitive advantage. *European Management Journal*, *28*(6), 479–490.

Kurtmollaiev, S. (2020). Dynamic capabilities and where to find them. *Journal of Management Inquiry*, *29*(1), 3–16.

Lestari, S. D., Leon, F. M., Widyastuti, S., Brabo, N. A., & Putra, A. H. P. K. (2020). Antecedents and consequences of innovation and business strategy on performance and competitive advantage of SMEs. *The Journal of Asian Finance, Economics and Business*, *7*(6), 365–378.

Lim, K. Y. H., Zheng, P., & Chen, C. H. (2020). A state-of-the-art survey of Digital Twin: Techniques, engineering product lifecycle management and business innovation perspectives. *Journal of Intelligent Manufacturing*, *31*, 1313–1337.

Macrinici, D., Cartofeanu, C., & Gao, S. (2018). Smart contract applications within blockchain technology: A systematic mapping study. *Telematics and Informatics*, *35*(8), 2337–2354.

Martín, C., Villar, L. B., Vigier, H. P., & Brignole, N. B. (2022). An evolutionary approach for the optimization of the beekeeping value chain. *Computers and Electronics in Agriculture*, *194*, 106787.

Mishra, V. (2022). Applications of Blockchain for vaccine passport and challenges. *Journal of Global Operations and Strategic Sourcing*, *15*(3), 345–362.

Mishra, V., & Madakam, S. (2022). Smart healthcare and IoT technologies: Academic and service provider review. In *Internet of Things and Data Mining for Modern Engineering and Healthcare Applications* (pp. 15–28). Chapman and Hall/CRC.

Mishra, V., & Rana, S. (2023). Future of marketing after disruptions and uncertainties: Physical, digital, or phygital? In *Contemporary trends in marketing: Problems, processes and prospects* (pp. 31–40). Springer Nature.

Mishra, V., Samuel, C., & Sharma, S. K. (2015). Use of machine learning to predict the onset of diabetes. *International Journal of Recent advances in Mechanical Engineering*, *4*(2), 9–14.

Mishra, V., & Sharma, M. G. (2022). Digital transformation evaluation of telehealth using convergence, maturity, and adoption. *Health Policy and Technology*, *11*(4), 100684. https://doi.org/10.1016/j.hlpt.2022.100684

Mishra, V., & Sharma, M. G. (2024). Factors affecting the implementation of digital lean in healthcare in the post-COVID world – Mixed-method approach. *The TQM Journal*. https://doi.org/10.1108/TQM-08-2023-0251

Oke, A. E., Kineber, A. F., Al-Bukhari, I., Famakin, I., & Kingsley, C. (2023). Exploring the benefits of cloud computing for sustainable construction in Nigeria. *Journal of Engineering, Design and Technology*, *21*(4), 973–990.

Olabode, O. E., Boso, N., Hultman, M., & Leonidou, C. N. (2022). Big data analytics capability and market performance: The roles of disruptive business models and competitive intensity. *Journal of Business Research*, *139*, 1218–1230.

Pal, A., Tiwari, C. K., & Haldar, N. (2021). Blockchain for business management: Applications, challenges, and potentials. *The Journal of High Technology Management Research*, *32*(2), 100414.

Rahman, K. S., & Thelen, K. (2019). The rise of the platform business model and the transformation of twenty-first-century capitalism. *Politics & Society*, *47*(2), 177–204.

Roy, V. (2021). Contrasting supply chain traceability and supply chain visibility: Are they interchangeable? *International Journal of Logistics Management*, *32*(3), 942–972.

Sahni, S., & Kaurav, R. P. S. (2023). What? Why? When? How? Where? of technology-based bibliometric review. In *Advancing methodologies of conducting literature review in management domain* (Vol. 2, pp. 79–101). Emerald Publishing Limited.

Sankar, S., Srinivasan, P., Luhach, A. K., Somula, R., & Chilamkurti, N. (2020). Energy-aware grid-based data aggregation scheme in routing protocol for agricultural Internet of things. *Sustainable Computing: Informatics and Systems*, *28*, 100422.

Shakeel, J., Mardani, A., Chofreh, A. G., Goni, F. A., & Klemeš, J. J. (2020). Anatomy of sustainable business model innovation. *Journal of Cleaner Production*, *261*, 121201.

Shrivastava, S. (2017). Digital disruption is redefining the customer experience: The digital transformation approach of the communications service providers. *Telecom Business Review*, *10*(1), 41.

Sincharoenkul, K. (2022). COVID-19 management and the effectiveness of government support of the tourism SMEs in Phuket. *Journal of International Studies*, *12*(2), 93–128.

Sunyaev, A., & Sunyaev, A. (2020). Cloud computing. *Internet Computing: Principles of Distributed Systems and Emerging Internet-Based Technologies*, 195–236.

Taboada, I., & Shee, H. (2021). Understanding 5G technology for future supply chain management. *International Journal of Logistics Research and Applications*, *24*(4), 392–406.

Taeihagh, A., Ramesh, M., & Howlett, M. (2021). Assessing the regulatory challenges of emerging disruptive technologies. *Regulation & Governance*, *15*(4), 1009–1019.

Täuscher, K., & Laudien, S. M. (2018). Understanding platform business models: A mixed methods study of marketplaces. *European Management Journal*, *36*(3), 319–329.

Thakuriya, P., Kaur, S., & Mishra, V. (2023). Assessment of blockchain technology as remedy to counterfeit drugs problem in pharmaceutical supply chain and implementation approach. *Operations Research Forum*, *4*(2), 1–16.

Vaska, S., Massaro, M., Bagarotto, E. M., & Dal Mas, F. (2021). The digital transformation of business model innovation: A structured literature review. *Frontiers in Psychology*, *11*, 539363.

Vial, G. (2021). Understanding digital transformation: A review and a research agenda. *Managing digital transformation*, 13–66.

Wang, C. L., & Ahmed, P. K. (2007). Dynamic capabilities: A review and research agenda. *International Journal of Management Reviews*, *9*(1), 31–51.

Wu, M., Kozanoglu, D. C., Min, C., & Zhang, Y. (2021). Unravelling the capabilities that enable digital transformation: A data-driven methodology and the case of artificial intelligence. *Advanced Engineering Informatics*, *50*, 101368.

Yildiz, T., & Aykanat, Z. (2021). The mediating role of organizational innovation on the impact of strategic agility on firm performance. *World Journal of Entrepreneurship, Management and Sustainable Development*, *17*(4), 765–786.

SECTION 1

DISRUPTIVE INNOVATIONS AND MARKET TRANSFORMATION

CHANGE MANAGEMENT IN THE ADOPTION OF DISRUPTIVE INNOVATION: A CRITICAL REVIEW

Gayatri Panda[a], Amarnath Padhi[a] and Manoj Kumar Dash[b]

[a]*NIST University, India*
[b]*ABV-IIITM, India*

ABSTRACT

In recent decades, organizations globally have faced challenges in adopting disruptive innovation. This chapter explores the relationship between change management and adopting disruptive innovations. Through a systematic analysis of existing literature, common themes and trends in this field are identified. The present study employs a bibliometric and content analysis of 77 publications to analyze the role of change management in the adoption of disruptive innovation. Additionally, a framework is presented to facilitate the understanding of how change management influences the adoption of disruptive innovations within organizations. The research highlights that embracing disruptive innovation is not straightforward; it demands a well-thought-out change management approach. This approach should emphasize cultivating an environment that encourages and nurtures innovation. Creating a culture that empowers employees to take risks and explore new ideas is crucial. Additionally, organizational culture, leadership, communication, and employee engagement emerge as critical factors for the successful adoption of disruptive innovations in the workplace. In summary, it is important to recognize that the successful adoption of disruptive innovations within organizations relies on the successful implementation of change management initiatives.

Keywords: Change management; disruptive; innovation; systematic literature review; bibliometric; Content analysis; visualization

Review of Technologies and Disruptive Business Strategies
Review of Management Literature, Volume 3, 19–45

ISSN: 2754-5865/doi:10.1108/S2754-586520240000003002

1. INTRODUCTION

In today's world, disruption is something we are all familiar with in various industries such as technology and health services. The challenge for organizations these days lies in the effective management of disruptive innovation – the introduction of new products or services that significantly alter existing methods and substitute current market offerings (Dissanaike, 2020). Change management plays an integral role from preimplementation to implementation transition of any innovative concept like the adoption of disruptive innovation. Organizations need to be comfortable enough to embrace changes within their structure while navigating different paradigms associated with disruptive ecosystems (Waddell et al., 2019); only then will they reap full rewards emerging from advantageous adoptions. As organizations face mounting competencies around developments concerning dynamic inventions impacting process flow operations on multiple levels, tackling those requires the reallocation of control structures through collaborative approaches toward implementing relatable solutions amid competition supremacy factors (Meaden et al., 2017). Subsequently, this serves ideally incentivize organizational progress by simultaneously adapting encouragingly to advancing digital technologies leading to intentional convergences among disintegrating industries forming value chains across geographic boundaries priming major successes upholding disrupted markets (Cobbo et al., 2019).

> "Innovation is the lifeblood of organizations in today's fast-paced and competitive landscape" (Drucker, 2014, p. 206).

This sentiment resonates strongly as organisations strive to remain relevant and seize new opportunities. Disruptive innovation powerfully impacts industries by challenging established players and shifting market dynamics. However, effectively adopting disruptive innovations in organizations requires careful consideration and change management strategies implementation (Hiatt & Creasey, 2012). Change management plays a crucial role in guiding organizations through disruptive innovation adoption complexities, using processes, methodologies, and practices that support transitioning individuals, teams, and the overall organization. Effective change management enhances adaptability, spurs innovation, and harnesses disruptive technologies and models' potential. This chapter explores the intersection of change management and disruptive innovation adoption, investigating the challenges, opportunities, and best practices for managing change in this context. According to Christensen (1997), disruptive innovations create new markets, disrupting existing ones. Adopting them necessitates significant organizational changes in structure, processes, and culture because they challenge the status quo, requiring embracing new ways of working to stay competitive. Communication is an essential change management component, creating awareness and understanding of expected impacts from the innovation so individuals and teams can prepare for change and adapt.

2. LITERATURE REVIEW

Innovation plays a pivotal role in an organization's ability to maintain competitiveness and stay ahead in their respective industries. By embracing innovation, organizations can introduce new products and services, explore untapped markets, and enhance their overall profitability. Furthermore, innovation enables organizations to enhance operational efficiency, resulting in cost reductions. This is accomplished by developing novel products and services, capitalizing on emerging markets, and embracing innovative business models that generate strategic advantages. The literature suggests that innovation has garnered significant attention from management practitioners and researchers due to its crucial role in organizational success and the attainment of a competitive edge. This chapter commences with an introduction to disruptive innovation, drawing upon the seminal work of Christensen (2015). The focus lies on its impact on established industries and incumbent players. Christensen's research emphasizes that organizations aiming to leverage disruptive innovation must be willing to re-evaluate existing processes and readily adapt to emerging technologies as they materialize. A fundamental facet explored in this section is the imperative nature of change management when adopting disruptive innovation and the significance of organizations adapting and evolving alongside technological advancements.

The role of change management in enabling organizations to successfully adopt disruptive innovations has received growing research attention in recent years (Rana et al., 2022; Sahni & Kaurav, 2023). As Kaurav and Gupta (2022) highlight, research interest in this area spans multiple disciplines reflecting its multidisciplinary relevance and importance. A technology-focused lens underpins the analysis, consistent with established approaches for bibliometric reviews on technological transformations in industries and functions like artificial intelligence (AI) in human resource management (Kaushal et al., 2023) and digital health (Mishra & Sharma, 2022). By gathering and appraising contributions across relevant management, innovation, information systems, and organizational change literature, this review seeks to advance conceptual and practical understanding of how to enable disruptive innovations through change management strategies and processes. Innovation enables organizations to enhance competitiveness and profitability through novel products, untapped markets, and efficient operations. Research underscores innovation's pivotal role in strategic advantage and organizational success. Drawing on Christensen (2015), adopting disruptive technologies necessitates change management, as organizations must adapt alongside advancing innovations. Essentially, staying competitive amid disruption requires embracing emerging technologies, which likely require process reconfiguration. Companies risk failure if unable to transition quickly. Smith and Jones' (2020) research reveals proactive change management, including clear communication, staff involvement, and training, enables successful disruptive innovation adoption. Recent research emphasizes the critical role of adaptive leadership in navigating organizational disruptions. A study by Su and Junge (2023) found that effective leaders, often termed "innovation catalysts," excel at identifying emerging trends and fostering a culture of change. These leaders distinguish themselves by prioritizing clear communication, employee preparedness, and cultivating support throughout the organization. The study highlights that companies led by such forward-thinking individuals are better positioned to thrive during periods of industry transformation, as they facilitate smoother transitions and capitalize on emerging opportunities.

Research shows blending top-down and bottom-up change management best enables disruptive innovation adoption (Brown & Lee, 2019). Essentially, employee involvement at all levels matters. Experts emphasize innovator cultures accepting of change, risk-taking, and experiments also smooth disruption implementation (Johnson & Christensen, 2019). However, existing cultures valuing stability over agility may hinder innovation by effective leadership (Cameron & Quinn, 2019). Leaders must selectively transform cultures alongside technologies. Overall, research makes clear that leadership-driven change management and innovation-supporting cultures are key to unlocking disruptive innovations' potential without being destabilized by their complexity (Kotter, 2020). Essentially, firm-wide flexibility and willingness to try new things allow organizations to ride waves of disruption. Leadership is crucial when adopting disruptive innovations. Jones and Brown (2019) show leaders provide clear vision and direction while inspiring staff to embrace change and facilitate successful disruption implementation. Likewise, O'Reilly and Tushman's (2008) concept of "organizational ambidexterity" suggests companies balance exploring disruptive opportunities while exploiting existing strengths, aligning with Helfat and Peteraf's (2003) "dynamic capabilities" model where firms nimbly reconfigure competencies to address changing environments. Essentially, research suggests adaptable, proactive leaders setting the course through clarity, inspiration, and support, in ambidextrous cultures flexibly shifting structures and processes, allowing organizations to smoothly ride waves of disruption versus being overwhelmed by them. Implementing disruptive innovations faces cultural resistance and employee fear (Souza & Korsunsky, 2003). Successful change management eases transition via senior leaders communicating implementation's benefits (Goodman, 2012), while training offerings demystify unfamiliar disruptive technologies. Guidance and incentives encouraging risk-taking further reduce anxiety. Additionally, feedback loops monitoring progress help spot adoption barriers early (Garcia, 2007). Essentially, research suggests change leaders quell disruption fears through vision sharing, knowledge building, transition support, and progress tracking. This perspectival and emotional transformation facilitates staff embracing innovations, allowing organizations to smoothly surf industry transformation waves.

Research also shows that disruptive innovations deliver consumer value while exposing companies to profit-rich opportunities (Obi, 2023). Effective change management is crucial for organizations to leverage disruptive innovations (Koll et al., 2024). By addressing adoption barriers, especially staff resistance, companies create receptivity to change. Strategies include reducing anxiety, building knowledge, and incentivizing participation. Change management ultimately determines organizational success in disruptive eras.

Research reveals that innovation-embracing cultures accepting of change and risk more successfully adopt disruptions (Brown & Wilson, 2021). Meanwhile, smooth user-centric integration of new technologies requires information technology (IT) infrastructure capabilities like storage scalability (Li et al., 2020). Essentially, organizational receptivity combined with technical readiness enables disruption adoption. This involves clear communication, visionary leadership, and multilevel participation facilitating employee acceptance (Roblek et al., 2021). Overall, studies emphasize cultivating agility, capabilities, and staff buy-in unlocks disruptive innovations' transformative potential. Organizations lacking these change management fundamentals risk being left behind amid eras of industry upheaval. The adoption of disruptive innovations requires organizations to undergo major changes to their technologies, processes, business models, and cultures (Christensen et al., 2015). Effective change management is critical for organizations to successfully transition to and leverage disruptive innovations, which often promise improved efficiency, productivity, and competitive positioning. Extant research on this phenomenon stems predominantly from IT companies and high-tech start-ups. However, with rapid advancements in areas like fintech, clean energy, AI and automation, quantum computing, biotechnology, and advanced manufacturing, an increasing number of organizations across banking, health care, energy, transportation, logistics, and other industries grapple with managing change during disruptive innovation adoption (Hopp et al., 2018; Yu & Hang, 2010). Researchers have studied various changes required during innovation transitions, including structural realignment, skill development, culture shifts toward creativity and risk-taking, and new performance metrics (Kane et al., 2015). Scholars have also proposed change management frameworks to guide organizations undergoing potentially transformational innovation-based transitions (Paehler, 2018).

While providing important theoretical insights, the extant literature has three key limitations. First, most empirical findings derive from small samples of start-ups and IT companies (Euchner, 2019; McAdam, 2003). More research across larger samples of brick-and-mortar companies transitioning core systems is needed. Second, there is little investigation into the scalability and transferability of change management approaches across industries with varying regulation, infrastructure maturity, access to skills, and innovation ecosystems. Researchers have called for contextualizing findings since change triggers and processes likely differ across industries (Huber, 2003). Finally, existing studies predominately highlight successful cases rather than exploring barriers or unsuccessful efforts, skewing understanding (Markard & Truffer, 2006). To advance scholarship, scholars should conduct critical studies investigating failed implementation attempts and challenges companies seeking to leverage disruptive innovation face when managing complex, transformational change initiatives. Though extant research explores effective change management frameworks, these prescriptive models often overlook implementation challenges that can derail innovation adoption efforts. Scholars argue change management models provide "idealistic rational pictures" yet fail to capture the messy realities of navigating complex transitions (By, 2005). The literature lacks a critical analysis of why many companies still struggle to leverage potentially transformative innovations despite the availability of change management best practices. Implementation barriers highlighted in isolated studies provide clues but deserve deeper investigation across contexts. Challenges include a lack of long-term commitment from leadership (Dooley & Sullivan, 2007), change fatigue from repeated failed efforts (Maurer, 2010), poor communication that increases uncertainty and cynicism (Elving, 2005), skill deficiencies despite training investments (Burnes & Cooke, 2013), and cultural inertia preventing widespread adoption of new processes (Kotlewski & Moeslein, 2020). Such barriers are embedded during implementation, often derailing meticulously planned change initiatives mid-stream after significant resource outlays (Appelbaum et al., 2012).

Scholars posit underlying reasons for failed efforts may involve misjudging the complexity of required structural, behavioral, and cultural transformations (Smets et al., 2012). Critics argue that prescribed change models cannot anticipate emergent obstacles like staff turnover, leadership changes, technology glitches, or flagging morale (By, 2005). Isolated insights suggest change leaders often struggle to "operate in the gray" when external or internal discontinuities disrupt implementation (Burnes, 2015). Yet the specific managerial challenges arising from nonlinear innovation journeys in different organizational contexts remain understudied. Advancing scholarship on leading change amid disruptive innovation requires expanding beyond normative prescriptions to critically examine implementation barriers arising from complex system-level interactions that delay or derail adoption efforts. Context-sensitive empirical research can elucidate common stumbling blocks during transitions and how multilayered social structures shape variable change outcomes across industries for theory building (Bartunek & Woodman, 2015). Such critical research holds vital insights for equipping managers to navigate inevitable emergent challenges that punctuate disruptive innovation adoption journeys.

Recently, scholars have critically examined failed or challenging digital transformation efforts in industries like health care and tourism that have seen massive disruptions from new technologies. Mishra and Sharma (2022) evaluated telehealth implementations, finding lack of technological maturity and poor clinical workflow integration limited adoption and convergence across healthcare systems. Similarly, Kaurav et al. (2020) used bibliometric analysis to reveal tourism and hospitality digitalization faced barriers including a lack of customer readiness, employee skill gaps in leveraging technologies like AI, and the inability to synchronize complex system changes. These findings highlight how innovation adoption models pushing new technologies underestimate socio-technical change requirements and overestimate the readiness of staff and customers. Researchers highlight that while disruptive innovations can allow organizations to dramatically improve products, services, and processes, the changes required to leverage such innovations involve substantial challenges (Govindarajan & Srivastava, 2022). Organizations need new skills, changes in culture, updated workflows, and operating models to capitalize on the potential of disruptive innovation (Tell et al., 2022). Studies indicate that weaknesses in change management are a key barrier to disrupted innovation success, whereas change management capabilities can act as a vital enabler (Appelbaum et al., 2012; Santos et al., 2022). As disruptive innovations often conflict with existing systems, processes, and employee mindsets, managing tensions and resistance during adoption phases is crucial (Besson & Løvas, 2022). Despite the acknowledgment of the pivotal role of change management, there remain knowledge gaps regarding specific change management strategies, leadership approaches, and cultural factors that can facilitate effective disruptive innovation adoption (Skog et al., 2022; Totterdill, 2020).

3. METHODOLOGY

This study utilized two major research methodologies – a systematic literature review (SLR) and bibliometric analysis. Bibliometric analysis measures three important criteria: review technique, relational technique, and evaluation technique. Review techniques include traditional methods such as SLRs and meta-analyses. Relational techniques examine the relationships between existing studies based on co-authorship, co-occurring keywords, citation, co-citation analysis, and bibliographic coupling. Lastly, the evaluation technique aims to explore the scientific performance or contributions of two or more individuals or groups. These methodologies help us gain a comprehensive understanding of the research landscape and the significant contributions made by researchers in a particular field. By employing these techniques, we can gain valuable insights into the current state of research and identify areas that require further investigation. When it comes to evaluating research, there are three main groups of techniques to consider. The first group is focused on measuring contributions, such as the number of papers authored by an individual, the number of papers produced in a given year, and the number of times a paper has been cited. The second group is all about impact metrics, including the total number of citations received, the number of citations per year, and usage log data that tracks the average usage rates for articles published in a journal. Finally, there are hybrid metrics that aim to capture both productivity and impact by providing a single figure, such as the average number of citations per paper or various indices designed to measure both factors simultaneously. With these techniques at our disposal, we can better understand the impact and value of research in a variety of fields.

The focus of our research was to conduct a comprehensive SLR and bibliometric analysis to identify the most prominent themes in the research area through clustering. Many studies utilize visualization tools such as Bibliometrix, Gephi, and Pajek. However, our team used the VOSviewer and Bibiloshiny package of R studio to develop and analyze data for various bibliometric techniques. Fig. 1 highlights the different bibliometric techniques and their strengths in research.

The SLR technique is a powerful tool for researchers looking to gain valuable insights into existing research on a particular topic (Paul & Barari, 2022). By analyzing and synthesizing various literature studies, an SLR can provide answers to research questions and help identify research gaps that can guide future studies. In this study, we followed the Preferred Reporting Items for Systematic Reviews and Meta-Analyses (PRISMA) guidelines, a widely accepted framework for identifying, screening, and including relevant articles for further

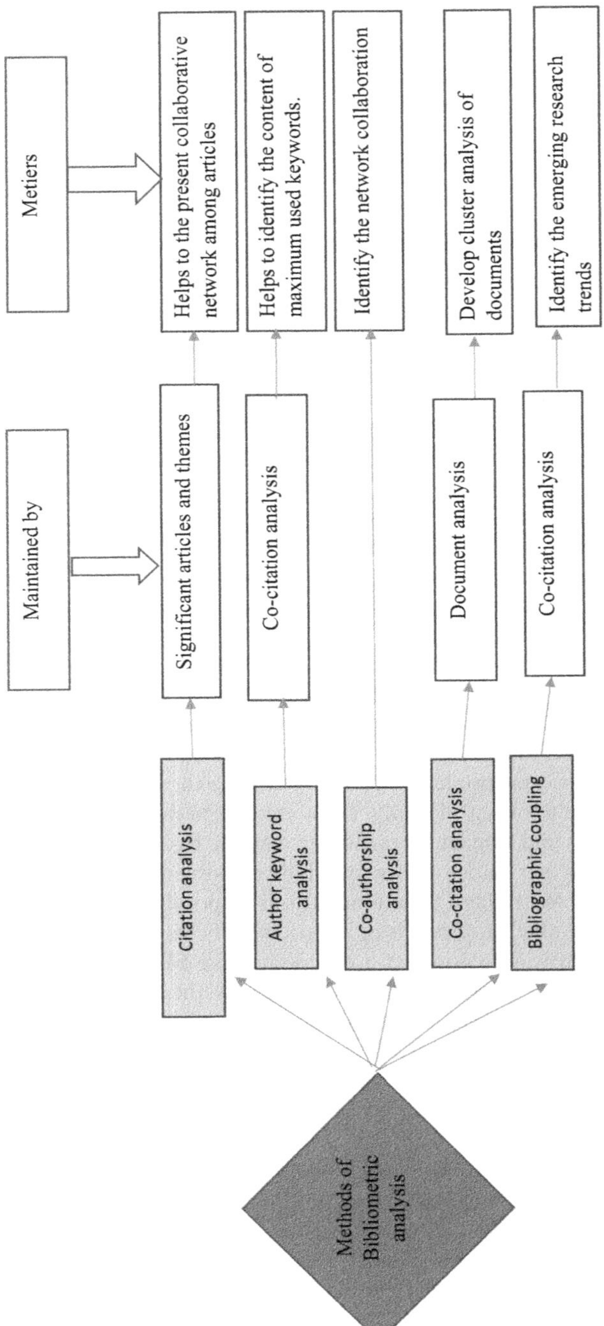

Fig. 1. Techniques of Visualization and Strength Analysis. *Source:* Created by authors.

review and analysis. The researchers aim to gain a comprehensive understanding of change management in the adoption of disruptive technology. Therefore, the researchers presented the key statistics in Table 1, which describe the current research status in the domain. Fig. 2 outlines our search and inclusion strategy for selecting research papers for our study.

3.1 Database Selection

For the present research work, the authors have used the Scopus database to extract the required articles for further analysis and synthesis of results. The major reason for the selection of the database is that it is considered one the largest databases to explore scientific publications. It provides a comprehensive review to analyze the literature and extract inferences as the research papers indexed in the Scopus database are carefully chosen for inclusion (Alka et al., 2023; Meyers et al., 2021).

Table 1. Key Statistics on Change Management in Adoption of Disruptive Innovation.

Description	Results
Key Statistics	
Duration	2001–2022
Sources (Journals)	77
Papers	77
Average publication years wise	1
Average citations per article	11
References	3,071
Document Type	
Article	58
Review	19
Document contents	
Keywords plus	637
Author's keywords	278
Authors	71
Existence of authors	54
One-authored documents	54
Multiple-authored documents	3
Collaboration of Authors	
One-authored papers	54
Document per Author	1
Coauthors per papers	1
Collaboration index	2.0

Source: Created by authors.

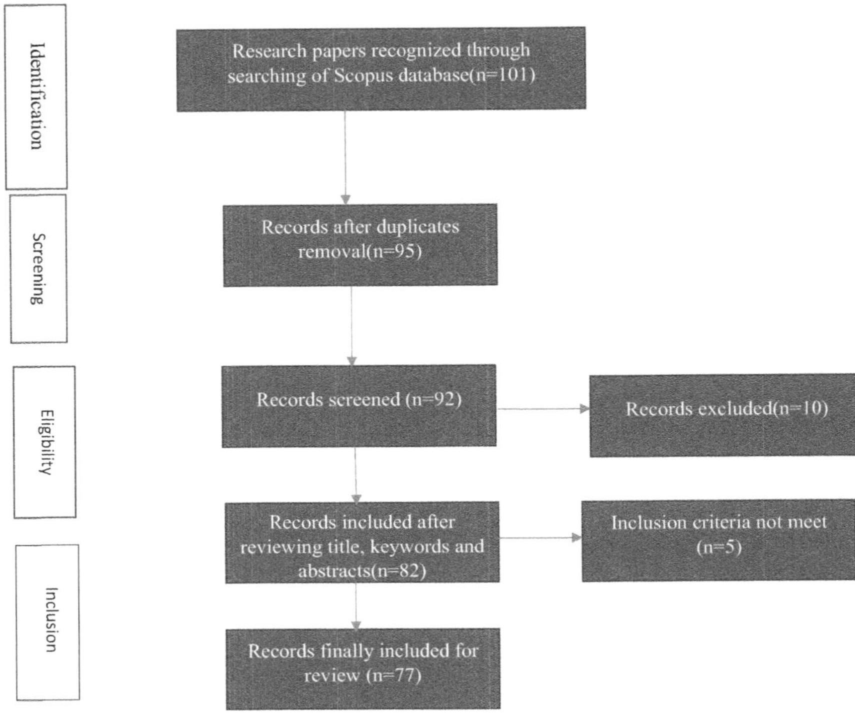

Fig. 2. Identification and Selection of Literature. *Source:* Created by authors.

3.2 Search Strategy

To identify suitable research articles, a comprehensive search was undertaken in the current research study by utilizing a variety of keywords pertinent to the research domain as follows ([“Change management” OR “Change management process” OR “Transformation management” OR “Innovation management” OR “Transition management”] AND TITLE-ABS-KEY [“Disruptive innovation” OR “Transformative innovation” OR “Revolutionary Innovation” OR “Break-through innovation”]). The present research study clarifies that the study considered the whole publications in the research domain. It does not create any time interval for extracting the intervals.

3.3 Article Extraction and Assessment

The initial search resulted in finding 101 articles from the Scopus database. The researchers took several steps to extract and retain the final data file, including selecting relevant articles that matched the research domain.

4. RESEARCH QUESTIONS

The primary objective of our study is to explore and gain a clear view of existing research trends on change management through the adoption of disruptive innovation. It measures what has been done and what future researchers can address in their studies. The present research work explores the research domain to identify the emerging themes that are beyond the traditional approaches, methods, and techniques. The study is a yardstick to gather insights into the domain with a perspective on addressing change management. Thus, the stated gaps motivated the researchers to develop the stated research questions:

RQ1. What is the publication trend, highly contributing authors, and highly cited sources in the research area?
RQ2. What are the current research trends in change management through the adoption of disruptive innovation?
RQ3. What are developed emerging themes through cluster analysis in change management through the adoption of disruptive innovation?
RQ4. What is the future research framework identifying the benefits, opportunities, and outcomes of change management through the adoption of disruptive innovation?

Based on the stated research questions, the following research objectives have been formulated to signify the present research work:

- To address the present research state of the condition through analyzing the extracted data from the Scopus database as well as developing network maps (i.e., keyword co-occurrence, citation, co-citation, and bibliographic coupling analysis).
- To identify the emerging themes and develop a framework for benefits, opportunities, and outcomes of change management through the adoption of disruptive innovation.

4.1 Answer to RQ1

4.1.1 Yearly Publication Trend Analysis

The publication trend measures the contribution of researchers in change management through the adoption of disruptive innovation. Fig. 3 discusses the yearly contribution of the researchers. The graph signifies that in the beginning, there was no momentum among researchers to develop academic literature for the field of research. However, from 2020, there is a growth trend in the literature which shows a significant interest and surge rise in the literature in the concerned research area. Hence, it signifies researchers are constantly driving hard to contribute to the field and explore new dimensions and antecedents for better results and focusing on understanding change management through innovative management.

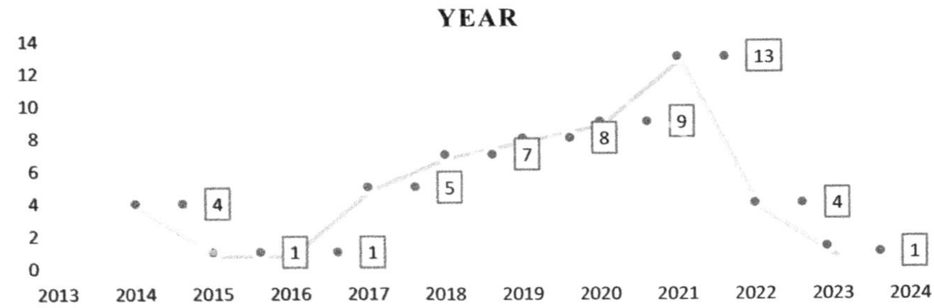

Fig. 3. Yearly Trend. *Source:* Created by authors.

4.1.2 Top Contributing Authors

The developed Fig. 4 analyses the top 10 author's statistics. In terms of the author's contribution, Weinreich. S has contributed three articles with the maximum contribution. Next to that, Asmar, L with two articles followed by Cubero, J. N. with two articles. Thus, the consecutive authors have made similar contributions to the research field.

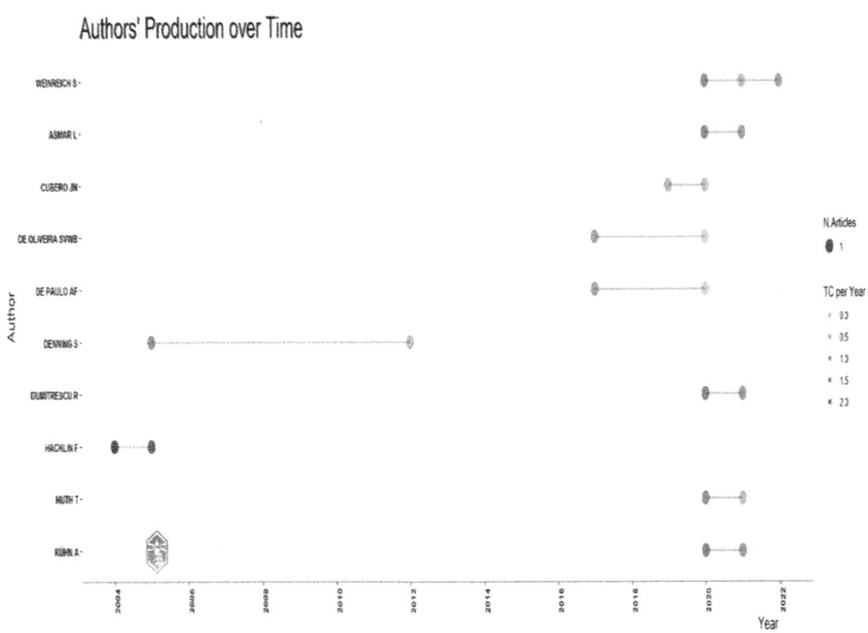

Fig. 4. Author Statistics. *Source:* Created by authors.

The developed diagram signifies future researchers can contribute significantly to the field and add value to the academic fraternity by exploring the existing literature and analyzing the different dimensions and applications through the adoption of change management in disruptive innovation.

4.1.3 Top Cited Sources

The analysis of the top 10 cited sources is explained in Fig. 5. It is signified from the developed figure that the *International Journal of Innovation and Technology Management* has the maximum publication, next to *Procedia CIRP*, followed by *Strategy and Leadership*. These are the three journals with the maximum publications. The researchers have restricted the analysis of 10 sources considering the space and word limit constraints. Table 2 provides an elaborative idea on the various aspects such as the number of publications, total citations, and publication start year regarding the top 10 sources to provide ideas to the upcoming researchers and provide better insight for the selection of publication scope and opportunity in journals.

Fig. 6 describes the analysis of a three-field plot diagram, or it is also called as "Sankey diagram." It shows a dynamic linkage between three elements of the study (keywords, countries, and journals). The researchers analyzed the 77 articles extracted from the Scopus database, through the Sankey diagram and provided a brief analysis to identify the linkage and analyze the noteworthy contributions to the research field. The plot area is divided into three sections, highlighting journals on the left, keywords in the middle, and the most contributing countries on the right-hand side. It is fascinating to note that Germany, the United States of America, and Spain are the top contributors in the research field. In terms of the linkage between the author's keyword and country, it states

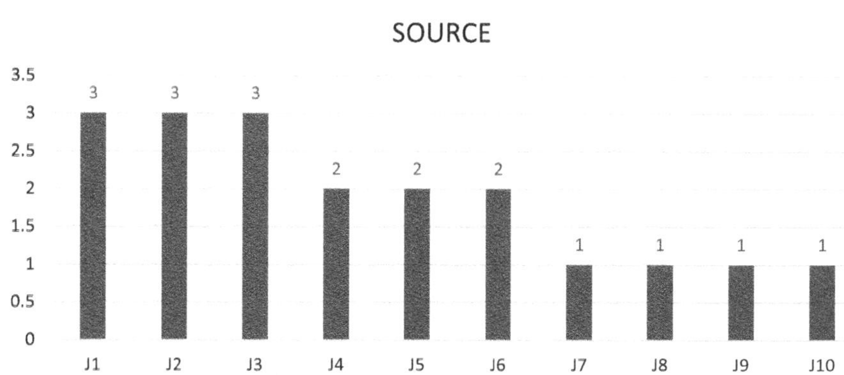

Fig. 5. Source Statistics. *Source:* Created by authors. *Note:* J1: *International Journal of Innovation and Technology Management*, J2: *Procedia CIRP*, J3: *Strategy and Leadership*, J4: *IEEE International Engineering Management Conference*, J5: *Journal of Product Innovation Management*, J6: *Research Technology Management*, J7: *Advances In Science Technology And Engineering Systems*, J8: *Built Heritage*, J9: *Business History Review*, J10: *California Management Review*.

Table 2 Source Statistics.

Source	No of Publications	*h*-index	TCI	Publication Start Year
J1	3	24	753	2004
J2	3	91	16,348	2012
J3	3	51	4,982	1996
J4	2	20	100	1996
J5	2	162	16,577	1984
J6	2	77	430	1988
J7	1	16	536	2016
J8	1	7	65	2017
J9	1	34	822	1926
J10	1	147	2,180	1970

Source: Created by authors.
Note: TCI – Total Citation Index.

keywords like "disruptive innovation," "innovation management," "change management," and "Innovation" are frequently used keywords by authors to publish research papers. The journals like the "International Journal of Technology and Management," "Procedia CIRP," and "Strategy and Leadership" are the journals having maximum publications in the research field.

4.2 Answer to RQ2

To analyze the stated *RQ2*, the researchers performed the network analysis. The network analysis is performed based on three criteria such as semantic analysis (based on keyword co-occurrence), Next to that, citation analysis is carried out to identify the emerging themes and trending topics in the area of research.

Lastly, co-citation analysis to analyze the author's collaboration network and the contribution to the research field.

4.2.1 Keyword Co-occurrence Analysis

The developed Fig. 7 describes the keyword co-occurrence statistics. It is identified that "disruptive innovation" is the keyword with the highest usage with 27 occurrences and a total strength link of 49, next to that "innovation management" and "change management" with occurrences of 25 and 14 and a total link strength (TLS) of 49 and 35, respectively. The researchers in the present research study identified 270 keywords; based on the set inclusion criteria of a minimum of 2 times occurrence of keywords, 38 keywords were retained for developing the visualization map using the VOSviewer visualization software. It can be observed from Fig. 7 the keyword co-occurrence map is connected through different nodes and classified in different colors for easy identification. Thus, Table 3 describes the top 10 highly used keywords and their occurrence and TLS in the research domain. Thus, future researchers can use the prominent keywords in their research studies and can navigate the field of research for better contributions and outcomes.

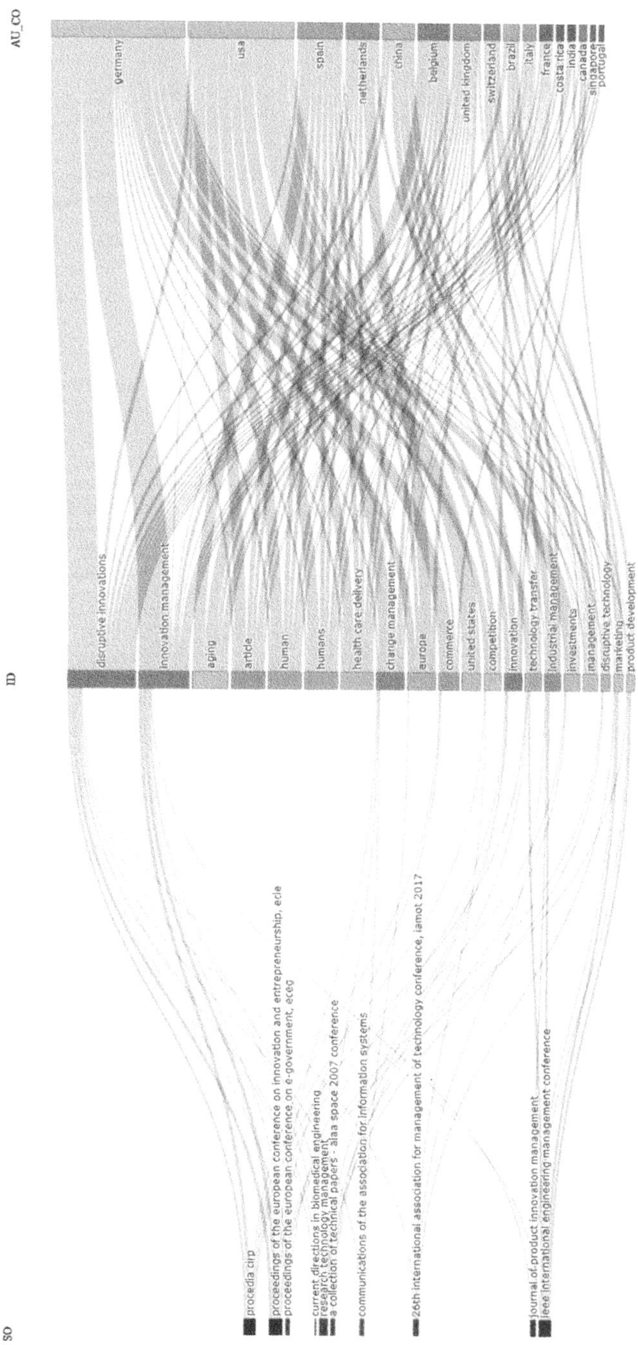

Fig. 6. Three-Field Plot Analysis Using Bibliometrix *R* Package. *Source:* Created by authors.

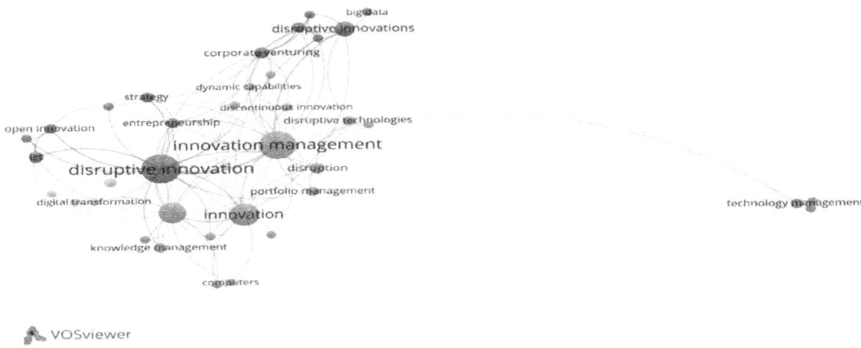

Fig. 7. Keyword's Co-occurrence Statistics. *Source:* Created by authors.

Table 3. Keyword Co-occurrence Statistics.

Keywords	Occurrence	Total Link Strength
Disruptive innovation	27	49
Innovation management	25	49
Change management	14	35
innovation	16	31
Corporate venturing	4	15
Discontinuous innovation	7	14
ICT	3	9
Entrepreneurship	3	8
Radical innovation	2	8

Source: Created by authors.

4.2.2 Citation Network Analysis (Based on Themes)

Citation analysis is a powerful tool that enables researchers to delve into the existing literature and uncover its conceptual structure. By identifying key themes, researchers can better understand the landscape of their chosen field and determine which areas require further exploration (Öberg, 2023). At the heart of this analysis is the thematic map, which is based on the centrality and density concept developed by Callon et al. (1991). This map is divided into two main themes: centrality, which measures the importance of a particular theme, and density, which tracks the growth and expansion of a theme over time (Alkhammash, 2023). To make sense of this map, researchers divide it into four quadrants: motor themes, which are the most important and influential; emerging or declining themes, which are on the rise or fall respectively; basic themes, which are the foundation of the field; and niche themes, which are specialized and often overlooked. Rectangular boxes represent the themes and subthemes in Fig. 8. Three subthemes, disruptive innovation, corporate venturing, and ambidexterity, are

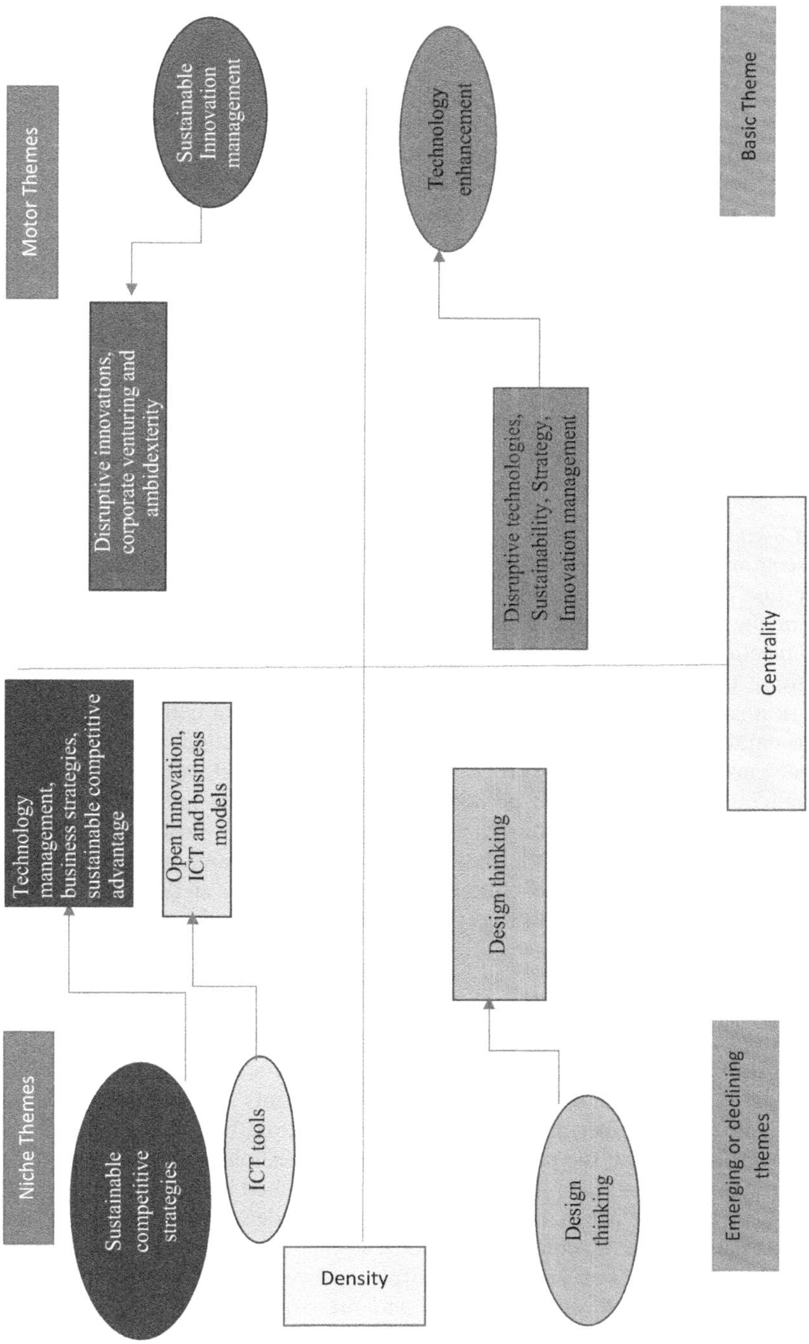

Fig. 8. Thematic Map. *Source:* Created by authors.

identified in the right top quadrant. These are grouped under "sustainable innovation management" and referred to as the motor theme. Since this is one of the highly contributing areas of research, it plays an immense role in analyzing the existing research studies. The left quadrant at the top is referred to as niche themes, it has two sets of themes and subthemes that are referred to as "sustainable competitive advantage," and it has subthemes such as technology management, business strategies, and sustainable competitive advantage; the next subthemes are open innovation, information and communications technology (ICT) tools, and business models, and it is grouped as "ICT tools." The next quadrant on the left below describes the emerging or declining which is grouped as "design thinking," whereas the last quadrant on the right below is termed as the basic theme which is named "technology enhancement" (Khare & Jain, 2022). The researchers identified the various themes and analyzed various quadrants to provide a pathway for future researchers. Therefore, future researchers and research studies can mobile the information and develop various qualitative and quantitative studies and add value to the academic field.

4.2.3 Co-citation Analysis

This section addresses the analysis of the co-citation network among authors. Co-citation occurs when multiple documents cite the same articles, and it reflects the combined impact of those articles (Boyack & Klavans, 2010). The strength of the connection between two publications is determined by the number of citations they share (White & McCain, 1998). For this research study, the co-citation network analysis was performed using VOSviewer with data extracted from the Scopus database. Figs. 9 and 10 illustrate the various connections between nodes, with each node representing an article. The links between nodes depict co-citation occurrences, and the distance between nodes indicates the relevance of their topics (Liu et al., 2013). The resulting map consists of three clusters: red, green, and blue. These clusters indicate that authors within the same cluster cite each other on similar themes. The clusters were automatically determined by the VOSviewer software based on subject relatedness or keyword similarity.

4.3 Answer to RQ3 *and* RQ4

4.3.1 Cluster Analysis (Bibliographic Coupling)

To address research questions 3 and 4, the research study conducted cluster analysis by utilizing bibliographic coupling of documents. The VOSviewer software was employed to perform the analysis and generate the clusters. Based on stated inclusion criteria, the researchers have set a threshold limit of 10 citations to a document to be included in the analysis which resulted in the identification of 23 documents, out of which 13 documents were considered as the largest set of connected items which are considered for developing the clusters. The clusters are grouped in five colors: red, green, blue, purple, and yellow. Table 4 describes the citations and TLS of developed clusters and the papers in the stated clusters. Thus, the below section describes the research contributions in each cluster and

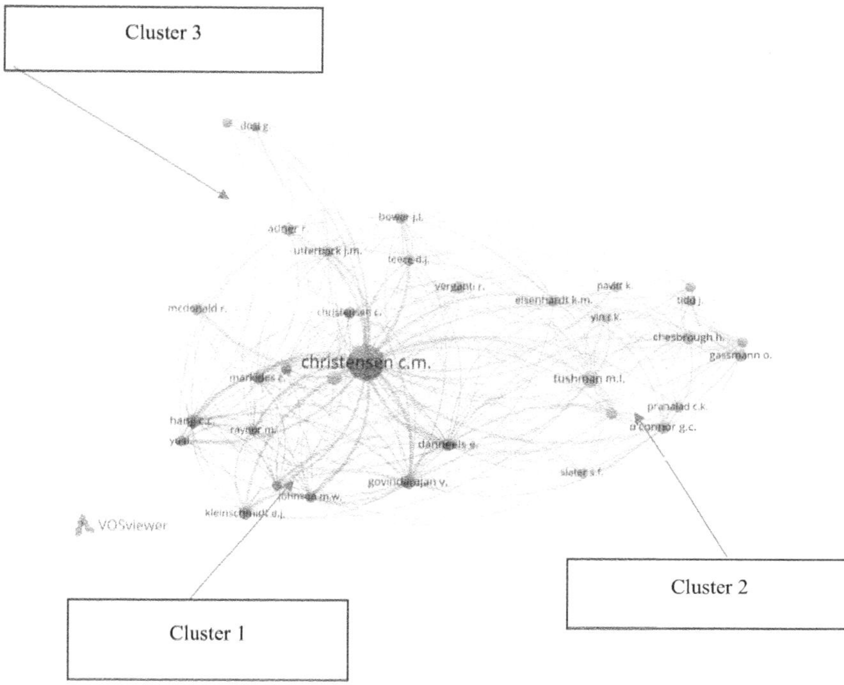

Fig. 9. Co-citation Network Map. *Source:* Created by authors.

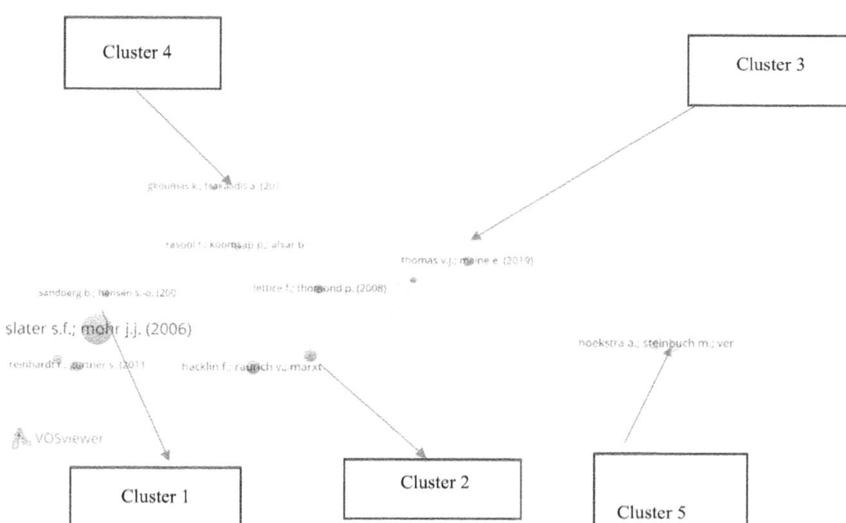

Fig. 10. Bibliographic Coupling of Documents. *Source:* Created by authors.

Table 4. Cluster Analysis of Documents.

Clusters	Citations	Total Link Strength
Cluster 1: Research for the Management of Disruptive Innovation		
Denning (2005)	22	2
Reinhardt and Gurtner (2011)	24	4
Sandberg and Hansén, (2004)	14	1
Slater and Mohr (2006)	*200*	*6*
Cluster 2: Organizational Resources are a Pathway for Handling Disruptive Innovation		
Hacklin et al. (2004)	*46*	*13*
Hacklin et al. (2005)	*37*	*21*
Lettice and Thomond (2008)	*22*	*3*
Cluster 3: Strategy Building Based on Market and Competitor's Plan		
Shang et al. (2019)	*12*	*13*
Thomas and Maine (2019)	*25*	*1*
Cluster 4: Framework to Develop Disruptive Innovation Strategies and Well-Being		
Rasool et al. (2018)	*41*	*3*
Gkoumas and Tsakalidis (2019)	*30*	*1*
Cluster 5: Management Support to Handle Crisis		
Hoekstra et al. (2017)	*13*	*1*
Novotny and Laestadius (2014)	*21*	*14*

Source: Created by authors.

analyzes the research papers for further understanding of the contribution to the research field. Each cluster is elaborated in different sections.

4.3.1.1 Cluster 1: Research for the Management of Disruptive Innovation. Cluster one is connoted as red color. Cluster one consists of five documents. Disruptive innovation is widely recognized as crucial in managing change, offering numerous opportunities and methods for understanding challenges and developing strategies to promote growth. An influential article by Slate and Mohr (2006) emphasizes the importance of evaluating an organization's capabilities and employee skill sets to manage disruptive innovation effectively. It also highlights the significance of exploring capabilities to achieve operational efficiency, gain a competitive advantage, and ensure long-term sustainability.

The second article was Reinhardt and Gurtner (2011) with a TLS 4 developed model that describes customer analysis as an important determinant to handling disruptive innovation; the model gave an insight that analyzing every possible mechanism is responsible for developing the right solutions for the problems faced. The third article by Denning (2005) with a TLS 2 discussed solving the paradox of innovation; it stated that dealing with disruptive innovation rethinking is a fundamental assumption. It is very important to examine the situation and develop methods to forecast the changing conditions and solutions. The fourth article in the cluster is by Sandberg and Hansén (2004); the authors explained the relationship between market proactiveness and disruptive innovations; it discussed various dimensions such as the scope of market proactiveness, idea generation, and development are generally very important for meeting the changing needs and achieve the organization-stated goals.

Based on the comprehensive review of various research papers discussed earlier, the following propositions are presented for future research studies:

P1. To emphasize other determinants of innovation variables such as rethinking, idea generation, and proactiveness in the context of national and international markets are necessary to meet the challenges.
P2. To examine through empirical research and identify the impact of innovation on change management for handling disruptive situations
P3. To analyze how change management through disruptive innovation in the long run results in a positive relationship with market conditions and organizational perspectives.
P4. To investigate the question "If disruptive innovation is not the main direction to change management, then what else is"?

4.3.1.2 Cluster2: Organizational Resources Are a Pathway for Handling Disruptive Innovation. Cluster two is connoted as red color. Cluster two consists of three documents. The top article was authored by Hacklin et al. (2005) with a TLS of 21; the researcher stated that operative decisions are very important in disruptive innovation as the economic and technological environment are very uncertain. Thus, the organization should develop a convergence approach for making corrective decisions. In the second article, with a TLS 13, Hacklin et al. (2004) stated that developing change management is a long-term process based on changing circumstances and technological changes. It should be a continuous phenomenon in every organization. The third article with TLC 3 by Lettice and Thomond (2008) stated that resource allocation is one of the prime factors for bringing and adopting innovation. Based on the previous discussions on existing literature, the following propositions are proposed for future research on this theme.

P5. To study the effects of disruptive innovation on organizational resources, and how it changes allocation, utilization, and investment patterns.
P6. To examine how organizational factors such as the management decision-making processes influence on change management process through disruptive innovation as well as employee well-being.
P7. To assess how disruptive innovation can be applied to assessing the change management benefits in short-run and long-run conditions.

4.3.1.3 Cluster 3: Strategy Building Based on Market and Competitor's Plan. Cluster three is connoted as blue color. Cluster two consists of two documents. The article by Shang et al. (2019) with TLS 13 identified eight key streams that are a major yardstick that brings disruptive innovation to an organization. The next article was authored by Thomas and Maine (2019), which discussed that disruptive innovation is not suitable to follow rather commercialization strategy is essential to monitor the market progress and handle competitive advantage over competitors. Based on the above-stated discussion of existing studies, the following propositions are formulated:

P8. To study the effects of disruptive innovation on creating competitive advantage and handling market demands.

P9. To examine factors economic and noneconomic factors responsible for the change management process through disruptive innovation.

4.3.1.4 Cluster 4: Framework to Develop Disruptive Innovation Strategies and Well-Being. Cluster four is denoted with purple color. The study by Rasool et al. (2018) presented a framework for developing innovation strategies within an organization using the existing setting of the incumbent firm, achieving the highest TLS 3. It suggests having a proactive approach toward developing innovations and also identifying those of competitors. The next article by Gkoumas and Tsakalidis (2019), titled "TLS 1," explores the topic of innovation management in the field of transport by focusing on the identification and evaluation of new and emerging technologies and trends. Building on the previous discussion of existing studies, the following propositions are formulated for further research:

P10. To examine the impact of frameworks developed to handle disruptive innovation for meeting challenges and market conditions.

P11. To analyze the trends responsible for the change management process through disruptive innovation.

4.3.1.5 Cluster 5: Management Support to Handle Crisis. Cluster five is denoted with yellow color. The article with maximum TLS 14 authored by Novotny and Laestadius (2014) stated that process innovations are tightly linked with product innovations. It is essential to identify the risks and uncertainties beforehand and management should develop plans to handle the crisis and provide with optimum solution. Hoekstra et al. (2017) stated that to develop profitable pathways through disruptive innovation, it is very important to have a heterogenous, learning, strategizing, and integrating culture, that will enable one to smoothly understand the changing conditions and prevailing a positive workflow in the organization. Based on the above-stated discussion of existing studies, the following propositions are formulated.

P12. To examine the process and product innovation to handle change management

P13. To analyze the implications of organizational culture for the change management process through disruptive innovation.

5. IMPLICATIONS

This research study has important implications for measuring the change management process through disruptive innovation. It highlights the importance of recognizing and identifying processes to facilitate organizations in developing clear and thoughtful plans and policies for making corrective decisions and ensuring the long-term sustainability and security of the organization. This study lays the foundation for further exploration by organizations, governments, policymakers, and researchers to assess current research conditions and investigate areas where the change management process can be implemented. Additionally, change management is a continuous process that addresses the needs of the market, customers, and organizations, making it an essential action for success. Future researchers can delve into developing more studies that provide practical pathways for implementing change management in the organizational context and leveraging the potential of innovation. Furthermore, applying disruptive innovation mechanisms can expand strategies and not only improve organizational well-being but also enhance employee well-being through skill enhancement programs and adequate training mechanisms for optimal outcomes.

6. CONCLUSION AND FUTURE RESEARCH DIRECTION

The present study conducted a SLR and bibliometric analysis using the PRISMA approach, utilizing data extracted from the Scopus database. Following a rigorous screening process, the study narrowed down the dataset to 77 research articles. The analysis provided comprehensive insights into significant publications, authors, journals, organizations, countries, co-citation patterns, and cluster analysis in the field of change management in the adoption of disruptive innovation. To facilitate the analysis, the study employed the Bibiloshiny data visualization tool in conjunction with R programming and VOSviewer. The research extensively covered various aspects of change management through disruptive innovation, including conceptual understanding derived from co-occurrence network analysis and thematic map analysis. By applying cluster analysis, the researchers identified five emerging research themes and put forward future research propositions within those particular themes, providing potential directions for future studies. The identified themes are management of disruptive innovation, pathway for handling disruptive innovation, strategy building based on market plans, framework to handle disruptive innovation and well-being, and management support to handle crises. To further expand the scope of this research area, future studies can broaden their focus by incorporating additional emerging keywords. Additionally, this study exclusively utilized a single database, and future research can explore other databases to gain a more comprehensive understanding of the research landscape. Moreover, the inclusion of quantitative tools like AHP, DEMATEL, and FUZZY-AHP can contribute to a deeper understanding of the subject matter and enrich the literature and academic community.

REFERENCES

Alka, M., Bancong, H., & Muzaini, M. (2023). Bibliometric analysis of Pedagogical Content Knowledge (PCK) publication trends in Scopus database from 2018 to 2022. *Studies in Learning and Teaching*, *4*(2), 306–318.

Alkhammash, E. Z. (2023). Viewing research themes through the lens of citation analysis: A methodological exploration. *Journal of Informetrics*, *17*(1), 101291.

Appelbaum, S. H., Habashy, S., Malo, J. L., & Shafiq, H. (2012). Back to the future: Revisiting Kotter's 1996 change model. *The Journal of Management Development*, *31*(8), 764–782.

Bartunek, J. M., & Woodman, R. W. (2015). Beyond Lewin: Toward a temporal approximation of organization development and change. *Annual Review of Organizational Psychology and Organizational Behavior*, *2*, 157–182.

Besson, P., & Løvas, B. (2022). Strategic change and innovation in incumbent firms: Managing tensions between present and future business models. *Long Range Planning*, *55*(4), 102311.

Boyack, K. W., & Klavans, R. (2010). Co-citation analysis, bibliographic coupling, and direct citation: Which citation approach represents the research front most accurately? *Journal of the American Society for Information Science and Technology*, *61*(12), 2389–2404.

Brown, A., & Lee, J. (2019). Mixing leadership approaches for disruptive innovation adoption. *Journal of Business Strategy*, *41*(4), 23–31.

Brown, L., & Wilson, H. (2021). Cultural predictors of disruptive innovation adoption. *Journal of Change Management*, *24*(4), 67–85.

Burnes, B. (2015). Understanding resistance to change–building on Coch and French. *Journal of Change Management*, *15*(2), 92–116.

Burnes, B., & Cooke, B. (2013). Kurt Lewin's Field theory: A review and re-evaluation. *International Journal of Management Reviews*, *15*(4), 408–425.

By, R. T. (2005). Organisational change management: A critical review. *Journal of Change Management*, *5*(4), 369–380.

Callon, M., Courtial, J. P., Turner, W. A., & Bauin, S. (1991). From translations to problematic networks: An introduction to co-word analysis. *Information (International Social Science Council)*, *22*(2), 191–235.

Cameron, K., & Quinn, R. (2019). Organizational culture assessment for disruptive innovation readiness. *Innovation Management Journal*, *22*(3), 79–96.

Christensen, C. M. (1997). *The innovator's dilemma: When new technologies cause great firms to fail*. Harvard Business Review Press.

Christensen, C. M. (2015). *The innovator's dilemma: When new technologies cause great firms to fail*. Harvard Business Review Press.

Christensen, C. M., Raynor, M. E., & McDonald, R. (2015). What is disruptive innovation? *Harvard Business Review*, *93*(12), 44–53.

Cobbo, S., Coughlin-Hill Ince Merlo Varuzzo, D. M., D'Esposito, M. R., Masullo, M., & Tresca, R. (2019). Emergent governance and disruptive technologies: The case of blockchain. *Entrepreneurship Research Journal*, *9*(4), 1–14.

Denning, S. (2005). Why the best and brightest approaches don't solve the innovation dilemma. *Strategy & Leadership*, *33*(1), 4–11.

Dissanaike, G. (2020). Disruptive innovation and management strategies. In *Applied psychology readings* (pp. 19–35). Springer.

Dooley, K., & Sullivan, W. (2007). Institutional strategy and decision making in the deregulation of the US railroad industry. *Research in the Sociology of Organizations*, *25*, 1–35.

Drucker, P. F. (2014). *Innovation and entrepreneurship*. Routledge.

Elving, W. J. (2005). The role of communication in organisational change. *Corporate Communications: An International Journal*, *10*(2), 129–138.

Euchner, J. (2019). Feature topic: Managing disruption. *Research-Technology Management*, *62*(2), 10–15.

Garcia, M. (2007). Monitoring the disruptive innovation adoption process. *Journal of Business Technology*, *23*(4), 46–60.

Gkoumas, K., & Tsakalidis, A. (2019). A framework for the taxonomy and assessment of new and emerging transport technologies and trends. *Transport*, *34*(4), 455–466.

Goodman, J. (2012). Leading disruptive change. *Advances in Management*, *5*(5), 4–8.

Govindarajan, V., & Srivastava, A. (2022). Why digital transformations fail. *Harvard Business Review*, *100*(2), 56–63.

Hacklin, F., Raurich, V., & Marxt, C. (2004). How incremental innovation becomes disruptive: The case of technology convergence. In *2004 IEEE International Engineering Management Conference (IEEE Cat. No. 04CH37574)* (Vol. 1, pp. 32–36). IEEE.

Hacklin, F., Raurich, V., & Marxt, C. (2005). Implications of technological convergence on innovation trajectories: The case of ICT industry. *International Journal of Innovation and Technology Management, 2*(03), 313–330.

Helfat, C., & Peteraf, M. (2003). The dynamic resource-based view: Capability lifecycles. *Strategic Management Journal, 24*(10), 997–1010.

Hiatt, J. M., & Creasey, T. J. (2012). *Change management: The people side of change*. Prosci Learning Center Publications.

Hoekstra, A., Steinbuch, M., & Verbong, G. (2017). Creating agent-based energy transition management models that can uncover profitable pathways to climate change mitigation. *Complexity, 2017*, 1–23.

Hopp, C., Antons, D., Kaminski, J., & Salge, T. O. (2018). Disruptive innovation: Conceptual foundations, empirical evidence, and research opportunities in the digital age. *Journal of Product Innovation Management, 35*(3), 446–457.

Huber, G. P. (2003). Disruptive technology: How Kodak missed the digital photography revolution. *Creativity at Work, 12*(1), 2–5.

Johnson, C., & Christensen, R. (2019). Building cultures of innovation to navigate market disruption. *MIT Sloan Executive Education Series on Disruption, 27*(5), 67–89.

Jones, J., & Brown, A. (2019). Leadership requirements for disruptive innovation adoption. *Journal of Leadership Studies, 14*(4), 20–42.

Kane, G. C., Palmer, D., Phillips, A. N., Kiron, D., & Buckley, N. (2015). Strategy, not technology, drives digital transformation. *MIT Sloan Management Review, 14*.

Kaur Kapoor, K., Meissner, P., & Cerri, J. (2022). Healthcare ecosystem transformation: A systematic literature review and future directions. *Technological Forecasting and Social Change, 175*, 121401.

Kaurav, R. P. S., Baber, R., & Rajput, S. (2020). Technology-driven tourism and hospitality industry as a tool for economic development: A bibliometric analysis. In *The Emerald handbook of ICT in tourism and hospitality* (pp. 469–486). Emerald Publishing Limited.

Kaurav, R. P. S., & Gupta, P. (2022). Trends in multidiscipline management research: past, present and future of FIIB business review. *FIIB Business Review, 11*(4), 382–404.

Kaushal, N., Kaurav, R. P. S., Sivathanu, B., & Kaushik, N. (2023). Artificial intelligence and HRM: Identifying future research Agenda using systematic literature review and bibliometric analysis. *Management Review Quarterly, 73*(2), 455–493.

Khare, A., & Jain, R. (2022). Mapping the conceptual and intellectual structure of the consumer vulnerability field: A bibliometric analysis. *Journal of Business Research, 150*, 567–584.

Koll, H., Esmark, K., & Jensen, A. (2024). 'Changing the course of a super tanker': A study of senior and junior managers' enactments of a transition narrative. *Journal of Change Management*, 1–18. https://doi.org/10.1080/14697017.2024.2346219

Kotlewski, C., & Moeslein, K. M. (2020). Coping with Bimodal IT. *MIS Quarterly Executive, 19*(1).

Kotter, J. P. (2020). *Accelerate: Leading disruptive change*. Harvard Business Review Press.

Lettice, F., & Thomond, P. (2008). Allocating resources to disruptive innovation projects: Challenging mental models and overcoming management resistance. *International Journal of Technology Management, 44*(1–2), 140–159.

Li, S., Da Xu, L., & Zhao, S. (2020). 5G internet of things: A survey. *Journal of Industrial Information Integration, 10*, 1–9.

Liu, X., Zhang, J., & Guo, C. (2013). Full-text citation analysis: A new method to enhance scholarly networks. *Journal of the American Society for Information Science and Technology, 64*(9), 1852–1863.

Markard, J., & Truffer, B. (2006). Innovation processes in large technical systems: Market liberalization as a driver for radical change? *Research Policy, 35*(5), 609–625.

Maurer, R. (2010). *Beyond the wall of resistance: Why 70% of all changes still fail—And what you can do about it*. Bard Press.

McAdam, R. (2003). Radical change: A conceptual model for research agendas. *The Leadership & Organization Development Journal*, *24*(4), 226–235.

Meaden, K., Simmons, T. K., Arva, B. G., & Alnuem, M. A. (2017). Creative pathway to disruptive innovations: A case study on Uber. *International Journal of Economics & Management Sciences*, *6*(431), 1–6.

Meyers, S. D., Azevedo, L., & Luther, M. E. (2021). A Scopus-based bibliometric study of maritime research involving the Automatic Identification System. *Transportation Research Interdisciplinary Perspectives*, *10*, 100387.

Mishra, V., & Sharma, M. G. (2022). Digital transformation evaluation of telehealth using convergence, maturity, and adoption. *Health Policy and Technology*, *11*(4), 100684.

Novotny, M., & Laestadius, S. (2014). Beyond papermaking: Technology and market shifts for wood-based biomass industries–management implications for large-scale industries. *Technology Analysis & Strategic Management*, *26*(8), 875–891.

Öberg, C. (2023). Neuroscience in business-to-business marketing research: A literature review, co-citation analysis and research agenda. *Industrial Marketing Management*, *113*, 168–179.

Obi, T. (2023). Assessing the strategic value of disruptive innovation. *Journal of Business Strategy*, *47*(1), 23–45.

O'Reilly, C., & Tushman, M. L. (2008). Ambidexterity as a dynamic capability: Resolving the innovator's dilemma. *Research in Organizational Behavior*, *28*, 185–206.

Paehler, K. (2018). Managing digital transformation requires mix of emergent and deliberate change. *MIS Quarterly Executive*, *17*(1).

Paul, J., & Barari, M. (2022). Meta-analysis and traditional systematic literature reviews—What, why, when, where, and how? *Psychology and Marketing*, *39*(6), 1099–1115.

Rana, S., Sakshi, & Singh, J. (2022). Presenting the POWER framework of conducting literature review. In *Exploring the latest trends in management literature* (pp. 1–13).

Rasool, F., Koomsap, P., Afsar, B., & Panezai, B. A. (2018). A framework for disruptive innovation. *Foresight*, *20*(3), 252–270.

Reinhardt, R., & Gurtner, S. (2011). Enabling disruptive innovations through the use of customer analysis methods. *Review of Managerial Science*, *5*, 291–307.

Roblek, V., Bach, M. P., Indihar Štemberger, M., & Eremenko, K. (2021). Disruptive technologies support a resilient and sustainable society: a case of digital transformation due to COVID-19. *Sustainability*, *13*(15), 8392.

Sahni, S., & Kaurav, R. P. S. (2023). What? Why? When? How? Where? of Technology-based bibliometric review. In *Advancing methodologies of conducting literature review in management domain* (Vol. 2, pp. 79–101). Emerald Publishing Limited.

Sandberg, B., & Hansén, S. O. (2004). Creating an international market for disruptive innovations. *European Journal of Innovation Management*, *7*(1), 23–32.

Santos, V. R., Lopes, A. I., Sousa, A., & Ramos, I. (2022). The relationship between disruptive innovation and change management in organisations. *Sustainability*, *14*(3), 1181.

Shang, T., Miao, X., & Abdul, W. (2019). A historical review and bibliometric analysis of disruptive innovation. *International Journal of Innovation Science*, *11*(2), 208–226.

Skog, D. A., Wimelius, H., & Sandberg, J. (2022). Technological discontinuities and disruptive innovation in large firms—A review of disruption management strategies and practices. *Technology Innovation Management Review*, *12*(1).

Slater, S. F., & Mohr, J. J. (2006). Successful development and commercialization of technological innovation: Insights based on strategy type. *Journal of Product Innovation Management*, *23*(1), 26–33.

Smets, M., Morris, T. I. M., & Greenwood, R. (2012). From practice to field: A multilevel model of practice-driven institutional change. *Academy of Management Journal*, *55*(4), 877–904.

Smith, A., & Jones, B. (2020). Change management for disruptive innovation adoption: Best practices and success factors. *Journal of Business Transformation*, *18*(4), 251–269.

Souza, D., & Korsunsky, E. (2003). Breaking the cycle of change resistance. *MIT Sloan Management Review*, *44*(4), 60–64.

Su, W., & Junge, S. (2023). Unlocking the recipe for organizational resilience: A review and future research directions. *European Management Journal*, *41*(6), 1086–1105.

Tell, J., Hoveskog, M., Ulvenblad, P., Ulvenblad, P. O., Barth, H., & Ståhl, J. (2022). Business model innovation in incumbent firms: A review of hindering and supporting factors. *Renewable and Sustainable Energy Reviews*, *156*, 112026.

Thomas, V. J., & Maine, E. (2019). Market entry strategies for electric vehicle start-ups in the automotive industry–Lessons from Tesla Motors. *Journal of Cleaner Production*, *235*, 653–663.

Totterdill, P. (2020). Closing the gap between theory and practice: Towards new innovation models for a fast-changing world. *International Journal of Innovation Management*, *24*(01), 2040002.

Waddell, D., Creed, A., Cummings, T. G., & Worley, C. G. (2019). *Organisational change: Development and transformation*. Cengage AU.

White, H. D., & McCain, K. W. (1998). Visualizing a discipline: An author co-citation analysis of information science, 1972–1995. *Journal of the American Society for Information Science*, *49*(4), 327–355.

Yu, D., & Hang, C. C. (2010). A reflective review of disruptive innovation theory. *International Journal of Management Reviews*, *12*(4), 435–452.

A SYSTEMATIC REVIEW OF THE HOSPITALITY AND TOURISM INDUSTRY THROUGH THE LENS OF DISRUPTIVE INNOVATIONS

Anoop Kumar[a], Anil Singh Parihar[b] and Pooja Jain[a]

[a]*Amity University, India*
[b]*Manipal University, India*

ABSTRACT

With the technological advancements in the sphere of hospitality and tourism, the significant development has been pragmatic in the industry structures, processes and practices. The worth of innovation in the tourism industry is multifaceted which not only resulted in costs reduction, enhance operational efficiency and service quality upgrade but also enhanced customer experience. This chapter aims to review the articles, papers and books chapters published in various journals in the hospitality and tourism industry area through the lens of technological developments and disruptive innovations. Preferred Reporting Items for Systematic Reviews and Meta-Analysis (PRISMA) protocol, VOSviewer and word cloud are the tools applied for papers selection, analysis and the visual representation of the most researched themes. The findings reveal that the many researches being conducted post 2016 in this sphere. The information and communications technology (ICT) devices usage, robotics, artificial intelligence (AI), Radio Frequency Identification (RFID), Blockchain technology (BCT), and digital payments are considered as the crucial factors. The study emphasizes to put on better understanding of innovative disruptions in this sphere, layout plan for future research, and enable the decision-makers and authorities to make futuristic policies to stay competitive.

Keywords: Disruptive technology; hospitality industry; tourism; literature review; innovation

Review of Technologies and Disruptive Business Strategies
Review of Management Literature, Volume 3, 47–63

Published under exclusive licence by Emerald Publishing Limited
ISSN: 2754-5865/doi:10.1108/S2754-586520240000003003

1. INTRODUCTION

It is well known that the expansion of the economy is strongly influenced by the latest innovations and the acquisition of sustainable competitive advantage (Damanpour & Wischnevsky, 2006; Nagano et al., 2014). Disruptions occur when conventional methods are disrupted with the modern methods to survive a change in the environment (Khan, 2020). Innovation in many ways has disrupted the traditional practices and such innovations named as Disruptive innovation. The term was first coined by (Christensen, 1997) and mentioned in a book named "The innovators dilemma." Post this the terminology of technological disruption was picked and presented in different ways by various researchers and practitioners in their academic work, in a manner whatever they prefer to hold true and put into practice, which resulted in the incorrect development and application of the theory in this domain (Christensen et al., 2017; Lindsay & Hopkins, 2010; Tellis, 2005). In its initial form, Christensen (1997) focused primarily on technological innovation and investigated how modern technologies eventually overcame outdated technologies that once appeared to be superior in a market. Researchers and practitioners are becoming more aware of and interested in the disruptive innovation. However, since Christensen (1997) only provided a broad definition of the term (Tellis, 2005; Weeks, 2015), the concept of disruptive innovation has frequently been interpreted and evaluated arbitrarily.

Si and Chen (2020) defined disruptive innovation as process where technologies, products or services are primarily not at par with the existing mainstream customers value, but these advancements are capable enough to attract and satisfy consumers in low-end or new markets with more advantages and higher performance attributes which may be ignored by mainstream markets. Disruptive innovation, according to (Buhalis et al., 2019), happens when new competitors and circumstances put industry structures and acting behavior under pressure and change them. The disruptive innovation theory rejects the notion that disruption is a fundamental aspect of innovation, instead emphasizing that what is disruptive is how it alters the existing market (Dogru et al., 2019). Christensen et al. (2015) expanded the term meaning over time to encompass not only technologies but also goods and enterprise models. For instance, low-cost or discount department stores, point-to-point airlines, affordable, mass-market goods like power tools, copiers, motorcycles, and online businesses like travel agencies, bookselling, education, brokerage, and online shopping platforms are all listed as examples of disruptive innovations.

The new business model strategies supported by the disruptive technological advancements must focus either on the market size intensification by attracting new consumers into the market or by motivating existing consumers to increase their consumption (Markides, 2006). An enterprise model revolution is beyond the invention of a completely novel approach of an organization's part, according to the requirement to expand the market. The hospitality industry utilizes numerous intricate processes, which are being greatly benefited from smart technologies that provide an abundance of extensively utilized applications. The availability and accessibility of such new platforms is being utilized by clients and service providers alike (Kanta et al., 2021; Khan, 2020).

In present scenario, the creation of goods and services is being revolutionized by information and communications technology (ICT). Smart environments are being created as a result of technological disruptions like the improved artificial intelligence (AI), virtual (VR) and augmented reality (AR), Internet of Things (IoT), and autonomous devices. These technologies are changing structures, procedures, and practices within the industry (Buhalis et al., 2019). In the travel and hospitality industry, information technology (IT) has been widely adopted to boost operational efficiency, reduce expenses, and – above all – improve customer satisfaction and service quality (Law et al., 2009). Due to the fierce competition in contemporary business ecosystem, the hospitality and tourism industries must work hard to maintain and increase their competitiveness. Tourism businesses are compelled to innovate constantly because of how quickly and easily their rivals can steal their winning strategies. It is crucial to find inventions that are challenging for rivals to imitate (Vila et al., 2011). The technological development in hospitality and tourism industry has attracted many researchers to explore and analyze more in this realm. Based on this discussion the following are the objectives and research questions framed for this study: -

1.1 Research Objectives

- To explore the articles published on the topic since 2013–2023.
- To review these articles systematically.

1.2 Research Questions

Q1. What are the publication trends for technological disruptions in tourism and hospitality (publication volume, journal categories, authorship country, focus country, and sector of research)?

Q2. Which papers have received the more citations?

Q3. Which countries have contributed more in this domain?

Q4. What are the discussions and trends in terms of technological disruptions in hospitality and tourism studies?

Q5. What could be the challenges in adoption of disruptive technologies and their solutions?

1.3 Technology Disruption in Hospitality Industry

The synthesis of technological disruption reveals that pertinency of the relevant technical progresses within the organization/customer domain is supported by a variety of facilitating technologies that could bring about a radical change. Technology advancements had an impact on the tourism and hospitality industry by providing businesses and other stakeholders with numerous opportunities to enhance their multidimensionality in their operations (Kaurav et al., 2020). These enabling technologies have a wide range of service innovations as a result of their unprecedented macro-societal and microlevel disruptions of industry structures (Buhalis et al., 2019; Edvardsson & Tronvoll, 2013; Tussyadiah, 2020).

The ongoing trend toward co-creating value between customers and businesses is being accelerated by technological advancements in many markets. During the traditional manufacturing epoch, businesses created almost all the value contained in the goods being traded. In the current setting, services, as opposed to manufacturing, are the primary means of generating economic value, and services typically necessitate value co-creation between customers and businesses (Guttentag & Smith, 2017).

The hospitality and tourism industry are the front-line service sectors that integrates updated information on technology developments into strategic planning procedures (Phillips & Moutinho, 2014), because service management and marketing will be greatly impacted by it.

2. METHODOLOGY

In the area of academic research, the literature review is considered as an essential component (Mishra & Mishra, 2023) which provides a comprehensive overview of a subject domain by synthesizing previous knowledge (Farrukh & Sajjad, 2023). This chapter emphasized to present the current state of academic work carried out around innovation in hospitality and tourism area. The SCOPUS database is chosen primarily because it is believed to be the one of the most extensive repository for academic publications and work (Vieira & Gomes, 2009). The database of SCOPUS has been explored for the papers published from 2013 to 2023. The article title search was carried out with keywords as "Hospitality," "Tourism" and "Disruptive innovations."

To systematically review the existing literature, the Preferred Reporting Items for Systematic Reviews and Meta-Analysis (PRISMA) protocol was incorporated which provides consistency, clarity and transparency (Baber et al., 2023; Mishra & Mishra, 2023; Page et al., 2021). Fig. 1 shows the PRISMA protocol applied in this chapter. The planning, organizing, writing, embedding, and reflecting (POWER) framework by Rana et al. (2022, 2023) is utilized for effective literature writing.

The search resulted in 5,788 papers. These papers were then filtered by the source and keywords "Big data analytics," "Robots," "Blockchain," "Virtual reality," "Disruptive," and "Internet." This resulted in a total of 313 items. These items are then filtered as per the relevance to the topic and removal of duplicates, which resulted in 297 items. These 297 articles are then considered and included for the review.

3. ANALYSIS

3.1 Articles Publication per Year

The sample is segregated year-wise for analysis of yearly distribution of samples. Fig. 2 shows the sample distribution of the articles published during the period along with

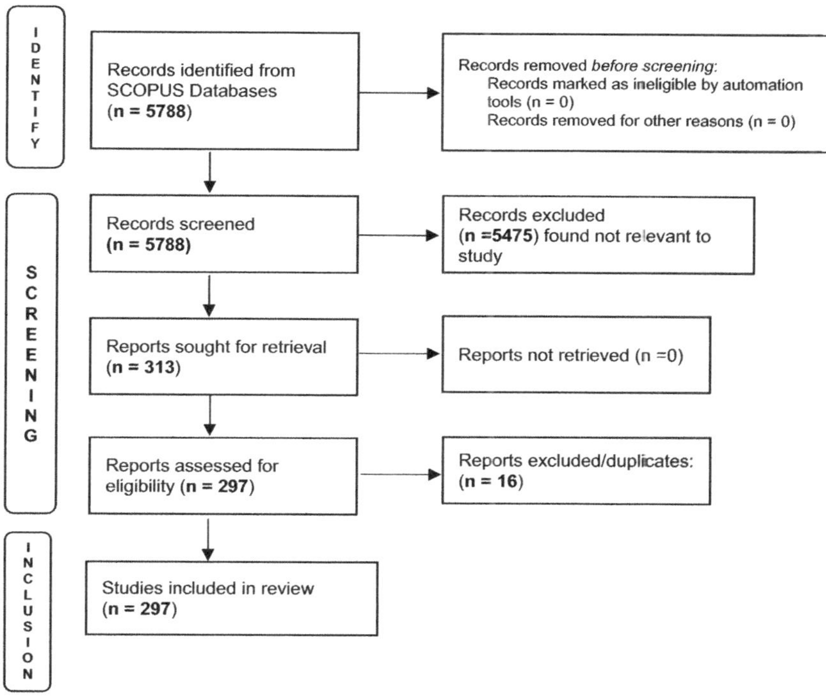

Fig. 1. PRISMA Protocol for Articles Selection. *Source:* Page et al. (2021).

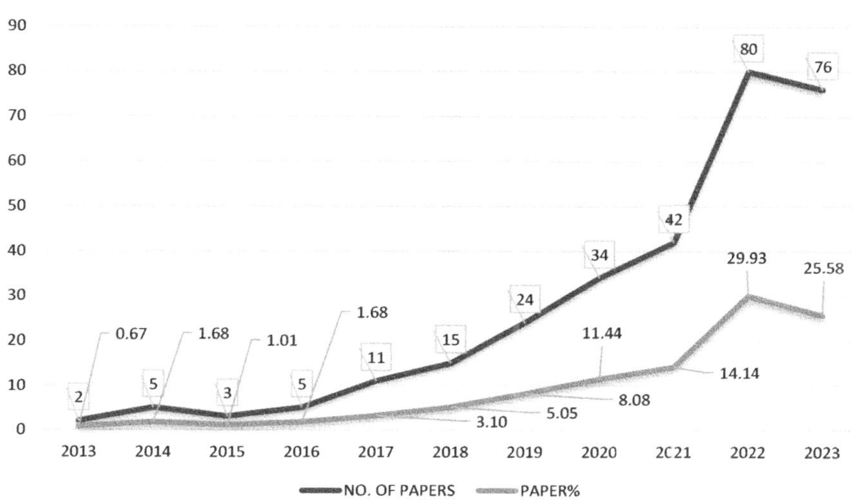

Fig. 2. Sample Distribution – Year of Publication. *Source:* Author's contribution.

the paper percentage. There is a growing trend of publications since 2016. The most publications on the subject were published in 2022 with a total of 80 articles and sample percentage of 29.93%. Forty-two papers were published in 2021 with publication percentage of 14.14%. Only few papers were published in the years 2013, 2014 and 2015. There are 76 publications already published in current year till May and it is expected that more papers will be published till year end.

3.2 Country-Wise Publication Analysis

The country-wise publications with the criteria as analysis type – Bibliographic Coupling, analysis unit – Country, counting method – Full counting, Minimum documents per country – One, Minimum citations of a country – Zero. The process resulted in 62 countries out of 66 countries and the network visualization is given in Fig. 3. These 62 countries are divided into 10 clusters. Cluster I has 10 following countries: Croatia, Iran, Jordan, Kazakhstan, Serbia, Slovakia, South Korea, Switzerland, United Arab Emirates, and Sweden (University West). Cluster II has 10 countries and includes China, Greece, Indonesia, Japan, Macao, the Netherlands, Norway, Pakistan, Taiwan, and the United States. Cluster III covers eight nations namely Bangladesh, Cyprus, India, Latvia, Malta, Qatar, Thailand, and Uzbekistan. Cluster IV consists of eight countries namely Czech Republic, Finland, Germany, Italy, Russian federation, Slovenia, Sweden, and Ukraine. Cluster V covers seven following nations: Costa Rica, Egypt, France, Oman, Poland, Saudi Arabia, and Singapore. Argentina, Australia, Canada, Malaysia, New Zealand, Romania, and the United Kingdom are under cluster VI. Six countries namely Brazil, Bulgaria,

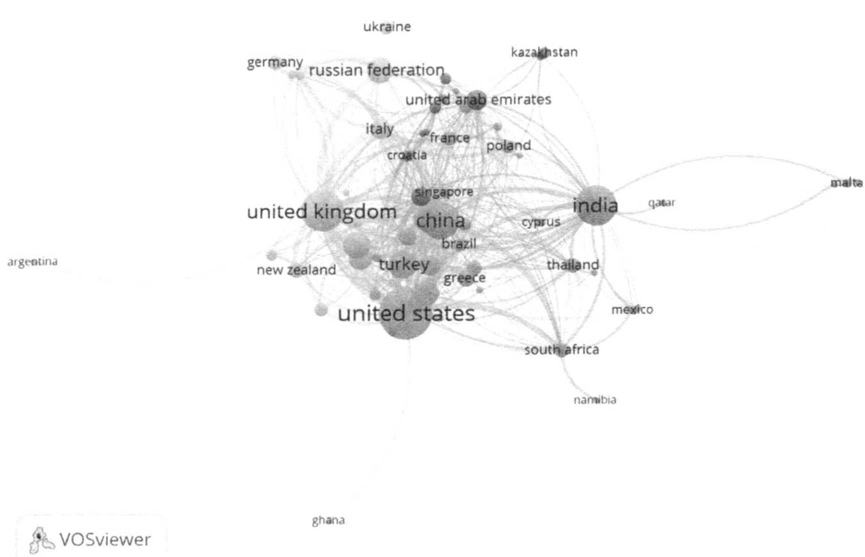

Fig. 3. Sample Distribution – Country-Wise. *Source:* VOSviewer analysis.

Hong Kong, Portugal, Spain, and Turkey comes under cluster VII and Ecuador, Mexico, Namibia, and South-Africa are under cluster VIII. Cluster IX and X consists of one nation each namely Ghana and Austria, respectively. The most contributing nations are the United States with 59 articles, the United Kingdom has 37 articles, India with 35 articles, China has 31 articles, and Turkey has 17 articles.

3.3 Word Cloud Analysis

The term "word cloud" or "tag cloud" refers to "visual representation of the set of words/tags in a systematic manner. In this presentation, various set words are formed which are based on the attributes of the text, such as size, weight, or color, and can be used to represent features (such as frequency) of the associated terms" (Halvey & Keane, 2007). It provides visual representation of knowledge that enables the viewer to grasp a text quickly and easily. High-level data can be easily shared using this tool without the user experiencing information overload (DePaolo & Wilkinson, 2014). The word cloud visualization is given in Fig. 4.

4. DISCUSSION

The technological advancements and intelligent machine systems greatly impacted the service industry. They provided platforms for the customers from all over the world to get connected from anywhere, anytime and could see the real-time availability of accommodation or tickets booking at any country; this not only increased accessibility but also exponentially increased availability of services (Buhalis et al., 2019). Guests' participation defines the service process and delivery in the hospitality industry, in contrast to other industries. The inclusion of such technological disruption especially customer-facing technology in businesses adds a new degree of interaction which is capable to create a positive change in the service dynamics (Huang et al., 2021). Based on the various

Fig. 4. Word Cloud Visualization. *Source:* Author's analysis.

technological developments we framed a theoretical structure for them under the domain of hospitality and tourism industry. The contribution by various researchers in the specific area of technological disruption is mentioned in Table 1.

Table 1. Technological Disruptions in Hospitality Industry.

Technology	Discussion	Author/s
ICT	The key areas of hospitality industry where ICT have significant impact: (i) operations, marketing and communication, (ii) customer service, (iii) relationship management.	DiPietro and Wang (2010)
	It is related to, among other things, the ease with which stakeholders can be contacted, the effectiveness of ICT as a distribution channel, and the effectiveness of ICT as a marketing forum. Both in developed and developing countries, ICT plays a substantial role in this realm.	Abir and Khan (2022)
	Smartphones and various applications allow user to generate online reviews pertains to a hotel property.	Buhalis and Foerste (2015)
	Smart apps simplify several daily tasks, as well as the provision and accessibility of hotel services, including picking a hotel, checking in and out, keyless pass to the accommodation, limiting the lights, and many others.	Praničević and Mandić (2020) Ozturk et al. (2012)
	The Internet significantly aids in the broadest possible diffusion of knowledge about the goods and services offered, especially for the hospitality sector. It also makes their merchandizing process easier.	Abir and Khan (2022)
	In the modern world, organizations involved in travel and hospitality have used ICT extensively.	Singh and Dhankhar (2020)
Radio Frequency Identification (RFID)	RFID enables: Contactless guestroom entry and enhanced door control which results in improved guest protection by preventing anyone who isn't authorized from entering the room. The environment in the room may already be configured to the visitors' personal preferences when they check in, including the lighting, window coverings, temperature, music, and TV channel.	Miller (2007)
	By utilizing the RFID technology which enable real-time consumer data support, the hotels can offer customize services to their customers.	Ozturk and Hançer (2015)
	The process of gathering the data required to successfully implement the loyalty program can be done using RFID technologies.	Ozturk et al. (2012)
	In some hotels RFID wristband is provided to their customers, which is connected to RFID cashless payment system that enables visitors to make purchases throughout the hotel.	Ozturk et al. (2012)
Robotics	After the COVID-19 pandemic, acceptance of service robots grew more than it had before.	Ladeira et al. (2023)

Table 1. (*Continued*)

Technology	Discussion	Author/s
	Robotic agents are also introduced in this domain.	Fan et al. (2019) Murphy et al. (2017)
	These frontier robots carry out waiter and concierge duties that traditionally required front-line employees to interact with customers on a limited basis.	Huang and Rust (2018) Belanche, Casaló, and Flavián (2020)
	How closely a robot resembles a human, a frequently studied aspect of its design, is less important than might be anticipated. Instead, customers' affinity for the robot is a better indicator of its likelihood to succeed.	Belanche, Casaló, Flavián, and Schepers (2020)
	The introduction of service robots are helpful in costs cutting and boosting business operations.	Ivanov and Webster (2018)
	Using service robots to welcome guests, improve service quality, or shorten wait times is another popular justification for doing so as to enhance the guest experience.	Lu et al. (2019)
AI	AI may lead to the technological substitute of human resources in several circumstances, requiring the tourism and hospitality sectors to redesign their operational practices and organizational configurations.	Saini and Bhalla (2022)
	Business customers will be satisfied by AI's help in locating and maximizing potential forthcoming trade prospects.	Lu et al. (2020) Kumar et al. (2021) Siripipatthanakul et al. (2021)
	The AI enabled systems and automation services can analyze vast amount of data and convert it into insightful enterprise data and offer prognosticative information about the future. Such systems are also able to minimize the human errors.	Limna (2023)
	This industry may progress toward becoming a smart hotel and tourism industry by the application and utilization of AI-enhanced operations and management systems.	Ruel and Njoku (2020)
	To synthesize key performance indicators, the hospitality sector has integrated AI support and computerized processes into systems like customer relationship management, property administration, and revenue management.	Mariani et al. (2018)
	AI-enabled systems offer numerous opportunities to the industry toward the improvement of daily operations and enduring plans, in addition to guarantee that their clients receive consistently high-quality goods and services.	Limna (2023)
	The organizations in this industry must utilize the most widespread applications which includes business intelligence tools driven by machine learning, VR and AR tools, individual customer service supports systems, chatbots and messaging tools, for enhancement of their on-site services and operations. Additionally, it's crucial to stay in touch with customers and fulfill their needs to maintain overall quality.	Citak et al. (2021)

(*Continued*)

Table 1. *(Continued)*

Technology	Discussion	Author/s
Big Data Analytics	Big data involves enormous, exhaustive, and varied datasets, and its analysis by a traditional database tool is not possible.	Elragal and Klischewski (2017)
	Big Data can improve tourism industry business intelligence, enabling decision-making and adding value in a better strategic and tactical approach.	Verhoef et al. (2016)
	Efficient use of big data is linked to tactical marketing objectives, marketplace analysis, revenue management, customer experience management, and reputation management in the tourism and hospitality industry.	Evans (2019) Guttentag (2019)
	Big data analytics are helping the hospitality sector to be more effective and efficient by defining new business models and implementing effective transformation.	Evans (2019)
Blockchain Technologies (BCT)	BCT's value to the hospitality sector lies in its capacity to reshape conventional digital marketing channels by verifying customer reviews as well as by identifying and removing phony and biased user observations posted on social media platforms.	Kwok and Koh (2018) Önder and Treiblmaier (2018) Sigala (2017)
	BCT can assist hospitality organizations in creating budgets by facilitating cashless payments, protecting financial transactions, and offering credit or investment options to both providers and customers.	www.amadeus.com
	Customer loyalty management presents numerous BCT use cases, making it particularly pertinent to the hospitality sector.	Kwok and Koh (2018)
	BCT can offer more timely and accurate information on business execution, including operative and environmental organization associated data, helping the investors and brand/franchise owners behind them to make (better) decisions.	www.hospitalitytech.com
	Due to data transparency and increased trust, BCT may further encourage competition (not feasible in conventional competition) among such businesses at a particular location.	Carson et al. (2018)
	When it comes to using BCT in the hospitality sector to support its (environmental) sustainability, supply-chain management, and logistics management (food) hold significant potential.	Poorigali (2018)
Digital Payments	A reality of service innovation is the growth of digital payments in tourist destinations. In tourist destinations, digital transactions are thought to improve the payment process.	Susanto et al. (2022)
	Smart tourist destinations are those that offer digital payment services because they are more effective at luring travellers there.	Novianti et al. (2022) Rafdinal (2021)

Source: Author's analysis.

4.1 Trends and Challenges

Khatri (2019) stated that due to intense competition observed in the tourism sector, success in the market depends on the organization's ability to modify its offerings to best suit with the transforming travel trends using innovative marketing technologies.

The applicability of disruptive technologies is rapidly increasing day by day (Reddy, 2006). These technological disruptions impact the workforce and job employment in the hospitality industry both positively and negatively. AI at one side enhance operations and management system but on the other side it poses risks as reduction in employment in low-tech industries, loss of control as a result of autonomous robots, concerns regarding privacy, safety, and security of data (Limna, 2023). The integration of cutting-edge technology, such as social or communicative robots, has significant implications for organizational strategies and human assets. In an organizational setup, human–robot interaction (HRI) necessitates modified policies and strategies due to shifting job tasks and a workforce that is primarily focused on general skills (Drexler & Lapré, 2019). Enhancing enterprise information management and establishing an internal data analytics system are two ways that organizations can prepare for the AI revolution. To optimize the efficacy of this framework and enhance the probability of success, managers must embrace an enduring perspective for its execution (Kaushal et al., 2023). The other important challenge for adopting the advancements in AI technology is the safety and security of data. The ICT devices utilized for AI application may store the travel history, purchase history which possess the challenge for data privacy and security issues (Kannan & Bernoff, 2019). Furthermore, these systems may be hacked or attacked by malware (Patawari & Bairwa, 2022).

The advanced feature embedded smartphones and other mobile devices, revolutionizing the tourism sector as they offer access to information to the tourists at any point of time (Jung et al., 2015). To capitalize on the internet's distribution capabilities, including sharing of content, gathering of feedback, reachability, communication, and one-to-one marketing, hotels are expected to establish a strong online presence (DiPietro & Wang, 2010). ICT devices provide the customers the best and unique experiences in hospitality sector through various means such as voice-controlled smart rooms, automated messaging, robotic guest service and using biometric authentication to check in (Bisoi et al., 2020) but on the other side they still cannot surpass the human intelligence (Laurent et al., 2015). The susceptibility of the industry to adopting AI varies depending on the kind of AI systems. Various systems such as search engines, booking platforms, virtual assistants, and chatbots are highly susceptible to adoption (Huang et al., 2021).

5. CONCLUSION

Technological disruptions are found in every domain and they are replacing the conventional methods of doing the things. Considering the current growth, using technology has a disruptive effect on service industry also. The objective of this analysis was to reconnoiter and review the insights of the academic work carried out in this domain, as such papers offer the reader a thorough, reliable, critical synopsis of a clearly defined area/topic in the format of a book review, conference review, or review of the literature (Kaurav & Gupta, 2022). We made a sincere effort to efficiently answer all the research questions.

The findings reveals that the more and more researches are being conducted post 2016 to assess/analyze various technological developments and disruptions in hospitality and tourism industry. The technological disruptions in the hospitality and tourism industries are largely attributable to ICT devices. Robotics, artificial intelligence, radio frequency identification devices, big data analytics, blockchain technology, and digital payments are among the latest disruptions which are not only affecting the dynamics of this industry but also revolutionizing this sector through enhanced customer satisfaction by ease of travel and accommodation booking and effective business operations through various means. However, there are certain challenges also associated with such technologies in terms of their high cost, data privacy concerns, image barriers, usage barriers, managing voluminous data, malware attacks and various other issues. There is also a major concern of job-loss of employees as these systems are able to perform their job.

This study is not without limitations, despite the extensive efforts, perhaps not every relevant paper was found during the literature search. The attempt was made to explore the SCOPUS indexed journals only and there is need for more paper to be explored on the subject from different databases. This chapter has only shown the trends, as prediction of most influential papers of the field in the future is not possible, because publication need time to show a significant impact.

5.1 Future Research Directions

Mnyakin (2023) identified that improved client support, customized advertising efforts, enhanced pricing tactics, rationalized processes, and stopping fraudulent activity can be achieved using big data analytics the industry. However, regulating the quantity and quality of data, sustaining data security, bridging the big data analytics skill gap, control over expenses, and integrating various software applications are some of the associated challenges.

However, these advancements are challenging due to reasons such as high cost, budgetary capacity, and estimate of organizations (Bisoi et al., 2020). Khanra et al. (2021) identified that usage barrier and image barriers, privacy concerns, and visibility are the crucial factors effecting the pertinence and adaptability of digital payments in the sector. Kılıçhan and Yilmaz (2020) argued that in general it is understood that these technologies can take the place of employees, but they should be considered as tools that uphold employees and improve the quality of services they provide.

For the purpose of safeguarding sensitive client information, hospitality organizations need to periodically assess and update their security protocols. In order to effectively use big data analytics tools, hospitality businesses must invest in employee training and hiring (Bandari, 2020, 2023; Mnyakin, 2023; Racherla, 2021; Sinclair & Ishmael, 2022; Vafin, 2021).

REFERENCES

Abir, T., & Khan, Y. H. (2022). Importance of ICT advancement and culture of adaptation in the tourism and hospitality industry for developing countries. In *Advances in business strategy and competitive advantage book series* (pp. 30–41). https://doi.org/10.4018/978-1-7998-8165-0.ch003

Baber, R., Upadhyay, Y., Baber, P., & Kaurav, R. P. S. (2023). Three decades of consumer ethnocentrism research: A bibliometric analysis. *Business Perspectives and Research, 11*(1), 137–158.

Bandari, V. (2020). Impact of data democratization and data literacy on employee productivity. *Sage Science Review of Educational Technology, 3*(1), 37–48. https://journals.sagescience.org/index.php/ssret/article/view/42

Bandari, V. (2023). Enterprise Data Security Measures: A comparative review of effectiveness and risks across different industries and organization types. *International Journal of Business Intelligence and Big Data Analytics, 6*(1), 1–11. https://research.tensorgate.org/index.php/IJBIBDA/article/view/3

Belanche, D., Casaló, L. V., & Flavián, C. (2020). Frontline robots in tourism and hospitality: Service enhancement or cost reduction? *Electronic Markets, 31*(3), 477–492. https://doi.org/10.1007/s12525-020-00432-5

Belanche, D., Casaló, L. V., Flavián, C., & Schepers, J. J. (2020). Robots or frontline employees? Exploring customers' attributions of responsibility and stability after service failure or success. *Journal of Service Management, 31*(2), 267–289. https://doi.org/10.1108/josm-05-2019-0156

Bisoi, S., Roy, M., & Samal, A. (2020). Impact of artificial intelligence in the hospitality industry. *International Journal of Advanced Science and Technology, 29*(5), 4265–4276.

Blockchain could revolutionize hospitality. (2017, December 6). *Hospitality Technology*. https://hospitalitytech.com/blockchain-could-revolutionize-hospitality

Buhalis, D., & Foerste, M. (2015). SoCoMo marketing for travel and tourism: Empowering co-creation of value. *Journal of Destination Marketing & Management, 4*(3), 151–161. https://doi.org/10.1016/j.jdmm.2015.04.001

Buhalis, D., Harwood, T., Bogicevic, V., Viglia, G., Beldona, S., & Hofacker, C. F. (2019). Technological disruptions in services: Lessons from tourism and hospitality. *Journal of Service Management, 30*(4), 484–506. https://doi.org/10.1108/josm-12-2018-0398

Carson, B., Romanelli, G., Walsh, P., & Zhumaev, A. (2018). *Blockchain beyond the hype: What is the strategic business value* (Vol. 1, pp. 1–13). McKinsey & Company.

Christensen, C. M. (1997). *The Innovator's dilemma: When new technologies cause great firms to fail.* Harvard Business School Press.

Christensen, C. M., McDonald, R., Altman, E. J., & Palmer, J. E. (2017). Disruptive Innovation: Intellectual history and future paths. *Proceedings – Academy of Management, 2017*(1), 14218. https://doi.org/10.5465/ambpp.2017.14218abstract

Christensen, C. M., Raynor, M. E., & McDonald, R. (2015). What is disruptive innovation. *Harvard Business Review*. https://procon.bg/article/what-disruptive-innovation

Citak, J., Owoc, M. L., & Weichbroth, P. (2021). A note on the applications of artificial intelligence in the hospitality industry: Preliminary results of a survey. *Procedia Computer Science, 192*, 4552–4559. https://doi.org/10.1016/j.procs.2021.09.233

Damanpour, F., & Wischnevsky, J. D. (2006). Research on innovation in organizations: Distinguishing innovation-generating from innovation-adopting organizations. *Journal of Engineering and Technology Management, 23*(4), 269–291. https://doi.org/10.1016/j.jengtecman.2006.08.002

DePaolo, C. A., & Wilkinson, K. (2014). Get your head into the clouds: Using word clouds for analyzing qualitative assessment data. *TechTrends, 58*(3), 38–44. https://doi.org/10.1007/s11528-014-0750-9

DiPietro, R. B., & Wang, Y. C. (2010). Key issues for ICT applications: Impacts and implications for hospitality operations. *Worldwide Hospitality and Tourism Themes, 2*(1), 49–67. https://doi.org/10.1108/17554211011012595

Dogru, T., Mody, M., & Suess, C. (2019). Adding evidence to the debate: Quantifying Airbnb's disruptive impact on ten key hotel markets. *Tourism Management*, *72*, 27–38. https://doi.org/10.1016/j.tourman.2018.11.008

Drexler, N., & Lapré, V. B. (2019). For better or for worse: Shaping the hospitality industry through robotics and artificial intelligence. *Research in Hospitality Management*, *9*(2), 117–120. https://doi.org/10.1080/22243534.2019.1689701

Edvardsson, B., & Tronvoll, B. (2013). A new conceptualization of service innovation grounded in S-D logic and service systems. *International Journal of Quality and Service Sciences*, *5*(1), 19–31. https://doi.org/10.1108/17566691311316220

Elragal, A., & Klischewski, R. (2017). Theory-driven or process-driven prediction? Epistemological challenges of big data analytics. *Journal of Big Data*, *4*(1). https://doi.org/10.1186/s40537-017-0079-2

Evans, N. (2019). *Strategic management for tourism, hospitality and events*. Routledge. https://doi.org/10.4324/9780429437601

Fan, A., Wu, L., Li, M., & Mattila, A. S. (2019). When does technology anthropomorphism help alleviate customer dissatisfaction after a service failure? – The moderating role of consumer technology self-efficacy and interdependent self-construal. *Journal of Hospitality Marketing & Management*, *29*(3), 269–290. https://doi.org/10.1080/19368623.2019.1639095

Farrukh, A., & Sajjad, A. (2023). A critical review of literature review methodologies. In S. Rana, J. Singh, & S. Kathuria (Eds.), *Advancing methodologies of conducting literature review in management domain. Review of management literature* (Vol. 2, pp. 103–123). Emerald Publishing Limited. https://doi.org/10.1108/S2754-586520230000002006

Guttentag, D. (2019). Transformative experiences via Airbnb: Is it the guests or the host communities that will be transformed? *Journal of Tourism Futures*, *5*(2), 179–184. https://doi.org/10.1108/jtf-04-2019-0038

Guttentag, D., & Smith, S. L. (2017). Assessing Airbnb as a disruptive innovation relative to hotels: Substitution and comparative performance expectations. *International Journal of Hospitality Management*, *64*, 1–10. https://doi.org/10.1016/j.ijhm.2017.02.003

Halvey, M., & Keane, M. T. (2007). An assessment of tag presentation techniques. In *World Wide Web Conference*. https://doi.org/10.1145/1242572.1242826

Huang, A., Cao, Y., De La Mora Velasco, E., Bilgihan, A., & Wei, W. (2021). When artificial intelligence meets the hospitality and tourism industry: An assessment framework to inform theory and management. *Journal of Hospitality and Tourism Insights*, *5*(5), 1080–1100. https://doi.org/10.1108/jhti-01-2021-0021

Huang, M. H., & Rust, R. T. (2018). Artificial intelligence in service. *Journal of Service Research*, *21*(2), 155–172. https://doi.org/10.1177/1094670517752459

Ivanov, S., & Webster, C. (2018). Adoption of robots, artificial intelligence and service automation by travel, tourism and hospitality companies – A cost-benefit analysis. *Social Science Research Network*. https://papers.ssrn.com/sol3/Delivery.cfm/SSRN_ID3007577_code657096.pdf?abstractid=3007577&mirid=1

Jung, T., Chung, N., & Leue, M. C. (2015). The determinants of recommendations to use augmented reality technologies: The case of a Korean theme park. *Tourism Management*, *49*, 75–86. https://doi.org/10.1016/j.tourman.2015.02.013

Kannan, P. V., & Bernoff, J. (2019). The future of customer service is AI-Human collaboration. *MIT Sloan Management Review*. https://sloanreview.mit.edu/article/the-future-of-customer-service-is-ai-human-collaboration

Kanta, K. N. M., Kaurav, R. P. S., Allam, U. S., & Srivalli, P. (2021). Wildlife tourism: A synthesis of past, present, and future research agenda. *Enlightening Tourism. A Pathmaking Journal*, *11*(2), 390–427.

Kaurav, R. P. S., Baber, R., & Rajput, S. (2020). Technology-driven tourism and hospitality industry as a tool for economic development: A bibliometric analysis. In *The Emerald handbook of ICT in tourism and hospitality* (pp. 469–486). Emerald Publishing Limited.

Kaurav, R. P. S., & Gupta, P. (2022). Trends in multidiscipline management research: Past, present and future of FIIB business review. *FIIB Business Review*, *11*(4), 382–404.

Kaushal, N., Kaurav, R. P. S., Sivathanu, B., & Kaushik, N. (2023). Artificial intelligence and HRM: Identifying future research Agenda using systematic literature review and bibliometric analysis. *Management Review Quarterly*, *73*(2), 455–493.

Khan, M. H. (2020). Technological disruptions in restaurant services: Impact of innovations and delivery services. *Journal of Hospitality & Tourism Research*, *44*(5), 715–732. https://doi.org/10.1177/1096348020908636

Khanra, S., Dhir, A., Kaur, P., & Joseph, R. P. (2021). Factors influencing the adoption postponement of mobile payment services in the hospitality sector during a pandemic. *Journal of Hospitality and Tourism Management*, *46*, 26–39. https://doi.org/10.1016/j.jhtm.2020.11.004

Khatri, I. (2019). Information technology in tourism & hospitality industry: A review of ten years' publications. *Journal of Tourism and Hospitality Education*, *9*, 74–87. https://doi.org/10.3126/jthe.v9i0.23682

Kılıçhan, R., & Yilmaz, M. (2020). Artificial intelligence and robotic technologies in tourism and hospitality industry. *Erciyes Üniversitesi Sosyal Bilimler Enstitüsü Dergisi*, *50*, 353–380. https://doi.org/10.48070/erusosbilder.838193

Kumar, S., Kumar, V., & Attri, K. (2021). Impact of artificial intelligence and service robots in tourism and hospitality sector: Current use & future trends. *Administrative Development: A Journal of HIPA, Shimla*, *8*(SI-1), 59–83. https://doi.org/10.53338/adhipa2021.v08.si01.04

Kwok, A. O. J., & Koh, S. G. M. (2018). Is blockchain technology a watershed for tourism development? *Current Issues in Tourism*, *22*(20), 2447–2452. https://doi.org/10.1080/13683500.2018.1513460

Ladeira, W. J., Perin, M. G., & De Oliveira Santini, F. (2023). Acceptance of service robots: A meta-analysis in the hospitality and tourism industry. *Journal of Hospitality Marketing & Management*, *32*(6), 694–716. https://doi.org/10.1080/19368623.2023.2202168

Laurent, P., Chollet, T., & Herzberg, E. (2015). *Intelligent automation entering the business world.* Deloitte. https://www2.deloitte.com/content/dam/Deloitte/lu/Documents/operations/lu-intelligent-automationbusiness-world.pdf. Accessed on March 5, 2018.

Law, R., Leung, R., & Buhalis, D. (2009). Information technology applications in hospitality and tourism: A review of publications from 2005 to 2007. *Journal of Travel & Tourism Marketing*, *26*(5–6), 599–623. https://doi.org/10.1080/10548400903163160

Limna, P. (2023). Artificial intelligence (AI) in the hospitality industry: A review article. *International Journal of Computing Sciences Research*, *7*, 1306–1317. https://doi.org/10.25147/ijcsr.2017.001.1.103

Lindsay, J., & Hopkins, M. (2010). From experience: Disruptive innovation and the need for disruptive intellectual asset strategy. *Journal of Product Innovation Management*, *27*(2), 283–290. https://doi.org/10.1111/j.1540-5885.2010.00715.x

Lu, L., Cai, R., & Gursoy, D. (2019). Developing and validating a service robot integration willingness scale. *International Journal of Hospitality Management*, *80*, 36–51. https://doi.org/10.1016/j.ijhm.2019.01.005

Lu, V. N., Wirtz, J., Kunz, W. H., Paluch, S., Gruber, T., Martins, A., & Patterson, P. G. (2020). Service robots, customers and service employees: What can we learn from the academic literature and where are the gaps? *Journal of Service Theory and Practice*, *30*(3), 361–391. https://doi.org/10.1108/jstp-04-2019-0088

Mariani, M. M., Baggio, R., Fuchs, M., & Höpken, W. (2018). Business intelligence and big data in hospitality and tourism: A systematic literature review. *International Journal of Contemporary Hospitality Management*, *30*(12), 3514–3554. https://doi.org/10.1108/ijchm-07-2017-0461

Markides, C. (2006). Disruptive innovation: In need of better theory. *Journal of Product Innovation Management*, *23*(1), 19–25. https://doi.org/10.1111/j.1540-5885.2005.00177.x

Miller, D. (2007). *Self-check-in hotels using RFID technology* (pp. 1–14). https://citeseerx.ist.psu.edu/document?repid=rep1&type=pdf&doi=e547bba870829b1d0f275e78eec4e25b4fcc0024

Mishra, V., & Mishra, M. P. (2023). PRISMA for review of management literature – Method, merits, and limitations – An academic review. In S. Rana, J. Singh, & S. Kathuria (Eds.), *Advancing methodologies of conducting literature review in management domain. Review of management literature* (Vol. 2, pp. 125–136). Emerald Publishing Limited. https://doi.org/10.1108/S2754-586520230000002007

Mnyakin, M. (2023). Big data in the hospitality industry: Prospects, obstacles, and strategies. *International Journal of Business Intelligence and Big Data Analytics*, *6*(1), 12–22.

Murphy, J., Hofacker, C. F., & Gretzel, U. (2017). Dawning of the age of Robots in Hospitality and tourism: Challenges for teaching and research. *European Journal of Tourism Research*, *15*, 104–111. https://doi.org/10.54055/ejtr.v15i.265

Nagano, M. S., Stefanovitz, J. P., & Vick, T. E. (2014). Innovation management processes, their internal organizational elements and contextual factors: An investigation in Brazil. *Journal of Engineering and Technology Management*, *33*, 63–92. https://doi.org/10.1016/j.jengtecman.2014.02.004

Novianti, S., Susanto, E. H., & Rafdinal, W. (2022). Predicting Tourists' behaviour towards smart tourism: The case in emerging Smart Destinations. *Journal of Tourism Sustainability*, *2*(1), 19–30. https://doi.org/10.35313/jtospolban.v2i1.30

Önder, I., & Treiblmaier, H. (2018). Blockchain and tourism: Three research propositions. *Annals of Tourism Research*, *72*, 180–182. https://doi.org/10.1016/j.annals.2018.03.005

Ozturk, A. B., & Hançer, M. (2015). The effects of demographics and past experience on RFID technology acceptance in the hospitality industry. *International Journal of Hospitality & Tourism Administration*, *16*(3), 275–289. https://doi.org/10.1080/15256480.2015.1054756

Ozturk, A. B., Palakurthi, R., & Hançer, M. (2012). Organizational-Level RFID technology adoption in the hospitality industry. *Tourism Analysis*, *17*(5), 629–642. https://doi.org/10.3727/108354212x13485873913967

Page, M. J., McKenzie, J. E., Bossuyt, P. M., Boutron, I., Hoffmann, T. C., Mulrow, C. D., Shamseer, L., Tetzlaff, J. M., Akl, E. A., Brennan, S. E., Chou, R., Glanville, J., Grimshaw, J. M., Hrobjartsson, A., Lalu, M. M., Li, T., Loder, E. W., Mayo- Wilson, E., McDonald, S., …, Moher, D. (2021). The PRISMA 2020 statement: An updated guideline for reporting systematic reviews. *Systematic Reviews*, *10*(1), 1–11.

Patawari, S., & Bairwa, M. K. (2022). Insights on the use of artificial intelligence in tourism & hospitality industry: A view. In *International Conference on Stalwart Management Practices: Sustenance in Covid Era*. https://www.researchgate.net/profile/Mahesh-Bairwa-2/publication/367519724_Insights_on_the_Use_of_Artificial_Intelligence_in_Tourism_Hospitality_Industry-a_View_Point/links/63d5f4d4c465a873a2678e2e/Insights-on-the-Use-of-Artificial-Intelligence-in-Tourism-Hospitality-Industry-a-View-Point.pdf

Phillips, P. A., & Moutinho, L. (2014). Critical review of strategic planning research in hospitality and tourism. *Annals of Tourism Research*, *48*, 96–120. https://doi.org/10.1016/j.annals.2014.05.013

Poorigali, S. (2018). The application of blockchain in the hospitality sector. https://www.hotel-online.com/press_releases/release/the-applicability-ofblockchain-in-the-hospitality-sector

Praničević, D. G., & Mandić, A. (2020). ICTs in the hospitality industry. *Tourism*, *68*(2), 221–234. https://doi.org/10.37741/t.68.2.9

Racherla, S. (2021). The drivers and barriers of adoption of people analytics: A review and empirical investigation. *Sage Science Review of Applied Machine Learning*, *4*(1), 1–11. https://journals.sagescience.org/index.php/ssraml/article/view/38

Rafdinal, W. (2021). Is smart tourism technology important in predicting visiting tourism destination? Lessons from West Java, Indonesia. *Journal of Tourism Sustainability*, *1*(2), 102–115. https://doi.org/10.35313/jtos.v1i2.20

Rana, S., Sakshi, & Singh, J. (2022). Presenting the POWER framework of conducting literature review. In S. Rana, Sakshi, & J. Singh (Eds.), *Exploring the latest trends in management literature. Review of management literature* (Vol. 1, pp. 1–13). Emerald Publishing Limited. https://doi.org/10.1108/s2754-586520220000001001

Rana, S., Singh, J., & Kathuria, S. (2023). Parameters and decision elements of writing effective literature review papers: Empirical evidence from multiple stakeholders on POWER Framework. In S. Rana, J. Singh, & S. Kathuria (Eds.), *Advancing methodologies of conducting literature review in management domain. Review of management literature* (Vol. 2, pp. 1–25). Emerald Publishing Limited. https://doi.org/10.1108/s2754-586520230000002001

Reddy, R. (2006). Robotics and intelligent systems in support of society. *IEEE Intelligent Systems*, *21*(3), 24–31. https://doi.org/10.1109/mis.2006.57

Ruel, H. J. M., & Njoku, E. (2020). AI redefining the hospitality industry. *Journal of Tourism Futures, 7*(1), 53–66. https://doi.org/10.1108/jtf-03-2020-0032

Saini, A., & Bhalla, R. (2022). Artificial intelligence and automation: Transforming the hospitality industry or threat to human touch. In *Handbook of research on innovative management using AI in Industry 5.0* (pp. 88–97). IGI Global.

Si, S., & Chen, H. (2020). A literature review of disruptive innovation: What it is, how it works and where it goes. *Journal of Engineering and Technology Management, 56*. 101568. https://doi.org/10.1016/j.jengtecman.2020.101568

Sigala, M. (2017). Collaborative commerce in tourism: Implications for research and industry. *Current Issues in Tourism, 20*(4), 346–355. https://doi.org/10.1080/13683500.2014.982522

Sinclair, D., & Ishmael, C. A. (2022). What innovations would enable the tourism and hospitality industry in Guyana to re-build? *Worldwide Hospitality and Tourism Themes, 14*(6), 541–548. https://doi.org/10.1108/whatt-05-2022-0062

Singh, L., & Dhankhar, D. (2020). ICT-based marketing and profitability in tourism and hospitality organizations in Indian scenario. In A. Hassan & A. Sharma (Eds.), *The Emerald handbook of ICT in tourism and hospitality* (pp. 311–330). Emerald Publishing Limited. https://doi.org/10.1108/978-1-83982-688-720201019

Siripipatthanakul, S., Phayaphrom, B., & Tong-On, P. (2021). The implementation of business intelligence using data analytics and its effects towards on performance in the hotel industry in Thailand. *Social Science Research Network*. https://autopapers.ssrn.com/sol3/papers.cfm?abstract_id=3944077

Susanto, E. H., Hendrayati, H., Rahtomo, W., & Prawira, M. F. A. (2022). Adoption of digital payments for travelers at tourism destinations. *DOAJ: Directory of Open Access Journals*. https://doi.org/10.46222/ajhtl.19770720.254

Tellis, G. J. (2005). Disruptive technology or visionary leadership?* *Journal of Product Innovation Management, 23*(1), 34–38. https://doi.org/10.1111/j.1540-5885.2005.00179.x

Tussyadiah, I. (2020). A review of research into automation in tourism: Launching the Annals of Tourism Research Curated Collection on Artificial Intelligence and Robotics in Tourism. *Annals of Tourism Research, 81*, 102883. https://doi.org/10.1016/j.annals.2020.102883

Vafin, A. (2021). The impact of remote work on firm's profitability: Optimizing virtual employee productivity and operational costs. *ResearchBerg Review of Science and Technology, 1*(1), 50–68.

Verhoef, P. C., Kooge, E., & Walk, N. (2016). *Creating value with big data analytics: Making smarter marketing decisions*. Routledge.

Vieira, E. S., & Gomes, J. (2009). A comparison of Scopus and Web of Science for a typical university. *Scientometrics, 81*(2), 587–600. https://doi.org/10.1007/s11192-009-2178-0

Vila, M., Enz, C. A., & Costa, G. (2011). Innovative practices in the Spanish hotel industry. *Cornell Hospitality Quarterly, 53*(1), 75–85. https://doi.org/10.1177/1938965511426562

Weeks, M. (2015). Is disruption theory wearing new clothes or just naked? Analyzing recent critiques of disruptive innovation theory. *Innovation: Management, Policy & Practice, 17*(4), 417–428. https://doi.org/10.1080/14479338.2015.1061896

https://prisma-statement.org/

https://amadeus.com/en/insights/research-report/blockchain-harnessing-its-potential-in-travel

SECTION 2

EVOLVING DIGITAL AND ARTIFICIAL INTELLIGENCE LANDSCAPE IN SERVICES AND MARKETING

DIGITAL ENIGMA: UNDERSTANDING ETHICAL DILEMMAS IN DESIGN AND MARKETING

Manoj Kumar Kamila[a], Sahil Singh Jasrotia[b] and Shagun Chib[c]

[a]*Jaipuria Institute of Management, India*
[b]*International Management Institute, India*
[c]*MIT World Peace University, India*

ABSTRACT

Operating ethically when developing and marketing a product or service is critical. An essential aspect of this process is ensuring that a company's guiding principles and values are congruent with its overarching goals. Concerns span from the veracity of marketing to the preservation of individual privacy to the impact of design on the natural world and human civilization. It also entails taking precautions if a product or advertising campaign has unforeseen repercussions. In today's interdependent and globalized world, it is more important than ever for firms to employ morally acceptable design and marketing tactics to acquire consumer trust and generate beneficial social and environmental benefits. This chapter offers insights for future researchers by offering a conceptual framework in ethics in design and marketing, which can be empirically tested. This study highlights several factors like privacy, manipulation, representation and diversity, accessibility, sustainability, social responsibility, and truth in advertising as important factors leading to ethical concerns in design marketing.

Keywords: Design; ethics; advertising; responsibility; digital age; marketing

Review of Technologies and Disruptive Business Strategies
Review of Management Literature, Volume 3, 67–82

Published under exclusive licence by Emerald Publishing Limited
ISSN: 2754-5865/doi:10.1108/S2754-586520240000003004

1. INTRODUCTION

The process of artistically creating a product or service's visual appeal and functioning is referred to as design. This includes a variety of factors, such as an application's user interface design, a brand's color palette, and the ergonomic considerations built into a device. On the other hand, marketing comprises the activities involved in promoting and distributing a particular product or service, including approaches such as advertising, branding, public relations, and sales strategies. Design and marketing must be integrated to provide a unified brand experience. A well-designed product catches the attention of potential buyers, while a well-executed marketing plan persuades them of its worth (Kamila & Jasrotia, 2023a). Apple is a prime example of this phenomenon, receiving international acclaim for its outstanding product design and powerful marketing methods. Apple has successfully integrated aesthetically beautiful and user-friendly technology by utilizing convincing marketing methods that drive consumer desire for their products despite their relatively higher cost. Previous studies have also explored consumer desire toward user-friendly and technology-oriented products (Mishra & Sharma, 2022; Sahni & Kaurav, 2023; Vyshnavi, 2022). Businesses must exhibit skills design and marketing skills to get a competitive advantage. In the context of design and marketing, ethics is critical. The underlying ideas and moral standards that govern the actions of designers and marketers are referred to as ethics. The design of a product has a significant impact on customer engagement and perception. Adherence to an ethical code in design ensures that products are inclusive, accessible, and safe for all users. Similarly, ethical marketing guarantees that honest and non-misleading promotional actions encourage customer trust and a positive brand image. The synergistic convergence of ethics, design, and marketing results in increased consumer happiness, strengthened brand loyalty, and, eventually, corporate prosperity.

Businesses may improve their relationships with customers and stakeholders by developing goods and services that value safety and inclusivity. Adopting marketing practices distinguished by honesty, transparency, and respect can also help develop strong partnerships (Kamila & Jasrotia, 2023b). This method fosters a climate of trust and integrity, allowing for the accomplishment of long-term and financially beneficial commercial activities. On the contrary, unethical practices in design and marketing can harm a company's reputation, resulting in customer and revenue loss. For example, companies that use misleading marketing strategies or produce biased products may see a drop in consumer confidence, resulting in lower sales and financial difficulty. Marketing ethics requires maintaining veracity, precision, and openness in promotional operations. Marketers should avoid misleading practices such as making incorrect or exaggerated claims about their products and resist using manipulative methods. Another critical ethical practice is respect for client privacy, particularly about data usage.

Furthermore, the ethical evaluation of marketing includes avoiding cultural appropriation and exploitation. Designers and marketers must considerably regard cultural diversity by ensuring that their product presentations and marketing methods are free of stereotyping or offending any specific population.

It is essential to include a diversified representation in marketing campaigns. Businesses have an inherent need to fulfill their community's social responsibility. This means conducting operations in a way that shows regard for societal and community requirements, emphasizing examining the potential impact of their products or services on the local economy or environment. A company's ethical commitment must be met by detecting and reducing negative repercussions.

2. METHODOLOGY

The methodology employed in this theoretical exploration of ethics in design marketing intends to provide a comprehensive framework for understanding and analyzing the critical intersections between ethical considerations, design principles, and marketing strategies (Pittman, 2023; Sahni & Kaurav, 2023). This chapter follows a conceptual approach. Conceptual studies do not offer data, instead they offer an integration of previous literature (Gilson & Goldberg, 2015). The research approach integrates a combination of literature review, conceptual analysis, and ethical framework application to establish a foundation for examining the complicated dimensions of ethical practices in the development and marketing of products and services (Farrukh & Sajjad, 2023). Based on the conceptual analysis, the study developed a conceptual framework to understand the area of design marketing and offer set of recommendations. As conceptual studies are nonempirical in nature and are descriptive, they lack the commonly accepted sample guidelines, we followed the approach as indicated and suggested by Hulland (2020) and Rana, Sakshi, et al. (2022). As per the guidelines, the study identified inconsistencies by assessing different concepts and justifying by offering appropriate examples. The study offers numerous examples on the concept of ethics in design marketing and then presents the need more clearly on why the study is important in ethics and design marketing. This chapter is executed in a twofold synthesis of literature. First, we tracked the evolution of ethics in design and marketing. The exercise led us to various factors that are of importance when it comes to ethics in design and marketing. The second step mapped the journey of ethics and marketing into creating a conceptual framework that can be essential for future researchers to contribute empirically and contribute to the area of ethics in design and marketing.

3. THE GROWTH IN ETHICS IN DESIGN MARKETING

Academic study that combines design, marketing, and ethics has gotten a lot of attention lately, so it needs to be looked at in more detail. It looks into issues like consumer privacy, economy, diversity, inclusion, and cultural appropriation, which are all linked. A big problem is protecting people's privacy, especially in this digital age of collecting a lot of data (Chawla & Kumar, 2022; Koul et al., 2022; Rana, Raut, et al., 2022). Establishing thorough data protection protocols and prioritizing transparency in how they handle data are ethical aspects of managing client data. This three-part study must include sustainability. An increasing number of studies have looked into the environmental effects of marketing and design activities, leading to a call for more eco-friendly and long-lasting methods to be used in these areas (Jasrotia et al., 2021, 2022; Kaurav & Gupta, 2022). When designing products, this means putting more emphasis on using eco-friendly materials and encouraging people to recycle in marketing materials.

Another thing that is clear in this area of study is the value of diversity and acceptance. According to studies by Misra et al. (2022) and Waller et al. (2005), design and marketing strategies that leave some people out can make bias or discrimination more likely to stay. Cultural elements from countries other than their own have been used by companies for marketing purposes, showing how important it is to be culturally sensitive so as not to offend people or spread stereotypes (Felix et al., 2017). More research needs to be done right away on the social and community effects of design and marketing choices, even though there are more and more studies in this area. For this reason, companies need to pay attention to these academic findings to make sure they run their businesses in a decent and socially acceptable way.

Businesses are now more aware of how their activities affect society and the world as a whole. So, they are working hard to make sure that their advertising and items are good for everyone. Businesses have also become more moral since rules were put in place to protect customer privacy, encourage environmentally friendly business practices, and lower racism (Schiff et al., 2020). You can't say enough good things about how important the internet is. Thanks to advances in technology, customers can now make better decisions about what to buy and speak out against bad business practices. This is possible thanks to a platform that makes information easy to find and pushes companies to think about ethics when they create and market their products (Rauschnabel et al., 2016). Table 1 shows the different important parts of ethics in design marketing.

Table 1. Key Aspects Among Ethics in Design Marketing.

Theme	Key Points	Implications
Consumer privacy	Massive data collection by companies raises privacy concerns (Chawla & Kumar, 2022; Koul et al., 2022; Rana, Raut, et al., 2022)	Firms must establish data protection protocols and prioritize transparency in handling consumer data
Sustainability	Environmental impact of design and marketing operations (Jasrotia et al., 2021, 2022; Kaurav & Gupta, 2022)	Emphasizing eco-friendly materials in design and promoting recycling in marketing is crucial
Diversity and inclusion	Exclusionary design and marketing can contribute to persisting bias or discrimination (Misra et al., 2022; Waller et al., 2005)	Diverse and inclusive teams are needed to create sensitive products and messaging is essential
Cultural appropriation	Firms exploit other cultures inappropriately for marketing objectives (Felix et al., 2017)	Cultural sensitivity is vital to avoiding offense or stereotypes

Source: Created by authors.

4. THE ETHICAL CONCERNS IN DESIGN MARKETING AND RESEARCH PROPOSITIONS

The design and marketing industries cancan have a significant impact on society and individuals in the commercial world. As a result, practitioners in these disciplines must evaluate the ethical implications of their work. Designers and marketers must be concerned about the following critical ethical considerations (Fig. 1).

4.1 Truth in Advertising/Deception

The marketing and advertising sector faces a tremendous ethical obligation due to its significant impact on customers' emotions and decision-making processes. According to Szabo and Webster (2021), marketers must be honest and cautious when presenting products and services to the public because misleading or

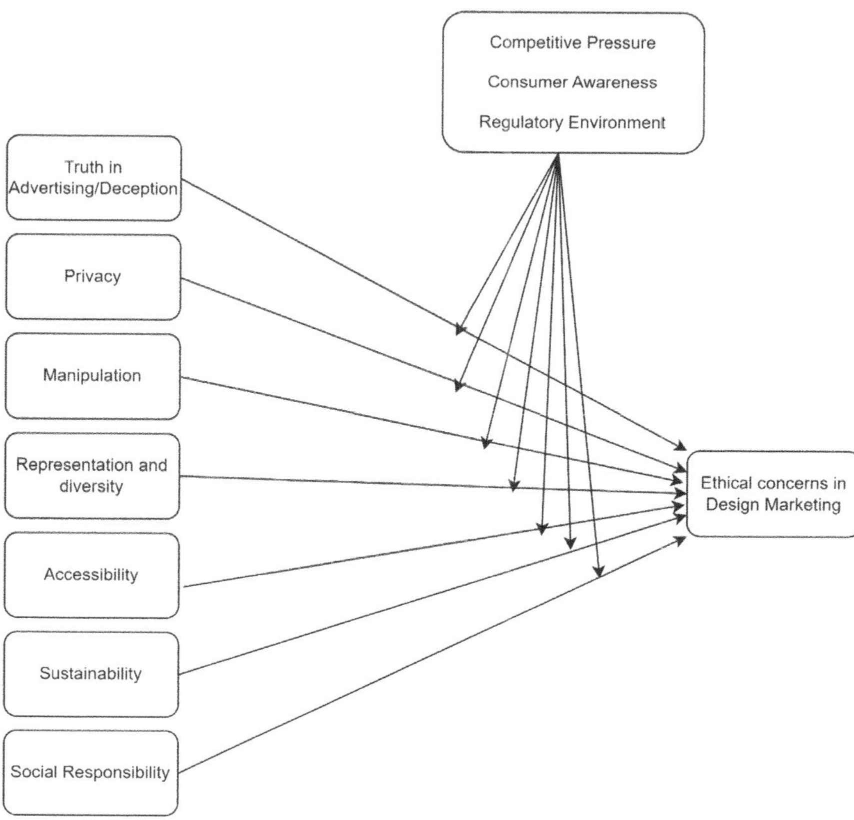

Fig. 1. Conceptual Model of Factors Leading to Ethical Concerns in Design Marketing. *Source:* Created by authors

deceptive advertising is ethically wrong and unlawful. Misusing such authority can have negative implications for society and individuals. Advertising has a substantial economic influence since it has the potential to shape consumer purchasing decisions and increase demand for a wide range of products and services (Kaurav et al., 2020; Sudha & Sheena, 2017). As a result, the transmission of false or inaccurate claims inside ads can mislead customers, affecting their decision-making in ways that may result in negative financial consequences, unhappiness, or even bodily harm. Deceptive advertising practices negatively influence customer trust in the marketplace and might potentially result in economic consequences.

In the United States, the Federal Trade Commission (FTC) and the Advertising Standards Authority (ASA) have both made laws to stop advertisers from misleading customers (Stewart, 2020). Advertising is a powerful way to get people to buy things, but it needs to be used with care and thought. According to Kotler et al. (2019), advertising must be completely honest and open in order for the market to be fair and competitive. Businesses need to show that they are committed to doing things in an honest and ethical way so that their clients are safe and the public doesn't lose trust in them. Following honesty, ethics, and responsibility rules is a basic moral duty in the marketing field, especially when it comes to telling the truth in ads. If marketers use this strategy, they might be able to build trust, keep the market's moral standards high, and balance out any bad effects that might happen to customers and society.

Based on the above understanding we formulate the first proposition as:

P1. Truth in advertising positively relates to ethics in design marketing practices.

4.2 Privacy

As the amount of personal data being collected grows, creators and marketers have a greater moral obligation to protect privacy rights. This includes making sure that methods for collecting data are clearly explained, getting informed permission, and keeping personal data safe. Designers and marketers are becoming more aware that privacy is a big social issue as technology and data collection methods improve quickly (Shmueli, 2017). Companies in the modern era of digital technology may easily collect, store, and use massive amounts of personally relevant data (Kaushal et al., 2023). While this ease has apparent benefits, it also comes with the duty of protecting individuals' right to privacy. Privacy is given much attention during the creation and promotion of products (Finn & Wright, 2016). Designers and marketers are responsible for protecting users' personal information from unauthorized access and exploitation and being forthright about the data-gathering methods they utilize. This involves the utilization of data in a manner that upholds individuals' rights to privacy and prevents the exploitative utilization of personal information that may result in negative consequences. The ethical considerations surrounding data utilization for targeted advertising are important. Signal, a prominent messaging application, distinguishes itself through the integration of state-of-the-art end-to-end encryption, underpinned by the open-source Signal Protocol. This encryption paradigm serves as a foundational design element, signifying a commitment to ensuring the confidentiality and integrity of user communications. Within this cryptographic framework, the communication channel is fortified to an extent where neither the service provider nor any external entities possess the capacity to intercept or decipher the transmitted messages or calls (Speak freely, 2024).

Businesses can create advertising campaigns that are highly focused by utilizing a growing amount of personal data. Nevertheless, this emerging phenomenon may raise concerns regarding the infringement of privacy and intrusion into individuals' spheres. Therefore, it is very important for marketers to make sure that personalized advertising campaigns protect people's privacy and give them control over how their data is used for targeting reasons. Using data for profiling and making decisions raises more worries because it could hurt people. Using personal information has led to unfair treatment of certain groups in areas like figuring out debt and job opportunities (Gillis & Spiess, 2019). It is very important for designers and marketers to fully understand these issues and take steps to make sure that their goods or campaigns don't lead to these kinds of bad results.

Concerns about privacy and ease of use must be taken into account by designers and marketers. As part of this, the privacy needs of people with disabilities must be taken into account when products and campaigns are being made. Privacy issues are very important from a social point of view in design and marketing, especially since companies are collecting more and more data. People who work in these fields need to know a lot about the possible outcomes of their actions and follow the right privacy rules. The things listed above include using clear methods to collect data, getting informed permission, keeping personal data safe, and lowering the chances that data will be misused or used to hurt people.

Based on the above understanding we formulate the second proposition as:

P2. Privacy positively relates to ethics in design marketing practices.

4.3 Manipulation

Researchers Key and Czaplewski (2017) say that both design and marketing can change how people think and act. According to moral standards, people who work in these fields should not lie or do dishonest things that take advantage of people's emotions or natural biases. The moral issues connected with design and marketing being able to change people's thoughts and actions are very important, as shown by the fact that they have a big impact on views and buying decisions (Szabo & Webster, 2021). Utilizing behavioral impact has a lot of power, but if it's not used correctly, it can have bad results. It's possible to use manipulative tactics in many ways, such as using subtle ways to persuade someone or directly appealing to their emotions or biases (Becher & Feldman, 2016). Emotional appeals are often used in marketing to get people to buy or use a product. These use visual and narrative methods to make people feel things like pleasure, security, or nostalgia. Even though these methods can help you connect deeply with your audience on an emotional level, it is very important not to use dishonest or manipulative methods. The use of "dark patterns", which are intentionally misleading or deceptive features built into the user interface, is another example of design manipulation. It is on purpose that dark designs are made to change people's behavior by hiding opt-out buttons or charges. Even though these methods may help in the short term, they can hurt someone's reputation and trustworthiness in the long term.

The marketing industry can be manipulated by using dishonest methods, like creating the illusion of urgency or shortage. The fear of missing out (FOMO) is a psychological phenomenon that marketers use to boost sales by playing on people's natural fear of being left out or ignored. Limiting offers or warning customers about limited supplies can create a sense of urgency, which could make them regret their buying decisions. According to Baker and Martinson (2001), designers and marketers have a moral duty to make sure that their goods and campaigns are made without lying or tricking people. This means making sure your goals are clear, giving accurate and honest information, and not lying to or taking advantage of customers during product or promotional demos. It's important to treat people with respect and not use emotional manipulation, bias, or making things seem more urgent than they really are. The moral problem that trickery creates is very important in design and marketing. Working in these areas requires professionals to fully understand the possible outcomes of their actions and be dedicated to meeting their professional duties. This means staying away from deceptive tactics, showing respect for the audience, and following moral standards. By taking this particular method, businesses can build trust and spread the idea of ethical behavior in the business world. So, this protects both customers and the community as a whole from bad things that might happen.

Based on the above understanding we formulate the third proposition as:

P3. Manipulation negatively relates to ethics in design marketing practices.

4.4 Representation and Diversity

People who work in marketing and design need to make sure that the stories and pictures they share with the public are inclusive of different experiences and points of view and don't support harmful stereotypes by accident (Du & Vieira, 2012). Diversity and representation have become big issues in design and marketing because the ideas that come from these fields have a big effect on what people think and believe (Sobočan et al., 2019). Negative stereotypes can get stronger when there isn't enough variety or influence. This can lead to more prejudice and push some groups to the edges of society.

The growth of negative stereotypes makes it very hard to decide how to show and include everyone in these fields (Borgerson & Schroeder, 2002). Using too sexualized images of women and showing certain ethnic groups in strange or scary places can spread damaging stereotypes, which can make discrimination and exclusion worse. As you can see, the above stereotypes can make bias and unfair treatment worse in many areas, such as job opportunities, housing, and schooling.

From 2011 to 2015, Access Icon worked on a project based on the ethics of inclusive design. The International Symbol of Access was changed as part of this project. The meaning of this sign, which is often found in wheelchair-accessible parking spots and buildings, was completely changed to better reflect people with disabilities. The original symbol showed a stick person sitting in a wheelchair that didn't move. The new symbol shows a moving representation. It shows a person's arms moving and their body leaning forward, giving the impression of being active and involved, like someone pushing or moving quickly in a wheelchair (Hendren, 2016).

Ethical design and marketing take into account how important diversity and participation are. To avoid adding to negative biases or stereotypes, people who work in these fields should make sure that diversity and representation are a top priority in their goods and marketing campaigns. This goal can be reached by taking a careful and thorough approach to expression, which means giving careful thought to the images and stories that are shown. Creative people who work in marketing and design can help make the world a better place by promoting diversity and fairness.

Based on the above understanding we formulate the fourth proposition as:

P4. Representation and diversity positively relate to ethics in design marketing practices.

4.5 Accessibility

According to Rivera et al. (2020), designers and marketers have a moral obligation to make sure that their campaigns and goods can be used by everyone, even people with disabilities. In both design and business, accessibility is a very important moral problem. For Kulkarni (2019), it's how well a lot of different people can use a thing, service, or place, no matter what their skills or limits are. Leaving disabled people out of campaigns and goods without trying to is a big ethical problem with accessibility. People who are deaf or hard of hearing can't see or hear the material or take part if a website doesn't work with screen readers or a marketing campaign doesn't have subtitles. If you leave people out by mistake, it could lead to more abuse and exclusion of disabled people.

Designers and marketers need to make sure that their products and campaigns are open to everyone around the world so that everything can be used by everyone. Follow well-known accessibility rules and best practices to make sure that people with disabilities can get to and use the site. In this case, people with disabilities need to have their specific needs met. You should also ask people with disabilities for help and feedback to make sure that their needs are met, and you should know what "accessibility" means in the context of your marketing or design work. They should also think about how to use words and pictures that everyone can understand when they talk about accessibility (Persson et al., 2015). So, talk about people with disabilities in a way that includes them and don't use words or pictures that support stereotypes or make people feel bad about themselves. If people in a lot of different fields show that they fully understand what makes something accessible, they can make sure that their marketing and goods are available for disabled customers. Microsoft's release of the Xbox Adaptive Controller shows that they are aware of the need to make designs more accessible. Microsoft created an adaptive touchpad controller because they knew that kids with physical disabilities, especially those who were missing limbs, had trouble using regular Xbox controls. This clever design not only met the needs of people with different disabilities, but it also created a space where people with different skills could play video games with their friends. The Xbox Adaptive Controller was designed with accessibility in mind, making sure that people with different kinds of disabilities can play games on the same level as their friends (Ads of Brands, 2019).

Based on the above understanding we formulate the fifth proposition as:

P5. Accessibility positively relates to ethics in design marketing practices.

4.6 Sustainability

In a world where environmental concerns are growing, designers and marketers need to think about how their goods and advertising might affect the environment. Sustainability has become an important ethical issue in design and marketing because it has a big effect on how natural resources are used and how the world is affected (Szabo & Webster, 2021). As concerns about the environment grow, professionals in all fields need to understand how their work affects the environment and use sustainability concepts in their daily work. Concerns about the morality of making products and running ads that hurt the environment are very important in the design and marketing fields (Szabo & Webster, 2021). Manufacturing things that use too much energy or depend on materials that won't last, for example, can have big effects on the environment and add to climate change.

In the same way, marketing tactics that encourage people to buy too many things or live wasteful lives can hurt the environment. Another thing that worries people is that sustainability is becoming more important in marketing and design (Ameen & Mourshed, 2019). Part of this could be helping designers and marketers learn more about sustainability standards and how the things and projects they make might affect the environment. Not doing this kind of critical thinking can lead to making and advertising goods and services that are bad for the environment.

Designers and marketers, according to Szabo and Webster (2021), have a moral duty to make sure that their campaigns and goods follow eco-friendly practices and don't make the environment worse. To do this, we need to follow sustainability standards and best practices and make sure that environmental factors are taken into account when products and projects are planned and carried out. Also, these professionals need to know why they need to use eco-friendly materials and push for eco-friendly methods in their goods and marketing (Green et al., 2019). Using biodegradable materials in packaging or advertising recycling can help the earth and encourage people to live in a way that doesn't harm it. Designers and marketers may have an effect on how eco-friendly goods and projects are marketed. This can be accomplished by identifying the environmental consequences of their business and adopting sustainable practices. Numerous corporate entities are presently aligning their strategies with circular design principles, a paradigmatic shift exemplified by enterprises such as 57th. design, specializing in the production of modular furniture. Concurrently, entities like AMP Robotics are actively engaged in programming recycling robots to enhance the efficiency of recycling processes. Companies such as PlasticRoad have also undertaken initiatives to repurpose plastic materials into modular components for road construction. This discernible shift toward circular design underscores a broader corporate commitment to sustainability and resource optimization (99pi, 2021).

Based on the above understanding we formulate the sixth proposition as:

P6. Sustainability positively relates to ethics in design marketing practices.

4.7 Social Responsibility

According to Raj et al. (2022), as representatives of commercial firms, designers and marketers are responsible for conducting their business in a way that serves society. This necessitates a detailed examination of their actions' broader social and economic consequences. Because businesses are obligated to conduct their operations in a way that benefits society, the concept of social responsibility as a moral imperative is especially significant in the domains of design and marketing. The ethical problem with social responsibility in design and marketing is manufacturing products and campaigns that have negative societal repercussions (Kim et al., 2020).

Marketing projects that deceive or manipulate people's existing beliefs could have negative consequences for all involved (Raj et al., 2022). Furthermore, it is crucial for the planning and marketing stages to have a deeper understanding and consideration of social responsibility (Zhang et al., 2019). It is essential to seek advice and assistance from groups and social responsibility experts, while also keeping informed about the most recent regulations and optimal approaches. Various professionals play a crucial role in contributing to the betterment of society through their work. Considering the impact of their decisions on others and the global economy is crucial. Contributing to social responsibility is a way for creators and advertisers to positively impact society (Amoako et al., 2021).

Designers and marketers have a big effect on how cultural views and behaviors are formed. They must follow high moral standards to make sure that their activities are good for people and the environment. People need to be careful about what they do and think about what might happen if they make a choice.

Based on the above understanding we formulate the seventh proposition as:

P7. Social responsibility positively relates to ethics in design marketing practices.

4.8 Competitive Pressure, Consumer Awareness, and Regulatory Environment as Moderators

Recently, researchers have looked at how ethical problems in design marketing are related to a number of other things, such as market competition, customer awareness, and business rules. To find out how these moderators effect the moral side of marketing strategies, researchers have looked at Szabo & Webster (2021), Feng et al. (2019), and Hari Adi and Adawiyah (2018). The competition has a big effect on marketing plans for ethical design. There is a chance that businesses will cheat to stay ahead when they have a lot of competitors (Ferguson et al., 2022). In places where people care about ethics, businesses may feel like they need to use more moral ways to sell themselves in order to stand out. Customers can do less illegal things in design marketing if they know more about it (Chatzopoulou & de Kiewiet, 2021). They are changing the way they sell to make sure they follow moral guidelines (Clementino & Perkins, 2021). This is because consumers are learning more about moral problems and building trust in brands more. Also, companies have to put ethical issues at the top of their design marketing efforts because more and more customers want companies to be open and responsible (Manuel & Herron, 2020). A big part of what shapes design marketing ethics is the legal landscape. Strong rules and ways to police them are put in place to stop unethical advertising practices (Bürger, 2023). If rules are too loose, companies may feel more free to do things that aren't right. Many times, businesses have to change how they advertise to meet the new social standards set by the rules. Based on the above understanding we formulate the eighth proposition as:

P8. Competitive pressure, consumer awareness and regulatory environment moderates' ethics in design marketing practices.

5. CONCLUSION

It is important for companies to consider the environmental impact of their products and take steps to address any issues that arise. It is crucial to promise customers that the company's services will always be transparent and free of any falsehoods or deceit. In the design and marketing fields, it's crucial to prioritize ethical practices in creating and promoting products and services. Adhering to these principles can result in numerous advantages, including increased customer trust, compliance with regulations, fulfilling social responsibilities, safeguarding the company's reputation, and fostering long-term sustainability. Considering the impact of products and services on both people and the world is crucial, and it's essential to take measures to minimize any negative consequences. In conclusion, integrating ethical concepts into design and marketing is crucial for safeguarding businesses' reputation and values, as well as promoting a mindful and eco-conscious society.

Establishing a corporate ethical code to regulate the production and promotion of goods and services is a current approach to addressing ethical concerns in design and marketing (Fig. 1). The code is intricately linked to the organization's goals and values, and it is thoroughly communicated to all stakeholders who require this information. It is crucial to conduct risk assessments to identify potential hazards associated with a product or marketing campaign and determine the most effective ways to minimize their impact. Examining the impact of products on society and the environment, along with the potential outcomes of marketing campaigns, businesses need to ensure that their products and advertising are free from any false or misleading information to maintain customer trust. Emphasizing the importance of prioritizing consumer privacy by implementing robust data security measures and transparent data collection and usage policies, it's important to regularly assess design and marketing methods to ensure alignment with ethical guidelines, the company's mission, and core values. Collaborating with organizations that advocate for ethical design and marketing, such as the Ethical Advertising and Marketing Alliance (EAMA) and the Ethical Marketing Forum (EMF), can be incredibly beneficial. Staying informed about evolving laws, trends, and regulations can be achieved through professional development courses.

In today's world, looking into ethical issues in marketing and design requires a strong commitment to morals and a steady desire to critically examine and improve methods. There will likely be big changes in the fields of design and marketing ethics because of new technologies, shifting consumer views, and stricter government rules. Companies need to carefully consider the moral issues connected with new technologies like AI and the Internet of Things (IoT), while also handling worries about data privacy and unintended outcomes. As people become more aware of how the goods and services they buy affect people's lives and the environment, companies that don't meet these standards risk losing customers and their brand. As a result, it is very important to follow the rules that are always changing and call for fair marketing and design. Companies need to keep up with changes in the law and be ready to show that they are committed to ethical standards. Including moral ideas in the design and marketing process is very important and needs careful consideration at all stages, from coming up with the idea and doing research to making the final product and running the advertising campaign. This means making sure the product is safe and works well, checking that claims are true, and including variety and respect in marketing materials. Being open and responsible during the process should be the rule, especially considering the social and environmental impacts. By addressing ethical problems in design and marketing, businesses can gain and keep customers' trust while also making the world a fairer and more environmentally conscious place to live.

REFERENCES

Ameen, R. F. M., & Mourshed, M. (2019). Urban sustainability assessment framework development: The ranking and weighting of sustainability indicators using analytic hierarchy process. *Sustainable Cities and Society*, *44*, 356–366.

Amoako, G. K., Doe, J. K., & Dzogbenuku, R. K. (2021). Perceived firm ethicality and brand loyalty: The mediating role of corporate social responsibility and perceived green marketing. *Society and Business Review*, *16*(3), 398–419.

Baker, S., & Martinson, D. L. (2001). The TARES test: Five principles for ethical persuasion. *Journal of Mass Media Ethics*, *16*(2–3), 148–175.

Becher, S. I., & Feldman, Y. (2016). Manipulating, fast and slow: The law of non-verbal market manipulations. *Cardozo Law Review*, *38*, 459.

Borgerson, J. L., & Schroeder, J. E. (2002). Ethical issues of global marketing: Avoiding bad faith in visual representation. *European Journal of Marketing*, *36*(5/6), 570–594.

Bürger, B. (2023). Public order policing: From theory to practice. In B. Bürger, T. D. Herold, & R. Lee (Eds.), *Public order policing*. Springer. https://doi.org/10.1007/978-3-031-43856-1_1

Chatzopoulou, E., & de Kiewiet, A. (2021). Millennials' evaluation of corporate social responsibility: The wants and needs of the largest and most ethical generation. *Journal of Consumer Behaviour*, *20*(3), 521–534.

Chawla, N., & Kumar, B. (2022). E-commerce and consumer protection in India: The emerging trend. *Journal of Business Ethics*, *180*(2), 581–604.

Clementino, E., & Perkins, R. (2021). How do companies respond to environmental, social and governance (ESG) ratings? Evidence from Italy. *Journal of Business Ethics*, *171*, 379–397.

Du, S., & Vieira, E. T. (2012). Striving for legitimacy through corporate social responsibility: Insights from oil companies. *Journal of Business Ethics*, *110*(4), 413–427.

Farrukh, A., & Sajjad, A. (2023). A critical review of literature review methodologies. In S. Rana, J. Singh, & S. Kathuria (Eds.), *Advancing methodologies of conducting literature review in management domain (Review of Management Literature)* (Vol. 2, pp. 103–123). Emerald Publishing Limited. https://doi.org/10.1108/S2754-586520230000002006

Felix, R., Rauschnabel, P. A., & Hinsch, C. (2017). Elements of strategic social media marketing: A holistic framework. *Journal of Business Research*, *70*, 118–126.

Feng, T., Wang, D., Lawton, A., & Luo, B. N. (2019). Customer orientation and firm performance: The joint moderating effects of ethical leadership and competitive intensity. *Journal of Business Research*, *100*, 111–121.

Ferguson, S. L., Flostrand, A., Lam, J., & Pitt, L. (2022). Caught in a vicious cycle? Student perceptions of academic dishonesty in the business classroom. *International Journal of Management in Education*, *20*(3), 100677.

Finn, R. L., & Wright, D. (2016). Privacy, data protection and ethics for civil drone practice: A survey of industry, regulators and civil society organizations. *Computer Law & Security Report*, *32*(4), 577–586.

Gillis, T. B., & Spiess, J. L. (2019). Big data and discrimination. *University of Chicago Law Review*, *86*(2), 459–488.

Gilson, L. L., & Goldberg, C. B. (2015). Editors' comment: so, what is a conceptual paper? *Group & Organization Management*, *40*(2), 127–130.

Green, K. M., Crawford, B. A., Williamson, K. A., & DeWan, A. A. (2019). A meta-analysis of social marketing campaigns to improve global conservation outcomes. *Social Marketing Quarterly*, *25*(1), 69–87.

Hari Adi, P., & Adawiyah, W. R. (2018). The impact of religiosity, environmental marketing orientation and practices on performance: A case of Muslim entrepreneurs in Indonesia. *Journal of Islamic Marketing*, *9*(4), 841–862.

Hendren, S. (2016). *The accessible icon project*. https://accessibleicon.org/. Accessed on January 11, 2024.

Hulland, J. (2020). Conceptual review papers: Revisiting existing research to develop and refine theory. *AMS Review*, *10*(1–2), 27–35.

Jasrotia, S. S., Darda, P., & Pandey, S. (2022). Changing values of millennials and centennials towards responsible consumption and sustainable society. *Society and Business Review*, *18*(2), 244–263.

Jasrotia, S. S., Kamila, M. K., & Patel, V. K. (2021). Impact of sustainable tourism on tourist's satisfaction: Evidence from India. *Business Perspectives and Research*, *11*(2), 173–189.

Kamila, M. K., & Jasrotia, S. S. (2023a). Ethics in product marketing: A bibliometric analysis. *Asian Journal of Business Ethics*, 1–24.

Kamila, M. K., & Jasrotia, S. S. (2023b). Ethics and marketing responsibility: A bibliometric analysis and literature review. *Asia Pacific Management Review*, *28*(4), 567–583.

Kaurav, R. P. S., Baber, R., & Rajput, S. (2020). Technology-driven tourism and hospitality industry as a tool for economic development: A bibliometric analysis. In *The Emerald handbook of ICT in tourism and hospitality* (pp. 469–486). Emerald Publishing Limited.

Kaurav, R. P. S., & Gupta, P. (2022). Trends in multidiscipline management research: Past, present and future of FIIB business review. *FIIB Business Review*, *11*(4), 382–404.

Kaushal, N., Kaurav, R. P. S., Sivathanu, B., & Kaushik, N. (2023). Artificial intelligence and HRM: Identifying future research agenda using systematic literature review and bibliometric analysis. *Management Review Quarterly*, *73*(2), 455–493.

Key, T. M., & Czaplewski, A. J. (2017). Upstream social marketing strategy: An integrated marketing communications approach. *Business Horizons*, *60*(3), 325–333.

Kim, J., Rundle-Thiele, S., Knox, K., Burke, K., & Bogomolova, S. (2020). Consumer perspectives on household food waste reduction campaigns. *Journal of Cleaner Production*, *243*, 118608.

Kotler, P., Kartajaya, H., & Setiawan, I. (2019). Marketing 3.0: From products to customers to the human spirit. In *Marketing wisdom* (pp. 139–156). Springer.

Koul, S., Jasrotia, S. S., & Mishra, H. G. (2022). Value co-creation in sharing economy: Indian experience. *Journal of the Knowledge Economy*, *13*(1), 387–405.

Kulkarni, M. (2019). Digital accessibility: Challenges and opportunities. *IIMB Management Review*, *31*(1), 91–98.

Manuel, T., & Herron, T. L. (2020). An ethical perspective of business CSR and the COVID-19 pandemic. *Society and Business Review*, *15*(3), 235–253.

Mishra, V., & Sharma, M. G. (2022). Digital transformation evaluation of telehealth using convergence, maturity, and adoption. *Health Policy and Technology*, *11*(4), 100684.

Misra, S., Pedada, K., & Sinha, A. (2022). A theory of marketing's contribution to customers' perceived value. *Journal of Creating Value*, *8*(2), 219–240.

Persson, H., Åhman, H., Yngling, A. A., & Gulliksen, J. (2015). Universal design, inclusive design, accessible design, design for all: Different concepts—One goal? On the concept of accessibility—Historical, methodological and philosophical aspects. *Universal Access in the Information Society*, *14*(4), 505–526.

Pittman, E. (2023). Realist synthesis: An innovative approach to literature review for complex management phenomena. In S. Rana, J. Singh, & S. Kathuria (Eds.), *Advancing methodologies of conducting literature review in management domain* (pp. 137–159). Emerald Publishing Limited. https://doi.org/10.1108/S2754-586520230000002008

Raj, V. A., Jasrotia, S. S., Rai, S. S., & Ansari, I. A. (2022). A bibliometric review of organic menus at restaurants: Research streams and future research path. *Journal of Quality Assurance in Hospitality & Tourism*, 1–27.

Rana, S., Raut, S. K., Prashar, S., & Quttainah, M. A. (2022). The transversal of nostalgia from psychology to marketing: What does it portend for future research? *International Journal of Organizational Analysis*, *30*(4), 899–932.

Rana, S., Sakshi, & Singh, J. (2022). Presenting the POWER framework of conducting literature review. *Exploring the latest trends in management literature*, 1–13.

Rauschnabel, P. A., Kammerlander, N., & Ivens, B. S. (2016). Collaborative brand attacks in social media: Exploring the antecedents, characteristics, and consequences of a new form of brand crises. *Journal of Marketing Theory and Practice*, *24*(4), 381–410.

Rivera, R. G., Arrese, A., Sádaba, C., & Casado, L. (2020). Incorporating diversity in marketing education: A framework for including all people in the teaching and learning process. *Journal of Marketing Education*, *42*(1), 37–47.

Sahni, S., & Kaurav, R. P. S. (2023). What? Why? When? How? Where? of technology-based bibliometric review. In S. Rana, J. Singh, & S. Kathuria (Eds.), *Advancing methodologies of conducting literature review in management domain (Review of Management Literature)* (Vol. 2, pp. 79–101). Emerald Publishing Limited. https://doi.org/10.1108/S2754-586520230000002005

Schiff, D., Biddle, J., Borenstein, J., & Laas, K. (2020, February). What's next for ai ethics, policy, and governance? A global overview. In *Proceedings of the AAAI/ACM conference on AI* (pp. 153–158). Ethics and Society.

Shmueli, G. (2017). Analyzing behavioral big data: Methodological, practical, ethical, and moral issues. *Quality Engineering*, *29*(1), 57–74.

Sobočan, A. M., Bertotti, T., & Strom-Gottfried, K. (2019). Ethical considerations in social work research. *European Journal of Social Work*, *22*(5), 805–818.

Speak freely. (2024). Signal messenger. https://signal.org/. Accessed on January 14, 2024.

Stewart, G. (2020). Trouble in paradise: Regulation of Instagram influencers in the United States and the United Kingdom. *Wis. Int'l LJ*, *38*, 138.

Sudha, M., & Sheena, K. (2017). Impact of influencers in consumer decision process: The fashion industry. *SCMS Journal of Indian Management*, *14*(3), 14–30.

Szabo, S., & Webster, J. (2021). Perceived greenwashing: The effects of green marketing on environmental and product perceptions. *Journal of Business Ethics*, *171*(4), 719–739.

Vyshnavi, P. (2022). Apple marketing strategy: The secret behind its simple yet effective marketing strategy. *StartupTalky*. https://startuptalky.com/apples-marketing-strategy/

Waller, D. S., Fam, K. S., & Erdogan, B. Z. (2005). Advertising of controversial products: A cross-cultural study. *Journal of Consumer Marketing*, *22*(1), 6–13.

Zhang, Q., Oo, B. L., & Lim, B. T. H. (2019). Drivers, motivations, and barriers to the implementation of corporate social responsibility practices by construction enterprises: A review. *Journal of Cleaner Production*, *210*, 563–584.

WEB REFERENCES

99pi. (2021). Mini-stories: Volume 10 – Page 3 of 3, 99% invisible. https://99percentinvisible.org/episode/mini-stories-volume-10/3/?_ga=2.122738946.863259434.1705740220-1255455478.1705740220. Accessed on January 20, 2024.

Ads of Brands. (2019). Microsoft: We all win, even advertising needs advertising. https://adsofbrands.net/en/ads/microsoft-we-all-win/10041. Accessed on January 13, 2024.

A BIBLIOMETRIC ANALYSIS AND VISUALIZATION OF MEDICAL ARTIFICIAL INTELLIGENCE RESEARCH

Yonghao Liu and Yu Mu*

Sichuan Agricultural University, China

ABSTRACT

In recent years, there has been an impressive increase in the use of artificial intelligence (AI) in medical treatment. Studies have explored many topics in the field of medical AI; however, few of them have systematically reviewed the overall area. This chapter retrieves 532 papers on medical AI from Social Sciences Citation Index core database of the Web of Science from 2013 to 2022. Two bibliometric and network analysis tools, including CiteSpace and HistCite, are used to identify the time-and-space knowledge map, research hotspots, emerging trends and key studies of medical AI research. A co-word network of medical AI is constructed to reveal that the field focuses more on the topic of machine learning. The analysis of the burst literature on medical AI indicates the research trends in the sub-sections such as law and ethics. Furthermore, the analysis of the co-citation uncovers the key studies in the field of medical AI. The results of bibliometric analysis illustrate the current situation, past evolution, and future trends in medical AI research, and identify hotspots and future research directions.

Keywords: Medical treatment; artificial intelligence; literature review; bibliometric analysis; visualization; CiteSpace; HistCite

*Corresponding author.

Review of Technologies and Disruptive Business Strategies
Review of Management Literature, Volume 3, 83–96

Published under exclusive licence by Emerald Publishing Limited
ISSN: 2754-5865/doi:10.1108/S2754-586520240000003005

1. INTRODUCTION

Artificial intelligence (AI) has recently and widely used to improve medical treatment. Medical AI refers to the application of AI technology in the area of medical treatment. Overall, AI empowers medical care to alleviate the shortage and imbalance of medical and health resources, by improving the efficiency of clinical diagnosis and the quality of medical treatment (Hosny & Aerts, 2019; Obermeyer & Emanuel, 2016; Yu et al., 2018). Medical AI primarily encompasses various subfields such as medical imaging, clinical decision support, precision medicine, health management, healthcare informatics, drug development, telehealth, and medical robotics (Mishra & Sharma, 2022). The core objectives of medical AI include reducing costs, increasing efficiency, improving diagnostic and treatment standards, enhancing patient experiences, and reducing the risk of illness. AI empowers all stages of healthcare, including pre-hospital, in-hospital, and post-hospital care. Medical institutions, scientific research institutes and enterprises jointly tackle the problem, hoping to learn from the successful experience of AI within translation, finance, and security to achieve major changes in the medical field (Obermeyer & Emanuel, 2016). For instance, deep learning is an emerging trend in multidiscipline management research (Kaurav & Gupta, 2022). The intervention of AI induces the applications of deep learning, intelligent machines, big data, and other digital technologies in the medical field. The deep integration of precision medicine and AI connects doctors, patients, medical apparatus, other medical stakeholders, and media. Technological innovation, as the basis, combines with institutional transformation, to promote the innovation research and development of medical AI.

Preventing and combating the COVID-19 underscores the original purpose of developing medical AI, that is, to help doctors rescue from repeat births and address the lack of high-quality medical resources. However, medical behavior per se is highly complex, uncertain, and risky. Accordingly, scientific and technological risks and medical needs will promote innovative changes in the policy ethics of AI regulation in terms of body, value, operation, and implementation. Particularly, there is an urgent need for the standardization and intelligence in medical big data.

The adjustment of robots, the governance of algorithmic ethics, and the improvement of access mechanisms lay a solid institutional foundation, and form a circle-type innovation alliance driven by the clinical application of outward AI, inward data feedback, and the reverse drive of underlying AI.

Recently, conducting literature review requires for more systematic procedure and analytical frameworks (Rana et al., 2022; Sahni & Kaurav, 2023). Bibliometric analysis is a quantitative statistical tool of indicating and monitoring research origins, pathways, and trends. Bibliometric analysis is currently and widely employed in a variety of medical treatment research areas (Bai et al., 2021; Chen et al., 2020; Li et al., 2020). Nevertheless, there is a dearth of a synthesis and an overview of the research distribution, the historical background, the research hotspots, and the future directions of medical AI research. As a result, it is critical to identify and define the current status of the entire medical AI research in order to offer a research foundation. This study conducted a systematically bibliometric analysis of medical AI research, by using CiteSpace and HistCite software and based on 532 articles of medical AI published from 2013 to 2022.

2. LITERATURE REVIEW

AI is increasingly used in various fields of science and technology. According to current research, more and more AI technologies are being used in medical treatment (Bitkina et al., 2023; Tang et al., 2023). However, Gaczek et al. (2023) find that consumers remain skeptical of the ability of AI to accurately evaluate their health status, and have reluctance to use health recommendations generated by AI. Gosak et al. (2022) investigate the effectiveness of AI within predicting complications associated with multimorbid diabetes mellitus through bibliometric studies. Mihevc et al. (2024) find that AI can be integrated into the platform to optimize the cost structure of remote monitoring of AH and T2D older adults in primary care. The ChatGPT tool is demonstrated as a somehow reliable information source for Spanish patients suffering chronic diseases; however, the readability of the information needs to be improved to enhance the usefulness for patients (Soto-Chávez et al., 2024). Lin et al. (2024) perform a systematic review of the impacts of technology in the area of speech-language pathology. Digital assistance systems based on AI in medical treatment (e.g., chatbots) play an increasingly essential role in the interaction and communication between doctors and patients in the future (Moldt et al., 2023).

Studies have explored many topics of medical AI. Bitkina et al. (2023) identify the current state of medical AI, based on the studies reporting evidence-based guideline. Graili et al. (2021) systematically discuss AI in outcomes research and cover the scope of AI techniques used in outcomes research to expend the knowledge of decision-makers. Gosak et al. (2022) adopt bibliometrics to investigate the effectiveness of AI in predicting diabetes-caused complications. Few studies systematically review the overall picture of medical AI.

With the deepening and expansion of medical AI research, many theoretical and empirical results are obtained. In terms of research content, in recent years, there have been many studies on a certain field of medical AI, such as the trend of electronic health development (Dinh-Le et al., 2019), the health information services for the elderly in libraries (Zhang et al., 2023), the important position and distribution of AI technology in medical information (Bitkina et al., 2023), the patent metric in medical AI (Yang et al., 2021), and the reasons for the trust and the reluctance to use medical AI (Gaczek et al., 2023). With regard to research methods, qualitative and quantitative research methods are divided, and most studies adopt qualitative research methods. In the quantitative studies, the WOS database is analyzed by using advanced analysis tools, e.g., CiteSpace and HistCite (Escobio-Prieto et al., 2023; Sahni & Kaurav, 2023). Accordingly, this chapter attempts to analyze and discuss the relevant problems of medical AI research based on WOS publication data and using CiteSpace and HistCite bibliometric tools.

3. METHOD

3.1 Research Instrument

Two most widely used bibliometric software, i.e., CiteSpace and HistCite, are employed as knowledge map analysis tools for medical AI research (Anlesinya &

Dadzie, 2023; Sahni & Kaurav, 2023). The application of bibliometric review, through a variety of methods to construct a more systematic analytical frameworks, can provide more valuable insights into the topic (Kaurav et al., 2020; Sahni & Kaurav, 2023).

CiteSpace refers to an information visualization tool that is widely used in the field of information graphics (Lab, 2013). In order to represent and analyze the information context of an area, visualization tools are used to propose the development history and structural links of the specific area. This study uses CiteSpace 5.7.R5 to obtain visualization that convey information about medical AI topic while also highlighting the domain's research boundaries and the knowledge base in important data.

HistCite, i.e., history of cite, is a citation map analyzing software, to visualize the citation links between numerous papers in a specific subject, identify notable documents in the field, and learn about the history of document development.

3.2 Data Collection

The bibliometric analysis relies on literature databases. WOS is regarded in academia as a highly renowned and prominent journal collection, with a core database containing over 10,000 well-known scientific journals from more than 10,000 area. As a result, the data source of this study is the Social Sciences Citation Index core databases of the WOS main database.

As the database updates day by day, this context seeks access to literature retrieval from WOS on 1 day to avoid bias (i.e., September 18, 2023). The search strategy includes the topic "medical artificial intelligence," and limits to the literature type "Article."

Articles published from 2013 to 2022 were retrieved. Finally, a total of 532 references were obtained. All bibliographic information of the publications is recorded for further processing data and the specific analyses.

4. RESULTS

4.1 Analysis of the Amount of Publications

To some degree, the time distribution of disciplinary publications can reflect the development trend and theoretical level of academic research in this field. As shown in result, during the period of 2018–2022, the annual amount of medical AI-related research exceeds 20 articles, indicating that the field of medical AI has attracted much attention since 2018. During the period of 2017–2022, the annual amount of articles is explosive and the attention continues to rise. In 2021, it reaches a peak, the annual amount of articles reaches as high as 182, the researchers push the medical AI-related research to a new height, and the research achievements are more remarkable. In contrast, the number of articles in 2022 dropped slightly, but the research results are more significant.

By plotting the trendline of the index, the *R*-squared value ($R^2 = 0.8863$) and the trendline formula ($Y = 0.5854e^{0.5891x}$) are used. The *R*-squared value is close to 1, which indicates that the trendline has a high degree of congruence and the reliability of the trendline is also high. The prediction derived from this is that in the next few years, medical AI research will remain in a constant state of flux, and research in this field will continue to grow at a high rate.

4.2 Analysis of Academic Journals and Core Authors

4.2.1 Analysis of Academic Journal

Relevant literature data are transferred to the CiteSpace software to obtain the academic journal map of the core journals of medical AI research. The color and thickness of the circle in the graph represent the time and the frequency of citation in the specific year. Each node represents the journal. The size of the citation shows the journal's citation frequency. The thicker the reference before the node, the greater the co-citation between journals.

The journals with highest citation frequency of medical AI are successively "Jama-Journal of the American Medical Association," "Jama-Journal of the American Medical Association," "Journal of International Medical Research," "Nature Medicine," "The New England Journal of Medicine," "Nature," "NPJ Digital Medicine," "BMJ-British Medical Journal," "Scientific Reports," and "International Journal of Medical Informatics." Respectively, these are journals in the field of medical disciplines, which are significant sources of medical AI research and play a critical supportive role in this research sector.

With regard to the field distribution of academic journals, the core journals of medical AI are mainly distributed in the subject field of medicine, and also involve the field of information technology. As the AI application in the medical field, medical AI inevitably involve multiple fields, particularly, in the field of medical treatment and information technology. Notably, the medical AI research has begun to set foot in the realms of law and ethics (Anishchenko et al., 2023), because the development of intelligent medical robot technology has also caused a series of ethical concerns. If the ethical issues of robots are not faced, this will undermine the society's confidence in medical AI, and even hinder the development and progress of medical science and technology. At the same time, the risks of applying medical algorithms are also gradually emerging (Ploug & Holm, 2023). For instance, the "Wei Zexi Incident" mistrusted the medical institutions promoted by algorithms, the "Gene Edited Baby Incident" abused algorithm technology to partially alter human genes, and other tragic events caused social chaos and reduced the public's trust in medical AI. Therefore, it is urgent to reflect on the ethical and legal issues caused by smart healthcare and find solutions to solve them.

4.2.2 Analysis of Core Authors

Relevant literature data are transferred to the CiteSpace software to obtain the core authors map of medical AI research. The author with the highest citation is Andre Esteva, as a key researcher of medical AI. His studies are mostly focused on medical diagnostics using AI and precision medicine. His publications have appeared on the covers of the journals Nature and Nature Medicine, and have appeared in Cell, The Lancet, Conference and Workshop on Neural Information Processing Systems, among others. His most famous book, "Dermatologist-level Classification of Skin Cancer with Deep Neural Networks," has been cited a total of 6,044 times. Others, such as Eric Jeffrey Topol, are renowned American cardiologists. His scientific focus is on the use of genomic and digital data, along with AI, to individualize medicine. He is also a practicing cardiologist. Fox Joseph has the highest centrality, with more than 20 publications in biology, physics, and other fields. Over the past decade, many authors have delved into topics related to medical AI, and they have been extremely instrumental in advancing medical AI research. They are more interested in the application of medical AI in clinical care, biological genes, and physical algorithms.

4.3 Analysis of Co-word Networks

The keywords in the domestic data are analyzed, the Node Type is set to Keyword, the threshold is set to T50, and the rest is defaulted, and the obtained knowledge graph of medical AI research hotspots is shown in Fig. 1. Keyword frequency analysis is used to clarify the research trends related to medical AI. After all, keywords stand for hot research topics, and burst word stands for a new frontier of research. A large node indicates a high keyword hit rate. As can be seen from Fig. 1, "artificial intelligence," "big data," "classification," "machine learning," "system," "deep learning," "technology," "model," "diagnosis," and "COVID-19" are relatively high with frequencies over 35 times.

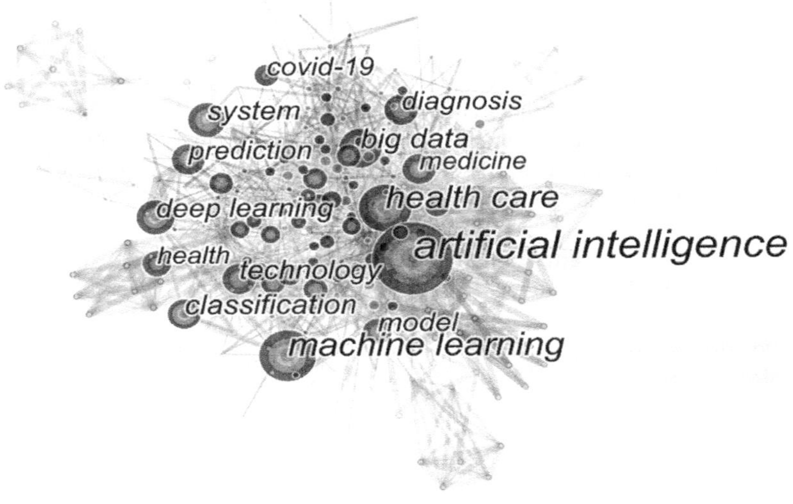

Fig. 1. The Co-word Network of Medical AI Research (CiteSpace). *Source:* Synthesized by the authors.

It is not difficult to see from Fig. 1 that the research objects of the past decade have mostly concentrated on the AI technology application in diagnosis and health management (Chang et al., 2022). At present, the application of medical AI has broad prospects and is a direction for future medical development. The application of AI in medical treatment follows its development in general. The research hotspots include the low price of healthcare, the resistance of consumers to medical AI, and the prediction of the results of machine learning in clinical diagnosis. In-depth and long-term research is need in these areas to drive the development of medical AI research. Therefore, a certain vacancy still exists in the studies on the application of medical AI that needs to be further explored by researchers.

Through the cluster analysis based on keyword co-occurrence graph, the research trends and hot issues in this field can be effectively revealed so as to have a deeper understanding of the research trend and frontier direction. CiteSpace is accepted to create a network in normal mode of 2013–2022. Slice length is 1 year. Node Select the node type is Keyword. The nodes are revised based on a given keyword match. The Log-likelihood (LLR) algorithm is applied to compute the clusters, then gained Fig. 2. The Modularity Q score is 0.5147. The Mean Silhouette score is 0.7057 ($N = 362$, $E = 1804$, density $= 0.0276$).

Clustering results mainly locate in "COVID-19 pandemic," "deep learning," "visualizing knowledge," "big data," "artificial intelligence perspective," "web-based intelligent tutoring system," "deliberative relational approach," "NILE virus," "artificial intelligence," "post-traumatic stress disorder," etc.

4.4 Analysis of Burst Literature

4.4.1 Analysis of Burst Keywords

"Burst words" refer to words that are regularly quoted over an extended period. In this context, the research limit is estimated using the keywords within the

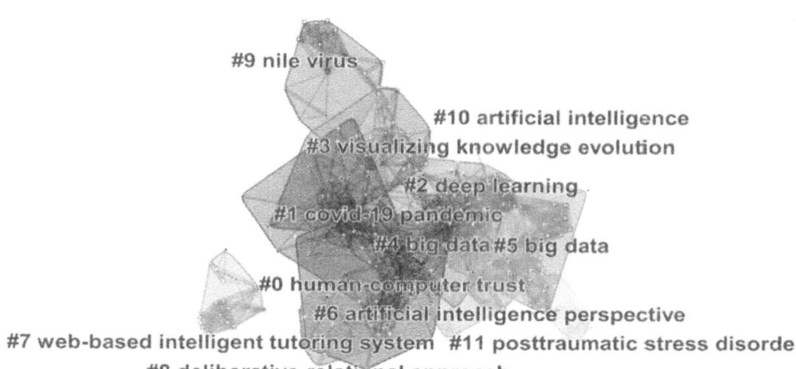

Fig. 2. Hot Topics of the Co-word Network of Medical AI Research (CiteSpace). *Source:* Synthesized by the authors.

highest citation burst. Table 1 shows the top 18 terms within the most citation burst emerging from 2013 to 2022. Fine line in the last column of Table 1 indicates that the specific keyword is quoted frequently; thick line indicates that the specific keyword is rarely put in quotation marks. Disorder and robot may be mentioned frequently in the coming years, reflecting new trends. In addition, emerging trends may also include E-health, decision-making, social media, and regression analysis.

- Disorder: During the COVID-19, there were relatively high rates (between 7% and 53.8%) of general post-traumatic stress disorder (PTSD) in many countries such as China, Spain, Italy, Iran, etc. (Xiong et al., 2020).
- Robot: Advancement of medical robots has the potential to revolutionize modern medicine and human well-being. The miniaturization of robotic platforms and system potentially improve medical treatment and patient diagnosis. The small robotic surgeons offer the access to distant and hard-to-reach parts of the body, and induce a variety of changes in medical treatment and procedures (Soto et al., 2020).
- E-health: E-health has grown exponentially, and more than 325,000 health applications are accessible in major app stores (Maramba et al., 2019).

Table 1. Burst Literature (Top 18) and Research Hotspots of Medical AI (CiteSpace).

Keywords	Year	Begin	End	2013–2022
Guideline	2013	2015	2018	
Medical informatics	2013	2016	2019	
Data mining	2013	2016	2017	
Artificial neural network	2013	2016	2018	
Electronic health record	2013	2017	2020	
Future	2013	2018	2020	
Technology	2013	2018	2018	
Dementia	2013	2018	2020	
Deep learning	2013	2018	2018	
Primary care	2013	2019	2020	
Support	2013	2019	2019	
Information	2013	2019	2020	
E-health	2013	2020	2020	
Decision-making	2013	2020	2020	
Social media	2013	2020	2020	
Regression	2013	2020	2020	
Disorder	2013	2021	2022	
Robot	2013	2021	2022	

Note: The fine line indicates the time interval, and the thick line represents the time period of the keyword burst.
Source: Synthesized by the authors.

- Decision-making: The clinical decision support system (CDSS) improves medical decisions through offering targeted and exact information of clinical, patient, and health information (Sutton et al., 2020).

4.4.2 Analysis of Thematic and Emerging Trends

This study makes the timeline view by the CiteSpace software. The results show that, in 2013 or earlier, the research on medical AI is a lot already and the keywords of that period are concentrated on "artificial intelligence," "health care," and "clinical decision support." Since 2016, research on medical AI has become more diverse, including "medical error," "cancer," "deep learning," "digital health," "neural network," "medical student" and "management," and accounts for large proportions. The evolutions have three main directions. The first one is the support technique for AI, like "system," "information technology," and "machine learning." The second is medical treatment, like "diagnosis," "personal medicine," and "COVID-19." The third one is reasonableness, like "ethics," "regulation," and "trust." This indicates that the medical AI was developing from a disease-centered model toward a patient-centered model.

Analyzing the research frontiers, it is found that recently, medical AI research has begun to involve research in the field of law and ethics (Anishchenko et al., 2023). There are also many research and analysis on the advancement of AI technology, human resource management (HRM) of medical AI, and its application (Kaushal et al., 2023). In addition, the research also covers issues such as patient privacy (Keshta & Odeh, 2021) and medical AI management (Chang et al., 2022). Medical AI relieves the labor pressure of doctors, facilitates doctors and patients, and reduces the cost of living. The consequent management, legal and ethical risks are one of the concerned themes (Ploug & Holm, 2023).

4.5 Analysis of Co-citation

The citation relationship between papers reveals the historical context of knowledge diffusion. In the early stage of research in some fields, citation relationships are relatively simple. With the expansion of research time and space, citation relationships have gradually developed into a huge citation network. Citation path evolution analysis has been widely used in bibliometric research (Lucio-Arias & Leydesdorff, 2014). In this chapter, the data processed by CiteSpace is imported into the HistCite software, and the first 60 digits are used to draw a citation chronology chart in local citations (LCS) order (Fig. 3). Each node in the illustration represents a document with a high citation rate. The larger node means the greater citation frequency. The arrows between the nodes indicate the citation path of document. The citation chronology chart can visually show the communication of research results and important research results.

Fig. 3 shows that the top 10 mostly cited documents are numbered 25, 79, 34, 38, 94, 126, 41, 155, 23, and 95. For instance, Yu et al. (2018) summarized the current status and influence of AI application in healthcare. Longoni et al. (2019)

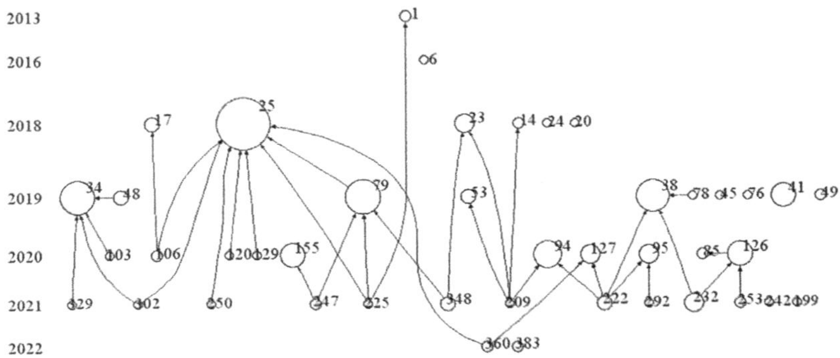

Fig. 3. The Literature Citation of Medical AI (HistCite).
Source: Synthesized by the authors.

Table 2. Statistics of Citation Frequency of Literature (Top 10) (HistCite).

Order	Number	First Author	Time	Theme	LCS
1	25	Yu KH	2018	AI in healthcare	37
2	79	Longoni C	2019	Resistance to medical AI	17
3	34	Price WN	2019	Privacy of medical big data	16
4	38	McDougall RJ	2019	Value-flexibility in medical AI	14
5	94	Reddy S	2020	Governance of AI in health care	10
6	126	Hatherley JJ	2020	Trust in medical AI	9
7	41	Gong B	2019	Influence of AI on preference	8
8	155	Fan WJ	2020	AI-based medical diagnosis support system (AIMDSS)	8
9	23	Laranjo L	2018	Conversational agents in healthcare	5
10	95	Ploug T	2020	Refusion of AI diagnostics and treatment	5

Source: Synthesized by the authors.

then examined consumer' resistance to medical AI and explored the reasons for its occurrence. Price and Cohen (2019) outlined the enormous challenges posed by big data to patient privacy and pointed out possible ways for the regulatory system. These studies are the classic literature and knowledge base of the Internet of Things (IoT) (see Table 2).

5. DISCUSSION

5.1 Findings

This research retrieves the core database of the WOS based on the search formula and retrieved data of 532 literature of medical AI research from 2013 to 2022. In this study, the amount of publications, core academic journals and authors, co-word networks, burst literature, and co-citation analysis of literature related to medical AI research are studied and discussed through the common review and analysis tools CiteSpace and HistCite. The main results are as follows:

- Through statistical analysis of the amount of publications, papers on medical AI research increases generally. In recent years, medical AI has been a research hotspot, and is assumed to continue gaining popularity. By plotting the R-squared value of the index, it can be predicted that medical AI research will remain in a constant state of flux in the coming years, and research in this field will continue to grow at a high rate.
- Through statistical analysis of academic journals, the core journals of medical AI are mainly distributed in the subject field of medicine, and will also involve the area of information technology. Medical AI research notably has begun to set foot in the fields of law and ethics. At the same time, the risks of the application of medical algorithms are also gradually emerging.
- Through statistical analysis of core authors, many authors have studied medical AI-related issues, and advanced the development of medical AI research. They are more interested in the application of medical AI in clinical care, biological genes, and physical algorithms.
- Through the statistical analysis of keywords and research frontiers based on high-frequency keyword analysis, the research objects in the past decade have mainly focused on the usage of AI technology in medical diagnosis and in health management. Through analyzing research frontiers, emerging trends include disorder, robot, E-health, decision-making, social media, and regression analysis. Analyzing the thematic and emerging trends, it is found that in recent years, the research of medical AI has begun to involve research in the field of law and ethics. In addition, the research also covers issues of patient privacy and medical AI management.
- Through statistical analysis of citation, the co-citation analysis of the medical AI research shows some important studies, which lay a solid foundation for the research of medical AI research. These important studies focus on the use of AI in healthcare (Yu et al., 2018), consumer' resistance to medical AI (Longoni et al., 2019), and the challenges that AI poses to patient privacy (Price & Cohen, 2019).

5.2 Implications

The research area of this chapter covers the entire medical AI. This study enriches the systematic review of the entire field of medical AI (Morrow et al., 2023). Through the overall overview of the medical AI research, this study is comprehensively considered and systematically planned with the overall aspects of the entire research field. The results provide a more intuitive overall perspective of medical AI for the whole society and the academia, and help understand and refer to research trends and gaps.

This chapter uses quantitative approach, specifically, by analyzing WOS data and using CiteSpace and HistCite software to discuss the relevant issues of medical AI research. Quantitative research has the advantage of a wide range of investigations, and is easy to summarize in the literature review (Pickering & Byrne, 2014). The results of quantitative research results are more objective and accurate, compared with those of qualitative research. This method makes this study easier and more clearly to be understood, and grasps the evolution trajectory and research frontiers of medical AI.

5.3 Limitations and Directions of Research

Although the reviews of medical AI research in the past decade are more targeted, and can usually provide evidence reference for scholars in the field, it is difficult to confirm whether these conclusions are general due to the limited sample size. Based on 532 literature, this chapter systematically reviews and summarizes the progress and historical context of existing medical AI research, and proposes potential future research directions. The relevant conclusions will help scholars in related fields to grasp the research progress, locate research interests, and bring inspiration for future research work. Medical AI research is still in the ascending stage. Along with the development of medical AI research, future research should include as much literature as possible and carry out a richer and more comprehensive review.

Future research can further promote the medical AI research around the following themes.

- Law and ethics of medical AI. Studies have shown that there is currently a lack of legislative work to simplify public relations related to the use of AI (Anishchenko et al., 2023; Ploug & Holm, 2023). Researchers can continue to explore the law and ethical regulations associated with the use of AI.
- Risks of medical AI. The problems and risks of AI systems in medical treatment have attracted great attention (Ploug & Holm, 2023). Researchers are recommended to have a comprehensive look at the risks of medical AI such as the external and internal risks and the related solutions.
- Management of medical AI. Some important management issues of medical AI remain to be solved (Chang et al., 2022). Future research can focus on issues such as the use of medical AI in health management and the management of medical AI equipment.
- Privacy of medical AI. At present, data management and privacy protection are research hotspots of medical AI (Keshta & Odeh, 2021). Researchers can study the effective mechanism of data use and security modes related to privacy protection to improve data security.

ACKNOWLEDGMENTS

This work is supported by Sichuan Science and Technology Program (Grant No. 2023NSFSC1050), and Innovation Training Planning Project of Sichuan University Students (Grant No. S202310626020).

REFERENCES

Anishchenko, M. A., Gidenko, I., Kaliman, M., Polyvaniuk, V., & Demianchuk, Y. V. (2023). Artificial intelligence in medicine: Legal, ethical and social aspects. *Acta Bioethica, 29*(1), 63–72.

Anlesinya, A., & Dadzie, S. A. (2023). Technology and the conduct of bibliometric literature reviews in management: The software tools, benefits, and challenges. In S. Rana, J. Singh, & S. Kathuria (Eds.), *Advancing methodologies of conducting literature review in management domain* (pp. 57–78). Emerald Publishing Limited.

Bai, X., Song, Z., Zhou, Y., Wang, X., Wang, Y., & Zhang, D. (2021). Bibliometrics and visual analysis of the research status and trends of postpartum depression from 2000 to 2020. *Frontiers in Psychology, 12*, 665181.

Bitkina, O. V., Park, J., & Kim, H. K. (2023). Application of artificial intelligence in medical technologies: A systematic review of main trends. *Digital Health, 9*. https://doi.org/10.1177/20552076231189331

Chang, C. Y., Jen, H. J., & Su, W. S. (2022). Trends in artificial intelligence in nursing: Impacts on nursing management. *Journal of Nursing Management, 30*(8), 3644–3653.

Chen, S., Lu, Q., Bai, J., Deng, C., Wang, Y., & Zhao, Y. (2020). Global publications on stigma between 1998–2018: A bibliometric analysis. *Journal of Affective Disorders, 274*, 363–371.

Dinh-Le, C., Chuang, R., Chokshi, S., & Mann, D. (2019). Wearable health technology and electronic health record integration: Scoping review and future directions. *JMIR mHealth and uHealth, 7*(9).

Escobio-Prieto, I., Blanco-Díaz, M., Pinero-Pinto, E., Rodriguez-Rodriguez, A. M., Ruiz-Dorantes, F. J., & Albornoz-Cabello, M. (2023). Quantitative ultrasound and bone health in elderly people, a systematic review. *Biomedicines, 11*(4), 1175.

Gaczek, P., Pozharliev, R., Leszczynski, G., & Zielinski, M. (2023). Overcoming consumer resistance to AI in general health care. *Journal of Interactive Marketing, 58*(2–3), 321–338.

Gosak, L., Martinovic, K., Lorber, M., & Stiglic, G. (2022). Artificial intelligence based prediction models for individuals at risk of multiple diabetic complications: A systematic review of the literature. *Journal of Nursing Management, 30*(8), 3765–3776.

Graili, P., Ieraci, L., Hosseinkhah, N., & Argent-Katwala, M. (2021). Artificial intelligence in outcomes research: A systematic scoping review. *Expert Review of Pharmacoeconomics & Outcomes Research, 21*(4), 601–623.

Hosny, A., & Aerts, H. J. W. L. (2019). Artificial intelligence for global health. *Science, 366*(6468), 955–956.

Kaurav, R. P. S., Baber, R., & Rajput, S. (2020). Technology-driven tourism and hospitality industry as a tool for economic development: A bibliometric analysis. In A. Hassan & A. Sharma (Eds.), *The Emerald handbook of ICT in tourism and hospitality* (pp. 469–486). Emerald Publishing Limited.

Kaurav, R. P. S., & Gupta, P. (2022). Trends in multidiscipline management research: Past, present and future of FIIB business review. *FIIB Business Review, 11*(4), 382–404.

Kaushal, N., Kaurav, R. P. S., Sivathanu, B., & Kaushik, N. (2023). Artificial intelligence and HRM: Identifying future research agenda using systematic literature review and bibliometric analysis. *Management Review Quarterly, 73*(2), 455–493.

Keshta, I., & Odeh, A. (2021). Security and privacy of electronic health records: Concerns and challenges. *Egyptian Informatics Journal, 22*(2), 177–183.

Lab, W. (2013). Review on the application of CiteSpace at home and abroad. *Journal of Modern Information, 33*(4), 99–103.

Li, R. R., Sun, J., Hu, H. T., Zhang, Q. F., Sun, R. H., Zhou, S. N., Zhang, H. J., & Fang, J. Q. (2020). Research trends of acupuncture therapy on knee osteoarthritis from 2010 to 2019: A bibliometric analysis. *Journal of Pain Research, 13*, 1901–1913.

Lin, C. J., Mubarok, H., Ramadhana, A. B. R., Gasperius, S., Liu, C. Y., Sawettanun, S., Meesomyut, K., & Zheng, L. R. (2024). Trends in technology-enhanced learning strategies in speech-language pathology solutions: A systematic review of journal publications from 2004 to 2023. *Interactive Learning Environments*. https://doi.org/10.1080/10494820.2023.2300011

Longoni, C., Bonezzi, A., & Morewedge, C. K. (2019). Resistance to medical artificial intelligence. *Journal of Consumer Research, 46*(4), 629–650.

Lucio-Arias, D., & Leydesdorff, L. (2014). Main-path analysis and path-dependent transitions in HistCite-based historiograms. *Journal of the Association for Information Science and Technology, 59*(12), 1948–1962.

Maramba, I., Chatterjee, A., & Newman, C. (2019). Methods of usability testing in the development of eHealth applications: A scoping review. *International Journal of Medical Informatics, 126*, 95–104.

Mihevc, M., Zavrnik, C., Mori, L. M., Virtic, P. T., Petek, S. M., Klemenc-Ketis, Z., & Poplas, S. A. (2024). Bottom-up analysis of telemonitoring costs: A case study in Slovenian primary care. *Zdravstveno Varstvo, 63*(1), 5–13.

Mishra, V., & Sharma, M. G. (2022). Digital transformation evaluation of telehealth using convergence, maturity, and adoption. *Health Policy and Technology, 11*(4), 100684.

Moldt, J. A., Festl-Wietek, T., Mamlouk, A. M., Nieselt, K., Fuhl, W., & Herrmann-Werner, A. (2023). Chatbots for future docs: Exploring medical students' attitudes and knowledge towards artificial intelligence and medical chatbots. *Medical Education Online, 28*(1), 2182659.

Morrow, E., Zidaru, T., Ross, F., Mason, C., Patel, K. D., Ream, M., & Stockley, R. (2023). Artificial intelligence technologies and compassion in healthcare: A systematic scoping review. *Frontiers in Psychology, 13*, 971044.

Obermeyer, Z., & Emanuel, E. J. (2016). Predicting the future – Big data, machine learning, and clinical medicine. *New England Journal of Medicine, 375*(13), 1216–1219.

Pickering, C., & Byrne, J. (2014). The benefits of publishing systematic quantitative literature reviews for PhD candidates and other early-career researchers. *Higher Education Research and Development, 33*(3), 534–548.

Ploug, T., & Holm, S. (2023). The right to a second opinion on artificial intelligence diagnosis-remedying the inadequacy of a risk-based regulation. *Bioethics, 37*(3), 303–311.

Price, W. N., & Cohen, I. G. (2019). Privacy in the age of medical big data. *Nature Medicine, 25*(1), 37–43.

Rana, S., Sakshi, & Singh, J. (2022). Presenting the POWER framework of conducting literature review. In S. Rana, Sakshi, & J. Singh (Eds.), *Exploring the latest trends in management literature* (pp. 1–13). Emerald Publishing Limited.

Sahni, S., & Kaurav, R. P. S. (2023). What? Why? When? How? Where? of technology-based bibliometric review. In S. Rana, J. Singh, & S. Kathuria (Eds.), *Advancing methodologies of conducting literature review in management domain* (pp. 79–101). Emerald Publishing Limited.

Soto, F., Wang, J., Ahmed, R., & Demirci, U. (2020). Medical micro/nanorobots in precision medicine. *Advanced Science, 7*(21), 2002203.

Soto-Chávez, M. J., Bustos, M. M., Fernández-Avila, D. G., & Muñoz, O. M. (2024). Evaluation of information provided to patients by ChatGPT about chronic diseases in Spanish language. *Digital Health, 10*. https://doi.org/10.1177/20552076231224603

Sutton, R. T., Pincock, D., Baumgart, D. C., Sadowski, D. C., Fedorak, R. N., & Kroeker, K. I. (2020). An overview of clinical decision support systems: Benefits, risks, and strategies for success. *NPJ Digital Medicine, 3*(1), 17.

Tang, L., Li, J. X., & Fantus, S. (2023). Medical artificial intelligence ethics: A systematic review of empirical studies. *Digital Health, 9*. https://doi.org/10.1177/20552076231186064

Xiong, J., Lipsitz, O., Nasri, F., Lui, L. M. W., Gill, H., Phan, L., Chen-Li, D., Iacobucci, M., Ho, R., Majeed, A., & McIntyre, R. S. (2020). Impact of COVID-19 pandemic on mental health in the general population: A systematic review. *Journal of Affective Disorders, 277*, 55–64.

Yang, X., Wang, M., & Zhou, Y. (2021). The development trend of artificial intelligence in medical: A potentiometric analysis. *Artificial Intelligence in the Life Sciences, 1*, 100006.

Yu, K. H., Beam, A. L., & Kohane, I. S. (2018). Artificial intelligence in healthcare. *Nature Biomedical Engineering, 2*(10), 719–731.

Zhang, Y., Xu, P. R., Sun, Q. N., Baral, S., Xi, L. J., & Wang, D. R. (2023). Factors influencing the e-health literacy in cancer patients: A systematic review. *Journal of Cancer Survivorship, 17*(2), 425–440.

METAVERSE MARKETING: A GUIDE TO REACHING THE NEXT GENERATION OF CONSUMERS

Piyush Gupta[a], Vivek Mishra[a], Anshuman Adarsh Sahu[a] and Priya Jindal[b]

[a]*Birla Global University, India*
[b]*Chitkara Business School, Chitkara University, India*

ABSTRACT

Metaverse is going to change the landscape in every field, sector, and business. This chapter aims to explore the role of marketing in the metaverse focusing on each sector and business. This chapter has adopted bibliometrics analysis to explore the importance of metaverse marketing. The results suggest that the publication and citation of articles have seen a huge jump from 2022 onwards. Keyword co-occurrence analysis shows that metaverse with blockchain, marketing, education, and virtual reality (VR) are hot words in the upcoming time. Metaverse marketing shows that innovation, mixed reality, and extended reality will change the landscape of marketing. Analysis suggests that China, the United States, South Korea, and India are the top contributing countries in the research of metaverse. By understanding the implications of the metaverse on purchaser conduct and promoting systems, organizations can draw in the main interest group and gain esteem in this new advanced scene.

Keywords: Metaverse; marketing; bibliometrics; virtual reality; mixed reality; India

1. INTRODUCTION

In recent times, people have become more familiar with an innovative concept called the metaverse that's been inspired by science fiction. In a nutshell, it's a digital world resembling real-life scenarios that provide users with an immersive feeling akin to being present physically in an interactive space (Kim, 2021).

Review of Technologies and Disruptive Business Strategies
Review of Management Literature, Volume 3, 97–113

ISSN: 2754-5865/doi:10.1108/S2754-586520240000003006

Operating as a shared environment where participants can meet each other virtually while engaging in various activities and voyaging across diverse realms using only their avatars as transport – the metaverse combines features of augmented reality along with internet technology allowing individuals to have immediate access to ongoing experiences remotely (Davis et al., 2009). Representing excellent prospects for transforming how we interact within the bounds of cybersecurity above all else (Pooyandeh et al., 2022).

1.1 Importance of Metaverse

The transformative possibilities that the metaverse presents are not lost on experts closely following technological advancements today. A crucial aspect worth considering is how it reshapes interpersonal relations by providing an innovative space that simulates the real world. Enabling people to connect seamlessly with each other globally beyond geographical boundaries, such platforms make it easier to create and foster new connections, share experiences, and build communities that transcend identity differences – improving intercultural understanding (Kim, 2021).

Immersive technologies with the potential to link diverse individuals in meaningful ways constitute a powerful tool for creating a sense of shared purpose among various social groups while promoting educational objectives, economic networking opportunities as well as mutual cultural exchange and strengthening communities (Han et al., 2023).

Furthermore, the metaverse opens up exciting new economic possibilities by providing access to virtual trade and digital markets. Individuals can engage in purely online transactions such as purchasing or selling goods or services using solely their avatar's presence. This includes opportunities like investing in digital assets such as private virtual property holdings, buying exclusive access to unique clothing options within the metaverse fashion industry, or even attending revolutionary events hosted entirely virtually (Sayem, 2022; Yilmaz et al., 2022).

The metaverse empowers makers and business visionaries, and endeavors to market their computerized items and contact an overall crowd, empowering new plans of action and pay sources to arise. It additionally gives broad information bits of knowledge and examination, considering designated promoting, customized encounters, and statistical surveying (Ni et al., 2023). What's more, the metaverse empowers individuals to communicate their computerized characters and participate in self-articulation (Chugh & Vyas, 2023). Clients might plan and customize computerized symbols that mirror their virtual characters. This gives space for imagination, individual marking, and the improvement of numerous characters. Inside the metaverse, virtual garments, frills, and customization prospects take into consideration self-articulation and portrayal. Clients might flaunt their abilities, participate in virtual occasions, and interface with others given similar interests and encounters, advancing a feeling of having a place and realness.

The metaverse offers immersive and interactive settings that go beyond traditional media in terms of experiences. Users can travel across virtual worlds, take part in virtual activities, and interact with computer-generated landscapes. This has far-reaching consequences for entertainment, gaming, education, training, and simulations. Within the metaverse, virtual concerts, exhibitions, and performances can be staged, providing unique and compelling experiences. Virtual classrooms, interactive simulations, and immersive educational experiences are also possible in the metaverse. Students can collaborate on projects, digitally visit historically significant sites, or perform scientific experiments in virtual settings, increasing the accessibility and efficacy of education (Tasa & Görgülü, 2010).

Within the metaverse, collaboration and invention are encouraged. It brings together individuals and organizations from various backgrounds, enabling virtual co-working, remote collaboration, and shared creative spaces. Within virtual environments, people may cooperate on projects, brainstorm ideas, and share information, resulting in cross-disciplinary cooperation and new solutions. The metaverse serves as a forum for the exchange of ideas, the promotion of creativity, and the exploration of what is possible (Hee-Jung & Jin-Woo, 2010).

The metaverse likewise handles worries of advanced openness and variety. It empowers better-computerized encounters as well as fair admittance to virtual universes and advanced assets. Inside the metaverse, virtual travel, social drenching, and admittance to encounters that sound troublesome or impossible in the real world become accessible. This has consequences for schooling, social trade, and self-awareness since people might get to and partake in computerized encounters no matter what their geological area or actual limitations (Shen et al., 2021).

1.2 Applications of Metaverse

The metaverse has a few applications in different areas, changing how we communicate with computerized content and virtual settings. Here are some significant metaverse applications:

Amusement and gaming: The metaverse offers rich and intuitive diversion and gaming encounters (Niu & Feng, 2022). Clients can investigate virtual universes, play multiplayer games, and take part in virtual encounters that obscure the differentiation between the physical and advanced universes (He, 2022). Virtual reality (VR) and augmented reality (AR) advancements further develop the gaming experience by permitting clients to associate progressively with virtual items and characters.

Virtual gatherings and occasions: The metaverse gives virtual gathering spaces and occasion settings where individuals may remotely assemble, coordinate, and go to meetings, workshops, shows, and displays. Virtual gatherings and occasions are a more practical and effective choice than in-person social events, considering overall cooperation while limiting the carbon impression related to movement (Hennig-Thurau et al., 2023).

Schooling and preparing: There are significant consequences for training and preparing in the metaverse. Vivid and drawing-in instructive encounters are given through virtual study halls, reenactments, and intuitive learning conditions.

Understudies can visit authentic areas, perform logical examinations, and go on virtual field outings to work on their perception and data maintenance. Experts can likewise master new abilities and data in a safe and directed climate by utilizing virtual preparation conditions (Rachmadtullah et al., 2023).

Virtual exchange: The metaverse gives a stage to virtual exchange and computerized markets. Clients can buy and sell virtual items, advanced resources, and land inside the metaverse. Virtual style, adornments, and collectables have filled in unmistakable quality, opening up new potential for online business and computerized business. Brands and ventures might make a presence in the metaverse to associate with clients and give one-of-a-kind computerized encounters (Şanlısoy & Çiloğlu, 2023).

Interpersonal interaction and correspondence: The metaverse increments person-to-person communication and correspondence by offering virtual regions for people to associate and convey. Inside virtual universes, clients might have continuous visits, construct networks, and take part in shared exercises. People can utilize virtual social stages to advance their inclinations, capacities, and characters, considering new sorts of social inclusion and articulation (Nagendran et al., 2022).

Engineering and plan: The metaverse has applications in engineering and configuration, permitting draftsmen and architects to make virtual portrayals of designs, scenes, and metropolitan regions. Programmatic experiences and 3D demonstrating permit draftsmen to envision and assess plans before genuine execution. This upgrades the effectiveness of the planning cycle and considers more precise input and support (Purahong et al., 2022).

Medical services and treatment: The metaverse can be utilized in medical care and treatment. Augmented reality-based treatments can be utilized to treat fears, post-awful pressure problems (PTSD), and nervousness issues. Virtual conditions may likewise be utilized for clinical preparation, permitting medical services professionals to rehearse troublesome tasks in a protected climate. Telemedicine and far-off medical care administrations can be improved by using the metaverse, which empowers virtual counsels and remote checking (Yang et al., 2022).

Social protection and the travel industry: There is potential for social conservation and the travel industry in the metaverse. Developing virtual duplicates of authentic landmarks and social resources is conceivable, permitting people to investigate and encounter them in a remote place. This advances social connection, the security of jeopardized locales, and admittance to social encounters that are generally inaccessible in the actual world (Gursoy et al., 2022).

2. REVIEW OF LITERATURE

2.1 Bibliometrics Analysis

Bibliometric analysis, a quantitative system used to focus on books, articles, and dispersions, has gained tremendous importance in the field of investigation and the academic world. It is immovably associated with scientific metrics, which revolve around exploring intelligent estimations and markers. By using genuine procedures, bibliometric assessment gives significant encounters into various pieces of canny work, making it an urgent gadget in surveying educational quality and understanding investigation designs (Donthu et al., 2021). One of the fundamental purposes of bibliometric assessment is to look over the academic impact and nature of journals or individual makers (Kaurav & Gupta, 2022). By seeing reference rates, h-record, and other significant estimations, researchers can quantitatively survey the effect and importance of scholarly responsibilities. These evaluations are instrumental in powerful cycles associated with progressions, residency appraisals, supporting entryways, and grant applications. Besides, bibliometric assessment plays a vital part in registering journal impact factors, which are by and large used as characteristics of journal greatness and importance inside unambiguous disciplines (Kaurav et al., 2020; Kaurav & Gupta, 2022; Kaushal et al., 2023; Mishra & Sharma, 2022; Rana et al., 2022; Sahni & Kaurav, 2023).

The bibliometric assessment has been applied to various fields, engaging researchers to follow research floats and separate appropriation plans. For example, it has been utilized in fields like desolation of the chiefs, nursing, chest illness, diabetes mellitus, white platelets, and spinal ultrasound (Kokol et al., 2021). By taking a gander at dissemination models and reference associations, researchers can procure pieces of information for the progression of assessment inside these spaces, perceive emerging examination districts, and predict future examples. These data uphold organizing investigation tries, working with participation, and apportioning resources effectively. Furthermore, bibliometric assessment grants researchers to design the insightful scene of a field. By examining co-reference associations, watchword repeat, and gathering techniques, experts can perceive interconnected research locales and explore interdisciplinary affiliations. This guides in planning data as well as advances joint endeavors between experts from different disciplines, provoking imaginative and successful investigation results.

2.2 Application of Bibliometrics Analysis

Bibliometric analysis, as a quantitative technique for concentrating on distributions and insightful results, has many uses across different fields. Some of the key applications of bibliometric analysis include:

Research assessment and execution appraisal: Bibliometric examination is usually used to evaluate the exploration result and effect of people, research gatherings, organizations, and, surprisingly, whole nations. It gives objective measures, for example reference counts, h-list, and diary influence factors, which are utilized to assess the quality and impact of examination commitments. These data are significant for settling on informed choices regarding advancements, residency assessments, subsidizing allotments, and examination coordinated efforts (Mukherjee et al., 2022).

Distinguishing exploration research patterns: Bibliometric examination helps in recognizing arising research patterns and areas of interest inside a specific field. By breaking down distribution designs, reference organizations, and co-reference bunches, specialists can acquire experiences in the heading of exploration and the rise of new points. These data are helpful for scientists, policymakers, and financing organizations to assign assets and back the improvement of promising regions (Kaurav & Gupta, 2022).

Planning scholarly design and information spaces: Bibliometric investigation permits specialists to plan the scholarly construction of a particular field or exploration area. By dissecting co-origin organizations, reference examples, and watchword co-events, it is feasible to recognize the central ideas, critical givers, and the interrelationships between various points. This aids in understanding the information scene and works with interdisciplinary joint efforts (Kaurav & Gupta, 2022).

Evaluating cooperation and organizations: Bibliometric examination gives experiences into research joint effort examples and organizations. By examining co-initiation organizations and co-reference designs, specialists can distinguish key teammates, research groups, and cooperative patterns. These data help cultivate joint efforts, distinguishing potential examination accomplices, and understanding the elements of information trade and cooperation inside a field (Kaurav & Gupta, 2022).

Assessing diaries and distributions: Bibliometric investigation is broadly used to assess the quality and effect of scholastic diaries and individual distributions. Diary influence factors, reference rates, and other bibliometric pointers help analysts, distributors, and per users survey the impact and permeability of diaries in their particular fields. It supports distinguishing high-influence diaries for distribution and empowers scientists to arrive at informed conclusions about where to distribute their work (Maulani et al., 2021).

Following exploration effect and spread: Bibliometric investigation permits specialists to follow the effect and dispersal of their examination. By checking reference counts, co-origin organizations, and elective measurements (for example Altmetrics), specialists can quantify the permeability and reach of their work. These data are significant for professional success and award applications, and shows the more extensive effect of exploration past customary reference measurements (Haustein et al., 2014).

Science strategy and direction: Bibliometric examination assumes a significant part in science strategy and navigation. Policymakers and subsidizing organizations use bibliometric information to assess research needs, evaluate the effect of examination financing, and illuminate strategy choices. It assists in relating to exploring holes, solid areas, and possible coordinated efforts to shape research plans and asset designations (Picard-Aitken et al., 2010).

Financing designation: Bibliometric examination is in many cases utilized in the distribution of exploration subsidizing. Subsidizing organizations can utilize bibliometric markers to distinguish high-carrying out scientists and foundations, as well as areas of examination that are creating critical effects. These data help in pursuing key subsidizing choices and coordinating assets toward research attempts that can yield significant results (Wang et al., 2019).

Benchmarking and relative investigation: Bibliometric examination takes into account benchmarking and similar investigations between various analysts, foundations, or nations. By looking at reference measurements, distribution results, and joint effort designs, partners can evaluate their general exhibition and distinguish regions for development. This examination can help in laying out objectives, distinguishing best practices, and cultivating solid rivalry among specialists and foundations (Goh & See, 2021).

Assessing exploration strategy and projects: Legislatures and research associations can utilize bibliometric investigation to assess the adequacy of examination approaches and projects. By breaking down bibliometric information, they can evaluate the effect of drives, for example research awards, impetus plans, and information move programs. This assessment helps with distinguishing fruitful systems and making proof-based acclimations to approaches and projects (Spanache et al., 2022).

Protected innovation and patent examination: Bibliometric investigation is utilized in protected innovation and patent investigation to distinguish patterns, innovation groups, and critical creators in a specific field. By inspecting reference examples and patent references, specialists and patent workplaces can evaluate the impact and effect of protected advances. These data are helpful for patent valuation, innovation moves, and going with informed choices regarding licensed innovation assurance (Sick et al., 2021).

Writing survey and information union: Bibliometric investigation is a significant device for directing precise writing audits and information blends. By utilizing bibliometric procedures, specialists can recognize pertinent examinations, investigate reference organizations, and guide the scholarly construction of an exploration region. This guides in summing up existing information, distinguishing research holes, and creating experiences for future exploration bearings (Chen et al., 2021).

All in all, the bibliometric examination has a large number of utilizations across research assessment, pattern investigation, joint effort evaluation, diary assessment, research influence following, science strategy, subsidizing designation, benchmarking, patent examination, writing survey, and information combination. Its quantitative methodology gives significant experiences that help analysts, policymakers, financing organizations, and different partners in pursuing informed choices, molding research plans, and progressing logical information.

3. RESEARCH METHODOLOGY

The flow of methodology with research questions is presented below:

- Selection of articles from Scopus database ($n = 676$) as of June 5, 2023
- Bibliometrics analysis of selected Scopus database
- Research questions dealt:
  - Publications of metaverse articles in business, accounting, social science, and decision sciences fields [*RQ1*]
  - Citation analysis [*RQ2*]

- Keyword analysis [*RQ3*]
- Metaverse marketing [*RQ4*]
- Top contributing authors [*RQ5*]
- Top contributing institutions [*RQ6*]
- Top contributing countries [*RQ7*]

*3.1 Publications Over the Years [*RQ1*]*

According to the bibliometric analysis of metaverse research from 2006 to 2021, there has been a considerable rise in publications on the metaverse in recent years. From zero in 2006 to more than 350 in 2022, the number of publications has expanded dramatically. The huge surge in publications can be observed in 2022 and 2023. This surge in publication corresponds to the metaverse's continuing development and expansion in breadth and popularity over the last many years. While there are several causes for this surge in publications, the rising popularity of VR and associated technologies is most certainly one of them. As VR becomes more widely available and accessible, more individuals are expected to investigate the potential benefit of the metaverse and write about their experiences there.

*3.2 Citations Analysis Over the Years [*RQ2*]*

The citation analysis shows that metaverse articles are hugely cited in 2022 (citations of 1,300) and 2023 (citations of 1,700). The sharp expansion in references to metaverse-related distributions lately shows the developing interest in this innovation. It likewise recommends that the metaverse is essentially affecting the examination of local areas. These distributions have fundamentally affected the innovative work of the metaverse in an extremely large manner. They truly have commonly helped shape our opinion on this innovation and it's for the most part possible effect on society, which shows that these distributions in a real sense have essentially influenced the innovative work of the metaverse in an unpretentious manner. The metaverse is a quickly developing field with the in every practical sense, potential to reform how we cooperate with our general surroundings in a very huge manner. The review of the metaverse literature over the years shows a decent momentum and quickly developing into a field having potential to upset how we fundamentally connect with our generally surroundings subtly.

*3.3 Top Cited Articles in Metaverse [*RQ2*]*

The new flood of interest in the metaverse is driven by its true capacity for vivid encounters, advanced economies, and worldwide availability. The quantity of references that a distribution gets decides its effect. In this way, to acquire a comprehension of the scholarly elements of the field, we examine the most powerful distributions in an examination field. The most referred-to articles from the assortment are uncovered in Table 1. The outcomes showed that the article published by Dwivedi et al. (2022), on the challenges, opportunities, and agenda for research, practice, and policy of metaverse arrived quickly at 148 citations within 1 year.

Authors have concentrated on the groundbreaking impact of the metaverse as well as cultural outcomes connected with social collaboration factors from expansive reception. Advertising, schooling, the travel industry, and medical care are among the businesses that may be moved by the metaverse (Dwivedi et al., 2022). Moreover, the paper investigated the instructive utilizations of the metaverse and inspected the conceivable outcomes and restrictions of the metaverse (Kye et al., 2021). The metaverse, an interoperable organization of virtual

Table 1. Top Cited Articles on Metaverse in Business, Accounting, Decisions, and Social Sciences.

Sl No	Publication Year	Document Title	Journal Title	2022	2023	Total
1	2022	Metaverse beyond the hype: Multidisciplinary perspectives on emerging challenges, opportunities, and agenda for research, practice, and policy	International Journal of Information Management	32	116	148
2	2021	Educational applications of metaverse: Possibilities and limitations	Journal of Educational Evaluation for Health Professions	64	58	122
3	2021	Advertising in the metaverse: Research agenda	Journal of Interactive Advertising	45	36	81
4	2017	A content service deployment plan for metaverse museum exhibitions – Centering on the combination of beacons and HMDs	International Journal of Information Management	38	33	71
5	2022	Facebook and the creation of the metaverse: Radical business model innovation or incremental transformation?	International Journal of Entrepreneurial Behavior and Research	42	30	72
6	2018	The social metaverse: Battle for privacy	IEEE Technology and Society Magazine	38	31	69
7	2022	Definition, roles, and potential research issues of the metaverse in education: An artificial intelligence perspective	Computers and Education: Artificial Intelligence	38	30	68
8	2022	The metaverse in the hospitality and tourism industry: An overview of current trends and future research directions	Journal of Hospitality Marketing and Management	23	32	55
9	2022	What is augmented reality marketing? Its definition, complexity, and future	Journal of Business Research	26	28	54
10	2022	Metaverse – The new marketing universe	Journal of Business Strategy	33	18	51

Source: Scopus Database.

settings that permits clients to draw in with another as symbols simultaneously for an enormous scope, is supposed to upset a few components of conventional publicizing (Rosário et al., 2023). Since the idea is still in its early stages, scholastic discussion on the metaverse is generally focused on characterizing it to the table for a beginning stage for the majority of these subjects (Dwivedi et al., 2022). The leftover most referenced articles examine Metaverse's current periods of purpose, impediments, exceptional issues, and potential.

*3.4 Keyword Analysis [*RQ3*]*

Eight clusters were featured utilizing the grouping approach. Fig. 1 portrays the rehashed watchwords that showed up in the logical articles. The cloud map shows the times the term shows up in the article and the connection between the watchwords. Each term in the organization is addressed as a circle, with the size of the circle relative to the number of distributions where the term shows up. Each tone represents a group of expressions, and the length of bent lines demonstrates the rough association of the term's redundancy, while the thickness of ones shows the strength of pairings of subject regions or catchphrases. The groups mirror the connection between the two subjects. Presented as in Fig. 1, the eventual outcome of the assessment was made out of eight gatherings. The metaverse watchword had the most hubs, i.e., seven. Moreover, the blockchain watchword in the red cluster was produced by six hubs. Three out of the eight clusters, i.e., green, blue, and red, are larger than the others. These zones contain metaverse games, retail, interaction, sustainability, extended reality, and other

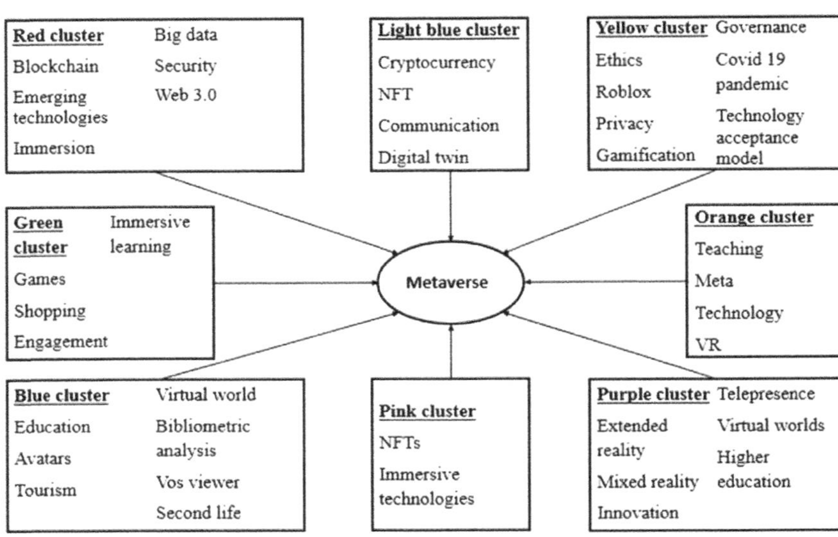

Fig. 1. Keyword Analysis. *Source:* Authors.

relevant issues. It is emphasized that metaverse technology can be accomplished using concepts such as extended, mixed and virtual realities.

The scholars of the paper underline the meaning of raising information about the advantages of the metaverse for innovation, instruction, and upgrading manageability. The green bunch addresses games, shopping, and engagement which can be transformed using the metaverse technologies. The metaverse gives a few opportunities for development, participation, and financial development. Clients can deliver and possess virtual resources, trade virtual labor and products, and take part in virtual economies. It sets out new open doors for amusement, instruction, correspondence, and business. Moreover, the metaverse presents significant issues like personality, protection, and morals. Decentralized character arrangements give buyers command over their information and permit them to make computerized personalities with confirmed qualifications. Protection and safety efforts are fundamental for safeguarding client data and guaranteeing a solid virtual climate.

Blockchain, enormous information, new advances, and Web 3.0 are the accentuation of the red group area. Blockchain is perhaps the main business that the metaverse has significantly impacted. Both the metaverse and blockchain can give a large number of outcomes progressively in situations. Involving large information in the metaverse empowers people and associations to have customized encounters, vivid examination, and information-driven bits of knowledge. 3.0 drives the metaverse, giving decentralized, vivid, and connected encounters by means of blockchain, computerized reasoning, and impending advances.

*3.5 Metaverse Marketing [*RQ4*]*

The metaverse and the promoting business are associated in various ways. Advertisers might utilize the metaverse to make vivid brand encounters, draw in clients through virtual communications, and further develop brand mindfulness through the situation of virtual things decisively. Joint efforts with virtual powerhouses in the metaverse grow advertising effort prospects. The gigantic amount of information made inside the metaverse might be utilized to make customized showcasing and designated crusades. Moreover, the metaverse gives virtual trade stages, customized encounters, story open doors, improved examination, and estimation capacities, all of which add to the moving showcasing scene in a carefully vivid climate.

*3.6 Top Contributing Authors [*RQ5*]*

According to Table 2, there were 24 distinct author partnerships. The greatest author collaboration included Wang, Hui, and Wang, as well as several additional writers that worked on this topic. The tiny cluster indicates which writers have collaborated the most.

Table 2. Top Contributing Authors.

Red Cluster	Other Clusters
Wang H.	Chen Z.
Hui P.	Lee J.
Wang Y.	Li Y.
Dark Blue Cluster	Bibri S. E.
Kim J.	Ayiter E.
Park J.	Alfaisal R.
Gray Cluster	Buhalis D.
Wang X.	Fu Y.
Tan T. M.	Chen J.
Wang J.	Kim H.
Zhao L.	Wiederhold B. K.
Lee S.	Chen C. D.
Wang S.	
Green Cluster	
Cali U.	
Gokasar I.	

Source: Authors.

*3.7 Top Contributing Institutions [*RQ6*]*

Through various audit fields, these foundations have added to the creation and data on the metaverse. They focused on increased production, extended reality, mixed reality, human–PC interface, PC plans, and striking developments. Their work routinely revolves around making distinctive experiences, surveying clients directly, building virtual settings, and examining the metaverse's social, social, and mechanical repercussions. These affiliations' assessment covers a wide assortment of metaverse applications, including but not limited to guidance, redirection, clinical benefits, story, and electronic humanities. They work to overhaul particular pieces of the metaverse like following, conveying, and correspondence moves close. They similarly research the metaverse's actual limit concerning novel kinds of correspondence, cooperation, and client experiences. It is fundamental to remember that each establishment's specific assignments and fields of study could be different, and individual researchers inside these affiliations could have their focal locales and expertise. These associations' joined undertakings help to impel human cognizance and push the unsettled areas of the metaverse in different fields (refer to Table 3).

*3.8 Top Contributing Countries [*RQ7*]*

There are four nations with foundations, and as per the number of papers, China, the United States, South Korea, and India are the most contributing countries in the field of metaverse as shown in Fig. 2.

Table 3. Top Contributing Institutions.

- Istanbul Technical University
- Department of Computer Engineering
- Jinan University Guangzhou
- School of Business and Economics
- Department of Business Administration
- Queensland University of Technology
- School of Information Systems
- Universidad de Cundinamarca, Colombia
- University of Bamberg, Germany
- Amity International Business School
- Faculty of Operation and Economics
- School of Business and Law
- University of Northumbria at Newcastle
- Live + Smart Research Lab, School of Systems Engineering
- Sun Yat-sen University
- Norwegian University of Science and Technology
- Smart Learning Institute of Beijing Normal University
- Symbiosis Center for Information Technology
- Department of Industrial Engineering, Istanbul Technical University
- Daden Limited, 103 Oxford Rd., Newbury, RG14 1LN, UK
- College of General Education, Nanjing University

Source: Authors.

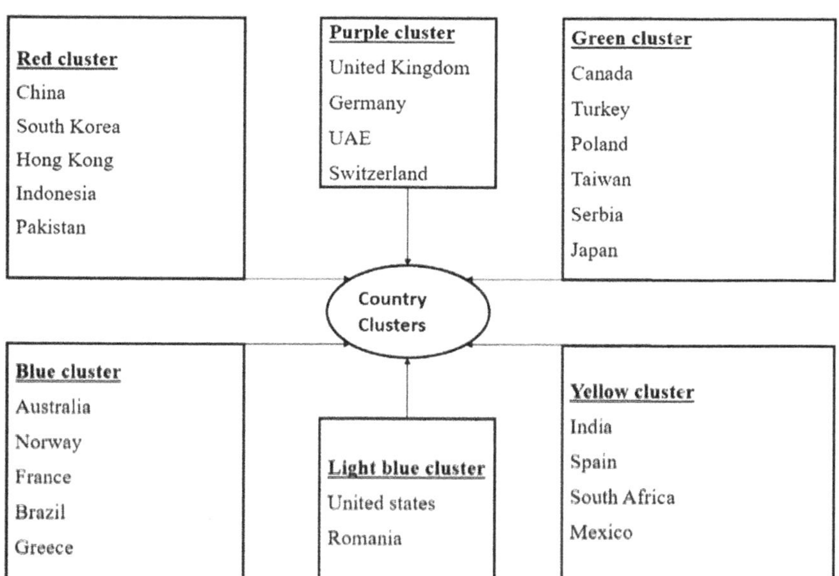

Fig. 2. Top Contributing Countries (Based on Six Documents per Country).
Source: Authors.

4. CONCLUSION

The idea of the metaverse, a computer-generated experience space where clients can connect with a computer-generated environment and different clients, has acquired significant consideration lately. This arising innovation can alter different businesses, including promoting and publicizing. The motivation behind this study is to investigate the amazing open doors and difficulties that the metaverse presents for arriving at the up-and-coming age of customers. By understanding the implications of the metaverse on purchaser conduct and promoting systems, organizations can draw in the main interest group and gain esteem in this new advanced scene. There is no precise definition of the metaverse for all intents and purposes because it is still in its early phases in a significant degree, allowing all intents and purposes, it may be best defined as an immersive virtual experience allowing users represented by avatars to interact and purchase things online, or so they believed. Some of the metaverse's genuine common components include that the metaverse is infinite and never ends. Consistently exists in real-time and allows people to have a virtual identity, presence, and independent agency. Users may build, own, largely invest in, and essentially sail in a fully functional cosmos consist of actual and virtual worlds. Products and content across platforms allow contributors to produce material and experience in a significant way. The arising idea of the metaverse presents an unrivalled chance for advertisers to draw in and associate with the up-and-coming age of shoppers in imaginative and vivid ways. As innovation proceeds to develop and reshape our communications with the computerized domain, organizations should adjust their promoting methodologies to stay pertinent and catch the consideration of a carefully local crowd.

All through this chapter, we have investigated the essential standards of metaverse showcasing, digging into its characterizing attributes, possible advantages, and different techniques for compelling execution. By embracing the metaverse, brands can rise above conventional limits, get through the commotion of the computerized scene, and lay out significant, enduring associations with shoppers. Notwithstanding, it is fundamental to recognize the difficulties that go with this change in perspective. Security concerns, moral contemplations, and the requirement for interoperability across various metaverse stages are among the obstacles that advertisers should address in their quest for metaverse achievement. A cooperative methodology between enterprises, controllers, and innovation engineers will be urgent in exploring these intricacies and forming a metaverse biological system that encourages trust and imagination. Considering these bits of knowledge metaverse showcasing isn't simply a passing pattern, but an extraordinary power that can reshape how we connect with brands and consume content. As the metaverse keeps on advancing, advertisers should stay versatile, receptive, and sensitive to the developing inclinations of the up-and-coming age of customers. By embracing the metaverse's prospects, brands can situate themselves at the very front of another period of promoting, fashioning further associations, and making significant encounters that rise above the limits of the physical and advanced universes. As we venture into this exciting frontier, the principles and strategies outlined in this guide will serve as a valuable compass for navigating the complex landscape of metaverse marketing and effectively engaging the consumers of tomorrow.

5. FUTURE OF METAVERSE MARKETING

According to McKinsey, the metaverse can dramatically alter business and general personal life, which is particularly significant. Investment in the metaverse effectively exceeded $120 billion in 2022 and is predicted to essentially create $5 trillion by 2030, or so they believed Games like Fortnite, Minecraft, and Axie Infinity are already combining components of the metaverse and offering an immersive experience to users, demonstrating the future of marketing in the metaverse. Similarly, businesses like Nike, Samsung, and Coca-Cola are already using the metaverse to reach out to their customers, demonstrating the future of marketing in the metaverse. It is not a stretch to say that digital marketing is dominating traditional marketing; with the addition of the metaverse, digital marketing is expected to evolve to a new level, demonstrating how the future of marketing in the Metaverse has the potential to impact both economic and personal life subtly. According to Gartner, by 2026, 25% of individuals will spend at least 1 hour every day in the metaverse for work, retail, education, social networking, and leisure. Marketers may use Metaverse to immerse and engage customers in a 3D digital experience that incorporates VR and AR. Brands may use the metaverse to establish their environment dedicated to a product or service, where customers can explore, engage, and make transactions using their avatars.

REFERENCES

Chen, W., Ahmed, M. M., Sofiah, W. I., Isa, N. A. M., Ebrahim, N. A., & Hai, T. (2021). A bibliometric statistical analysis of the fuzzy inference system-based classifiers. *IEEE Access*, *9*, 77811–77829.

Chugh, M., & Vyas, S. (2023). Exploring the incredible potential and opportunity of the metaverse world. In *Strategies and opportunities for technology in the metaverse world* (pp. 34–47). IGI Global.

Davis, A., Murphy, J., Owens, D., Khazanchi, D., & Zigurs, I. (2009). Avatars, people, and virtual worlds: Foundations for research in metaverses. *Journal of the Association for Information Systems*, *10*(2), 1.

Donthu, N., Kumar, S., Mukherjee, D., Pandey, N., & Lim, W. M. (2021). How to conduct a bibliometric analysis: An overview and guidelines. *Journal of Business Research*, *133*, 285–296.

Dwivedi, Y. K., Hughes, L., Baabdullah, A. M., Ribeiro-Navarrete, S., Giannakis, M., Al-Debei, M. M., Dennehy, D., Metri, B., Buhalis, D., Cheung, C. M. K., Conboy, K., Doyle, R., Dubey, R., Dutot, V., Felix, R., Goyal, D. P., Gustafsson, A., Hinsch, C., Jebali, I., ... & Wamba, S. F. (2022). Metaverse beyond the hype: Multidisciplinary perspectives on emerging challenges, opportunities, and agenda for research, practice and policy. *International Journal of Information Management*. https://doi.org/10.1016/j.ijinfomgt.2022.102542

Goh, K. H., & See, K. F. (2021). Twenty years of water utility benchmarking: A bibliometric analysis of emerging interest in water research and collaboration. *Journal of Cleaner Production*, *284*, 124711.

Gursoy, D., Malodia, S., & Dhir, A. (2022). The metaverse in the hospitality and tourism industry: An overview of current trends and future research directions. *Journal of Hospitality Marketing & Management*, *31*(5), 527–534.

Han, E., Miller, M. R., DeVeaux, C., Jun, H., Nowak, K. L., Hancock, J. T., Ram, N., & Bailenson, J. N. (2023). People, places, and time: A large-scale, longitudinal study of transformed avatars and environmental context in group interaction in the metaverse. *Journal of Computer-Mediated Communication*, *28*(2), zmac031.

Haustein, S., Peters, I., Bar-Ilan, J., Priem, J., Shema, H., & Terliesner, J. (2014). Coverage and adoption of altmetrics sources in the bibliometric community. *Scientometrics*, *101*, 1145–1163.

He, T. (2022). From single-player games to metaverse: A futuristic analysis of challenging legal issues in the video game industry in China. *GRUR International*, *71*(10), 952–966.

Hee-Jung, K., & Jin-Woo, K. (2010). The influence of temporal attributes on spatial co-design in creative communities. *Archives of Design Research*, *23*(3), 285–296.

Hennig-Thurau, T., Aliman, D. N., Herting, A. M., Cziehso, G. P., Linder, M., & Kübler, R. V. (2023). Social interactions in the metaverse: Framework, initial evidence, and research roadmap. *Journal of the Academy of Marketing Science*, *51*(4), 889–913.

Kaurav, R. P. S., Baber, R., & Rajput, S. (2020). Technology-driven tourism and hospitality industry as a tool for economic development: A bibliometric analysis. In *The Emerald handbook of ICT in tourism and hospitality* (pp. 469–486). Emerald Publishing Limited.

Kaurav, R. P. S., & Gupta, P. (2022). Trends in multidiscipline management research: Past, present and future of FIIB business review. *FIIB Business Review*, *11*(4), 382–404.

Kaushal, N., Kaurav, R. P. S., Sivathanu, B., & Kaushik, N. (2023). Artificial intelligence and HRM: Identifying future research agenda using systematic literature review and bibliometric analysis. *Management Review Quarterly*, *73*(2), 455–493.

Kim, J. (2021). Advertising in the metaverse: Research agenda. *Journal of Interactive Advertising*, *21*(3), 141–144.

Kokol, P., Blažun Vošner, H., & Završnik, J. (2021). Application of bibliometrics in medicine: A historical bibliometrics analysis. *Health Information & Libraries Journal*, *38*(2), 125–138.

Kye, B., Han, N., Kim, E., Park, Y., & Jo, S. (2021). Educational applications of metaverse: Possibilities and limitations. *Journal of Educational Evaluation for Health Professions*, *18*.

Maulani, G., Musu, E. W., Soetikno, Y. J. W., & Aisa, S. (2021). Education management using blockchain as future application innovation. *IAIC Transactions on Sustainable Digital Innovation (ITSDI)*, *3*(1), 60–65.

Mishra, V., & Sharma, M. G. (2022). Digital transformation evaluation of telehealth using convergence, maturity, and adoption. *Health Policy and Technology*, *11*(4), 100684.

Mukherjee, D., Lim, W. M., Kumar, S., & Donthu, N. (2022). Guidelines for advancing theory and practice through bibliometric research. *Journal of Business Research*, *148*, 101–115.

Nagendran, A., Compton, S., Follette, W., Golenchenko, A., Compton, A., & Grizou, J. (2022). Metaversal learning environments: Measuring, predicting and improving interpersonal effectiveness. arXiv preprint arXiv:2205.02875. https://doi.org/10.48550/arXiv.2205.02875

Ni, P., Zhu, J., & Wang, G. (2023). *Activity-oriented production promotion utility maximization in metaverse social networks*. IEEE/ACM Transactions on Networking.

Niu, X., & Feng, W. (2022). Immersive entertainment environments-from theme parks to metaverse. In *International conference on human-computer interaction* (pp. 392–403). Springer International Publishing.

Picard-Aitken, M., Campbell, D., & Côté, G. (2010). The use of multiple bibliometric indicators in science policy to support the development of collaboration strategies. In *Eleventh International Conference on Science and Technology Indicators*, Leiden, the Netherlands, 9–11 September 2010 (p. 213).

Pooyandeh, M., Han, K. J., & Sohn, I. (2022). Cybersecurity in the AI-based metaverse: A survey. *Applied Sciences*, *12*(24), 12993.

Purahong, B., Anuwongpinit, T., Kanjanasurat, I., Chansuthirangkool, M., Singto, K., Somdock, N. P., Damrongsak, P., Khunthawiwone, P., & Archevapanich, T. (2022). Engineering education roadmap of the future trend of basic metaverse based on VR with cooperation between the government and the private sector. In *2022 7th international STEM education conference (iSTEM-Ed)* (pp. 1–5). IEEE.

Rachmadtullah, R., Setiawan, B., Wasesa, A. J. A., & Wicaksono, J. W. (2023). Elementary school teachers' perceptions of the potential of metaverse technology as a transformation of interactive learning media in Indonesia. *International Journal of Innovative Research and Scientific Studies, 6*(1), 128–136.

Rana, S., Sakshi, & Singh, J. (2022). Presenting the POWER framework of conducting literature review. *Exploring the Latest Trends in Management Literature*, 1–13.

Rosário, A. T., Lopes, P. R., & Rosário, F. S. (2023). How the metaverse can leverage the business world. In *Handbook of research on AI-based technologies and applications in the era of the metaverse* (pp. 51–82). IGI Global.

Sahni, S., & Kaurav, R. P. S. (2023). What? Why? When? How? Where? of technology-based bibliometric review. In *Advancing methodologies of conducting literature review in management domain* (Vol. 2, pp. 79–101). Emerald Publishing Limited.

Şanlısoy, S., & Çiloğlu, T. (2023). A view of the future of the metaverse economy on the basis of the global financial system: New opportunities and risks. *Journal of Corporate Governance, Insurance, and Risk Management, 10*(1), 28–41.

Sayem, A. S. M. (2022). Digital fashion innovations for the real world and metaverse. *International Journal of Fashion Design, Technology and Education, 15*(2), 139–141.

Shen, B., Tan, W., Guo, J., Zhao, L., & Qin, P. (2021). How to promote user purchase in metaverse? A systematic literature review on consumer behavior research and virtual commerce application design. *Applied Sciences, 11*(23), 11087.

Sick, N., Merigó, J. M., Krätzig, O., & List, J. (2021). Forty years of World Patent Information: A bibliometric overview. *World Patent Information, 64*, 102011.

Spanache, I., Irimia, A., & Curaj, A. (2022). New approaches in research assessment-from bibliometrics to goals-oriented approaches. The case of researchers' assessment for hiring and career development in Romania. *Europolity, 16*(2).

Tasa, U. B., & Görgülü, T. (2010). Meta-art: Art of the 3-D user-created virtual worlds. *Digital Creativity, 21*(2), 100–111.

Wang, Z., Wang, Y., Peng, S., Niu, B., Cui, C., & Wu, J. (2019). Mapping the research of energy subsidies: A bibliometric analysis. *Environmental Science and Pollution Research, 26*, 28817–28828.

Yang, D., Zhou, J., Chen, R., Song, Y., Song, Z., Zhang, X., Wang, Q., Wang, K., Zhou, C., Sun, J., Zhang, L., Bai, L., Wang, Y., Wang, X., Lu, Y., Xin, H., Powell, C. A., Thuemmler, C., Chavannes, N. H., ... & Bai, C. (2022). Expert consensus on the metaverse in medicine. *Clinical eHealth, 5*, 1–9.

Yilmaz, M., Hacaloğlu, T., & Clarke, P. (2022, August). Examining the use of non-fungible tokens (NFTs) as a trading mechanism for the metaverse. In *European conference on software process improvement* (pp. 18–28). Springer International Publishing.

SECTION 3

SECTOR-SPECIFIC TECHNOLOGICAL DISRUPTIONS

A REVIEW OF SELF-SERVICE TECHNOLOGY ADOPTION IN THE TOURISM AND HOSPITALITY INDUSTRY

Surabhi Gore

Rosary College of Commerce and Arts, India

ABSTRACT

Self-Service Technology (SST) is a disruptive technology that has reshaped customer interactions, increased efficiency, and enabled data-driven decision-making. Its impact continues to evolve as technology advances and customer expectations change, making it a key consideration for businesses in a dynamic landscape. This chapter delves into critical findings regarding the adoption and implications of SST in tourism and hospitality. The relevant studies are sourced from the Scopus database. A mixed literature review methodology was employed to review papers. The literature review findings show facets of SST adoption, shedding light on the intricate relationships between consumer readiness variables, context-specific influences, preferred SST features, and psychological attributes. The study reveals consumer preferences, including convenience, ease of use, and speed of service, as primary drivers of the adoption of SST. The bibliometric analysis reveals the scope for developing SST literature in tourism and hospitality. Collaborations among scholars, research and funding institutions could help provide the impetus. Research in SST security, sustainability, and resilience could help enhance the SST literature. Comparative studies evaluating SST's social and economic implications are also suggested.

Keywords: Self-service technology; SST; SST usage; tourism; hospitality; kiosk

Review of Technologies and Disruptive Business Strategies
Review of Management Literature, Volume 3, 117–135

Published under exclusive licence by Emerald Publishing Limited
ISSN: 2754-5865/doi:10.1108/S2754-586520240000003007

1. INTRODUCTION

Self-service technologies (SST) have revolutionized the tourism and hospitality industry by providing improved customer experience, streamlining operations, saving cost, and providing 24/7 access. SST is a technological interface that empowers customers to access services without requiring direct involvement from employees (Meuter et al., 2005). SSTs are considered disruptive as they challenge traditional models and norms of the industry (Shin & Perdue, 2019). They allow new ways of interacting with customers, changing the dynamics of hotels, restaurants, transport industry and even tourist destination operations (Gummerus et al., 2019). Consumers today have high awareness and adoption behavior toward SST. They use SSTs to perform routine tasks such as booking flights, accommodations, and transportation. Convenience, time-saving, and trust in technology are the motivating factors (Molina-Collado et al., 2022).

Online booking platforms like websites and mobile apps, self-check-in/check-out kiosks found in airports and hotels, automated baggage tagging and drop systems at airports, mobile check-in and digital key access at hotels, information or concierge kiosks, automated ticket vending machines used by transport organizations, museums, and theme parks, in-room tablets, language translation apps, contactless payment systems, virtual reality (VR) and augmented reality (AR) experiences, automated tour guides like audio guides or smartphone apps with GPS, and ordering menu kiosks are examples of SSTs used in tourism and hospitality industry.

The research in SST in services dates back to when Meuter et al. (2005) analyzed the likelihood of consumers using SSTs and showed that consumer readiness mediates between adoption and the likelihood of trial. Kincaid and Baloglu (2006) evaluated the impact of SST on restaurant operations. Oyedele and Simpson (2007) and Stockdale (2007) evaluated SSTs in hotels and e-tourism, respectively. Stockdale (2007) developed a framework emphasizing the benefits of enhancing customer loyalty and achieving cost savings. Chen and Chen (2008) found that optimism and innovativeness influence attitude, subjective norms, and perceived behavioral control toward SST. Victorino et al. (2009) proposed the technology readiness index as a segmentation tool. SST research gained popularity post-2010 when many scholars began investigating consumer behavior, attitude, perception, and readiness while others developed frameworks, models, and scales to measure SST usage. Authors proposed trust and self-efficacy influencing SST use (Fan et al., 2020; Lema, 2009). Studies also concluded that anxiety plays a significant role across different contexts with SSTs (Hong & Ahn, 2023; Suwannakul, 2021). Consumer preferences for SST features, including convenience, ease of use, and speed of service, are identified as critical drivers (Wang & Wu, 2014; Yang, Lai, et al., 2021). Furthermore, age, education, occupation, income, SST types, and travel frequency contribute to differences in technology readiness and its dimensions. Security and privacy are crucial for the excellence of tourist services (Safaeimanesh et al., 2021). Authors also discuss SST being a cause of disruption (Chiu & Nguyen, 2022; Molina-Collado et al., 2022; Wang, Harris, & Patterson, 2017). Kaurav et al. (2020) suggest mobile technology, AR, application-based analysis, virtual assistants, and prescriptive analysis as technology-based solutions for tourism operations.

The literature review papers highlight less consideration given to SST research in tourism and hospitality (Iranmanesh et al., 2022; Molina-Collado et al., 2022; Saputra & Anggarawati, 2022; Shiwen et al., 2022; Shin & Perdue, 2019). The authors suggest continued research focusing on different sectors within the tourism and hospitality industry. Thus, this chapter presents a mixed literature review combining bibliometric and Theory, Context, Characteristics, Methodology-based analysis (TCCM) on SST, specifically within tourism and hospitality. This chapter addresses the following objectives.

(1) To track the evolution and current trends in SST research in tourism and hospitality.
  - What is the distribution of publications?
  - What are the major research areas/topics?
  - What is the level of co-authorship among researchers?
  - How are the studies bibliographically linked to each other?

(2) To analyze SST research based on TCCM.
(3) To suggest future research avenues.

2. METHODOLOGY

Bibliometric analysis is a method of analyzing scientific data involving quantitative examination of academic publications to identify patterns, trends, and relationships within a specific field or research domain. It provides insights into the growth of knowledge, research collaboration, and the impact of research publications. Bibliometric analyses use various metrics and visualization tools to assess the scholarly impact of research papers, authors, journals, and institutions (Sahni & Kaurav, 2023). It helps to identify the impact of publications and authors. It also allows one to find research gaps and visualize the research topics (Donthu et al., 2021). The analysis consists of evaluative and relational techniques. The evaluative technique assesses the distribution of studies, journals, most contributing authors, highest citations, and keywords. The relational techniques include analysis of co-authorship, co-citation, and bibliometric coupling (Ülker et al., 2023). Sahni and Kaurav (2023) report wide acceptance of bibliometrics within business management and social sciences.

Paul and Rosado-Serrano (2019) proposed the TCCM framework for literature review analysis, in which *T* stands for theory, C for context, C for characteristics, and *M* for methodology. This method analyses the origin, evolution, current research areas, and future interests in the subject area. Farrukh and Sajjad (2023) stress that narrative, descriptive, and critical reviews bring out the author's skills in logical reasoning, content analysis, literature mapping, critical writing, and ethical consideration.

2.1 Data Collection

The data on SST publications was obtained from the Scopus database. The search parameters are provided in Table 1. The MS Excel file (.CSV) having $n =$ 189 papers was downloaded. The database was scanned to check the relevancy of articles and duplicate entries. Articles on SST in tourism and hospitality were selected for the review ($n = 133$). The analysis was done using Vos Viewer.

2.2 Tracking the Evolution of SST Research

Assessing the distribution of publications: The chart illustrating the progression of publications and citations was created utilizing MS Excel. A co-author analysis was conducted using VOS viewer to assess the connections between researchers. Co-author analysis examines collaborations among scholars (Mavric et al., 2021; Ülker et al., 2023). It helps identify research cohorts and institutions involved, and provides insights into the framework of scientific communication.

Evaluation of themes: Co-word analysis was employed to assess shifts in thematic content. Co-word analysis uncovers frequently used terms within the article and helps to identify the evolution and trends on a given topic (Ülker et al., 2023). Additionally, it aids in pinpointing potential areas for future research exploration. Further, TCCM analysis was performed on the abstracts of the papers, and the data was tabulated in MS Excel.

Table 1. Search Parameters for Papers From Scopus Database.

Keywords	Self-Service Technolog*
OR	Self-Service Technolog*
AND	Hospitalit*
OR	Hotel
OR	Tourism
OR	Airlin*
OR	Trave*
OR	Transpor*
OR	Destinatio*
OR	Restauran*
OR	Disruptio*
Time frame	Anytime
Subject area	Social Sciences, Management, Arts and Humanities, Multi-disciplinary, Economics
Document type	Articles, Conference Papers, Book Chapters
Source type	Journal, Conference Proceedings, Books
Language	English
Search date	September 2, 2023

Source: Scopus database.

denotes the variable part or multiple characters that may be added to the word for example Technolog may include variations like technology, technologies, or technological.

2.3 Evaluating the Level of Co-Authorship

Co-authorship is evaluated based on citation analysis. In citation analysis, authors are assumed to cite papers pertinent to their research and substantially influence the field (Uysal, 2010; Ülker et al., 2023). This analysis helps identify the most frequently cited authors, studies, and journals, often considered highly influential (Uysal, 2010).

2.4 Bibliometric Coupling

Two studies are bibliometrically coupled when referencing the same third study (Kessler, 1963). The degree to which two documents cite the same third document signifies the intensity of their connection. A higher degree of coupling suggests that the documents share similarities (Ülker et al., 2023).

The future research areas are determined based on the research gaps analyzed from the literature.

3. FINDINGS

3.1 Bibliometric Analysis

3.1.1 Evolution and Distribution of Publications

The study identified 133 articles published in 82 journals and conference proceedings from 2005 to 2023. A descriptive analysis of the publications is presented in Fig. 1. The figure indicates a steady increase in the publication, with an average of seven publications per year. The citations show a decreasing trend line with an average of 200 citations annually. Fig. 2 depicts the most impactful journals belonging to tourism and multi-disciplinary fields. Journal of Marketing has the most citations, while most publications are from the International Journal of Hospitality Management. No co-citation links were identified between the sources, suggesting that very few studies cite similar work.

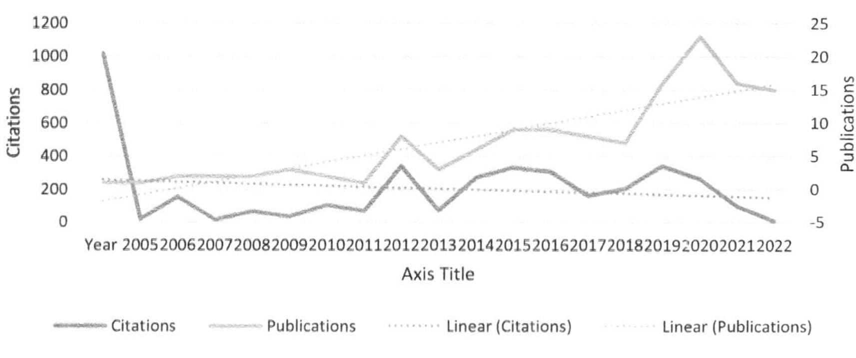

Fig. 1. Year-Wise Publication and Citation Trend. *Source:* Scopus database.

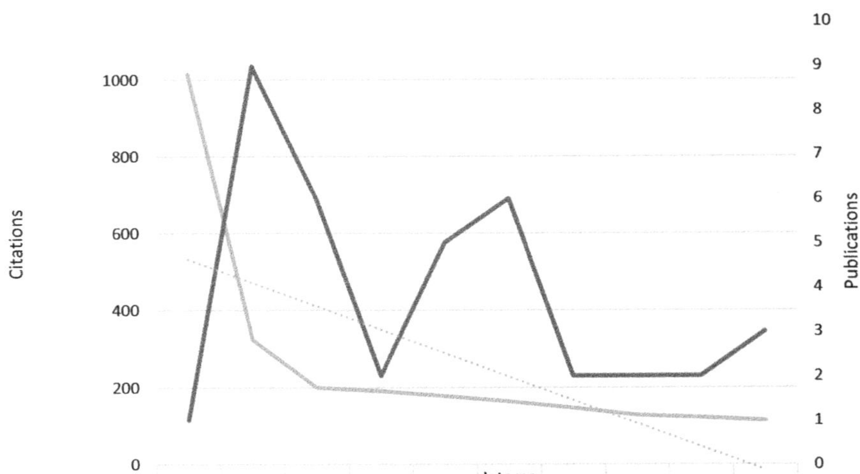

	Journal of Marketing	International Journal of Hospitality Management	Journal of Hospitality Marketing and Management	Journal of Business Research	Journal of Hospitality and Tourism Research	International Journal of Contemporary Hospitality Management	Computers in Human Behavior	Tourism Management Perspectives	Management Science	Journal of Travel and Tourism Marketing
Citations	1015	324	200	191	178	164	147	128	122	114
Publications	1	9	6	2	5	6	2	2	2	3

Fig. 2. Top 10 Journals and Their Impact on SST Research. *Source:* Scopus database; the dotted line represents the linear (average) citations.

3.1.2 Evolution of Keywords

The co-occurrence of keyword analysis helps to recognize the development of knowledge on the topic and current research trends. Fig. 3 presents the overlay of keywords from 2005 to 2023. Six clusters with 57 keywords were identified. The main keywords in cluster one were automation, customer experience, innovation, kiosk, service failure, and technology acceptance. Cluster two included air transport, customer loyalty and satisfaction, sales, and surveys. The words in cluster three were design, enjoyment, marketing perception, and service. Behavior Research, consumption, information system, usefulness, value, service quality, and technology readiness belong to cluster four. Cluster five had COVID-19, hospitality, and security, while Cluster six had hotels and restaurants.

3.1.3 Co-Authorship and Citation Analysis

Co-authorship refers to the scientific collaborations that authors make with each other. The co-authorship analysis revealed six clusters of authors with more than

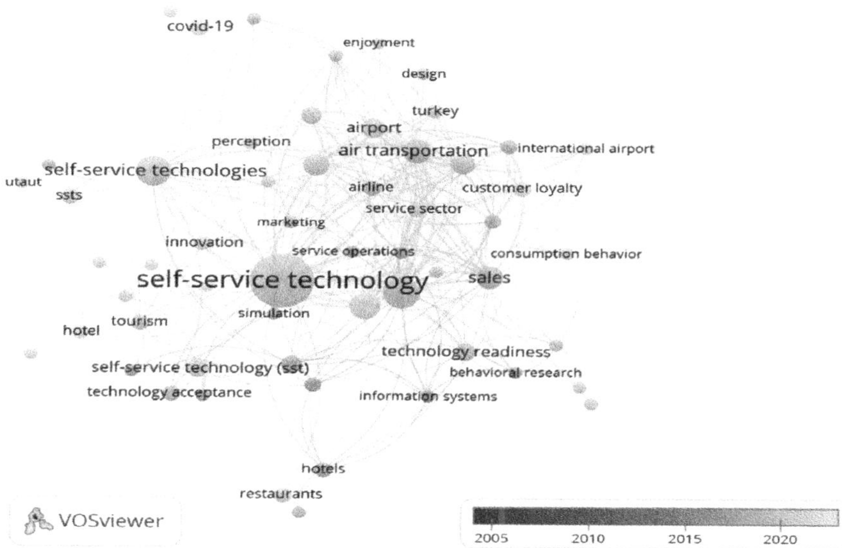

Fig. 3. Overlay of Keywords. *Source:* VOSviewer and Scopus database.

one publication but zero intergroup links (Garg, 2021, 2022; Kaushik & Rahman, 2016, 2017; Kelly et al., 2013, 2017, 2019; Kokkinou & Cranage, 2011, 2013, 2015; Liu & Yang, 2021, 2022; Ueda & Kurahashi, 2017, 2018). Thus, the analysis highlights a dearth of collaborations among authors. Most co-authorship publications are from the United States. The largest cluster of co-authorships has seven countries: Australia, Malaysia, Greece, Lithuania, Oman, Philippines, and Spain.

Citation analysis identifies how often other scholarly publications have cited a particular work. High citation counts are an indicator of a work's influence and importance. The citation analysis of authors with more than 10 citations shows 64 individual clusters but no links. Table 2 presents the top five cited authors and their publications.

3.1.4 Bibliometric Coupling

Bibliographic coupling is a method of grouping documents. It shows if two separate documents cite the same third document (Kessler, 1963). The citing document is called bibliographically coupled (Ferreira, 2018). If the strength of the coupling is high, it indicates similarities between the articles (Ülker et al., 2023). Fig. 4 shows seven clusters with 48 documents with a link strength of 589 and 305 links. The findings show that there is scope to increase the strength of bibliometric coupling by forming collaborations among authors, funding institutions, and research organizations.

Table 2. Top 10 Cited Authors and Publications.

Authors	Title	Year	Source Title	Cited By
Meuter M.L.; Bitner M.J.; Ostrom A.L.; Brown S.W.	Choosing among alternative service delivery modes: An investigation of customer trial of self-service technologies	2005	Journal of Marketing	1015
Kaushik A.K.; Agrawal A.K.; Rahman Z.	Tourist behavior toward self-service hotel technology adoption: Trust and subjective norm as key antecedents	2015	Tourism Management Perspectives	126
Oh H.; Jeong M.; Baloglu S.	Tourists' adoption of self-service technologies at resort hotels	2013	Journal of Business Research	124
Oyedele A.; Simpson P.M.	An empirical investigation of consumer control factors on intention to use selected self-service technologies	2007	International Journal of Service Industry Management	106
Chen C.-F.; Wang J.-P.	Customer participation, value co-creation and customer loyalty - A case of airline online check-in system	2016	Computers in Human Behavior	103

Source: Scopus database.

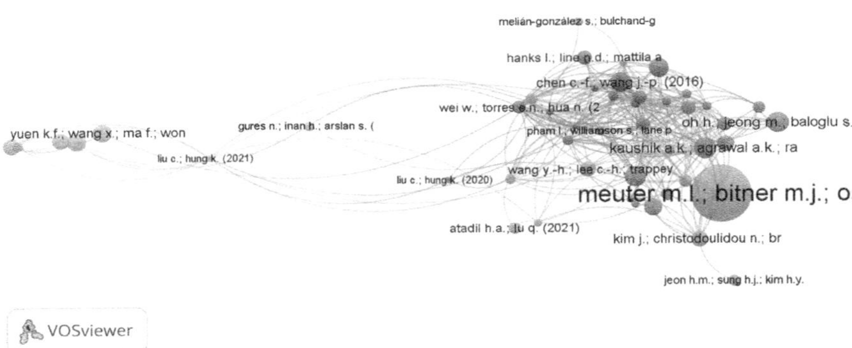

Fig. 4. Bibliometric Coupling of Authors. *Source:* VOSviewer and Scopus database.

3.2 TCCM Analysis

3.2.1 Theories

Authors have used different theories to evaluate the SSTs. The most used theories are related to consumer behavior (Kim & Chen, 2023; Kokkinou & Cranage, 2011; Safaeimanesh et al., 2021; Shim et al., 2020; Xu et al., 2020) and technology acceptance and readiness (Islam, 2023; Lien et al., 2021; Suwannakul, 2021; Wu & Phung, 2021; Yang, Choi, & Chung, 2021). The unified theory of acceptance and use of technology (UTAUT 1 & 2) (Asenso et al., 2021; Chanmatakulvat & Chaveesuk, 2020; Fan et al., 2020; Garg, 2021, 2022; Jeon et al., 2020; Melián-González et al., 2021; Nilsson et al., 2021; Susskind & Curry, 2016; Yang, Lai, et al., 2021) and diffusion of innovations theory (Kaushik & Rahman, 2017; Lin et al., 2023) is frequently used among scholars.

Authors have used theories from various disciplines to evaluate SSTs. The organizational and marketing theories used are the theory of inventive problem-solving (Wang, Lee, & Trappey, 2017), service delivery and processes (Kelly et al., 2017; Kelly & Lawlor, 2021; Wang, Lee, & Trappey, 2017), role and script theory (Susskind & Curry, 2016), customer relationship management (Hanks et al., 2016), and Sanpo-Yoshi principle (Her, 2021). Self-determination (Chiu & Nguyen, 2022; Hong & Ahn, 2023), self-efficacy (Fan et al., 2020), theory of planned behavior (Islam, 2023; Lien et al., 2021), stimulus organism response framework (Ahn & Seo, 2018), social psychology (Batouei et al., 2020; Wang, Harris, & Patterson, 2017), prosocial self-identity and warm glow (Giebelhausen et al., 2017), and gamification (Lee & Lu, 2023) are some of the analyzed psychology theories. The economic theories include utility theory (Safaeimanesh et al., 2021), transaction cost economics (Yuen et al., 2019), theory of consumption values (Wei et al., 2017; Yuen et al., 2019; Zaitouni & Murphy, 2023), resource matching (Yuen et al., 2019), costly signaling theory (Hanks et al., 2016), and error correction model (Chanmatakulvat & Chaveesuk, 2020).

The social exchange theory is the only social theory used to study SST (Atadil & Lu, 2021; Pant, 2022). The service quality and quality function deployment (Park et al., 2021, 2022; Shim et al., 2020; Wang, Lee, & Trappey, 2017; Wong et al., 2022) and loyalty (Ayodeji & Rjoub, 2021; Chen & Wang, 2016; Huang, 2021; Kokkinou & Cranage, 2011) theories are gaining popularity.

3.2.2 Context

Context refers to the firm or the country where the research is performed. Most research is done in the hospitality sector, followed by restaurants and airlines, while some studies have focused on SST services in different industries. Eight studies focused on SST usage during the COVID-19 pandemic. Few studies have analyzed SSTs at tourist destinations/attractions. (Her, 2021; Melián-González et al., 2021).

3.2.3 Characteristics

Characteristics refer to the variables that are evaluated. Most studies measure consumer's attitude (Chiu & Nguyen, 2022; Graham et al., 2020; Kim & Park, 2024; Nilsson et al., 2021; Shim et al., 2020; Xu et al., 2022), behavior (Garg, 2022; Ma et al., 2024; Yuen et al., 2019), experience (Hong & Ahn, 2023; Nam et al., 2023; Zaitouni & Murphy, 2023), impact (Hong & Ahn, 2023; Kim & Park, 2024; Lee & Lu, 2023), perception (Garg, 2021; Xu et al., 2022), satisfaction (Kim & Chen, 2023; Safaeimanesh et al., 2021; Suksutdhi, 2022), acceptance (Garg, 2022; Jeon et al., 2020; Kim, Joe, & Erdem, 2023), readiness (Nilsson et al., 2021; Shim et al., 2020), loyalty (Chen & Wang, 2016; Kim & Chen, 2023), willingness, or decision-making among consumers (Kokkinou & Cranage, 2015). Few studies examine the stakeholder's perspective (Her, 2021; Wong et al., 2022).

Some have also focused on tourists (Graham et al., 2020; Islam, 2023; Pant, 2022) and employees (Lema, 2009; Melián-González & Bulchand-Gidumal, 2020).

SST usage (Graham et al., 2019; Kelly et al., 2019; Kim, Kim, & Lee, 2023; Liu & Hung, 2020; Sagala & Putro, 2020; Wu & Phung, 2021), its framework (Chanmatakulvat & Chaveesuk, 2020; Wei et al., 2017), and process (Batouei et al., 2020; Henderson et al., 2023; Kaushik & Rahman, 2016; Tan & Netessine, 2020) is also assessed. Technology adoption by organizations (Liu & Hung, 2021; Saputra & Anggarawati, 2022), waiting time (Ayodeji et al., 2023; Kokkinou & Cranage, 2013), technological advantages and failures (Liu & Hung, 2022; Um et al., 2020), service quality (Park et al., 2022; Rolim et al., 2021), hotel SST capabilities (Kim, Joe, & Erdem, 2023; Liu & Yang, 2021), and Bar Code and QR code techniques (Anitha et al., 2019; Cheong et al., 2017) are some of the other variables that are evaluated.

3.2.4 Methodology

SST research has used both qualitative (Girija et al., 2023; Gupta & Sharma, 2021; Kelly et al., 2017; Kelly & Lawlor, 2021; Liu & Hung, 2020, 2021; Liu & Yang, 2021; Pant, 2022; Sagala & Putro, 2020; Wong et al., 2022) and quantitative approaches (Fan et al., 2020; Garg, 2022; Graham et al., 2020; Hong & Ahn, 2023; Jeon et al., 2020; Kim & Chen, 2023; Kim, Joe, & Erdem, 2023; Melián-González & Bulchand-Gidumal, 2020; Oliveira et al., 2021; Safaeimanesh et al., 2021; Tan & Netessine, 2020; Xu et al., 2020, 2022; Yang, Lai, et al., 2021). Many studies use structures equation modeling (Ayodeji & Rjoub, 2021; Chiu & Nguyen, 2022; Kim, Kim, & Lee, 2023; Pham et al., 2020; Shim et al., 2020; Suksutdhi, 2022; Wu & Phung, 2021; Yang, Choi, & Chung, 2021) and partial least square analysis (Ayodeji et al., 2023; Islam, 2023; Kim, Kim, & Lee, 2023; Ma et al., 2024; Melián-González et al., 2021; Nam et al., 2023; Suksutdhi, 2022; Yang, Lai, et al., 2021; Zaitouni & Murphy, 2023). Authors have also used experiments and simulations (Lee & Lu, 2023; Tang et al., 2022; Um et al., 2020). Conceptual frameworks are suggested for SST research (Batouei et al., 2020; Chanmatakulvat & Chaveesuk, 2020; Cserdi & Kenesei, 2021; Kelly et al., 2019; Park et al., 2022; Stockdale, 2007; Wong et al., 2022; Zaitouni & Murphy, 2023). Very few studies focus on mixed methods (Gupta & Sharma, 2021; Kim & Park, 2024; Liu & Hung, 2022; Nilsson et al., 2021) and scenario-based quantitative framework (Kokkinou & Cranage, 2015; Tang et al., 2022).

4. FUTURE RESEARCH AREAS

While there has been substantial research on Self-Service Technology (SST) in the tourism and hospitality industry, several research gaps and areas require further investigation.

4.1 Research Areas Originating From Bibliometric Analysis

More research is required in the area of SST in the tourism and hospitality domain itself, and such publications are very few compared to other domains like SSTs in businesses. Tourism and hospitality journals need to publish more papers in this area. Only six of the top ten most impactful journals belong to the tourism and hospitality field. Journal editors could push for more SST-based research. The bibliometric analysis highlights the lack of collaborations between scholars involved in SST research. Collaborative research in SST for tourism and hospitality requires an impetus. Conferences and seminars promoting SST research in tourism and hospitality could be organized. Authors also need to cite one other, thus supporting each other's research and adding value to the literature.

COVID-19 has changed the way consumers use SST. The keyword analysis highlights security as one of the issues with SSTs. Research into security in SSTs at hotels, airlines, airports, and restaurants could be done. Such studies could address privacy concerns related to SST usage, including data protection, identity theft, and cybersecurity measures. There is also a need to examine the environmental impact of SSTs, including their energy consumption and carbon footprint. Research on sustainable and eco-friendly SST solutions is not seen while reviewing papers. Studies on how SSTs can be utilized effectively in crisis management and disaster response situations in the tourism and hospitality industry are limited. SST's role in communication and recovery efforts could be ascertained.

Exploring the economic and social impacts of SSTs on local communities and economies in tourist destinations can shed light on both positive and negative consequences. Kim, Joe, and Erdem (2023) and Fan et al. (2018) found that men and women assess kiosk technologies differently and suggested research into the underlying causes of the differences. The use of artificial intelligence (AI) and SST has not been analyzed much. Investigating the potential impact of emerging technologies like AI, AR, VR, and blockchain on SSTs in the tourism and hospitality industry is an area ripe for exploration (Huang, 2021; Iranmanesh et al., 2022).

4.2 Future Research Areas Originating From TCCM Analysis

4.2.1 Theory

SST research lacks comprehensive research, leading to theory development. Though the technology acceptance model (Islam, 2023), UTAUT and UTAUT 2 are popular with SST research (Fan et al., 2020; Garg, 2021), no theory has been solely developed and accepted for tourism and hospitality services. Scholars could collaborate to work on this aspect. Social theories could help study how society and social relationships affect behavior and attitude toward SST (Atadil & Lu, 2021; Pant, 2022). Core business theories from marketing and strategic management, like resource-based view, customer journey mapping, hedonic versus utilitarian value and brand equity, could also be tested with SST (Alvarez et al., 2020; Susskind & Curry, 2016).

4.2.2 Context

While there is extensive research on SSTs in mainstream tourism, there is a gap in understanding their role and effectiveness in niche tourism markets, such as adventure tourism or ecotourism (Her, 2021; Melián-González et al., 2021). SST research in the domain of tourism and hospitality could look at researching different settings like destinations (islands and mainland or cities and villages) or types of tourist areas (religious or mountains or beaches). It will provide a different perspective on SST usage and help evaluate the challenges restricting SST growth. Research on developing and third-world countries would also provide more understanding of SST effectiveness. Cross-cultural studies can provide insights into how SST usage varies across cultures and regions. It could help businesses tailor their SST offerings to specific customer segments (Lee et al., 2022).

4.2.3 Variable

Much research on SST looks at the consumer point of view. However, research on employees and stakeholders is fewer. Research can include examining scenarios where customers prefer employee assistance alongside SSTs. Research that can help integrate stakeholder's perspectives will help add value. Yang, Choi, and Chung (2021) suggest technology acceptance factors such as accuracy, speed, and budget to be evaluated for future research. The authors also stress studying the human service factor. Her (2021) suggests evaluating value correspondence through mobile AR. Evaluation of motivational aspects and SST attributes are also suggested (Hong & Ahn, 2023; Park et al., 2021). Research is needed to explore how SSTs can be personalized to cater to tourist's unique preferences and needs; for example, studies on personalized recommendations for accommodations, activities, and dining options could be undertaken. There is a gap in research related to the long-term impact and return on investment for businesses that implement SSTs. Studying the sustainability of SST investments and their contribution to the bottom line is critical (Bai et al., 2020). Research on SST usage's regulatory and legal aspects, including compliance with data protection laws, accessibility standards, and international regulations, could be undertaken (McLeay et al., 2021). Ma et al. (2024) propose evaluating the role of different types of regulations and the motivation of customers with SST difficulties. Scholars also suggest the assessment of different moderating and mediating variables.

4.2.4 Methodology

SST research has many studies involving quantitative and qualitative methodologies. Action research, simulations, and scenario-based research are gaining popularity among scholars. The research based on mixed methods needs to be done. Islam (2023) recommends longitudinal studies on tourist behavior with SST. The authors suggest qualitative approaches and comparative analysis of tourist response toward SSTs. Lee and Lu (2023) suggest a comparative investigation into gamified services across restaurants.

5. CONCLUSION

SST has emerged as a disruptive force in tourism and hospitality, offering myriad benefits to businesses and consumers. Its adoption has reshaped customer interactions, saved costs, increased efficiencies, and tweaked business models. SST has empowered consumers with convenience and control over their experiences, from booking flights and accommodations to checking in and accessing services. It has streamlined operations and enabled businesses to collect valuable data, personalize services, and adapt to changing customer preferences.

The COVID-19 pandemic accelerated the adoption of SSTs. The significance of SSTs became even more pronounced as they offered a unique blend of personalization and hygiene. Emotional values played a pivotal role, with customers experiencing varying degrees of stress and motivation when interacting with SST. SST's situational and functional aspects, combined with innovative menu designs reminiscent of gaming menus, aimed to create seamless and engaging experiences.

The practical implementation of SST requires a delicate balance between automation and human interaction. While SSTs excel in routine and transactional tasks, personalized and complex service situations require a human touch. Customer's attitudes toward SST were influenced by factors such as waiting time, emphasizing the need for efficient and user-friendly SST solutions. The findings highlight the relationships between technology, customer satisfaction, loyalty, and innovation in tourism and hospitality. They emphasize the need for businesses in these industries to adapt to emerging technologies.

The analysis of the evolution of publications has provided valuable insights into the SST dynamics. The domain needs collaborative research across stakeholders, institutions, and countries through dialogues, seminars, and conferences. SST research could examine the sociocultural and economic impacts on tourist destinations and hospitality organizations.

REFERENCES

Ahn, J. A., & Seo, S. (2018). Consumer responses to interactive restaurant self-service technology (IRSST): The role of gadget-loving propensity. *International Journal of Hospitality Management*, *74*, 109–121.

Alvarez, J., Léger, P. M., Fredette, M., Chen, S. L., Maunier, B., & Senecal, S. (2020). An enriched customer journey map: How to construct and visualize a global portrait of both lived and perceived users' experiences? *Designs*, *4*(3), 29.

Anitha, M., Babel, A., Kumar, A., Rauniyar, A., & Zahid, K. (2019). Cloud-based secured QR code for self-service access control system at resort and hotels. In *Computing and network sustainability: Proceedings of IRSCNS 2018* (pp. 387–395). Springer Singapore.

Asenso, G. B., Asamoah, D., & Agyei-Owusu, B. (2021). Exploring the factors that drive use of self-service technologies in air-travel in an African country. *International Journal of Logistics Systems and Management*, *39*(3), 273–291.

Atadil, H. A., & Lu, Q. (2021). An investigation of underlying dimensions of customers' perceptions of a safe hotel in the COVID-19 era: Effects of those perceptions on hotel selection behavior. *Journal of Hospitality Marketing & Management, 30*(6), 655–672.

Ayodeji, Y., & Rjoub, H. (2021). Investigation into waiting time, self-service technology, and customer loyalty: The mediating role of waiting time in satisfaction. *Human Factors and Ergonomics in Manufacturing & Service Industries, 31*(1), 27–41.

Ayodeji, Y., Rjoub, H., & Özgit, H. (2023). Achieving sustainable customer loyalty in airports: The role of waiting time satisfaction and self-service technologies. *Technology in Society, 72*, 102–106.

Bai, C., Dallasega, P., Orzes, G., & Sarkis, J. (2020). Industry 4.0 technologies assessment: A sustainability perspective. *International Journal of Production Economics, 229*, 107776.

Batouei, A., Iranmanesh, M., Mustafa, H., Nikbin, D., & Ping, T. A. (2020). Components of airport experience and their roles in eliciting passengers' satisfaction and behavioural intentions. *Research in Transportation Business & Management, 37*, 100585.

Chanmatakulvat, N., & Chaveesuk, S. (2020). Continuance intention to use self-service technology of mass rapid transit system in Thailand: A conceptual framework. In *Proceedings of the 10th international workshop on computer science and engineering (WCSE 2020)* (pp. 259–266). ISBN 978-981-14-4787-7.

Chen, S. C., & Chen, H. H. (2008). The influence of technology readiness on the theory of planned behaviour with self-service technologies. In *Proceedings of the WMSCI The 12th world multi-conference on systemics, cybernetics and informatics, Orlando, FL* (Vol. 6, pp. 85–90).

Chen, C. F., & Wang, J. P. (2016). Customer participation, value co-creation, and customer loyalty – A case of airline online check-in system. *Computers in Human Behavior, 62*, 346–352.

Cheong, S. N., Ling, H. C., Teh, P. L., Ahmed, P. K., & Yap, W. J. (2017). Encrypted quick response scheme for hotel check-in and access control system. *International Journal of Engineering Business Management, 9*. https://doi.org/10.1177/1847979017720039

Chiu, Y. T. H., & Nguyen, D. M. (2022). Service failure and self-recovery in tech-based services: Self-determination theory perspective. *The Service Industries Journal, 42*(13–14), 1075–1100.

Cserdi, Z., & Kenesei, Z. (2021). Attitudes to forced adoption of new technologies in public transportation services. *Research in Transportation Business & Management, 41*, 100611.

Donthu, N., Kumar, S., Mukherjee, D., Pandey, N., & Lim, W. M. (2021). How to conduct a bibliometric analysis: An overview and guidelines. *Journal of Business Research, 133*, 285–296.

Fan, A., Wu, L., & Mattila, A. S. (2018). Gender differences in the intentions to voice complaints across different service failure modes. *Journal of Foodservice Business Research, 21*(1), 22–32.

Fan, A., Wu, L., Miao, L., & Mattila, A. S. (2020). When does technology anthropomorphism help alleviate customer dissatisfaction after a service failure? – The moderating role of consumer technology self-efficacy and interdependent self-construal. *Journal of Hospitality Marketing & Management, 29*(3), 269–290.

Farrukh, A., & Sajjad, A. (2023). A critical review of literature review methodologies. In S. Rana, J. Singh, & S. Kathuria (Eds.), *Advancing methodologies of conducting literature review in management domain. Review of management literature* (Vol. 2, pp. 103–123). Emerald Publishing Limited. https://doi.org/10.1108/S2754-586520230000002006

Ferreira, F. A. (2018). Mapping the field of arts-based management: Bibliographic coupling and co-citation analyses. *Journal of Business Research, 85*, 348–357.

Garg, A. (2021). The technology acceptance and use of tablet menu among young adults: An empirical study based on UTAUT 2 model. *International Journal of Hospitality & Tourism Systems, 14*(1), 41–50.

Garg, A. (2022). Investigating the moderating effects of age and gender on customers' use of tablet menu in casual dining restaurants. *Journal of Quality Assurance in Hospitality & Tourism, 23*(6), 1509–1547.

Giebelhausen, M., Lawrence, B., Chun, H. H., & Hsu, L. (2017). The warm glow of restaurant check-out charity. *Cornell Hospitality Quarterly, 58*(4), 329–341.

Girija, S., Sharma, D. R., & Kaushal, V. (2023). Exploring dimensions of the customer experience at budget hotels during the COVID-19 pandemic: A netnography approach. *Qualitative Market Research: An International Journal, 26*(4), 320–344.

Graham, A., Budd, L., Ison, S., & Timmis, A. (2019). Airports and ageing passengers: A study of the UK. *Research in Transportation Business & Management*, *30*, 100380.

Graham, A., Kremarik, F., & Kruse, W. (2020). Attitudes of ageing passengers to air travel since the coronavirus pandemic. *Journal of Air Transport Management*, *87*, 101865.

Gummerus, J., Lipkin, M., Dube, A., & Heinonen, K. (2019). Technology in use–characterizing customer self-service devices (SSDS). *Journal of Services Marketing*, *33*(1), 44–56.

Gupta, K., & Sharma, S. (2021). Kiosks as self-service technology in hotels: Opportunities and challenges. *Worldwide Hospitality and Tourism Themes*, *13*(2), 236–251.

Hanks, L., Line, N. D., & Mattila, A. S. (2016). The impact of self-service technology and the presence of others on cause-related marketing programs in restaurants. *Journal of Hospitality Marketing & Management*, *25*(5), 547–562.

Henderson, H., Grace, K., Gulbransen-Diaz, N., Klaassens, B., Leong, T. W., & Tomitsch, M. (2023). From parking meters to vending machines: A study of usability issues in self-service technologies. *International Journal of Human-Computer Interaction*, 1–15.

Her, J. J. (2021). Engaging locals in rural areas: Value correspondence in placemaking through mobile augmented reality. *Digital Creativity*, *32*(3), 215–233.

Hong, E., & Ahn, J. (2023). The role of autonomy, competence, and relatedness in motivation to use self-service technology (SST) among customers with difficulties in SST. *Journal of Hospitality and Tourism Technology*, *14*(4), 630–642.

Huang, S. M. (2021). The effect of self-service technology of the service quality on customer loyalty for Resort hotels in Taiwan-customer satisfaction as mediator. In *The 9th international conference on orange technology (ICOT)* (pp. 1–4). IEEE.

Iranmanesh, M., Ghobakhloo, M., Nilashi, M., Tseng, M. L., Yadegaridehkordi, E., & Leung, N. (2022). Applications of disruptive digital technologies in the hotel industry: A systematic review. *International Journal of Hospitality Management*, *107*, 103304.

Islam, M. N. (2023). Factors affecting adoption of self-service E-ticketing technology: A study on heritage sites in Bangladesh. *Heliyon*, *9*(3), e14691.

Jeon, H. M., Sung, H. J., & Kim, H. Y. (2020). Customer's acceptance intention of self-service technology of restaurant industry: Expanding UTAUT with perceived risk and innovativeness. *Service Business*, *14*, 533–551.

Kaurav, R. P. S., Baber, R., & Rajput, S. (2020). Technology-driven tourism and hospitality industry as a tool for economic development: A bibliometric analysis. In *The Emerald handbook of ICT in tourism and hospitality* (pp. 469–486). Emerald Publishing Limited.

Kaushik, A. K., Agrawal, A. K., & Rahman, Z. (2015). Tourist behaviour towards self-service hotel technology adoption: Trust and subjective norm as key antecedents. *Tourism Management Perspectives*, *16*, 278–289.

Kaushik, A. K., & Rahman, Z. (2016). Self-service innovativeness scale: Introduction, development, and validation of scale. *Service Business*, *10*, 799–822.

Kaushik, A. K., & Rahman, Z. (2017). An empirical investigation of tourist's choice of service delivery options: SSTs vs service employees. *International Journal of Contemporary Hospitality Management*, *29*(7), 1892–1913.

Kelly, P., & Lawlor, J. (2021). Adding or destroying value? User experiences of tourism self-service technologies. *Journal of Hospitality and Tourism Insights*, *4*(3), 300–317.

Kelly, P., Lawlor, J., & Mulvey, M. (2013). Customer decision-making processes and motives for self-service technology usage in multi-channel hospitality environments. *International Journal of Electronic Customer Relationship Management*, *7*(2), 98–116.

Kelly, P., Lawlor, J., & Mulvey, M. (2017). Customer roles in self-service technology encounter in a tourism context. *Journal of Travel & Tourism Marketing*, *34*(2), 222–238.

Kelly, P., Lawlor, J., & Mulvey, M. (2019). Self-service technologies in the travel, tourism, and hospitality sectors: Principles and practice. In *Robots, artificial intelligence, and service automation in travel, tourism, and hospitality* (pp. 57–78). Emerald Publishing Limited.

Kessler, M. M. (1963). Bibliographic coupling between scientific papers. *American Documentation*, *14*(1), 10–25.

Kim, B., & Chen, Y. (2023). Empowering consumers through self-service technology: A comparative analysis. *Journal of Hospitality & Tourism Research*. https://doi.org/10.1177/10963480231182959

Kim, J., Joe, S., & Erdem, M. (2023). The bright and dark sides of hotel kiosks: An empirical study. *Journal of Hospitality and Tourism Insights*, *6*(2), 1043–1065.

Kim, M., Kim, Y., & Lee, G. (2023b). Effect of situational factors (control, convenience, time pressure, and order complexity) on customers' self-service technology choices. *Journal of Hospitality Marketing & Management*, 649–669.

Kim, G., & Park, S. A. (2024). Understanding restaurant users' attitudes towards self-service ordering via kiosks during the COVID-19 pandemic: An application of the theory of anxiety. *Tourism and Hospitality Research*, *24*(1), 80–94. https://doi.org/10.1177/14673584221133666

Kincaid, C. S., & Baloglu, S. (2006). An exploratory study on the impact of self-service technology on restaurant operations. *Journal of Foodservice Business Research*, *8*(3), 55–65.

Kokkinou, A., & Cranage, D. A. (2011). Modelling human behaviour in customer-based processes: The use of scenario-based surveys. In *Proceedings of the 2011 winter simulation conference (WSC)* (pp. 683–689). IEEE.

Kokkinou, A., & Cranage, D. A. (2013). Using self-service technology to reduce customer waiting times. *International Journal of Hospitality Management*, *33*, 435–445.

Kokkinou, A., & Cranage, D. A. (2015). Why wait? Impact of waiting lines on self-service technology use. *International Journal of Contemporary Hospitality Management*, *27*(6), 1181–1197.

Lee, W., & Lu, L. (2023). Designing gamified interactions with self-service technology at restaurants. *International Journal of Hospitality Management*, *113*, 103503.

Lee, S. S., Park, K., & Kim, Y. (2022). Self-service versus human interaction in private consumption: The moderating role of brand personality. *Social Behavior and Personality: An International Journal*, *50*(4), 1–10.

Lema, J. D. (2009). Preparing hospitality organizations for self-service technology. *Journal of Human Resources in Hospitality & Tourism*, *8*(2), 153–169.

Lien, C. H., Hsu, M. K., Shang, J. Z., & Wang, S. W. (2021). Self-service technology adoption by air passengers: A case study of fast air travel services in Taiwan. *The Service Industries Journal*, *41*(9–10), 671–695.

Lin, P. M., Peng, K. L., Au, W. C. W., Qiu, H., & Deng, C. D. (2023). Digital menus innovation diffusion and transformation process of consumer behaviour. *Journal of Hospitality and Tourism Technology*, *14*(5), 732–761.

Liu, C., & Hung, K. (2020). A comparative study of self-service technology with service employees: A qualitative analysis of hotels in China. *Information Technology & Tourism*, *22*(1), 33–52.

Liu, C., & Hung, K. (2021). A multilevel study on preferences for self-service technology versus human staff: Insights from hotels in China. *International Journal of Hospitality Management*, *94*, 102870.

Liu, C., & Hung, K. (2022). Improved or decreased? Customer experience with self-service technology versus human service in hotels in China. *Journal of Hospitality Marketing & Management*, *31*(2), 176–204.

Liu, C., & Yang, J. (2021). How hotels adjust technology-based strategy to respond to COVID-19 and gain competitive productivity (CP): Strategic management process and dynamic capabilities. *International Journal of Contemporary Hospitality Management*, *33*(9), 2907–2931.

Ma, H., Kwon, J., & Ahn, J. (2024). The impact of regulations and motivations on behavioural intentions of customers with self-service technology difficulties. *Current Issues in Tourism*, *27*(1), 142–153.

Mavric, B., Öğretmenoğlu, M., & Akova, O. (2021). Bibliometric analysis of slow tourism. *Advances in Hospitality and Tourism Research*, *9*(1), 157–178.

McLeay, F., Osburg, V. S., Yoganathan, V., & Patterson, A. (2021). Replaced by a robot: Service implications in the age of the machine. *Journal of Service Research*, *24*(1), 104–121.

Melián-González, S., & Bulchand-Gidumal, J. (2020). Employment in tourism: The jaws of the snake in the hotel industry. *Tourism Management*, *80*, 104–123.

Melián-González, S., Gutiérrez-Taño, D., & Bulchand-Gidumal, J. (2021). Predicting the intentions to use chatbots for travel and tourism. *Current Issues in Tourism*, *24*(2), 192–210.

Meuter, M. L., Bitner, M. J., Ostrom, A. L., & Brown, S. W. (2005). Choosing among alternative service delivery modes: An investigation of customer trial of self-service technologies. *Journal of Marketing*, *69*(2), 61–83.

Molina-Collado, A., Gómez-Rico, M., Sigala, M., Molina, M. V., Aranda, E., & Salinero, Y. (2022). Mapping tourism and hospitality research on information and communication technology: A bibliometric and scientific approach. *Information Technology & Tourism*, *24*(2), 299–340.

Nam, J., Kim, S., & Jung, Y. (2023). Elderly users' emotional and behavioral responses to self-service technology in fast-food restaurants. *Behavioral Sciences*, *13*(4), 284.

Nilsson, E., Pers, J., & Grubbström, L. (2021). Self-service technology in casual dining restaurants. *Services Marketing Quarterly*, *42*(1–2), 57–73.

Oh, H., Jeong, M., & Baloglu, S. (2013). Tourists' adoption of self-service technologies at resort hotels. *Journal of Business Research*, *66*(6), 692–699.

Oliveira, A., Maia, M., Fonseca, M., & Moraes, M. (2021). Customer preferences and self-service technologies: Hospitality in the pandemic context. *Anatolia*, *32*(1), 165–167.

Oyedele, A., & Simpson, P. M. (2007). An empirical investigation of consumer control factors on intention to use selected self-service technologies. *International Journal of Service Industry Management*, *18*(3), 287–306.

Pant, P. (2022). Technology social practices by Millennials and Gen Z at airport departure terminals. *Tourism Management Perspectives*, *43*, 100978.

Park, S., Kwun, D. J., Park, J. Y., & Bufquin, D. (2022). Service quality dimensions in hotel service delivery options: Comparison between human interaction service and self-service technology. *International Journal of Hospitality & Tourism Administration*, *23*(5), 931–958.

Park, S., Lehto, X., & Lehto, M. (2021). Self-service technology kiosk design for restaurants: An QFD application. *International Journal of Hospitality Management*, *92*, 102757.

Paul, J., & Rosado-Serrano, A. (2019). Gradual internationalization vs born-global/international new venture models: A review and research agenda. *International Marketing Review*, *36*(6), 830–858. https://doi.org/10.1108/IMR-10-2018-0280

Pham, L., Williamson, S., Lane, P., Limbu, Y., Nguyen, P. T. H., & Coomer, T. (2020). Technology readiness and purchase intention: Role of perceived value and online satisfaction in the context of luxury hotels. *International Journal of Management and Decision Making*, *19*(1), 91–117.

Rolim, P. S. W., Correia, A. R., & Borille, G. M. R. (2021). A method to evaluate determinant factors on airport check-in level of service. In *Proceedings of the institution of civil engineers-transport* (Vol. 174(4), pp. 254–266). Thomas Telford Ltd.

Safaeimanesh, F., Kılıç, H., Alipour, H., & Safaeimanesh, S. (2021). Self-service technologies (SSTs) – The next frontier in service excellence: Implications for the tourism industry. *Sustainability*, *13*(5), 2604.

Sagala, N. T. M., & Putro, E. (2020). The development of a self-service application at Martabak Air Mancur restaurant. *Journal of Physics: Conference Series*, *1566*(1), 012056.

Sahni, S., & Kaurav, R. P. S. (2023). What? Why? When? How? Where? of technology-based bibliometric review. In *Advancing methodologies of conducting literature review in management domain* (Vol. 2, pp. 79–101). Emerald Publishing Limited.

Saputra, F. E., & Anggarawati, S. (2022). Will self-service technologies be widely adopted in travel, tourism, and hospitality industries during and after COVID-19? *International Journal of Sustainable Development and Planning*, *17*(6), 1937–1942.

Shim, H. S., Han, S. L., & Ha, J. (2020). The effects of consumer readiness on the adoption of self-service technology: Moderating effects of consumer traits and situational factors. *Sustainability*, *13*(1), 95.

Shin, H., & Perdue, R. R. (2019). Self-service technology research: A bibliometric co-citation visualization analysis. *International Journal of Hospitality Management*, *80*, 101–112.

Shiwen, L., Kwon, J., & Ahn, J. (2022). Self-service technology in the hospitality and tourism settings: A critical review of the literature. *Journal of Hospitality & Tourism Research*, *46*(6), 1220–1236.

Stockdale, R. (2007). Managing customer relationships in the self-service environment of e-tourism. *Journal of Vacation Marketing*, *13*(3), 205–219.

Suksutdhi, T. (2022). Self-Service Technology (SST) implication toward intention to revisit in small hotels: A case study of Nakhon Ratchasima Province, Thailand. *Geo Journal of Tourism and Geosites*, *41*(2), 523–530.

Susskind, A. M., & Curry, B. (2016). An examination of customers' attitudes about tabletop technology in full-service restaurants. *Service Science*, *8*(2), 203–217.

Suwannakul, E. (2021). Role of technology readiness in airline passengers' perceptions of self-service technology quality. *African Journal of Hospitality, Tourism and Leisure*, *10*(2), 670–681.

Tan, T. F., & Netessine, S. (2020). At your service on the table: Impact of tabletop technology on restaurant performance. *Management Science*, *66*(10), 4496–4515.

Tang, Y. E., Yang, L., & He, Y. (2022). My phone, my zone: Restaurant consumers' territorial responses to unsolicited recommendations on their smartphones. *International Journal of Hospitality Management*, *101*, 103–115.

Ueda, K., & Kurahashi, S. (2017). The passenger decision-making mechanism of self-service kiosk at the airport. In *New frontiers in artificial intelligence: JSAI-isAI 2016 workshops, LENLS, HAT-MASH, AI-Biz, JURISIN and SKL, Kanagawa, Japan, November 14–16, 2016, Revised selected papers* (pp. 159–175). Springer International Publishing.

Ueda, K., & Kurahashi, S. (2018). Agent-based self-service technology adoption model for air-travelers: Exploring best operational practices. *Frontiers in Physics*, *6*, 5.

Ülker, P., Ülker, M., & Karamustafa, K. (2023). Bibliometric analysis of bibliometric studies in the field of tourism and hospitality. *Journal of Hospitality and Tourism Insights*, *6*(2), 797–818.

Um, T., Kim, T., & Chung, N. (2020). How does an intelligence chatbot affect customers compared with self-service technology for sustainable services? *Sustainability*, *12*(12), 5119.

Uysal, O. O. (2010). Business ethics research with an accounting focus: A bibliometric analysis from 1988 to 2007. *Journal of Business Ethics*, *93*(1), 137–160.

Victorino, L., Karniouchina, E., & Verma, R. (2009). Exploring the use of the abbreviated technology readiness index for hotel customer segmentation. *Cornell Hospitality Quarterly*, *50*(3), 342–359.

Wang, C., Harris, J., & Patterson, P. G. (2017). Modelling the habit of self-service technology usage. *Australian Journal of Management*, *42*(3), 462–481.

Wang, Y. H., Lee, C. H., & Trappey, A. J. (2017). Service design blueprint approach incorporating TRIZ and service QFD for a meal ordering system: A case study. *Computers & Industrial Engineering*, *107*, 388–400.

Wang, H. Y., & Wu, S. Y. (2014). Factors influencing behavioural intention to patronize restaurants using iPad as a menu card. *Behaviour & Information Technology*, *33*(4), 395–409.

Wei, W., Torres, E. N., & Hua, N. (2017). The power of self-service technologies in creating transcendent service experiences: The paradox of extrinsic attributes. *International Journal of Contemporary Hospitality Management*, *29*(6), 1599–1618.

Wong, I. A., Huang, J., Lin, Z., & Jiao, H. (2022). Smart dining, smart restaurant, and smart service quality (SSQ). *International Journal of Contemporary Hospitality Management*, *34*(6), 2272–2297.

Wu, C. H. J., & Phung, T. B. (2021). The antecedents of tourists' continuous usage intention of self-service technology in Taiwan. *International Journal of Business Information Systems*, *38*(2), 281–298.

Xu, Y., Jeong, E., & Baiomy, A. E. (2022). Enjoyment, convenience, or both? Investigating key attributes for consumers to use interactive self-service technology in restaurants. *Anatolia*, *33*(1), 164–167.

Xu, Y., Jeong, E., Baiomy, A. E., & Shao, X. (2020). Investigating onsite restaurant interactive self-service technology (ORISST) use: Customer expectations and intentions. *International Journal of Contemporary Hospitality Management*, *32*(10), 3335–3360.

Yang, K., Choi, J. G., & Chung, J. (2021). Extending the Technology Acceptance Model (TAM) to explore customer's behavioural intention to use Self-Service Technologies (SSTs) in Chinese budget hotels. *Global Business & Finance Review (GBFR)*, *26*(1), 79–94.

Yang, T., Lai, I. K. W., Fan, Z. B., & Mo, Q. M. (2021). Interactive service quality on the acceptance of self-service ordering systems for the restaurant industry. *Journal of Hospitality and Tourism Technology*, *12*(2), 271–286.

Yuen, K. F., Wang, X., Ma, F., & Wong, Y. D. (2019). The determinants of customers' intention to use smart lockers for last-mile deliveries. *Journal of Retailing and Consumer Services, 49*, 316–326.

Zaitouni, M., & Murphy, K. S. (2023). Self-Service Technologies (SST) in the US Restaurant industry: An evaluation of consumer perceived value, satisfaction, and continuance intentions. *Journal of Foodservice Business Research*, 1–32.

SUSTAINABLE COMPETITIVE ADVANTAGE IN HERITAGE TOURISM: LEVERAGING CULTURAL LEGACY IN A DATA-DRIVEN WORLD

Aditi Nag and Smriti Mishra

Birla Institute of Technology Mesra, India

ABSTRACT

This research explores sustainable competitive advantage (SCA) in heritage tourism, focusing on authenticity, cultural preservation, and visitor experience. It examines the role of data in transforming visitor experiences through personalization, marketing insights, and predictive analytics. This chapter also examines the impact of technology, such as mobile applications, augmented reality (AR), and virtual reality (VR), on heritage tourism experiences. It emphasizes the importance of balancing modernization and cultural preservation, emphasizing ethical considerations and safeguarding heritage site authenticity. This chapter also highlights the significance of sustainability in heritage tourism, including eco-conscious practices, community engagement, and resource allocation. It discusses feedback mechanisms, documentation of cultural and historical assets, and heritage preservation as fundamental elements in SCA. The research encourages collaborative innovation within the heritage tourism domain, encouraging academics and industry professionals to explore emerging research topics. This chapter advocates for a future where heritage tourism offers unparalleled and sustainable experiences while safeguarding and celebrating the enduring treasures of the past.

Keywords: Artificial intelligence; cultural legacy; data-driven; heritage; sustainable competitive advantage; tourism

Review of Technologies and Disruptive Business Strategies
Review of Management Literature, Volume 3, 137–162

Published under exclusive licence by Emerald Publishing Limited
ISSN: 2754-5865/doi:10.1108/S2754-586520240000003008

1. HERITAGE TOURISM IN A DATA-DRIVEN WORLD: AN INTRODUCTION

Heritage tourism, also known as cultural or historical tourism, is a significant sector within the tourism industry that involves exploring and experiencing cultural, historical, and natural heritage sites and activities (Alsahafi et al., 2023; Yuan et al., 2016). These sites hold immense value for their historical and cultural significance (Del Vecchio et al., 2018) and potential economic and sociocultural impact (Kontogianni & Alepis, 2020). However, heritage tourism is at a crossroads in today's data-driven world, as the data-driven economy presents transformative opportunities and challenges (Zhuang & Liu, 2010). This review paper explores the evolving landscape of heritage tourism within a data-driven world, focusing on the intersection of tradition and technology, where the rich tapestry of history meets the power of data analytics. The review aims to bridge the gaps in heritage tourism and explore its historical roots, economic importance, cultural preservation, and role in fostering cross-cultural understanding. The study also analyses the emerging gaps in this dynamic domain and how it aims to bridge them.

Heritage tourism, originating from the Grand Tour of Europe, emerged in the 20th century to protect historical sites from destruction during war and urbanization. It is a significant economic force, contributing significantly to the tourism industry's global revenue (Silva et al., 2022). Tourists travel long distances to experience heritage sites, often choosing destinations based on their historical and cultural appeal (Li et al., 2023). This preference leads to infrastructure development, local economic growth, and employment opportunities (Nekmahmud et al., 2022). Heritage tourism can extend tourist seasons, reducing seasonality-related economic fluctuations, especially for regions heavily reliant on tourism (Wang, Wang, et al., 2020). Local artisans benefit from increased demand for traditional products and souvenirs, generating income for individuals and communities (Bibri, 2021). Heritage tourism is crucial in preserving cultural identity and fostering community belonging, particularly in indigenous communities. It contributes to intercultural dialogue and understanding, promoting global harmony and cross-cultural appreciation (Ahvenniemi et al., 2017). Sustainable practices and responsible tourism approaches are essential to ensure heritage sites and their communities thrive while safeguarding the integrity of our shared human heritage for generations to come (Angelidou et al., 2018).

2. RESEARCH METHODOLOGY

The research methodology involved a systematic literature review, starting with specific research questions about the impact of data-driven strategies on heritage tourism. The search used keywords and phrases related to data-driven approaches in heritage tourism, including peer-reviewed journals, conference proceedings, and reputable books (refer to Table 1).

Table 1. Keywords and Associated Phrases.

Keywords	Associated Phrases
Tourism	Urban tourism product model, special events, infrastructure, resources, leisure, choice
Tourism management	Development, job prospects, economic growth, tourist satisfaction, tourist experience, recurring visits
Heritage	Tourism system, WHS, cultural legacy, cultural heritage, development, identity
Artificial intelligence	Algorithm, clustering, AR, machine learning, problem-solving, VR, decision-making, cognitive science, 5G, chatbots, image recognition, creative solutions

Source: Authors.

After selecting the keywords and identifying the associated phrases, literature selection was carried out (refer to Fig. 1) from Elsevier and ScienceDirect, among others. Only studies published in English within the last decade were considered.

The selected literature had to focus explicitly on data-driven strategies in heritage tourism management. Relevant information, key findings, and methodologies were extracted from the selected literature. A detailed synthesis was conducted to identify patterns, gaps, and overarching themes related to the

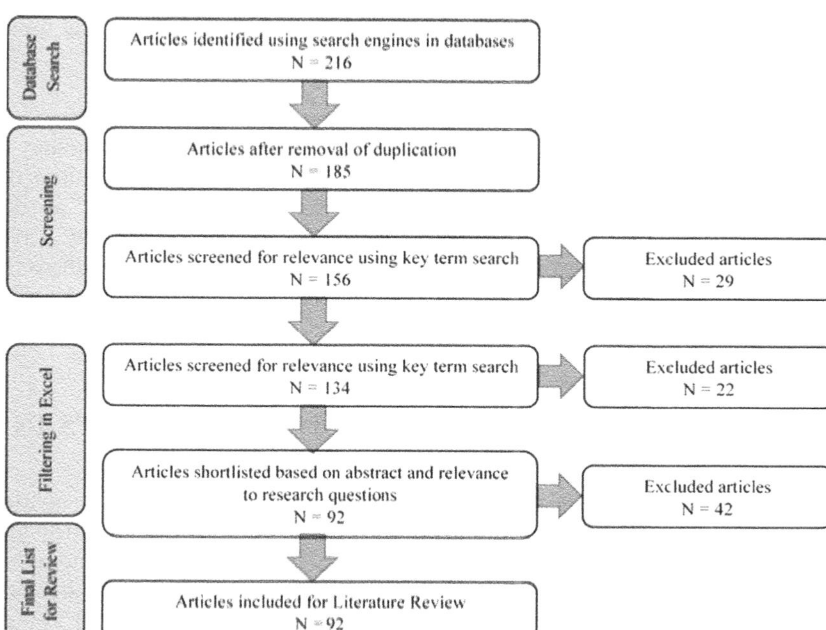

Fig. 1. SLR Literature Selection as Per PRISMA Flow Diagram. *Source:* Authors.

impact of data-driven strategies on heritage tourism. The literature chosen was critically assessed for quality and relevance, with high-quality studies holding more weight in the synthesis process. Data analysis involved synthesizing and interpreting information from the selected literature, using tools like content analysis and thematic synthesis to identify overarching themes and trends.

As heritage tourism evolves, several critical gaps and questions emerge:

- How can heritage tourism leverage data and technology to enhance visitor experiences while preserving the authenticity and integrity of cultural sites?
- In a world increasingly conscious of sustainability, what are the best practices for heritage sites and destinations to adopt eco-friendly measures, engage local communities, and promote responsible tourism?
- How is the data revolution transforming the management of visitor experiences at heritage sites, and what are the ethical considerations and implications of this transformation?
- What strategies can heritage destinations employ to balance integrating modern technologies, such as augmented reality (AR) and mobile apps, with the imperative of cultural preservation?
- What does the future hold for heritage tourism, considering emerging trends like artificial intelligence (AI), 5G connectivity, and AR, and how can heritage destinations stay ahead in this dynamic landscape?
- How can academics, industry professionals, and policymakers collaborate to drive innovation in heritage tourism, particularly in exploring emerging topics that align with sustainability and technology?

This review paper addresses these gaps by comprehensively analyzing heritage tourism in a data-driven world. It will explore the role of data and technology in heritage preservation, the ethical considerations that come into play, and the strategies for achieving sustainable competitive advantage (SCA) in this ever-evolving sector. By weaving together research, insights, and practical recommendations, this paper aims to guide stakeholders toward a future where the treasures of our past remain intact and enriched by the possibilities of a data-driven age.

3. DIVERSE CULTURAL AND HISTORICAL ASSETS IN HERITAGE TOURISM

Heritage tourism stands out as a captivating and distinctive mode of travel, inviting explorers to traverse time and immerse themselves in the world's varied and enthralling heritage. This unique form of tourism encompasses a rich mosaic of cultural and historical treasures, including historical sites, museums, architectural marvels, cultural festivals, UNESCO World Heritage Sites, cultural routes, pilgrimage trails, and indigenous cultural heritage (Batty et al., 2012). Historical sites function as time capsules, transporting visitors to bygone eras and offering profound insights into the events, cultures, and civilizations that have shaped our global narrative. Museums serve as custodians of invaluable artifacts and cultural treasures, allowing visitors to explore the artistic achievements of civilizations throughout history (Bibri, 2019). Cultural festivals, deeply rooted in heritage, enable travelers to participate in celebrations, fostering cross-cultural exchanges and leaving indelible impressions of encountered cultures (Bibri, 2020). UNESCO's recognition of World Heritage Sites acknowledges their extraordinary cultural, historical, scientific, or natural significance (Refer to Appendix A). Cultural routes and pilgrimage trails facilitate transformative journeys, retracing ancient trade routes, religious pilgrimages, or historical migrations (Adie et al., 2018). Pilgrimage trails, particularly imbued with spiritual significance, offer travelers profound and introspective experiences connecting them with history and spirituality (Grover et al., 2018). Indigenous cultural tourism emphasizes respectful interactions with indigenous communities, promoting cultural preservation, economic empowerment, and cross-cultural understanding (Angelidou & Stylianidis, 2020). Through this lens, travelers gain insights into indigenous peoples' history, traditions, and worldviews, fostering a deep appreciation for the cultural diversity that enriches our shared global heritage. Heritage tourism is a testament to humanity's diverse cultural and historical legacy, offering a distinctive and immersive experience that transcends temporal and geographical boundaries.

4. SCA IN HERITAGE TOURISM

SCA in heritage tourism is a destination's strategic advantage over its competitors by effectively leveraging its unique cultural, historical, and natural assets. It ensures the destination can consistently attract and satisfy tourists, ensuring its long-term appeal and viability in the competitive tourism market (Buhalis et al., 2019). SCA involves maintaining and enhancing a destination's distinctiveness, authenticity, and attractiveness to set it apart from others and allow it to thrive over time. It involves a holistic approach that combines cultural and historical heritage preservation, memorable visitor experiences, and sustainable management to ensure the destination's continued relevance in the tourism industry.

4.1 SCA: An Overview

"SCA" refers to a heritage destination's capacity to uphold its allure and competitive advantage over time. It involves harnessing distinctive cultural and historical assets to attract and retain tourists while ensuring the destination's economic viability and cultural authenticity. SCA encompasses various essential elements in heritage tourism that collectively contribute to a destination's enduring competitiveness and appeal (Buhalis et al., 2019). These elements operate synergistically to set the heritage site or destination apart from others in the tourism industry.

One fundamental aspect of SCA is "Authenticity and Preservation," where authenticity, at the heart of SCA in heritage tourism, necessitates the genuine representation of a destination's cultural identity. Preserving heritage sites, exemplified by the cases of Venice and Angkor Wat, involves striking a delicate balance between safeguarding historical assets and providing accessible, living history encounters (Alvesson & Sandberg, 2013). "Cultural Authenticity and Identity" constitute another pivotal element of SCA. This extends beyond physical artifacts, encompassing language, oral traditions, and traditional crafts. Initiatives such as the revival of the Welsh language in Wales and the preservation of textile crafts in India contribute to authentic cultural experiences, enriching heritage tourism (Burton et al., 2020). "Visitor Experience and Sustainability" form the third key component of SCA. A positive visitor experience, crucial for SCA, relies on authenticity and education. Tourists engaging with local communities in Kyoto and experiencing immersive virtual reality (VR) encounters in Athens amplify cultural understanding. Implementing sustainable tourism practices in destinations like Machu Picchu and Bhutan enhances visitor experiences and drives economic sustainability, ensuring a vibrant heritage tourism sector (de-Lima-Santos et al., 2022).

In summary, SCA in heritage tourism is realized through the meticulous orchestration of authenticity, cultural preservation, and visitor experience. This strategic approach creates a distinctive, economically sustainable, culturally authentic heritage destination. By preserving historical and cultural integrity and offering authentic, educational, and sustainable experiences, heritage destinations can distinguish themselves in the competitive tourism landscape and guarantee the long-term preservation of cultural and historical legacies.

5. DATA AS A STRATEGIC ASSET FOR HERITAGE TOURISM

Heritage tourism has undergone a significant transformation driven by integrating data-driven technologies. This shift empowers heritage sites and destinations to use data innovatively, enhancing visitor experiences, engagement, preservation efforts, accessibility, and sustainability. Data-driven insights and technologies, such as personalization, predictive analytics, digital storytelling, and accessibility enhancements, are crucial in transforming heritage tourism (Elgendy et al., 2022). Analyzing visitor data enables tailored experiences, from guided tours to interactive exhibits, fostering engagement and supporting data-driven preservation efforts (Amankwah-Amoah & Adomako, 2019). Predictive analytics anticipates visitor trends, optimizing resource allocation, enhancing satisfaction, and preparing sites for emergencies (Nag et al., 2023). Embracing technologies like digital storytelling and AR, heritage sites provide immersive historical narratives, enhance accessibility, aid conservation, and offer educational opportunities (McLoughlin et al., 2021). Initiatives for accessibility and inclusivity, including wheelchair ramps and multilingual interpretation, ensure equal access, creating a positive experience that respects diversity (Mention, 2019). Preservation and conservation efforts are integral to data-driven heritage tourism, protect architectural features, and involve community participation (Waitt & Gibson, 2009). Digital marketing, through virtual tours and engaging content, expands global reach, promoting sustainability and enhancing engagement (Loukissas, 2019). Efficient resource allocation, sustainability planning, and continuous improvement guided by visitor feedback contribute to managing visitor flow and preserving heritage sites (Otero, 2022; Yu Chung Wang et al., 2022). Cultural and historical documentation is critical in preserving knowledge, fostering collaborations, and strengthening the bond between communities and their heritage (Abd Hamid, 2023). In the pursuit of data-driven excellence, historic sites revolutionize through personalized experiences, understanding visitor behavior, and employing sophisticated marketing strategies (Yathiraju & Bhatia, 2023).

6. LEVERAGING TECHNOLOGY FOR COMPETITIVE ADVANTAGE

Heritage tourism is at the intersection of tradition and modernity, with technology such as mobile apps, AR, and VR playing a crucial role in reshaping visitor experiences. Mobile apps serve as interactive guides, providing comprehensive information about heritage sites, exhibits, and artifacts. They also serve as navigation aids, allowing visitors to explore without fear of getting lost (Kiráľová, 2019).

AR technology combines the real and virtual worlds, providing unique insights into the past through games and scavenger hunts. It aids education by simplifying complex historical concepts. VR offers heritage tourism experiences beyond physical boundaries, allowing virtual tours of remote sites. It excels in historical reconstruction, offering realistic perspectives, time-travel experiences, and immersive storytelling (Kiráľová, 2019; Sangchumnong & Kozak, 2020). It also enhances accessibility for individuals with mobility challenges, allowing them to experience heritage sites that may be difficult to access physically. Technology, including mobile apps, AR, and VR, is revolutionizing heritage tourism by making it more engaging, informative, and accessible. As technology advances, the possibilities for enhancing heritage exploration are boundless, promising an exciting future for heritage tourism (Chhabra, 2010).

Digital innovations have significantly transformed heritage tourism, enhancing visitor experiences through mobile apps, AR, VR, and interactive exhibits. Examples include the Louvre Museum in Paris, Machu Picchu in Peru, and the British Museum in London. Alcatraz Island in San Francisco uses cell house audio tours, while the Acropolis Museum in Athens uses 3D reconstructions and AR on tablets. The Ellis Island National Museum of Immigration in New York uses interactive exhibits and a genealogy research center. The National Museum of Singapore uses digital storytelling techniques for dynamic engagement with cultural heritage. Chichen Itza in Mexico provides VR archaeological reconstructions, providing detailed insights into the ancient Maya civilization. These examples demonstrate the global integration of technology into heritage tourism, ensuring a more immersive, educational, and engaging experience while preserving these destinations' cultural and historical significance. In doing so, these sites facilitate connections for visitors of all ages and backgrounds with the rich heritage they represent (Kiráľová, 2019; Mensah & Boakye, 2023; Sangchumnong & Kozak, 2020).

7. CELEBRATING HERITAGE IN THE DIGITAL AGE: HOW DATA AND TECHNOLOGY SHAPE SUSTAINABLE TOURISM

In the dynamic landscape of heritage tourism, the fusion of historical charm with digital innovation has become paramount, transforming heritage sites into dynamic spaces where tradition harmonizes with cutting-edge technology (D'Auria, 2009; Okumus et al., 2012). Examining case studies from renowned destinations worldwide illustrates the transformative influence of data and technology.

The Vatican Museums in Vatican City use data analytics for efficient visitor management, ensuring a seamless experience and effective crowd control. They offer immersive experiences through virtual tours and AR guides, enhancing historical context. Angkor Wat in Cambodia uses high-resolution imaging and 3D scanning for digital preservation, preserving the site's legacy for future generations. The Smithsonian Institution in Washington, D.C., uses visitor feedback to curate engaging exhibits and extends its educational reach globally. The Great Barrier Reef in Australia uses real-time environmental monitoring to detect stress signs and promote sustainable tourism practices. The Tower of London in the United Kingdom enhances the visitor experience with interactive exhibits and a mobile app, fostering a deeper connection with the site's history. Digital preservation strategies, including artifact replicas, protect cultural heritage and enhance educational value. These case studies demonstrate how heritage sites effectively leverage data and technology for SCA. Through data-driven insights and immersive experiences, these destinations not only thrive in the competitive tourism landscape but also fulfill their crucial role as custodians of unique cultural heritage (D'Auria, 2009; Okumus et al., 2012).

Balancing modernization with cultural preservation in heritage tourism is a complex task that requires careful implementation. Technology can enhance visitor experiences without compromising authenticity, using AR and VR to provide historical context while preserving the site's physical integrity. Interpretation and storytelling are crucial, with local guides, storytellers, and cultural experts playing a vital role in fostering a deeper connection between visitors and the heritage (Yu Chung Wang et al., 2022). Sustainable conservation practices, such as noninvasive scanning techniques and high-resolution imaging, minimize physical impact on historical artifacts and structures while creating digital records for conservation and research (Boyd & Crawford, 2012). Community involvement is also crucial, ensuring cultural insights and traditions are respected and incorporated into the tourism experience. Accessibility and education are central to this equilibrium, with digital content catering to various age groups and educational backgrounds. Renewable energy sources can power data centers and technology installations, reducing their environmental footprint (Arnott & Pervan, 2008). Regulatory frameworks, including heritage protection regulations, guide the use of technology within heritage sites, ensuring clear guidelines support and enhance heritage preservation while preserving cultural significance.

8. SAFEGUARDING CULTURE: THE KEY TO SCA IN HERITAGE TOURISM

Balancing technology integration with preserving authenticity and cultural integrity at heritage sites entails navigating a complex web of ethical concerns, a crucial endeavor addressed by scholars (Balaguer & Cantavella-Jorda, 2002; Nag & Mishra, 2023b). The ethical challenge involves maintaining heritage site authenticity while augmenting it with technology, such as AR, necessitating a balanced approach (Balaguer & Cantavella-Jorda, 2002; Nag & Mishra, 2023b). Ethical considerations include ensuring technology-enhanced experiences are accessible without over-commercializing sites, emphasizing fair pricing, and prioritizing local communities and educational groups (Nag & Mishra, 2023a). Privacy and data security pose ethical dilemmas in collecting visitor data, requiring strict regulations, transparency, consent, and anonymization for ethical data use (Sharma et al., 2021). Ensuring technological inclusivity is essential, avoiding the exclusion of visitors without smartphones or with disabilities through traditional options and adherence to accessibility standards (Ranjbari et al., 2021). Minimizing the environmental impact of technology is a crucial ethical consideration, demanding eco-friendly solutions like low-energy infrastructure and responsible e-waste management (Stoica et al., 2022). Addressing concerns related to cultural appropriation involves collaboration with local communities and cultural experts to ensure accuracy and sensitivity (Girard & Nijkamp, 2009; Tresna & Nirmalasari, 2018). Technology should not encourage disrespectful behavior, necessitating guidelines, education, and staff enforcement for responsible tourism and respect for cultural significance (Harfst et al., 2021; Hausmann, 2007).

The integration of technology into heritage sites requires a thoughtful approach to preserve authenticity and cultural integrity, offering opportunities to enhance, educate, and make heritage more accessible (Ranjbari et al., 2021). By conscientiously addressing these ethical concerns, heritage sites can strike a balance between tradition and digital opportunities, ensuring the enduring preservation of cultural and historical treasures for future generations.

Cultural preservation is crucial for heritage tourism destinations to maintain their competitive edge. It ensures authenticity, attracts genuine travelers, and fosters a strong local connection. This approach encourages return visits and loyalty, highlighting the responsibility of heritage destinations to preserve unique cultural traditions. Preserved sites gain global recognition, leading to partnerships and increased visibility. Cultural preservation also enriches educational experiences, providing a deeper understanding of history and traditions. Thus, it is essential for heritage tourism (Koutsi & Stratigea, 2021).

9. DATA-DRIVEN MARKETING AND PROMOTION

Data are crucial in heritage tourism, guiding destinations to create precise and enticing marketing strategies. Through meticulous data analysis, heritage sites can create detailed profiles of their visitors, incorporating demographic details, travel preferences, and more. This comprehensive understanding forms the basis for tailored marketing messages that align with the preferences and characteristics of different visitor groups (Ranjbari et al., 2021).

Segmentation is another powerful tool in heritage tourism, allowing destinations to categorize the tourism market into distinct segments based on unique interests, motivations, and behaviors. This segmentation enables heritage sites to craft campaigns and packages that resonate with each segment, ensuring their offerings resonate on a personal level (Abbas et al., 2021). Personalized marketing is another crucial aspect of heritage tourism, leveraging past behaviors and preferences to create intimate connections with potential patrons. Geographic precision is crucial, as data-driven insights can pinpoint the origin of heritage tourists and allocate resources with precision. Data enhance content creation, as destinations can craft engaging and informative materials that resonate with potential tourists. In the age of social media, data are increasingly important as it fuels engagement on platforms, providing insights into trending topics and potential visitors' sentiments (Sharma et al., 2021). Data-driven advertising can be strategically displayed based on online behavior, ensuring marketing resources are directed toward individuals actively seeking heritage experiences. Data also enrich on-site experiences, with real-time data guiding visitors through interactive exhibits and self-guided tours and optimizing site layouts. Postvisit data are also pivotal, providing feedback on visitor satisfaction and areas for improvement (Kerdpitak et al., 2022).

9.1 Crafting Authentic Narratives: The Role of Storytelling and Content Marketing in Heritage Tourism

Heritage tourism is a crucial industry that preserves historical artifacts and cultural legacies while fostering emotional connections. Storytelling and content marketing are essential in this context, creating lasting memories and preserving intangible cultural heritage (Nag & Mishra, 2023a). These narratives offer interpretive insights, helping visitors contextualize their experiences and appreciate the heritage on display. Differentiation is key in heritage tourism, as storytelling enables destinations to create unique identities. Visitors become emotionally connected to a destination's narrative, inspiring them to return. Accessibility and inclusivity are fundamental principles in heritage tourism, with storytelling transcending language barriers and presenting content in diverse formats (Richards, 2018). Marketing and promotion are essential for attracting tourists, and community engagement and local pride are additional dimensions of heritage tourism (Chang & Liu, 2009). By involving local communities in storytelling, heritage sites create narratives that resonate with residents, fostering a sense of ownership and pride.

9.2 Sustaining the Past for the Future: Sustainable Practices in Heritage Tourism

In heritage tourism, a profound confluence of the past and the future occurs. Here, the significance of preserving cultural and historical treasures is inexorably intertwined with the imperative of embracing sustainable practices. There exists a delicate equilibrium that heritage sites must strike – a balance that ensures the authenticity, cultural richness, and historical value of these cherished destinations remain intact while simultaneously guaranteeing their long-term vitality in a rapidly evolving world (Benur & Bramwell, 2015). This exploration is significant as it unveils the strategies, innovations, and ethical considerations that enable heritage destinations to honor their past, cater to the needs of present-day travelers, and safeguard their legacy for the generations yet to come.

9.2.1 Preserving Our Heritage: The Sustainability Imperative in Cultural Tourism

Sustainability in heritage tourism encompasses a comprehensive approach, interweaving practices and principles to preserve cultural and historical treasures, minimize environmental impact, and engage local communities (Panasiuk, 2021; Peters et al., 2011). This enduring framework emphasizes eco-friendly practices like energy-efficient lighting and waste recycling (Jenkins & Graves, 2022). Conservation efforts include controlled visitor access and guided tours for cultural and ecological preservation (Allam & Newman, 2018). Active community engagement fosters economic opportunities and collaborative support for heritage site preservation (Umachandran & Said, 2022). Responsible tourism education encourages minimal environmental impact and respectful interactions (Russo-Spena et al., 2022). Economic benefits arise as responsible travelers contribute to the local economy, supporting sustainable accommodations and cultural activities (Buhalis et al., 2023). The long-term sustainability of heritage tourism integrates various practices, ensuring these unique treasures endure as cultural landmarks (Stoica et al., 2022).

Sustainability in heritage tourism is a forward-thinking approach to preserving cultural, historical, and natural assets (Paskaleva-Shapira, 2007). This specialized industry safeguards authenticity, attracting conscientious travelers and fostering a loyal following. Sustainability practices generate organic recommendations, strengthening destinations competitively. Operational efficiency yields long-term cost savings, reinvested in site preservation and community engagement (Hawkins, 2013; Liao & Chuang, 2020; Wacker, 1998). Sustainability equips heritage destinations to mitigate environmental and social risks, maintaining their reputation (Stoica et al., 2022).

10. HERITAGE TOURISM 2.0: THE TRANSFORMATIVE POTENTIAL OF AI, 5G, AND AR

The future of heritage tourism is poised for a transformative shift propelled by AI, 5G connectivity, and AR, ushering in sustainable and immersive experiences

(Stăncioiu et al., 2011; Wang et al., 2020). These technological advancements are set to redefine cultural exploration, with AI-driven personalization tailoring tours based on visitor data, immersive AR experiences bringing history to life, and 5G connectivity enabling real-time engagement with AR and VR applications. Digital twins, powered by AI, will play a pivotal role in creating detailed replicas for preservation, research, and educational purposes, allowing virtual exploration of historical sites. Gamification will transform heritage tourism by engaging younger generations with historical puzzles and hidden stories. At the same time, sustainable practices, such as solar power and eco-friendly transportation, will promote responsible travel and environmental preservation. Virtual Cultural Exchange through VR will foster global connections and cross-cultural understanding, and multimedia storytelling incorporating videos, podcasts, and AR-enhanced exhibits will provide rich, multisensory experiences at heritage sites. The integration of Internet of Things (IoT) technology will optimize crowd management, safety, and ticketing, offering real-time site availability and nearby attraction recommendations. In contrast, collaborative preservation efforts among heritage sites, cultural organizations, universities, and tech companies will drive research and innovative experiences (Barns et al., 2017).

However, the promising advancements in heritage tourism also pose challenges, including data privacy concerns, addressing the digital divide, and balancing revenue generation with preservation goals. Cultural sensitivity is crucial to prevent misrepresentation or appropriation, and a thoughtful approach is needed to avoid over-reliance on technology, ensuring deeper visitor engagement (Panasiuk & Wszendybył-Skulska, 2021). Strategic planning is essential to preserve digital assets, and eco-friendly solutions and responsible infrastructure development are necessary to minimize environmental impact (Mendola & Volo, 2017). Navigating these complexities requires collaborative efforts among heritage site managers, technology providers, policymakers, and local communities to ensure that technology is an enabler rather than a disruptor in heritage tourism.

11. FORGING SCA: THE DATA, TECHNOLOGY, AND SUSTAINABILITY TRIAD IN HERITAGE TOURISM

The integration of advanced technologies, including AI, 5G connectivity, and AR, has ushered in a transformative era for heritage tourism, reshaping visitor experiences and emphasizing sustainability, ethical data use, and a delicate balance between preservation and technology (Risteskia et al., 2012). Envisioning the future of heritage tourism involves maintaining the accessibility and relevance of past treasures for contemporary travelers. Sustainability is at the forefront, with eco-friendly initiatives and responsible tourism strategies central to the transformation (Ribeiro, 2019). Essential aspects include ethical data handling, the equilibrium between preservation and technology, inclusivity, cultural sensitivity, and environmental responsibility (Blake & Sinclair, 2003; Josefsson & Steinthorsson, 2021). Collaboration with local communities ensures authenticity in technology-driven experiences, fostering a respectful and sustainable heritage tourism landscape. Balancing the delicate interplay of data utilization, technology integration, and commitment to sustainable practices is crucial for maintaining SCA in heritage tourism.

Strategically, data are a crucial asset in heritage tourism, providing insights into visitor preferences and trends for customized experiences that resonate and build connection and loyalty (Ristić, 2018). Technology is an enabler through AR, VR, mobile apps, and interactive displays, bridging the past and present, enhancing engagement, and digitizing cultural treasures for future generations (Fernández et al., 2020). Sustainability is a core value, emphasizing responsible tourism practices that respect local cultures and minimize environmental impact, aligning with ethical values and appealing to environmentally conscious travelers (Li & Du, 2021). Data, technology, and sustainability synergy empower SCA, enabling heritage destinations to enhance practices and experiences through eco-friendly transportation and energy-efficient infrastructure (Rodríguez-Díaz & Pulido-Fernández, 2021). Long-term adaptability and resilience are fostered by integrating data, technology, and sustainability, ensuring relevance in a dynamic landscape by staying attuned to visitor expectations and emerging technologies (Hysa et al., 2021). Ultimately, SCA in heritage tourism is a dynamic and sustainable endeavor, recognizing the pivotal roles of data, technology, and sustainable practices in preserving cultural legacies and captivating modern travelers.

12. ELEVATING HERITAGE TOURISM: PRACTICAL RECOMMENDATIONS FOR STAKEHOLDERS

Heritage tourism involves stakeholders such as heritage site managers, destination marketers, and policymakers. They must work together to preserve cultural legacies and ensure sustainable growth in a digital age. This requires strategically integrating data, technology, and sustainable practices (Selim et al., 2021). Practical recommendations can guide these stakeholders in preserving and celebrating past treasures responsibly, data-driven, and sustainably. Table 2 depicts the practical recommendations for heritage site managers, destination marketers, and policymakers to enhance heritage tourism sustainably, leveraging data, technology, and sustainable practices.

When implemented collaboratively by heritage site managers, destination marketers, and policymakers, these recommendations can create a harmonious balance between technology, sustainability, and cultural preservation in heritage tourism.

12.1 Fostering Collaboration and Innovation: A Path to Sustaining Heritage Tourism

The future of cultural preservation and visitor engagement relies on collaboration and innovation. This involves stakeholders from various sectors, including

Table 2. Practical Recommendations to Enhance Tourism Sustainably.

Stakeholders	Practical Recommendations	References
For heritage site managers	Heritage site visitor experience enhancement strategy • Invest in technology like AR apps and virtual tours to preserve cultural integrity. • Implement data-driven decision-making systems for tailored experiences and optimized resource allocation. • Integrate sustainability into the strategy, focusing on eco-friendly infrastructure and waste reduction. • Provide educational programs to highlight the site's historical and cultural significance. • Collaborate with local communities for informed decision-making and site ownership.	Maja & Letaba, 2022; Ribeiro, 2019; Mrđa & Carić, 2019
For destination marketers	Heritage marketing strategy • Utilize visitor data for personalized campaigns. • Craft digital stories to connect visitors to destinations. • Emphasize sustainable tourism and responsible travel. • Highlight technology-driven features like AR-guided tours. • Foster collaborations with heritage sites for mutual benefits.	Nag & Mishra, 2023b; Langen et al., 2022
For policymakers	Promoting responsible tourism and sustainable development near heritage sites • Implement effective regulations and enforcement. • Address overcrowding, waste management, and environmental impact. • Provide financial incentives and tax breaks for eco-friendly practices. • Implement data protection laws for responsible data collection. • Invest in sustainable infrastructure and energy-efficient technologies. • Facilitate collaborative dialogs for mutual benefits and cultural heritage preservation.	Mishra et al., 2022; Sanders, 2014

Source: Authors' compilation.

heritage site managers, local communities, policymakers, entrepreneurs, and creative minds (Caciora et al., 2021). By combining tradition and technology, these efforts enhance visitor experiences and fuel the sustainability of heritage tourism in a digital age. Practical steps are needed to nurture collaboration and innovation, paving the way for a future where the past is cherished, celebrated, and continually reimagined. Encouraging collaboration and innovation in heritage tourism is crucial for driving positive change and ensuring the long-term sustainability of cultural legacies (Vasile & Login, 2013).

To promote innovation in heritage tourism, cross-sector partnerships between heritage site managers, local communities, businesses, and educational institutions are crucial. Technology incubators, cocreation workshops, research grants, digital archives, and cultural exchange programs are essential. Innovation challenges, training programs, and recognition awards are also essential. Networking events and crowdsourcing can engage the public, emphasizing sustainability metrics. These strategies harness collective creativity and expertise to preserve cultural legacies while embracing technology and sustainable practices. This collaborative spirit enriches visitor experiences and ensures heritage tourism thrives in an ever-changing world.

13. NAVIGATING UNCHARTED TERRITORY: RESEARCH HORIZONS IN HERITAGE TOURISM AND SCA

Heritage tourism is a complex and evolving field that seeks to achieve SCA by preserving cultural heritage for future generations. This requires research into critical aspects such as the impact of technology on authenticity, sustainability metrics, visitor behavior, ethical dilemmas in technology-driven experiences, innovative marketing approaches, policies, resilience strategies against external shocks, technology for accessibility, and long-term economic benefits of sustainable practices.

Research in these areas can deepen our understanding of how heritage tourism can achieve SCA while preserving cultural heritage for future generations. It can also inform the development of policies, strategies, and practices that ensure the longevity and vitality of heritage destinations in an ever-evolving tourism landscape. Encouraging academics and industry professionals to explore emerging topics is crucial for heritage tourism's continued growth and evolution. Strategies to advance research in emerging areas include establishing dedicated research grants and scholarships, interdisciplinary conferences, specialized journals, interactive workshops, webinars, networking events, industry advisory boards, student involvement, mentorship programs, and international collaborations.

By implementing these strategies, the heritage tourism community can cultivate an environment where academics and industry professionals are inspired, empowered, and supported in pursuing emerging topics. This collective effort drives innovation, enriches our understanding of heritage tourism, and ensures that this vibrant sector remains at the forefront of sustainable and culturally enriching travel experiences.

14. RESULTS

Heritage tourism is a dynamic sector that combines static and ever-changing factors, influencing its trajectory (refer to Table 3). It combines cultural significance, authenticity, and sustainability with the forces of data, technology, and evolving visitor expectations. The balance between tradition and innovation is crucial in heritage tourism, as it must adapt to the digital age while embracing the unchanging. The appeal of heritage tourism lies in harmonizing past treasures with future possibilities. While some foundational elements remain steadfast,

Table 3. Static and Ever-Changing Factors in Heritage Tourism.

Static Factors	Cultural Significance	The enduring cultural and historical significance of heritage sites remains a static factor. These sites serve as custodians of our collective memory, bearing witness to the passage of time.
	Authenticity	The intrinsic value of authenticity in heritage tourism remains unyielding. Travelers are drawn to experiences that offer a genuine connection to the past, rooted in the traditions and narratives of a bygone era.
	Sustainability	The imperative of sustainability, encompassing responsible tourism practices and environmental stewardship, is an enduring element. Sustainable practices are not merely trends but integral to preserving heritage for future generations.
Ever-Changing Factors	Data and Technology	The data-driven revolution continues to reshape heritage tourism. Technology remains in constant flux, from data analytics shaping visitor experiences to integrating AR and mobile apps.
	Visitor Expectations	Traveler expectations are ever-evolving, driven by technological advancements and changing demographics. Today's visitors seek personalised, immersive, and sustainable experiences, reshaping how heritage sites are managed and marketed.
	Emerging Trends	Trends like AI, 5G connectivity, and AR introduce new dimensions to heritage tourism. These trends redefine how we engage with cultural heritage and open doors to innovative possibilities.
	Collaboration and Innovation	The collaboration between academics, industry professionals, and policymakers is dynamic. It propels innovation and fuels the exploration of emerging topics that bridge the gaps between tradition and technology.

Source: Authors.

others rapidly evolve, highlighting the need for a delicate balance between tradition and innovation.

The dynamic interplay between static and ever-changing factors in various sectors creates a narrative of continuity and transformation. Static factors serve as timeless foundations, representing core values, principles, and traditions that define a sector's identity and purpose. They provide stability, offering a steady framework for the industry. On the other hand, ever-changing factors represent the fluid elements of innovation, adaptation, and progression. These factors, influenced by the static foundations, reflect the sector's ability to evolve and respond to external stimuli, such as technological advancements, societal shifts, and economic trends. The dynamic nature of these ever-changing factors challenges existing norms and pushes the boundaries of what is possible within the established framework. The enduring principles and values embedded in the static factors serve as beacons, guiding the direction of change. This interaction results in constant adaptation and refinement, ensuring the sector preserves its heritage while embracing future opportunities. This delicate balance between enduring and evolving elements propels the industry forward, allowing it to navigate the complexities of the modern world while honoring its foundational principles.

Sustainability is a concept that aims to meet present needs without compromising future generations' ability to meet their own. However, its definition can change based on technological advancements, social norms, economic conditions, and environmental challenges. This dynamic nature ensures that sustainability remains relevant and effective over time, aligning with our world's evolving needs and challenges. The interlinking of static and ever-changing factors creates a symbiotic relationship (refer to Fig. 2), allowing the system to preserve its fundamental identity while embracing necessary transformations to stay relevant in a constantly evolving world.

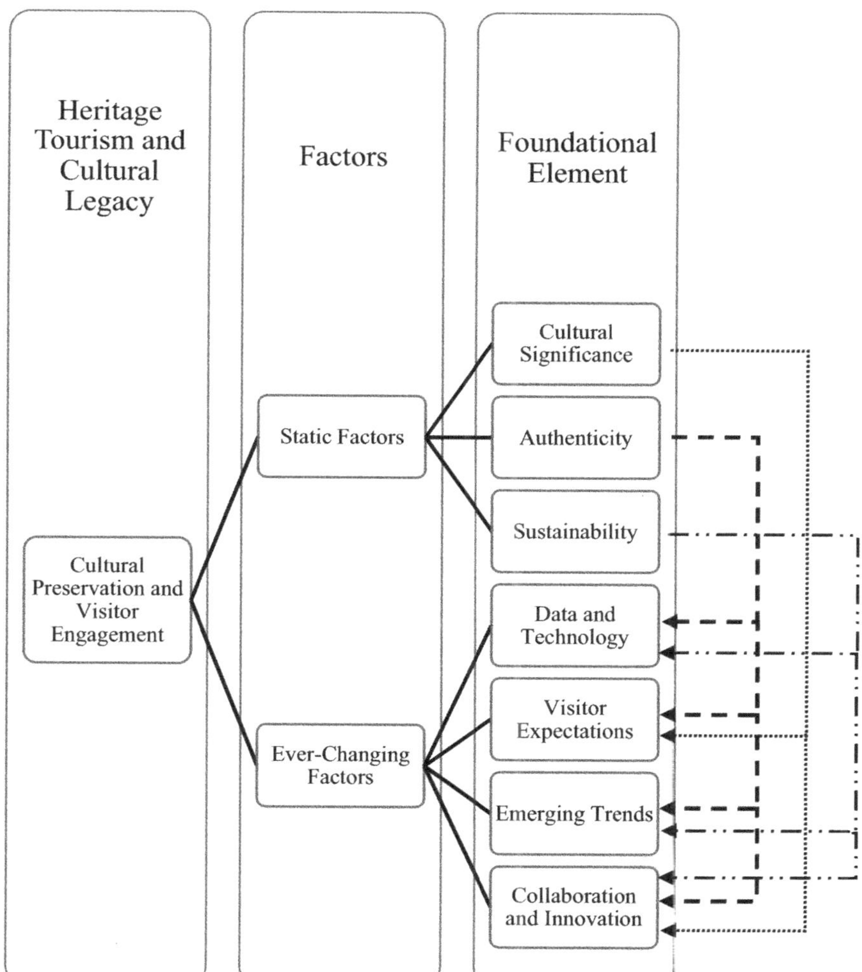

Fig. 2. Relationship Between Static and Ever-Changing Factors. *Source:* Authors.

Heritage tourism showcases the resilience of cultural legacies in a dynamic world, combining timeless appeal with digital opportunities. A sustainable future for heritage tourism requires balancing static and ever-changing factors, ensuring tradition and technology coexist harmoniously. This ensures the preservation of historical treasures, enriching travelers' experiences and preserving them for future generations.

15. CONCLUSION

Heritage tourism stands as a testament to humanity's rich and diverse cultural legacies, offering travelers a unique and immersive journey through time. As the sector continues to evolve, it faces the dual challenge of preserving its timeless essence while embracing the opportunities presented by technological advancements and changing visitor expectations. The delicate balance between tradition and innovation is essential for ensuring the sustainability and relevance of heritage tourism in the modern era.

Heritage tourism can maintain its allure for tourists by utilizing data, technology, and sustainable practices to improve visitor experiences and safeguard cultural heritage for future generations, all while retaining its historical richness. Working together, stakeholders – including managers of heritage sites, destination marketers, legislators, and local communities – can help navigate the ever-changing terrain and protect the integrity of heritage tourism.

As we look toward the future, it is imperative that heritage tourism remains committed to its core values of authenticity, cultural preservation, and responsible stewardship. By embracing change while staying true to its roots, heritage tourism can continue to thrive as a vibrant and enduring expression of humanity's shared heritage and cultural identity.

16. FUTURE RESEARCH SCOPE

Future research in heritage tourism can explore the impact of emerging technologies like AI, VR, AR, and blockchain on visitor experiences, preservation efforts, and sustainability practices. In-depth studies on visitor behavior and satisfaction levels are needed to understand the role of technology in shaping these interactions. Engaging local communities in heritage tourism management can help understand their contributions and potential for collaboration. Sustainability and environmental conservation are critical areas of investigation, with research on mitigating the environmental impact of tourism activities and promoting sustainable practices. Policy and governance frameworks for heritage tourism should ensure cultural preservation and equitable access to resources. Heritage tourism's role in cross-cultural exchange, diplomacy, and peacebuilding can foster mutual understanding and cooperation between diverse communities and nations. Addressing these research areas can advance heritage tourism as a sustainable, inclusive, and transformative force for cultural preservation and economic development.

17. COMPETING INTEREST

The authors declare no competing interest.

18. DATA AVAILABILITY

The literature cited in the work has been published in several journals and proceedings and acknowledged and cited in the reference list.

19. FUNDING STATEMENT

This work was supported by the Department of Science and Technology – Inspire [Grant number IF210191, 2022], Ministry of Science and Technology, Government of India.

REFERENCES

Abbas, J., Mubeen, R., Iorember, P. T., Raza, S., & Mamirkulova, G. (2021). Exploring the impact of COVID-19 on tourism: Transformational potential and implications for a sustainable recovery of the travel and leisure industry. *Current Research in Behavioral Sciences*, *2*, 100033. https://doi.org/10.1016/j.crbeha.2021.100033

Abd Hamid, N. F. (2023). A systematic literature review of the digital transformation of cultural heritage assets during the COVID-19 pandemic. *International Journal of Real Estate Studies*, *17*(1), 107–119. https://doi.org/10.11113/intrest.v17n1.212

Adie, B. A., Hall, C. M., & Prayag, G. (2018). World heritage as a placebo brand: A comparative analysis of three sites and marketing implications. *Journal of Sustainable Tourism*, *26*(3), 399–415. https://doi.org/10.1080/09669582.2017.1359277

Ahvenniemi, H., Huovila, A., Pinto-Seppä, I., & Airaksinen, M. (2017). What are the differences between sustainable and smart cities? *Cities*, *60*, 234–245. https://doi.org/10.1016/j.cities.2016.09.009

Allam, Z., & Newman, P. (2018). Redefining the smart city: Culture, metabolism and governance. *Smart Cities*, *1*(1), 4–25. https://doi.org/10.3390/smartcities1010002

Alsahafi, R., Alzahrani, A., & Mehmood, R. (2023). Smarter sustainable tourism: Data-driven multi-perspective parameter discovery for autonomous design and operations. *Sustainability*, *15*(5), 4166. https://doi.org/10.3390/su15054166

Alvesson, M., & Sandberg, J. (2013). Has management studies lost its way? Ideas for more imaginative and innovative research. *Journal of Management Studies*, *50*(1), 128–152. https://doi.org/10.1111/j.1467-6486.2012.01070.x

Amankwah-Amoah, J., & Adomako, S. (2019). Big data analytics and business failures in data-rich environments: An organizing framework. *Computers in Industry*, *105*(2019), 204–212. https://doi.org/10.1016/j.compind.2018.12.015

Angelidou, M., Psaltoglou, A., Komninos, N., Kakderi, C., Tsarchopoulos, P., & Panori, A. (2018). Enhancing sustainable urban development through smart city applications. *Journal of Science and Technology Policy Management*, *9*(2), 146–169. https://doi.org/10.1108/JSTPM-05-2017-0016

Angelidou, M., & Stylianidis, E. (2020). Cultural heritage in smart city environments: The update. *ISPRS Annals of the Photogrammetry, Remote Sensing and Spatial Information Sciences*, *2*, 957–964. https://doi.org/10.5194/isprs-annals-V-2-2020-957-2020

Arnott, D., & Pervan, G. (2008). Eight key issues for the decision support systems discipline. *Decision Support Systems*, *44*(3), 657–672. https://doi.org/10.1016/j.dss.2007.09.003

Balaguer, J., & Cantavella-Jorda, M. (2002). Tourism as a long-run economic growth factor: The Spanish case. *Applied Economics*, *34*(7), 877–884. https://doi.org/10.1080/00036840110058923

Barns, S., Cosgrave, E., Acuto, M., & Mcneill, D. (2017). Digital infrastructures and urban governance. *Urban Policy and Research*, *35*(1), 20–31. https://doi.org/10.1080/08111146.2016.1235032

Batty, M., Axhausen, K. W., Giannotti, F., Pozdnoukhov, A., Bazzani, A., Wachowicz, M., Ouzounis, G., & Portugali, Y. (2012). Smart cities of the future. *The European Physical Journal Special Topics*, *214*(1), 481–518. https://doi.org/10.1140/epjst/e2012-01703-3

Benur, A. M., & Bramwell, B. (2015). Tourism product development and product diversification in destinations. *Tourism Management*, *50*, 213–224. https://doi.org/10.1016/j.tourman.2015.02.005

Bibri, S. E. (2019). On the sustainability of smart and smarter cities in the era of big data: An interdisciplinary and transdisciplinary literature review. *Journal of Big Data*, *6*(1), 2–64. https://doi.org/10.1186/s40537-019-0182-7

Bibri, S. E. (2020). A methodological framework for futures studies: Integrating normative backcasting approaches and descriptive case study design for strategic data-driven smart sustainable city planning. *Energy Informatics*, *3*(1), 31. https://doi.org/10.1186/s42162-020-00133-5

Bibri, S. E. (2021). Data-driven smart eco-cities of the future: An empirically informed integrated model for strategic sustainable urban development. *World Futures*, 1–44. https://doi.org/10.1080/02604027.2021.1969877

Blake, A., & Sinclair, M. T. (2003). Tourism crisis management: US response to September 11. *Annals of Tourism Research*, *30*(4), 813–832. https://doi.org/10.1016/S0160-7383(03)00056-2

Boyd, D., & Crawford, K. (2012). Critical questions for big data: Provocations for a cultural, technological, and scholarly phenomenon. *Information, Communication & Society*, *15*(5), 662–679. https://doi.org/10.1080/1369118X.2012.678878

Buhalis, D., Harwood, T., Bogicevic, V., Viglia, G., Beldona, S., & Hofacker, C. (2019). Technological disruptions in services: Lessons from tourism and hospitality. *Journal of Service Management*, *30*(4), 484–506. https://doi.org/10.1108/JOSM-12-2018-0398

Buhalis, D., O'Connor, P., & Leung, R. (2023). Smart hospitality: From smart cities and smart tourism towards agile business ecosystems in networked destinations. *International Journal of Contemporary Hospitality Management*, *35*(1), 369–393. https://doi.org/10.1108/IJCHM-04-2022-0497

Burton, J. W., Stein, M. K., & Jensen, T. B. (2020). A systematic review of algorithm aversion in augmented decision making. *Journal of Behavioral Decision Making*, *33*(2), 220–239. https://doi.org/10.1002/bdm.2155

Caciora, T., Herman, G. V., Ilieş, A., Baias, Ş., Ilieş, D. C., Josan, I., & Hodor, N. (2021). The use of virtual reality to promote sustainable tourism: A case study of wooden churches historical monuments from Romania. *Remote Sensing*, *13*(9), 1758. https://doi.org/10.3390/rs13091758

Chang, L. Y., & Liu, W. (2009). Temple fairs in Taiwan: Environmental strategies and competitive advantage for cultural tourism. *Tourism Management*, *30*(6), 900–904. https://doi.org/10.1016/j.tourman.2008.12.002

Chhabra, D. (2010). *Sustainable marketing of cultural and heritage tourism*. Routledge.

D'Auria, A. (2009). Urban cultural tourism: Creative approaches for heritage-based sustainable development. *International Journal of Sustainable Development*, *12*(2–4), 275–289. https://doi.org/10.1504/IJSD.2009.032782

de-Lima-Santos, M. F., Mesquita, L., de Melo Peixoto, J. G., & Camargo, I. (2022). Digital news business models in the age of industry 4.0: Digital Brazilian news players find in technology new ways to bring revenue and competitive advantage. *Digital Journalism*, 1–25. https://doi.org/10.1080/21670811.2022.2037444

Del Vecchio, P., Mele, G., Ndou, V., & Secundo, G. (2018). Creating value from social big data: Implications for smart tourism destinations. *Information Processing & Management*, *54*(5), 847–860. https://doi.org/10.1016/j.ipm.2017.10.006

Elgendy, N., Elragal, A., & Päivärinta, T. (2022). DECAS: A modern data-driven decision theory for big data and analytics. *Journal of Decision Systems*, *31*(4), 337–373. https://doi.org/10.1080/12460125.2021.1894674

Fernández, J. A. S., Azevedo, P. S., Martín, J. M. M., & Martín, J. A. R. (2020). Determinants of tourism destination competitiveness in the countries most visited by international tourists: Proposal of a synthetic index. *Tourism Management Perspectives*, *33*, 100582. https://doi.org/10.1016/j.tmp.2019.100582

Girard, L. F., & Nijkamp, P. (Eds.). (2009). *Cultural tourism and sustainable local development*. Ashgate Publishing Ltd.

Grover, V., Chiang, R. H., Liang, T. P., & Zhang, D. (2018). Creating strategic business value from big data analytics: A research framework. *Journal of Management Information Systems*, *35*(2), 388–423. https://doi.org/10.1080/07421222.2018.1451951

Harfst, J., Sandriester, J., & Fischer, W. (2021). Industrial heritage tourism as a driver of sustainable development? A case study of Steirische Eisenstrasse (Austria). *Sustainability*, *13*(7), 3857. https://doi.org/10.3390/su13073857

Hausmann, A. (2007). Cultural tourism: Marketing challenges and opportunities for German cultural heritage. *International Journal of Heritage Studies*, *13*(2), 170–184. https://doi.org/10.1080/13527250601121351

Hawkins, D. E. (2013). Sustainable tourism competitiveness clusters: Application to World Heritage sites network development in Indonesia. In *Cultural and heritage tourism in Asia and the Pacific* (pp. 299–312). Routledge.

Hysa, B., Karasek, A., & Zdonek, I. (2021). Social media usage by different generations as a tool for sustainable tourism marketing in society 5.0 idea. *Sustainability*, *13*(3), 1018. https://doi.org/10.3390/su13031018

Jenkins, J., & Graves, L. (2022). Do more with less: Minimizing competitive tensions in collaborative local journalism. *Digital Journalism*, 1–20. https://doi.org/10.1080/21670811.2022.2026237

Josefsson, M. Y., & Steinthorsson, R. S. (2021). Reflections on a SMART urban ecosystem in a small island state: The case of SMART Reykjavik. *International Journal of Entrepreneurship and Small Business*, *42*(1–2), 93–114. https://doi.org/10.1504/IJESB.2021.112260

Kerdpitak, C., Kerdpitak, N., Pongpeng, T., & Pungnirund, B. (2022). Development of historical and cultural tourism areas for the competitive business of U-don Thani Province. *International Journal of Health Sciences*, *V*, 271–285. https://doi.org/10.53730/ijhs.v6nS5.5226

Kiráľová, A. (2019). Sustainable tourism marketing strategy: Competitive advantage of destination. In *Sustainable tourism: Breakthroughs in research and practice* (pp. 183–206). IGI Global. https://doi.org/10.4018/978-1-5225-7504-7.ch010

Kontogianni, A., & Alepis, E. (2020). Smart tourism: State of the art and literature review for the last six years. *Array*, *6*, 100020. https://doi.org/10.1016/j.array.2020.100020

Koutsi, D., & Stratigea, A. (2021). Sustainable and resilient management of underwater cultural heritage (UCH) in remote mediterranean islands: A methodological framework. *Heritage*, *4*(4), 3469–3496. https://doi.org/10.3390/heritage4040192

Langen, T., Falk, K., & Mansouri, M. (2022). A systems thinking approach to data-driven product development. *Proceedings of the Design Society*, *2*, 1915–1924. https://doi.org/10.1017/pds.2022.194

Li, S., & Du, S. (2021). An empirical study on the coupling coordination relationship between cultural tourism industry competitiveness and tourism flow. *Sustainability*, *13*(10), 5525. https://doi.org/10.3390/su13105525

Li, J., Lee, T. J., Chen, N., & Park, K. S. (2023). Pro-environmental behaviour of the residents in sensitive tourism destinations. *Journal of Vacation Marketing*, *29*(2), 291–308. https://doi.org/10.1177/13567667221101406

Liao, C. S., & Chuang, H. K. (2020). Tourist preferences for package tour attributes in tourism destination design and development. *Journal of Vacation Marketing*, *26*(2), 230–246. https://doi.org/10.1177/1356766719880250

Loukissas, Y. A. (2019). *All data are local: Thinking critically in a data-driven society*. MIT Press.

Maja, M. M., & Letaba, P. (2022). Towards a data-driven technology roadmap for the bank of the future: Exploring big data analytics to support technology roadmapping. *Social Sciences & Humanities Open*, *6*(1), 100270. https://doi.org/10.1016/j.ssaho.2022.100270

McLoughlin, S., Maccani, G., Puvvala, A., & Donnellan, B. (2021). An urban data business model framework for identifying value capture in the smart city: The case of organicity. In *Smart cities and smart governance: Towards the 22nd century sustainable city* (Vol. 37, pp. 189–215). Springer. https://doi.org/10.1007/978-3-030-61033-3_9

Mendola, D., & Volo, S. (2017). Building composite indicators in tourism studies: Measurements and applications in tourism destination competitiveness. *Tourism Management*, *59*, 541–553. https://doi.org/10.1016/j.tourman.2016.08.011

Mensah, E. A., & Boakye, K. A. (2023). Conceptualizing post-COVID-19 tourism recovery: A three-step framework. *Tourism Planning & Development*, *20*(1), 37–61. https://doi.org/10.1080/21568316.2021.1945674

Mention, A. L. (2019). The future of fintech. *Research-Technology Management*, *62*(4), 59–63. https://doi.org/10.1080/08956308.2019.1613123

Mishra, U. C., Sarkar, S., & Nag, A. (2022). Measuring social acceptance of resettlement colonies for the post COVID-affected migrants in India. *Journal of the Anthropological Survey of India*, *71*(1), 105–124. https://doi.org/10.1177/2277436X221087834

Mrđa, A., & Carić, H. (2019). *Models of heritage tourism sustainable planning* (pp. 165–180). Cultural Urban Heritage: Development, Learning and Landscape Strategies. https://doi.org/10.1007/978-3-030-10612-6_14

Nag, A., Choudhary, N., Sinha, D., Sinha, A. P., & Mishra, S. (2023). Predictive analytics-new business intelligence in SCM. *International Journal of Value Chain Management*, *14*(3), 325–345. https://doi.org/10.1504/IJVCM.2023.133078

Nag, A., & Mishra, S. (2023a). Stakeholders' perception and competitiveness of heritage towns: A systematic literature review. *Tourism Management Perspectives*, *48*, 101156. https://doi.org/10.1016/j.tmp.2023.101156

Nag, A., & Mishra, S. (2023b). Destination competitiveness and sustainability: Heritage planning from the perspective of the tourism industry stakeholders. In *Cases on traveler preferences, attitudes, and behaviors: Impact in the hospitality industry* (pp. 1–32). IGI Global. https://doi.org/10.4018/978-1-6684-6919-4.ch001

Nekmahmud, M., Ramkissoon, H., & Fekete-Farkas, M. (2022). Green purchase and sustainable consumption: A comparative study between European and non-European tourists. *Tourism Management Perspectives*, *43*, 100980. https://doi.org/10.1016/j.tmp.2022.100980

Okumus, F., Avci, U., Kilic, I., & Walls, A. R. (2012). Cultural tourism in Turkey: A missed opportunity. *Journal of Hospitality Marketing & Management*, *21*(6), 638–658. https://doi.org/10.1080/19368623.2012.627231

Otero, J. (2022). Heritage conservation future: Where we stand, challenges ahead, and a paradigm shift. *Global Challenges*, *6*(1), 2100084. https://doi.org/10.1002/gch2.202100084

Panasiuk, A. (2021). Marketing orientation of entities on the tourism market. *Sustainability*, *13*(21), 12040. https://doi.org/10.3390/su132112040

Panasiuk, A., & Wszendybył-Skulska, E. (2021). Social aspects of tourism policy in the European Union. The example of Poland and Slovakia. *Economies*, *9*(1), 16. https://doi.org/10.3390/economies9010016

Paskaleva-Shapira, K. A. (2007). New paradigms in city tourism management: Redefining destination promotion. *Journal of Travel Research*, *46*(1), 108–114. https://doi.org/10.1177/0047287507302394

Peters, M., Siller, L., & Matzler, K. (2011). The resource-based and the market-based approaches to cultural tourism in alpine destinations. *Journal of Sustainable Tourism*, *19*(7), 877–893. https://doi.org/10.1080/09669582.2010.547198

Ranjbari, M., Esfandabadi, Z. S., Zanetti, M. C., Scagnelli, S. D., Siebers, P. O., Aghbashlo, M., ... & Tabatabaei, M. (2021). Three pillars of sustainability in the wake of COVID-19: A systematic review and future research agenda for sustainable development. *Journal of Cleaner Production*, *297*, 126660. https://doi.org/10.1016/j.jclepro.2021.126660

Ribeiro, L. E. (2019). Investment management: Competing in a data-driven world. *Applied Marketing Analytics*, *5*(1), 54–59.

Richards, G. (2018). Cultural tourism: A review of recent research and trends. *Journal of Hospitality and Tourism Management*, *36*, 12–21. https://doi.org/10.1016/j.jhtm.2018.03.005

Risteskia, M., Kocevskia, J., & Arnaudov, K. (2012). Spatial planning and sustainable tourism as basis for developing competitive tourist destinations. *Procedia-Social and Behavioral Sciences*, *44*, 375–386. https://doi.org/10.1016/j.sbspro.2012.05.042

Ristić, Z. (2018). Cultural tourism as a unique form of sustainable tourism–cultural resources as tourism offer factors. *Zbornik radova Ekonomskog fakulteta u Istočnom Sarajevu*, *17*, 63–71.

Rodríguez-Díaz, B., & Pulido-Fernández, J. I. (2021). Analysis of the worth of the weights in a new travel and tourism competitiveness index. *Journal of Travel Research*, *60*(2), 267–280. https://doi.org/10.1177/0047287519899982

Russo-Spena, T., Tregua, M., D'Auria, A., & Bifulco, F. (2022). A digital business model: An illustrated framework from the cultural heritage business. *International Journal of Entrepreneurial Behavior & Research*, *28*(8), 2000–2023. https://doi.org/10.1108/IJEBR-01-2021-0088

Sanders, N. R. (2014). *Big data driven supply chain management: A framework for implementing analytics and turning information into intelligence*. Pearson Education.

Sangchumnong, A., & Kozak, M. (2020). Sustainable cultural heritage tourism at ban Wangka Village, Thailand. In *Culture and cultures in tourism* (pp. 25–35). Routledge.

Selim, M. A., Abdel-Fattah, N. A., & Hegazi, Y. S. (2021). A composite index to measure smartness and competitiveness of heritage tourism destination and historic building. *Sustainability*, *13*(23), 13135. https://doi.org/10.3390/su132313135

Sharma, G. D., Thomas, A., & Paul, J. (2021). Reviving tourism industry post-COVID-19: A resilience-based framework. *Tourism Management Perspectives*, *37*, 100786. https://doi.org/10.1016/j.tmp.2020.100786

Silva, B., Moro, S., & Marques, C. (2022). Sensing the impact of COVID-19 restrictions from online reviews: The cases of London and Paris unveiled through text mining. In J. L. Reis, E. P. López, L. Moutinho, & J. P. M. D. Santos (Eds.), *Marketing and smart technologies. Smart innovation, systems and technologies* (Vol. 279). Springer. https://doi.org/10.1007/978-981-16-9268-0_18

Stăncioiu, A. F., Teodorescu, N., Pârgaru, I., Vlădoi, A. D., & Băltescu, C. (2011). Tourism heritage – An important dimension for assessing/shaping a city's image. Study case: Bucharest. *Theoretical and Applied Economics*, *4*(4), 159.

Stoica, G. D., Andreiana, V. A., Duica, M. C., Stefan, M. C., Susanu, I. O., Coman, M. D., & Iancu, D. (2022). Perspectives for the development of sustainable cultural tourism. *Sustainability*, *14*(9), 5678. https://doi.org/10.3390/su14095678

Tresna, P. W., & Nirmalasari, H. (2018). Sustainable competitive advantage strategies of tourism products in Pangandaran district. *Review of Integrative Business and Economics Research*, *7*, 34–47.

Umachandran, K., & Said, M. M. T. (2022). The Internet Influences Asian Tourism In *Handbook of technology application in tourism in Asia* (pp. 49–65). Springer Nature Singapore.

Vasile, V., & Login, I. (2013). Innovative interpretation of cultural heritage and local sustainable entrepreneurship development. Case study on Romania – In (di) visible Bucharest. *European Research Development in Horizon 2020*, 573–593.

Wacker, J. G. (1998). A definition of theory: Research guidelines for different theory-building research methods in operations management. *Journal of Operations Management*, *16*(4), 361–385. https://doi.org/10.1016/S0272-6963(98)00019-9

Waitt, G., & Gibson, C. (2009). Creative small cities: Rethinking the creative economy in place. *Urban Studies*, *46*(5–6), 1223–1246. https://doi.org/10.1177/0042098009103862

Wang, S. L., Li, Y. C., & Zhang, C. P. (2020). Analysis of the effect of social support on sustainable competitive advantage in tourism industry-based on the perspective of living-ecology production integrated space. *Revista de Cercetare şi Intervenţie Socială*, *71*, 250–263.

Wang, S., Wang, J., Li, J., & Yang, F. (2020). Do motivations contribute to residents' engagement in pro-environmental behaviors? Resident-destination relationship and pro-environmental climate perspective. *Journal of Sustainable Tourism*, *28*(6), 834–852. https://doi.org/10.1080/09669582.2019.1707215

Yathiraju, N., & Bhatia, B. (2023). Predicting the future of heritage conservation for sustainable resource allocation. *International Journal of Sustainable Development Through AI, ML and IoT, 2*(1), 1–12.

Yu Chung Wang, W., Pauleen, D., & Taskin, N. (2022). Enterprise systems, emerging technologies, and the data-driven knowledge organisation. *Knowledge Management Research and Practice, 20*(1), 1–13. https://doi.org/10.1080/14778238.2022.2039571

Yuan, H., Xu, H., Qian, Y., & Li, Y. (2016). Make your travel smarter: Summarizing urban tourism information from massive blog data. *International Journal of Information Management, 36*(6), 1306–1319. https://doi.org/10.1016/j.ijinfomgt.2016.02.009

Zhuang, X., & Liu, H. (2010). Some suggestions for community-based ecotourism management. In *International conference on management and service science, Wuhan* (pp. 1–4). https://doi.org/10.1109/ICMSS.2010.5577145

APPENDIX A

Fig. A1. Timeline for Leveraging Cultural Legacy in a Data-Driven World. *Source:* Authors, created using Preceden.com.

Table A1. Technological Advancements, Cultural Legacy, and Data-Analysis Timeline for Leveraging Cultural Legacy in a Data-Driven World.

Timeline		*Technological Advancements*
1956	Introduction of AI	The development of AI in 1956 revolutionized automated decision-making and machine learning, enabling the processing of vast amounts of data, pattern detection, and insights, thus enhancing cultural legacy in a data-driven world.
1960s	Development of GIS technology	Developed in the 1960s, GIS technology is a powerful tool for analyzing and visualizing spatial data, enabling organizations to explore relationships between cultural heritage, demographics, and the environment spatially.
1969	Birth of the internet	ARPANET, the precursor to the internet, was established on October 9, 1969, revolutionizing computer networking and laying the groundwork for the World Wide Web, transforming global information sharing and access.
2004	Rise of social media	Facebook's launch in 2004 marked the start of the social media era, revolutionizing global communication and information sharing. Social media platforms promote cultural heritage, storytelling, and memory preservation.
2010s	AI-based language translation	It significantly reduced language barriers in a data-driven world, enabling instant translation of text and speech across languages and promoting cultural exchange and accessibility to heritage.
Timeline		*Cultural Legacy*
1972	UNESCO World Heritage Convention	The UNESCO World Heritage Convention, adopted in 1972, aims to safeguard and preserve cultural and natural sites of universal value, emphasizing the significance of cultural legacy in fostering global understanding and appreciation of diverse civilizations.
1980s	Establishment of digital humanities	Digital humanities, originating in the 1980s, integrates humanities studies with digital tools, promoting interdisciplinary collaborations for research, preservation, and interpretation of cultural artifacts in the digital age.
1980s	Digitization of music	The rise of CDs and digital formats significantly transformed the music industry, enhancing preservation efforts, increasing accessibility, and transforming how people consume and interact with global musical heritage.
1990s	Creation of digital libraries	In the 1990s, digital libraries emerged as centralized repositories of digitized texts, images, and audio-visual materials, enhancing accessibility, preservation, and dissemination of cultural legacies for educational and research purposes.
21st century	Cultural heritage documentation	The 2000s saw the advent of advanced digital imaging and documentation techniques, which significantly improved the preservation and accessibility of cultural heritage, thereby ensuring their long-term preservation.
21st century	Digitization of archives	Organizations and institutions digitize archives to preserve historically significant documents, enabling easier access, widespread dissemination, and enhanced preservation for future generations.

(Continued)

Table A1. *(Continued)*

Timeline		*Data Analysis*
1980s	Development of big data	In the 1980s, researchers explored large datasets and introduced "big data," enabling increased computing power to collect, store, and analyze vast amounts of information, driving data-driven decision-making across industries.
1990s	Formation of data mining methods	In the 1990s, data mining emerged as a field for uncovering patterns and insights from large datasets. It became a valuable tool for businesses to gain a competitive edge and effectively leverage their data.
21st century	Data Visualization tools	Big data has revolutionized data visualization, making complex information more understandable and actionable by creating visual representations and enhancing communication of cultural patterns and trends within vast datasets.
2009	Open data initiatives	In 2009, governments and organizations worldwide began embracing open data initiatives, making datasets accessible for public analysis, promoting transparency and innovation, and enabling researchers to explore innovative ways to leverage cultural legacy.
2010s	Data privacy and ethics regulations	The GDPR, introduced in 2018, aimed to regulate data privacy, ensure responsible handling of personal information, protect individuals' rights, and balance data-driven advancements with respect for cultural legacy as data volume increased.

Source: Authors.

TRANSFORMATIVE INFLUENCE OF DISRUPTIVE INNOVATIONS ON MARKETS AND BUSINESS PERFORMANCE

Sumit Narula[a] and Dhruv Sabharwal[b]

[a]*Amity University Gurugram, India*
[b]*Sharda University, India*

ABSTRACT

Researchers, business professionals, and policymakers are now focusing on how disruptive innovations affect markets and business performance in the quickly changing business landscape of today. This study investigates the complexity of disruptive innovations and how they alter established organizational strategies and market structures. The study explores the core traits of disruptive innovations and looks at how they upend established business models and alter the structure of entire industries. This study employs a comprehensive literature review to identify the primary motivators behind disruptive innovations and their diverse impacts on market dynamics. It looks into how disruptive change is sparked by evolving consumer behavior, flexible business models, and emerging technologies. Additionally, research examines how businesses use internal reorganizations and strategic alliances among other tactics to capitalize on and adjust to disruptive innovations. It also examines how market leaders deal with these difficulties in an effort to stay competitive, shedding light on the possible risks and uncertainties related to disruptive innovations. It also highlights how crucial it is for organizations to have innovative cultures and proactive adaptation in order to prosper in a time of swift technological advancements.

Keywords: Disruptive innovations; business performance; transformation; emerging technologies; organizational culture

Review of Technologies and Disruptive Business Strategies
Review of Management Literature, Volume 3, 163–184

ISSN: 2754-5865/doi:10.1108/S2754-586520240000003009

1. INTRODUCTION

This comprehensive review delves into the profound effects of disruptive innovations on both markets and the performance of businesses operating within them. By exploring the concept of disruptive innovation and its theoretical underpinnings, this study aims to illuminate the transformative power these innovations wield across various industries (Reardeon, 2019). Through an analysis of case studies and empirical evidence, we investigate how disruptive technologies have reshaped market dynamics and impacted the strategies and financial outcomes of key players. Additionally, we explore the role of regulations in fostering or hindering the adoption of these innovations, providing insights into the future outlook for businesses in an ever-evolving landscape. This review concludes with actionable lessons and best practices for business leaders and investors navigating the disruptive terrain to capitalize on its vast potential (Streaming media, 2020).

The theory of disruptive innovation (Bower & Christensen, 2022) has proven to be a compelling framework for understanding how innovation drives growth. Recent trends indicate that new entrants enjoy significant advantages in navigating new networks of value, as disruptive innovation disrupts established paths of technological growth. The vulnerability of incumbent companies stems from their inability to adjust strategies rather than technology (Rosenbloom & Christensen, 1994). Consequently, many executives in large, well-established companies, such as Intel, Microsoft, Google, and others, rely on disruptive innovations as their guiding principle.

These leaders consistently emphasize their efforts to anticipate "disruptive developments" that may impact their competitive positions (Tan et al., 2016). By avoiding performance domination and preserving competitiveness, businesses seek to disrupt their own models, evaluating their offerings, production, distribution, financing methods, and target markets. While technology alone may not predict the future, businesses must prepare for groundbreaking changes (Paap & Katz, 2004).

Innovators in business models do not always originate entirely new products or services; instead, they redefine existing ones and transform the way they reach end consumers (Trojan et al., 1993). A prime illustration of this is Amazbook didn't invent book shopping but rather reimagined the entire service, reshaped the customer experience, and redefined the role of customers as contributors through their intended purchases (Women, 2015).

In contrast, disruptive product technologies, as elucidated by Markides, bring about value innovations that profoundly reshape consumer preferences and behaviors. Some companies excel by introducing innovative new products, as seen in creative industries such as film, books, and music (Markides, 2006). This distinction underscores the varied approaches to innovation, with business model innovators focusing on redefining delivery and experience, while disruptive product technologies bring forth innovations that reshape consumer dynamics (Richter, 2013).

2. OBJECTIVES

This chapter examines major disruptive technologies that have occurred over the last three decades, focusing on their unique customer benefits, revolutionary drivers, and revenue-boosting potential. Furthermore, this chapter provides insightful information about a range of disruptive technologies and their significant effects on businesses.

3. THEORY AND LITERATURE REVIEW BACKGROUND

Bower and Christensen (2022) define disruptive innovation as the process through which a smaller, usually financially strapped company challenges an established organization (also known as an incumbent). This problem arises when a smaller business targets the bottom of the market and advances gradually.

Usually, this tactic goes through multiple phases:

- Established businesses focus on inventing and developing products or services to cater to the needs of the most demanding and profitable consumers, often neglecting the requirements of the lower end market segment.
- Smaller entrants enter the market and address the overlooked segment by offering products or services at a lower cost compared to incumbent providers.
- Despite the emergence of these new competitors, the incumbents do not react and continue to concentrate on their more lucrative divisions.

Eventually, the newcomers advance by providing solutions that the established companies' mainstream clientele find appealing. Disruption occurs when the traditional customer of the established firm is drawn to these new entrants (Christensen et al., 2006). Potential customers' wants could not be initially satisfied by disruptive technologies as easily as by traditional goods or services. They might be devoid of certain features or functionalities included in current offers. But they frequently shine in terms of cost, mobility, and speed, drawing in new or less picky clients. For example, Southwest Airlines pioneered low-cost, no-frills flights, which first drew in leisure travelers with few other options for reasonably priced air travel.

The impact of disruptive technologies has been evident across various consumer processes, from transportation to retail, electronics, connectivity, and social change processes. The social changes brought about by technological developments are often unintended consequences, arising from the pursuit of commercial opportunities. However, catalytic innovations deliberately aim to drive global change (Schmidt & Druehl, 2008).

It has been difficult for multinational corporations to successfully implement radical technologies. Successful development of radical technologies is hampered by several fundamental variables, which can be represented by different clusters of connected and partially interdependent inhibitors (Nunno & Warner, 2020). A company's unwillingness to relearn outmoded conceptual models, an excessively dominant architecture, a strict competitive definition, and a risk-averse organizational culture are a few examples of these inhibitors (Assink et al., 2006). The concept of disruptive innovation potential provides valuable insights into comprehending the interdependencies among these fundamental limitations. A company's growth plan should include bridging the gap between the mission and actual transformative innovativeness (Kaurav & Gupta, 2022; Yu & Hang, 2010).

Well-known businesses are using automated technologies and Applied Analytics (AA) to obtain real-time insights into field operations (Rammal, 2023). They use strategies like dynamic field dispatching and remote support to maximize real-time deployment (Page et al., 2021). By improving technological performance and cutting response times, these disruptive technologies enable industrial organizations to gradually enhance their practices, which in turn increases consumer loyalty (Fig. 1).

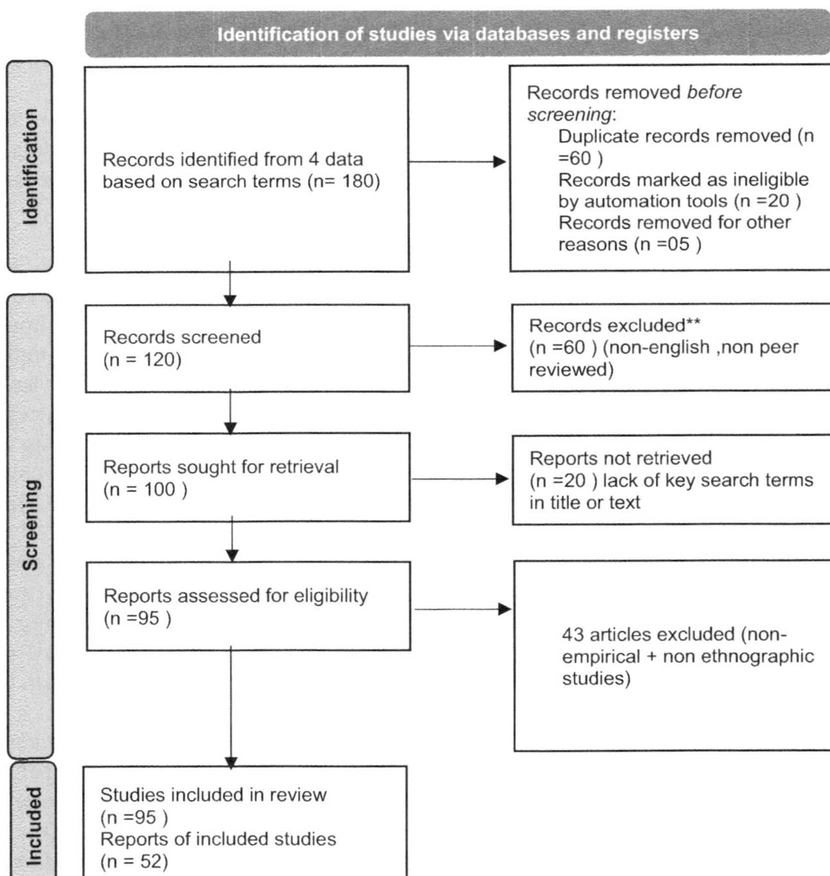

Fig. 1. PRISMA Framework for Selection of the Paper. *Source:* Author's own work.

4. METHODS-INNOVATION REVIEW

A variety of things can cause disruption, such as innovation that upsets established markets. Low-end disruptive strategies focus on businesses that provide appropriate products to customers at the bottom of the market (Psotka, 2013). The incumbent usually shifts its focus upstream as a result of these low-end disruptions because they often target lower profit segments for the incumbent. Conversely, nonconsumption-focused new market disruptions focus on industries with smaller profit margins (Rammal, 2023). Like low-end disruptions, the new business makes a profit at much lower pricing, and the products are regarded as valued (Moreau, 2013). The main difference is that new-market disruptions target underserved consumers, whereas low-end disruptions concentrate on overserved people.

Tapping into two categories of markets that traditional players ignore opens the door for disruptive technologies (Mordor, 2020). Companies prioritize constantly changing goods and services for their most profitable and combative customers, giving less attention to less demanding consumers, which leads to the emergence of low-end footholds. Because of this, incumbents' offerings frequently surpass the latter's efficiency standards, giving disruptors a chance to serve these lower end customers.

Uber is an example of a business that has had extraordinary success. Uber is a popular ride-sharing service that uses a mobile app to match passengers with drivers in the area. Uber's success may defy the conventional disruptive innovation paradigm, despite its rapid expansion and substantial market capitalization. Uber is upending the taxi industry, but it might not have a completely negative impact on other forms of transportation (Castellano, 2020).

In conclusion, disruptive innovation can manifest in multiple forms, each impacting different market segments and consumers. While Uber's success is noteworthy, its disruptive nature remains a subject of debate, highlighting the complexities and nuances of the disruptive innovation phenomenon (Mookerjee & Rao, 2021).

Tables 1 and 2 provide an overview of disruptive technologies, their origins, recent sales figures, and customer satisfaction levels. The following detailed explanations cover the first five advancements, including current and projected sales forecasts (Kale et al., 2007).

4.1 New Business Models

Traditional notions of hospitality are being reshaped by new business models such as HouseTrip, Airbnb (Guttentag, 2015) (Global), Zostel (Pandya et al., 2019) (India), and ride-sharing applications like Uber (Global), OLA (India) (Joshi, 2018; Kaurav et al., 2020; Yeh & Walter, 2017). According to Yeh and Walter (2017), some of these changes include the growing popularity of self-service cashiers, cashless payment methods in supermarkets, and mobile app-based meal ordering at airports and other locations. The landscape of hospitality is undergoing a profound transformation, propelled by innovative business models that challenge traditional norms (Global banking & Finance Review, 2023). Platforms such as HouseTrip and Airbnb (as discussed by Guttentag in

Table 1. Trends of Disruptive Innovation.

S.No.	New Trends	Description	Impact	Benefits
1	By 2025, more than half of the population is expected to be self-employed.	Innovative areas that may offer freelance jobs are, among others, AI, ML, IOT, and Modeling.	To minimize repair and maintenance time by 10%–25%. The cost of labor and other manpower would see a 5%–20% cut.	Increased flexibility, autonomy, and potentially higher earnings for self-employed individuals.
2	Around 40%–50% of production is expected to be carried out with AI, as a key component by 2035.	Compared to the past and current industrial scenario, the workforce is used more in the service sector than in manufacturing or packaging.	10%–20% increase in efficiency.	Improved productivity, reduced error rates, and cost savings for businesses adopting AI in production processes.
3	Using a mobile camera, augmented reality (AR) enhances the live view with visual features. Virtual reality (VR) alludes to a fully immersive experience that obscures the outside world. Forecasts indicate that the AR and VR industries will surpass US$ 108 billion by FY 2021.	The service sector is anticipating the expected defects and needs of consumers with a constructive customer solution.	Reduction in repair time by 30%–40% and 10%–20% improvement in customer satisfaction.	Enhanced customer experiences, improved problem-solving, and increased customer loyalty through AR and VR technologies.
4	Rapid advancement in AI and automation may lead to job displacement and loss of traditional employment opportunities.	Traditional job roles may become obsolete as AI and automation take over tasks, potentially leading to unemployment and economic instability.	Disruption of traditional employment sectors and potential socioeconomic challenges.	Increased efficiency, reduced operational costs, and innovation in industries adopting AI and automation technologies.

Source: Adopted and modified from Ananthakrishnan et al. (2020).

2015) have redefined the concept of accommodation, enabling individuals to share their homes with travelers worldwide. Similarly, in India, Zostel, as highlighted by Pandya et al. in 2019, has pioneered a unique hostel experience, tapping into the growing trend of experiential travel.

The evolution isn't limited to accommodation alone. The emergence of ride-sharing applications like Uber (on a global scale) and OLA (in India), explored by Joshi in 2018, and Yeh and Walter in 2017, has revolutionized transportation, offering convenient and often cost-effective alternatives to traditional taxis (Haddaway et al., 2022). These platforms leverage technology to connect drivers with riders, introducing a level of efficiency and convenience that has reshaped urban mobility.

Table 2. Analysis of a Few Disruptive Innovations in the Last 30 Years.

Driver of Disruptive Innovation	Area of Application	Product Names Introducers	Year	Origin Country	Significant Benefit to Consumer
Apple Vision Pro Unleashes the Power of Spatial Computing	Digital	Apple Vision Pro Apple	2023	USA	Apple Vision Pro promises to enable users to seamlessly integrate virtual elements into their physical surroundings, unlocking unparalleled immersion and productivity.
ChatGPT Redefines Human–Computer Interaction			2022	USA	Developed by Open AI, this groundbreaking language model harnessed the power of the GPT-3.5 architecture to revolutionize human–computer interactions.
Biometric	Healthcare and Security Systems	Face recognition, iris scan, finger print, etc.	1960, 1969	USA	Increase in security, safety, productivity.
Floating Agriculture	Agriculture	Floating and vertical agriculture	2012	Netherlands	Introduction of new technology.
Budget Hostels and Homestays	Tourism and Hospitality	Airbnb, HouseTrip, Zostel	2008	USA	Cheaper options of hotel stay and traveling at lower costs.
Web Streaming (OTT)	Entertainment	Bigflix, Netflix, YouTube, Amazon prime, etc.	1990	USA	Introduction of new technology in entertainment at home.
Digital Photography	Travel and Entertainment	Digital cameras, phone cameras, digital photography Nokia	1990	UK	Advancement in photography
3D Printers Revolutionize			2019	USA	This disruptive technology appeared in 2019 as part of predictive maintenance in manufacturing. Smart sensors helped identify potential

(Continued)

Table 2. (*Continued*)

Driver of Disruptive Innovation	Area of Application	Product Names Introducers	Year	Origin Country	Significant Benefit to Consumer
					problems, and 3D printers built new parts before needing to be needed.
Artificial Intelligence	Multidisciplinary	From 19th& 20th century beginning, 1950 Turning Test was first AI based machine test.	1950	UK	Replication n of human intelligence, leading to accuracy in forecasts and ability to predict customer actions.

Source: Modified by authors, adapted from Mookerjee & Rao (2021).

Furthermore, the changes extend beyond the hospitality and transportation sectors. Yeh and Walter (2017) note additional shifts in consumer behavior, such as the increasing prevalence of self-service cashiers in retail outlets. Cashless payment methods are becoming the norm in supermarkets, reflecting a broader global trend toward digital transactions for enhanced convenience and efficiency (Krotov & Junglas, 2008). Additionally, mobile app-based meal ordering is transforming dining experiences, not only at restaurants but also in unconventional locations such as airports.

This evolution in hospitality and service industries reflects a broader societal shift toward embracing technology for enhanced convenience and personalized experiences. These changes not only provide consumers with more choices and flexibility but also challenge established norms, fostering a culture of innovation and adaptation (Lucas & Goh, 2009). As these new business models continue to gain traction, the hospitality industry is navigating a dynamic landscape where traditional boundaries are continually being redefined, offering both challenges and opportunities for businesses and consumers alike (Miltgen et al., 2013).

4.2 Internet of Things (IoT)

According to Petrovic et al. (2017), the IoT undermines traditional engineering domains by connecting devices in cyber-physical ecosystems. With an annual compound growth rate of 11%, there were around 7 billion active IoT devices by the end of 2019. By 2030, this number is expected to increase quickly to 24.1 billion (Morrish et al., 2020). The advent of the IoT has ushered in a transformative era, challenging traditional engineering domains by interlinking devices within vast cyber-physical ecosystems, as highlighted by Petrovic et al. in 2017. The exponential growth of IoT is reflected in the staggering statistics: the number of active IoT devices surpassed 7 billion by the end of 2019, propelled by an annual compound growth rate of 11%. The rapid proliferation of connected devices is indicative of the profound impact IoT is having on diverse sectors, ranging from smart homes and health care to industrial automation and beyond.

As we look ahead, the trajectory of IoT expansion is set to soar even higher. Projections by Morrish et al. in 2020 estimate that by 2030, the number of active IoT devices will skyrocket to an astonishing 24.1 billion. This forecast underscores the pervasive integration of IoT into our daily lives and across industries. The seamless connectivity and data exchange facilitated by IoT are fostering a paradigm shift in how we perceive and interact with the world around us.

This explosive growth is fueled by advancements in sensor technologies, communication protocols, and the increasing prevalence of edge computing, enabling devices to process data locally. The implications are far-reaching, influencing not only consumer technologies like smart homes and wearables but also industrial processes, supply chain management, and urban infrastructure.

The sheer scale of the IoT ecosystem introduces both unprecedented opportunities and challenges. The vast amount of data generated by interconnected devices holds the potential to drive innovation, optimize operations, and enhance user experiences. Simultaneously, concerns about privacy, security, and the effective management of these data deluge necessitate careful consideration.

In conclusion, the trajectory of IoT growth, from 7 billion active devices in 2019 to a projected 24.1 billion by 2030, signifies a fundamental shift in the technological landscape. The interconnectedness of devices is reshaping how we live and work, with IoT emerging as a cornerstone of the digital revolution. As we navigate this interconnected future, addressing the evolving challenges and harnessing the vast potential of IoT will be key to unlocking its full transformative impact across diverse domains.

4.3 Artificial Intelligence (AI)

From 2020 to 2027, the global AI market is expected to increase at a compound annual growth rate (CAGR) of 42.2%, from its anticipated 2019 value of USD 39.9 billion. Many industries, including the automotive, medical, hotel, financial, and manufacturing sectors, are being revolutionized by AI (Lee, 2017). AI is becoming a crucial component at the heart of businesses, influencing software and systems in a variety of industries (Grand View Research, 2020). From 2020 to 2027, the global AI market is poised for remarkable growth, projected to surge at an impressive CAGR of 42.2%, building upon its anticipated value of USD 39.9 billion in 2019 (source). This astronomical growth is indicative of the transformative impact that AI is having across diverse industries.

Several sectors are experiencing a profound revolution, thanks to the integration of AI technologies. The automotive industry is leveraging AI for autonomous vehicles and advanced driver assistance systems, while the medical field benefits from AI in diagnostics, personalized medicine, and drug discovery. In the hotel and hospitality sector, AI is enhancing customer experiences through personalized services and efficient management systems. Financial institutions are utilizing AI for fraud detection, risk management, and customer service optimization. Additionally, AI is playing a pivotal role in the manufacturing sector by optimizing production processes, predictive maintenance, and quality control (Lee, 2017).

AI is not merely an auxiliary element but is evolving into a central and indispensable component for businesses worldwide. Its influence extends across software and systems, permeating various industries and transforming traditional modes of operation (Sabharwal et al., 2023). The integration of AI is not only about automating tasks but also about fostering innovation, improving decision-making processes, and unlocking new realms of possibilities in areas such as natural language processing, computer vision, and machine learning.

The insights derived from AI-driven analytics and predictive modeling have become instrumental in shaping strategic business decisions. As businesses across the globe recognize the potential of AI, investments in research and development, as well as AI implementation, continue to rise. The evolution of AI from a novel technology to a fundamental driving force in the business landscape underscores its capacity to revolutionize how industries operate and deliver value to consumers (Grand View Research, 2020).

In conclusion, the projected growth of the global AI market signifies a paradigm shift across industries, where AI is not merely a technological advancement but a transformative force shaping the future of business and innovation. As businesses increasingly integrate AI into their operations, the next decade holds the promise of unprecedented advancements, efficiency gains, and new possibilities across a spectrum of industries.

4.4 3D Printing

3D printing, which is upending the commercial tool design and manufacturing sector, had sales of USD 13.7 billion by the end of 2019 and is predicted to grow at a CAGR of 29.48% to reach USD 63.46 billion by 2025 (Hahn et al., 2014). In addition to providing a variety of options for contemporary architectural styles, building techniques, and materials, it permits the production of intricate artifacts (Mordor Intelligence, 2020). The transformative impact of 3D printing on the commercial tool design and manufacturing sector is unmistakable, with sales reaching USD 13.7 billion by the close of 2019. The trajectory of this technology continues to ascend, with a forecasted CAGR of 29.48%, projecting a market value of USD 63.46 billion by 2025, as highlighted by Hahn et al. in 2014. This exponential growth underscores the pivotal role that 3D printing is playing in reshaping how products are designed, prototyped, and manufactured.

Beyond the sheer economic metrics, 3D printing is revolutionizing the very fabric of industries by offering an array of options for contemporary architectural styles, innovative building techniques, and diverse materials (Francke et al., 2014). This technology's versatility enables the creation of intricate artifacts that were previously challenging or impossible to produce through traditional manufacturing methods, as emphasized by Mordor Intelligence in 2020.

One of the distinctive features of 3D printing lies in its ability to bring digital designs to life layer by layer, offering unparalleled precision and customization. This not only streamlines the prototyping process but also facilitates the production of highly complex and customized components for a myriad of applications (Eun, 2018). Industries ranging from aerospace and automotive to health care and consumer goods are harnessing the potential of 3D printing to optimize manufacturing processes, reduce costs, and unlock new possibilities in product design.

In the realm of architecture, 3D printing is pushing boundaries by enabling the construction of intricate structures with unprecedented speed and efficiency (Anshari et al., 2019). The technology allows architects and designers to explore innovative shapes and designs that were once constrained by traditional construction methods (Dinh & Thai, 2018). This not only enhances the aesthetics of contemporary architecture but also contributes to sustainability efforts through more efficient use of materials.

As 3D printing continues to evolve, it is poised to disrupt traditional manufacturing paradigms, ushering in an era of on-demand, customized production (Gallazzini, 2020). The technology's impact extends beyond individual industries, influencing supply chains, business models, and even societal norms (Fernandez & Aman, 2018). The dynamic growth and transformative potential of 3D printing underscore its status as a key driver of innovation in the manufacturing landscape, with implications that extend far beyond its current applications.

4.5 Blockchain

By 2022, global investment in blockchain solutions is expected to surpass $11.7 billion. The commercial demand for blockchain technology is projected to generate $20 billion in revenue by 2024. Active blockchain wallets reached 47.14 million in the first quarter of 2020 (Petrov, 2020). The technology is set to reduce infrastructure costs for banks by 30% and could save financial services companies up to $12 billion annually. The incorporation of blockchain into health care is forecasted to accelerate to $5.61 billion by 2025. Additionally, 55% of healthcare systems are expected to implement blockchain for commercial use by 2025, and 60% of chief information officers (CIOs) plan to integrate Block chain into their networks by the end of 2020. Blockchain is predicted to save banks' infrastructure expenses by 30%. Blockchain can save financial services firms up to $12 billion annually. By 2025, net funding for implementing blockchain technology in the healthcare industry is expected to reach $5.61 billion. Fifteen percent of all bitcoins in the world are owned by the FBI. By 2025, blockchain technology will be commercially implemented in 55% of healthcare systems. By the end of 2020, 60% of CIOs want to incorporate blockchain technology into their networks (Petrov, 2020).

5. RESULTS

Disruptive technologies have had a big impact on marketing and accounting, among other corporate operations. Over the past few decades, disruptive technology has ingrained itself into our daily lives, changing the way we interact and live (fwpr.com, 2020). Examples of these breakthroughs include the internet and cell phones.

We have analyzed Accounts Functions and Human Resources.

5.1 Accounts Function

Disruptive breakthroughs such as AI, blockchain, smart contracts, robotic process automation (RPA), and advanced analytics have completely changed the accounting industry and opened the door to new business models (DiGregorio, 2009). Accounting teams have benefited greatly from the automation of manual accounting tasks, and it is anticipated that AI-based solutions will further automate tasks in areas like treasury, management information system (MIS), tax planning, vendor payments, payroll, billing, banking, and audits (floqast.com, 2020). Furthermore, technology facilitates better decision-making, allowing companies to minimize back-end administrative work and concentrate on strategic initiatives (accountancyage.com, 2020).

The accounting industry is rapidly evolving as a result of emerging technologies like big data, business intelligence, research, and the IoT spreading across numerous business sectors. Automation has grown to be a major component of accounting services, enabling improved viewpoints, thorough research, and more fruitful collaborations (accountingdepartment.com, 2020).

The next wave of disruptive breakthroughs is being paved by the merging of present technology. Businesses can automate procedures, streamline operations, increase worker productivity, and strengthen customer loyalty by combining RPA with AI, machine learning, and cloud services (fwpr.com, 2020). Reducing costs by 25%–50%, RPA can work error-free around the clock and is more affordable than hiring people. The technology is revolutionary for company operations because it provides a specified, repeatable, and rule-based process execution without deviations (Peterson & George, 2020).

The impact of RPA and AI on businesses is expected to be substantial, but the trend is still in its early stages. Service providers are responding to the changing landscape by integrating RPA and AI functions. The automation of processes leads to improved data collection, predictive analytics, and streamlined operations, enhancing business performance (Fernandez & Aman, 2005). The anticipated impact of RPA and AI on businesses is poised to be nothing short of transformative, yet the full extent of this paradigm shift is still unfolding in its early stages. Across industries, service providers are proactively adapting to this evolving landscape by integrating RPA and AI functions into their operations.

One of the key advantages of RPA lies in the automation of routine and rule-based processes, which not only reduces manual effort but also ensures accuracy and efficiency. AI, on the other hand, brings a layer of intelligence to automation, enabling systems to learn and adapt to complex scenarios. Together, RPA and AI facilitate improved data collection, predictive analytics, and streamlined operations, all of which contribute to enhanced business performance.

The automation of processes through RPA enables businesses to free up valuable human resources from mundane tasks, allowing employees to focus on more strategic and creative aspects of their roles. This, in turn, fosters a more dynamic and innovative work environment. Moreover, the integration of AI augments this efficiency by providing the capability to analyze vast datasets, recognize patterns, and make data-driven predictions.

Fernandez and Aman (2005) highlight how this shift toward automation, driven by RPA and AI, has the potential to fundamentally reshape business processes. The improved speed and accuracy of tasks, combined with the ability to extract actionable insights from data, contribute to more informed decision-making (Srivastav, 2023). Predictive analytics powered by AI allows businesses to anticipate trends, identify opportunities, and mitigate risks in real-time, fostering a proactive rather than reactive approach to business operations.

The combination of RPA and AI is not merely a technological evolution but a strategic imperative for businesses looking to stay competitive in the digital era (Desjardins, 2020). As this trend matures, the synergy between human intelligence and technological capabilities is expected to unlock unprecedented efficiencies, innovation, and value creation (Dhiman et al., 2023). The ongoing integration of RPA and AI functions is not just a response to change but a proactive step toward shaping a more agile, intelligent, and responsive business landscape.

RPA complements accountants' work, offering real-time access to financial data and improving overall productivity. Key accounting functions, like accounts receivable and account credits, are significantly influenced by the automated data entry process, but accountants still play critical roles in paperwork control (SPANICCIATI, 2020).

Overall, disruptive innovations in various functions, including accounting, are reshaping business models, enabling efficiency gains, and transforming industries through technology-driven advancements.

RPA offers the capability to automate various accounting processes, enabling robots to efficiently handle operational accounting, accounting, and collections. Using RPA, account reconciliations can be executed with accuracy and speed. Robots can handle accounts payable and accounts receivable, reconciling transactions with consumers and suppliers in one-way or two-way interactions (cigen.com.au, 2020).

RPA or digital operation allows for simple configuration and automation of manual tasks. RPA can perform activities such as data copying and pasting between applications, data reconciliation and cross-referencing across different systems, and high-level actions. In addition to automating checks, RPA presents significant potential for enhancing internal audits (cigen.com.au, 2020).

RPA can effectively track and monitor key risk indicators (KRIs), generate structured reports and design dashboards, and format balanced scorecards, among other activities. However, to fully harness the strengths of RPA, implementation should be approached with the same discipline and consideration as any other technical project. When used strategically, RPA becomes a valuable technology tool for internal audit, leading to cost savings and improved risk coverage for businesses (cigen.com.au, 2020).

By automating many manual labor tasks previously performed by human workers, RPA significantly lowers the threshold for increased productivity. While this presents an excellent opportunity for time and cost savings, it is essential to address various industry-specific challenges related to RPA implementation (Price Waterhouse Coopers, 2020) (Fig. 2).

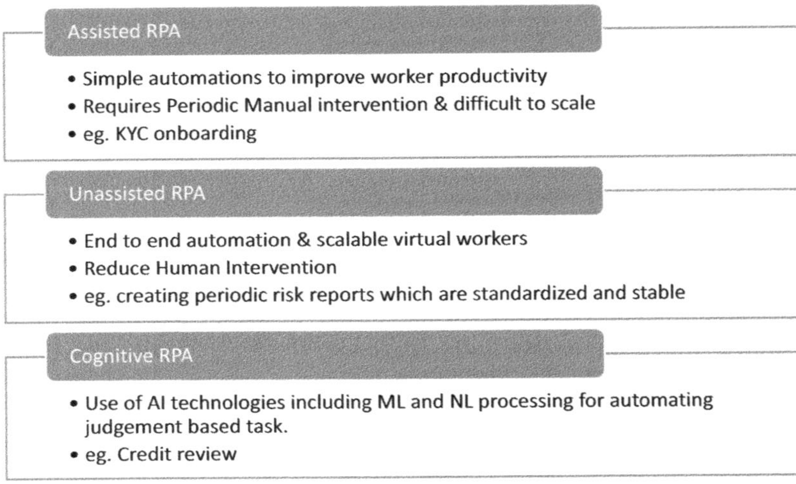

Fig. 2. Typical RPA Adoption Framework. *Source:* Author's own work.

5.1.1 Challenges in RPA Adoption

Every change is not without its difficulties; in the case of the banks' adoption of RPA, these are the main obstacles they must overcome.

The usage of RPA solutions is subject to unclear regulations. Banks are adopting RPA technology cautiously since regulators have not established any explicit rules or guidelines for its use for automation.

Unstable business processes: Banks find it challenging to use RPA solutions since many of their manual processes are not well-documented or stable.

Banks are still in the process of setting up an enterprise-wide RPA adoption strategy and governance structure, as the majority of the early RPA adoption occurred in silos.

Since RPA technologies are still developing, they are changing quickly.

5.2 Human Resources (HR)

Human Resources has witnessed significant advancements with the integration of AI in day-to-day operations across various industries. AI's ability to analyze vast amounts of data and leverage machine learning for improved decision-making has resulted in numerous applications for HR. These applications range from enhancing worker engagement and eliminating unconscious biases to improving employee health care and streamlining recruitment processes (hrtechnologist.com, 2020).

Predictive analytics is one of the latest breakthroughs in HR technology, enabling HR teams to leverage big data to identify potential candidates, even those who may not be actively seeking employment. This technology has revolutionized HR practices and empowered businesses with reliable and timely analysis (randstad.ca, 2020).

As AI and disruptive technologies continue to reshape various business functions, businesses must be prepared to adapt to the rapid changes in customer support, product development, and delivery (Sandström et al., 2009). AI can be described as computerized systems that collect data and use it to activate intelligent beings in the best possible way (Sabharwal et al., 2022). In the realm of HR, digital technology is transforming company structures and employee adaptations. New approaches to organizing work and learning through technology are also emerging, while social implications, such as technical unemployment, are being addressed. The innovations will also impact the purpose, work, and effectiveness of HR functions themselves (disruptive.asia, 2020).

RPA has proved to be an effective automation solution for reducing costs and improving processes (fwpr.com, 2020). The technology allows for greater quality control, monitoring, versatility, and workflow options. As RPA is cost-effective and has nonfinancial benefits like error reduction, it has become widely adopted across various industries (fwpr.com, 2020) (Fig. 3).

Disruptive technology is not just innovative; it challenges established performance norms and brings about major changes. By automating repetitive operations, firms that adopt digital transformations and technologies such as RPA gain increased productivity and reliability (fwpr.com, 2020). While big businesses frequently find it difficult to adapt to disruptive innovations, mid-sized businesses are better positioned to use these technologies. Christensen emphasizes the necessity for radical change and technical capabilities for sustainable success in his visionary views on creativity and technical business (Christensen, 2013). These views have the potential to be transformative.

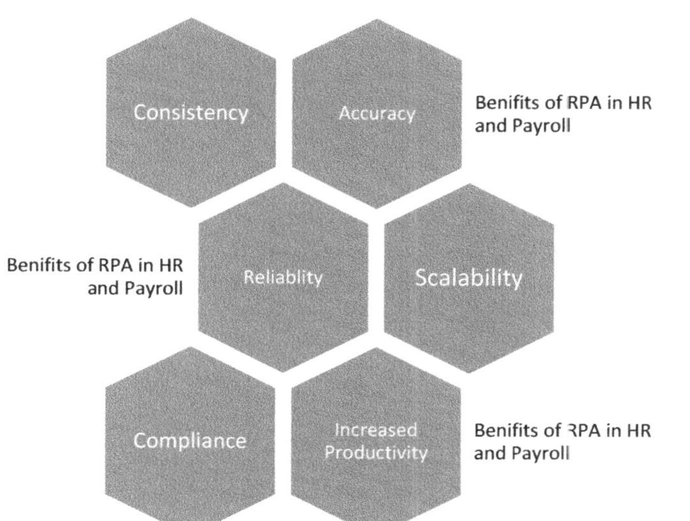

Fig. 3. Benefits of RPA in HR and Payroll. *Source:* Author's own work.

At any point during the hiring process, many HR professionals lack the technology necessary to find, contact, identify, and engage with possible applicants. It also provides quantifiable and tracked performance metrics, target descriptions, feedback gathering, and engagement surveys. When new technologies are developed to replace their current technologies, this reliance causes them to become disruptive. One of the newest innovations in HR technology is predictive analytical methods – revolutionary technology at work. The volume of big data that businesses are dealing with has increased the demand for accurate, quick analysis. These days, HR departments use analytics to search social media and online data findings.

5.3 Some Negative Impact of Disruptive Innovation

While disruptive innovations hold immense potential for transforming industries and driving progress, they are not without their share of negative aspects. One prominent concern revolves around the potential for significant job displacement. As automation and AI technologies advance, certain job roles may become obsolete, leading to unemployment and the need for reskilling in the workforce. This shift can exacerbate economic inequalities and pose challenges for individuals in traditional job sectors.

Ethical concerns also loom large in the realm of disruptive technologies. For instance, the rapid advancement of AI raises questions about privacy, data security, and the ethical use of algorithms. Issues such as biased decision-making, discrimination, and the unintended consequences of algorithmic systems pose serious ethical challenges that demand careful consideration and regulation. Striking a balance between technological advancement and ethical considerations is crucial to ensure that disruptive innovations contribute positively to society without compromising fundamental values and principles. Addressing these negative aspects is pivotal for achieving a more equitable and sustainable integration of disruptive technologies into our evolving socioeconomic landscape.

6. DISCUSSION

Disruptive technology is a persistent force in the modern economy that goes beyond simple innovation and improves upon current processes. Disruptions are now inevitable, consistently exceeding and extending the bounds of accepted performance criteria. Significant changes are about to reshape the landscape; therefore, it will be necessary to have a transformative mentality and be open to trying new things.

It takes trial and error to achieve transformation, especially when developing a creative attitude. It's interesting to note that, in contrast to their colleagues in larger organizations, proprietors of mid-sized businesses are better positioned to adopt disruptive technologies. An important turning point in this history has been made possible by the introduction of RPA, which has made it easier to automate repetitive processes. The main goal of RPA is to replace the labor-intensive, prone-to-error parts of physical labor with the efficiency and dependability of virtual automation technology.

Christensen's perspectives on creative and technical business were truly visionary. He emphasized that successful companies thrived by adapting to customer needs and consistently investing in technological advancements and innovations. Concurrently, major corporations grappled with the same goal, making considerable efforts to respond to their customers and persuade them. In contrast to the traditional business school model, which advocated doing everything possible to please consumers, Christensen's insights were groundbreaking and forward-thinking.

It has recognized that companies required distinct technical capabilities for radical change. While existing companies demonstrated sensitivity, aggressiveness, and creativity in terms of sustainable technology and developments, they often hesitated to embrace radical changes as per Christensen's model. This reluctance stemmed from a declining perception of the need for change and a certain inertia in adapting to new trends.

In reality, established companies were adept at recognizing and adopting transformative technologies when initially established. However, over time, they seemed to gradually lose their agility and responsiveness to emerging markets and evolving technologies. This reluctance to undergo necessary changes persisted and hindered their ability to keep pace with the dynamic business landscape. Christensen's insights shed light on the paradox wherein companies, despite their initial success and innovation, could struggle to maintain that momentum and adaptability over the long term.

Digitization is a catalyst for innovation as well as an engine for it. Data technology and the explosive development of new, core technologies present fresh chances to produce major advantages for consumers. Several corporations have benefited from RPAs' assistance in cutting costs through a redistribution of human capital. In addition to its nonfinancial advantages – such as improved, stable, and error-free processes – RPA technology is incredibly cost-effective. RPA is a flexible automation solution that offers numerous opportunities for workflow customization, monitoring, and quality enhancement.

The majority of businesses currently use RPA technology since it drastically reduces expenses and frees up other resources. It's an economical method that offers benefits that are not monetary, such as more precise, dependable processes that are less prone to mistakes. The majority of businesses utilize RPA to evaluate a particular application and get rid of outdated testing methods because of its restrictions. Apart from the apparent reduction in human resources, RPA will yield other advantages for the organization. On the surface, it could seem as though RPA wants to further reduce the company's expenses. Leaders will take advantage of RPA's ability to improve customer engagement and strategically strengthen their competitive standing in addition to its critical role in reducing operating expenses.

In our rapidly evolving world, technology remains in a perpetual state of reinvention. Client priorities and demands undergo constant change, necessitating enterprises to undergo dynamic transformations to remain competitive.

The corporate sector has come to a profound realization that the efficient business models of today are likely to become obsolete tomorrow. This awareness stems from the understanding that new technologies and advancements continually emerge, wielding the power to significantly reshape revenue streams.

Companies find themselves at a critical crossroads, faced with the imperative to choose between preserving their existing market positions and refining current practices or aligning themselves with emerging business models and disruptive innovations. The decision-making process involves navigating a delicate balance, as organizations weigh the risks of holding onto familiar territory against the potential rewards of embracing transformative change.

In this landscape, adaptability becomes a key factor for sustained success. Enterprises that can pivot swiftly in response to technological shifts and changing market dynamics are better poised to thrive amid uncertainty. The ability to anticipate and embrace disruptive innovations positions companies to not merely survive but to lead in an environment where staying ahead of the curve is paramount.

Moreover, recognizing the transient nature of efficient business models underscores the need for a proactive approach. Enterprises are increasingly inclined toward continuous innovation, striving not only to meet current market demands but also to anticipate and shape future trends. This forward-thinking mindset becomes a driving force, propelling organizations toward a future where they are not just responsive to change but actively shaping and defining the evolving landscape. Ultimately, the choice between preserving the status quo and embracing disruption becomes a defining factor in a company's ability to not only survive but to thrive in an ever-changing business ecosystem.

7. FUTURE RESEARCH SCOPE

In conclusion, the transformative influence of disruptive innovations on markets and business performance is a compelling narrative in the ever-evolving landscape of commerce. The relentless march of technological progress and the advent of groundbreaking innovations continually challenge established norms, reshaping industries and redefining the rules of competition. From the swift rise of disruptive technologies like 3D printing and AI to the dynamic shifts in business models exemplified by companies like Airbnb and Uber, the impact is undeniable.

Disruptive innovations force businesses to confront a choice – adapt or risk obsolescence. The ability to embrace change, foster innovation, and anticipate evolving market needs becomes a strategic imperative. The narratives of successful companies navigating these disruptions often highlight a willingness to discard conventional paradigms, experiment with new ideas, and pivot in response to emerging trends.

Moreover, the transformative influence extends beyond individual businesses to reshape entire markets. As industries adapt to disruptive innovations, consumer expectations evolve, regulatory frameworks adjust, and traditional barriers to entry are dismantled. The dynamic interplay between technological advancements and market dynamics creates an environment where agility, creativity, and adaptability are not merely desirable traits but essential for survival.

In this transformative era, companies that cultivate a forward-thinking mindset, continually reassess their strategies, and proactively engage with disruptive forces are better positioned to thrive. The journey is not without challenges – resistance to change, uncertainty, and the need for strategic foresight, all come into play. However, the stories of successful adaptation and the creation of new market leaders underscore the potential for organizations to not only weather disruptions but to leverage them as catalysts for growth, innovation, and lasting success in the ever-evolving landscape of business.

REFERENCES

Ananthakrishnan, B., Rüßmann, M., Schmieg, F., & Andersen, P. (2020). Technology and advanced analytics are revolutionising services – And creating new sources of value for industrial companies that know how to use them. Here's a road map that works. https://www.mckinsey.com/business-functions/mckinsey-digital

Anshari, M., Almunawar, M. N., Masri, M., & Hamdan, M. (2019). Financial technology and disruptive innovation. In *Association of Southeast Asian Nations*. IGI Global. https://doi.org/10.4018/978-1-5225-7793-5

Assink, M., van der Put, C. E., Hoeve, M., de Jong, N. M., Stams, G. J. J. M., & Oort, F. J. (2006). Risk factors for persistent delinquent behavior among juveniles: A meta-analytic review. *Clinical Psychology Review*, *26*(3), 322–340.

Bower, J., & Christensen, C. M. (2022). Disruptive technologies: Catching the wave. *Harvard Business Review*, 75–76.

Castellano, F. (2020). Commercial drones are revolutionizing business operations. toptal.com. https://www.toptal.com/finance/market-research-analysts/drone-market

Christensen, C. M. (2013). *The Innovator's Dilemma: When New Technologies Cause Great Firms to Fail*. Harvard Business Review Press.

Christensen, C. M., Baumann, H., Ruggles, R., & Sadtler, T. M. (2006). Disruptive innovation for social change. *Harvard Business Review*, *84*(12), 94–101.

Desjardins, J. (2020). The hyperloop: Disrupting the transportation industry. Visual Capitalist. https://www.visualcapitalist.com/hyperloop-disruptingtransportation-industry/

Dhiman, R., Srivastava, V., Srivastava, A., Rajni, & Uppal, A. (2023). How to plan and write for systematic literature review papers in management domain. In S. Rana, J. Singh, & S. Kathuria (Eds.), *Advancing methodologies of conducting literature review in management domain. Review of management literature* (Vol. 2, pp. 37–55). Emerald Publishing Limited. https://doi.org/10.1108/S2754-586520230000002003

DiGregorio, B. E. (2009). Biobased performance bioplastic: Mirel. *Chemistry and Biology*, *16*, 1–2. PubMed: 19171300. https://doi.org/10.1016/j.chembiol.2009.01.001

Dinh, T. N., & Thai, M. T. (2018). AI and blockchain: A disruptive integration. *Computer*, *51*, 48–53. https://doi.org/10.1109/MC.2018.3620971

Eun, A. & P. (2018). Business strategies of Korean TV player in the age of over top video service. *International Journals of Communication*, *12*(4), 567–589.

Fernandez, R. A., & Aman, J. (2005). Trends in global marketing and implications for business strategies. *Journal of Marketing Trends*, *42*(1), 45–59.

Fernandez, D., & Aman, A. (2018). Impacts of robotic process automation on global accounting services. *Asian Journal of Accounting and Governance*, *9*, 123–132. https://doi.org/10.17576/AJAG-2018-09-11

Francke, E., Smith, J., & Johnson, L. (2014). Disruptive innovation: Imperatives for business. *Management Dynamics*, *23*(3), 233–245.

Gallazzini, C. M. (2020) Science – Technology – Innovation: Closing the gender gap to meet the SDGs. https://www.empowerwomen.org/en/community/discussions/2017/04/science–technology–innovation–closing-thegender-gap-to-meet-the-sdgs

Global Banking & Finance Review: Banking: Finance. (2023, September 27). *Finance. Technology*. https://www.globalbankingandfinance.com/

Guttentag, D. (2015). Airbnb: Disruptive innovation and the rise of an informal tourism accommodation sector. *Current Issues in Tourism*, *18*, 1192–1217. https://doi.org/10.1080/13683500.2013.827159

Haddaway, N. R., Page, M. J., Pritchard, C. C., & McGuinness, L. A. (2022). PRISMA2020: An R package and Shiny app for producing PRISMA 2020-compliant flow diagrams, with interactivity for optimised digital transparency and Open Synthesis Campbell. *Systematic Reviews*, *18*(e1230). https://doi.org/10.1002/cl2.1230

Hahn, F., Jensen, S., & Tanev, S. (2014). Disruptive innovation vs disruptive technology: The disruptive potential of the value propositions of 3D printing technology start-ups. *Technology Innovation Management Review*, *4*, 27–36. [Review]. https://doi.org/10.22215/timreview/855

Joshi, K. (2018). Sustainable business strategies in a global economy. *Journal of Sustainable Business Practices*, *15*(4), 233–249.

Kale, G., Kijchavengkul, T., Auras, R., Rubino, M., Selke, S. E., & Singh, S. P. (2007). Compostability of bioplastic packaging materials: An overview. *Macromolecular Bioscience*, *7*, 255–277. PubMed: 17370278. https://doi.org/10.1002/mabi.200600168

Kaurav, R. P. S., Baber, R., & Rajput, S. (2020). Technology-driven tourism and hospitality industry as a tool for economic development: A bibliometric analysis. In *The Emerald handbook of ICT in tourism and hospitality* (pp. 469–486). Emerald Publishing Limited.

Kaurav, R. P. S., & Gupta, P. (2022). Trends in multidiscipline management research: Past, present and future of FIIB business review. *FIIB Business Review*, *11*, 382–404. https://doi.org/10.1177/23197145221136966

Krotov, V., & Junglas, I. (2008). RFID as disruptive innovation. *Journal of Theoretical and Applied Electronic Commerce Research*, *3*, 44–59. https://doi.org/10.4067/S0718-18762008000100005

Lee, I. (2017). An exploratory study of the impact of the Internet of Things (IoT) on business model innovation: Building smart enterprises at Fortune 500 companies. *Internet of Things*, 423–440.

Lucas, H. C., & Goh, J. M. (2009). Disruptive technology: How Kodak missed the digital photography revolution. *Journal of Strategic Information Systems*, *18*, 46–55. https://doi.org/10.1016/j.jsis.2009.01.002

Markides, C. (2006). Disruptive innovation: In need of better theory. *Journal of Product Innovation Management*, *23*, 19–25. https://doi.org/10.1111/j.1540-5885.2005.00177.x

Miltgen, C. L., Popovič, A., & Oliveira, T. (2013). Determinants of end-user acceptance of biometrics: Integrating the Big 3 of technology acceptance and privacy context. *Decision Support Systems*, *56*, 103–114. https://doi.org/10.1016/j.dss.2013.05.010

Mookerjee, J, & Rao, O. R. S. (2021). A review of the impact of disruptive innovations on markets and business performance of players. *International Journal of Grid and Distributed Computing*, *14*, 605–630.

Mordor. (2020). Intelligence. *3D printing market growth, trends, and forecasts (2020–5)*. Mordor Intelligence. https://www.mordorintelligence.com/industry-reports/3d-printing-market

Moreau, F. (2013). The disruptive nature of digitization: The case of the recorded music industry. *International Journal of Arts Management*, 18–31.

Morrish, J., Smith, A., & Johnson, L. (2020). *Global IoT Forecast Insight Report 2020*. Transform insights. https://transformainsights.com/research/reports/global-iot-forecast-insightreport-2020

Nunno, R., & Warner, C. (2020). Fact sheet: High speed rail development worldwide. eesi.org. https://www.eesi.org/papers/view/fact-sheet-high-speed-raildevelopment-worldwide

Paap, J., & Katz, R. (2004). Anticipating disruptive innovation. *Research-Technology Management*, *47*, 13–22. https://doi.org/10.1080/08956308.2004.11671647

Page, M. J., McKenzie, J. E., Bossuyt, P. M., Boutron, I., Hoffmann, T. C., Mulrow, C. D., Moher, D., Tetzlaff, J., Akl, E. A., Brennan, S. E., Chou, R., Glanville, J., Grimshaw, J. M., Hróbjartsson, A., Lalu, M. M., Loder, E. W., Mayo-Wilson, E., McDonald, S., McGuinness, L. A., ... & Thomas, J. (2021). The PRISMA 2020 statement: An updated guideline for reporting systematic reviews. *BMJ*, *372*, n71. https://doi.org/10.1136/bmj.n71

Pandya, V. M., Shukla, A. K., & Mehta, M. M. (2019). Digital transformation in the manufacturing sector: Key challenges and solutions. *International Journal of Production Research*, *57*(15–16), 4903–4916.

Peterson, J. L., & George, K. M. (2020). Advances in AI and their impact on business models. *AI & Society*, *35*(2), 307–319.

Petrov, A. (2020). Cybersecurity trends in 2020: What to expect. *Journal of Information Security*, *9*(2), 78–92.

Petrovic, D., Jovanovic, M., & Markovic, S. (2017). The role of big data in modern business environments. *Journal of Business Analytics*, *23*(4), 385–401.

Price Waterhouse Coopers. (2020). The future of work: Reshaping business and society. https://www.pwc.com

Psotka, J. (2013). Educational games and virtual reality as diruptive technology. *Journal of Education Technology & Society*, 69–80.

Rammal, H. G. (2023). Systematic literature reviews: Steps and practical tips. In S. Rana, J. Singh, & S. Kathuria (Eds.), *Advancing methodologies of conducting literature review in management domain. Review of management literature* (Vol. 2, pp. 27–35). Emerald Publishing Limited. https://doi.org/10.1108/S2754-586520230000002002

Rao, O. R. S. (2022). *Transformative technologies: Opportunities and risks* (pp. 101–106). Tech Innovate Press.

Reardeon, T. (2019). Rapid transformation of food system in develiping regions: Highlighting the rile of agriculture research and innovation. *Agricultural Systems*, 47–59.

Richter, M. (2013). Business model innovation for sustainable energy: German utilities and renewable energy. *Energy Policy*, *62*, 1226–1237. https://doi.org/10.1016/j.enpol.2013.05.038

Rosenbloom, R. S., & Christensen, C. M. (1994). echnological discontinuities, organisational capabilities, and strategic commitments. *Industrial and Corporate Change*, *3*, 655–685. https://doi.org/10.1093/icc/3.3.655

Sabharwal, D., Kabha, R., & Srivastava, K. (2023). Artificial Intelligence (AI)-powered virtual assistants and their effect on human productivity and laziness: Study on students of Delhi-NCR (India) & Fujairah (UAE). *Journal of Content, Community & Communication*, *17*, 162–174. https://doi.org/10.31620/JCCC.06.23/12

Sabharwal, D., Verma, M., & Sood, R. (2022). Studying the relationship between artificial intelligence and digital advertising in marketing strategy. *Journal of Content, Community & Communication*, *16*, 118–126. https://doi.org/10.31620/JCCC.12.22/10

Sandström, C., Magnusson, M., & Jörnmark, J. (2009). Exploring factors influencing incumbents' response to disruptive innovation. *Creativity and Innovation Management*, *18*, 8–15. https://doi.org/10.1111/j.1467-8691.2009.00507.x

Schmidt, G. M., & Druehl, C. T. (2008). When is a disruptive innovation disruptive? *Journal of Product Innovation Management*, *25*(4), 347–369.

Spanicciati, M. (2020). Emerging technologies and their implications for business strategy. *Technology Innovation Management Review*, *10*(5), 15–25.

Srivastav, R. (2023). The impact of remote work on organizational culture. *Journal of Organizational Behavior*, *44*(1), 102–118.

Streaming media. (2020). *OTT TV & video revenues reached $83bn in 2019*. streamingmedia.com. https://www.streamingmedia.com

Tan, A., Ashrafian, H., Scott, A. J., Mason, S. E., Harling, L., Athanasiou, T., & Darzi, A. (2016). Robotic surgery: Disruptive innovation or unfulfilled promise? A systematic review and meta-analysis of the first 30 years. *Surgical Endoscopy*, *30*, 4330–4352. PubMed: 26895896. https://doi.org/10.1007/s00464-016-4752-x

Trojan, J., Johnson, T. R., Rudin, S. D., Ilan, J., Tykocinski, M. L., & Ilan, J. (1993). Treatment and prevention of rat glioblastoma by immunogenic C6 cells expressing antisense insulin-like growth factor I RNA. *Science*, *259*, 94–97. PubMed: 8418502. https://doi.org/10.1126/science.8418502

Women, U. N. (2015). Financing: Why it matters for women and girls. unwomen.org. https://www.unwomen.org/en/news/in-focus/financing-for-gender-equality

Yeh, Y. H., & Walter, R. J. (2017). The influence of social media on consumer behavior. *Journal of Consumer Marketing*, *34*(3), 239–248.

Yu, D., & Hang, C. C. (2010). A reflective review of disruptive innovation theory. *International Journal of Management Reviews*, *12*, 435–452. https://doi.org/10.1111/j.1468-2370.2009.00272.x

A LITERATURE SURVEY OF TECHNOLOGICAL DISRUPTIONS IN THE SERVICE SECTOR

Sheereen Fauzel, Verena Tandrayen-Ragoobur and Shashi Jeevita Matadeen

University of Mauritius, Mauritius

ABSTRACT

The service sector has witnessed an important transformation due to technological disruption. The widespread adoption of digital technologies has enabled service providers to automate various tasks and processes. Blockchain technology, for instance, has transformed payments, remittances, and financial transactions in the financial services sector by providing greater transparency and security. The travel and hospitality industry has also seen changes through online booking platforms, review aggregators, and AI-driven recommendations. Other activities like entertainment, education, logistics, and transportation as well as retail have been disrupted by technologies leading to increased accessibility and efficiency and shaping the service economy into a customer-centric business model. This literature survey reviews the technological disruption in the services sector, including the health, education, financial, transport, tourism, and communications sectors. Across the subsectors reviewed, an average of 30 articles were reviewed and analyzed during the period 2000–2023.

Keywords: Technological disruptions; digital technologies; services sector; systematic literature review; process automation

1. INTRODUCTION

In today's world, the concept of "disruption" is becoming very important. The pioneering work of Christensen (1997) highlights how disruptive innovation and thereby disruptive technology can capture a whole industry. New entrants

Review of Technologies and Disruptive Business Strategies
Review of Management Literature, Volume 3, 185–202

Published under exclusive licence by Emerald Publishing Limited
ISSN: 2754-5865/doi:10.1108/S2754-586520240000003010

exploring a niche market may launch a product or service which initially has low performance on the market but later takes over the traditional mainstream market and becomes the dominant firm or the most competitive one. Emerging artificial intelligence (AI) is a form of disruptive innovation. In essence, existing firms need to constantly innovate and learn as well as adopt new technologies to stay in business.

There is an overwhelming degree of innovation in the services sector. In the realm of the financial services sector in particular, robotics, blockchain, and AI have played a vital role in expanding the industry. Customers as well are very enthusiastic about AI, robotics, and blockchain, though they do show some concerns over the risks inherent in disruptive digital technologies (Reynolds et al., 2019)[1]. Even the hospitality industry is becoming highly digitalized. There are now contactless solutions, such as mobile check-in, self-service kiosks, and smart room functionality. If these innovations are not adopted, hoteliers run the risk of losing a significant market share. In the transport industry, the Internet of Things (IoT), AI, and drones which have changed the way this sector is managed, hence paving the way for new services and business models. Communication technologies have also evolved and have become highly digitalized. This sector plays an important role in national security and welfare. This industry has transitioned from wired telephony to wireless services in the technological area (Zhohov & Sharma, 2022). Technology-driven disruption in the healthcare industry cannot be ignored. There are new medical applications used which are influenced by algorithm-based AI systems which is changing the way medical services are provided (Corrales et al., 2020). If these new methods are not adopted, the traditional medical facilities may go out of business. Similarly, within the education sector, the adoption of online learning platforms, AI-guided learning as well as collaborative platforms centered on chat interfaces and the integration of virtual and augmented reality have transformed the way knowledge and skills are passed on to students.

The concept of disruptive technologies in the services sector is explored in the chapter. Section 2 analyses the existing theoretical and empirical literature on disruptive technology. The next section reviews the concept of disruptive innovation relevant to the theory of disruptive technologies, followed by the review of empirical studies undertaken on technology disruption in key services sectors. Section 4 concludes with relevant policy recommendations, while the last section sets out the possibilities of future research on technological disruptions in the services sector.

2. LITERATURE REVIEW

2.1 Theory of Disruptive Technology

The pioneering theory of disruptive innovation can be applied to most technology-related industries (Christensen, 1997). The theory explains the reason behind the failure of dominant firms in the hard drive industry as a result of new entrants. The concept was primarily referred to as the disruptive technology which points toward the kind of technology which is inferior compared to the mainstream technology valued by consumers, but at the same time focuses on some neglected attributes in technology. With time, the new technologies can overcome the one used by the dominant firms in specific markets. More so, the disruptive technology may not be the best one. In fact, the new technology is generated through a process of social, economic, and political negotiations and selections. Firms adopting these technologies will not only ensure their survival, but also their growth in the future. On the other hand, firms failing to adopt these emerging technologies will have a high probability of failure (Nair & Ahlstrom, 2003).

The disruptive innovation concept can be explained via different perspectives. At least four perspectives are discussed in the literature and are outlined below (Fig. 1).

From the disruptive business model innovation perspective (Gilbert & Bower, 2002; Markides, 2006), disruptive innovation implies the implementation of new and unconventional business models which depart from traditional methods normally adopted by industry leaders. It is different from the well-established business models, and this new model is said to disrupt the existing ones and redefines the meaning of value creation. Within the first perspective, disruptive technology innovation relates to the introduction of new technologies that change and restructure existing markets. It encompasses the development of new

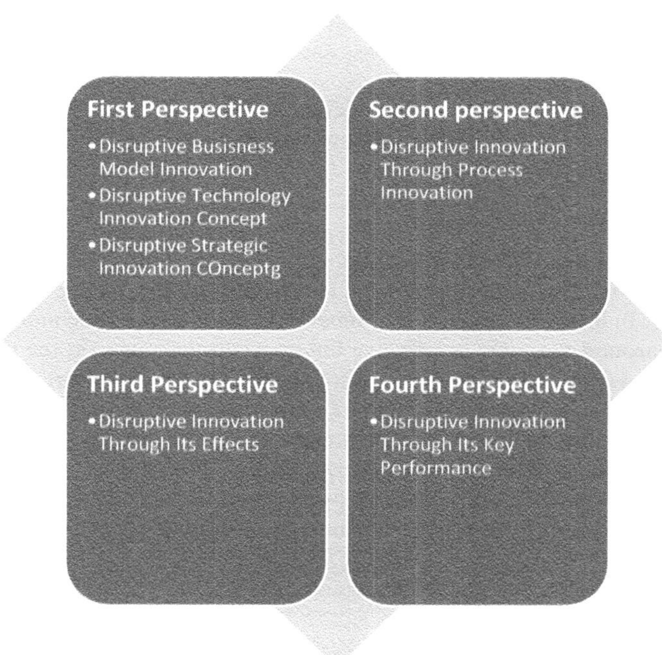

Fig. 1. Definition of Disruptive Innovation. *Source:* Authors' compilation.

technologies, which arise in niche markets but gradually expands to other sectors. These technologies are often simple, accessible, and cost-effective (Christensen, 1997; Danneels, 2004). Disruptive strategic innovation in turn includes new and original approaches to business strategies and processes, and these bring about an important shift in the competitive dynamics.

The next element in the model of disruptive innovation focusses on process innovation. It is a gradual process that is, for instance, transform the methods via which commodities are produced, delivered, and managed, instead of an outcome (Ansari et al., 2016; Christensen & Raynor, 2003; Schmidt & Druel, 2008). It involves the introduction of new and efficient ways of business operations and brings about a significant transformation in the industry. If a new process has faults, then it is not classified as a disruptive innovation. The innovative process, product, or service is initially inferior and neglected by the mainstream customers. However, when these processes, products, and services are launched by new firms and developed further, they are valued by customers. New groups of customers are attracted to the innovation and gradually take over a significant market share and may even become more competitive in the market and rule the industry (Guttentag & Smith, 2017).

The third perspective relates to the effects of disruptive innovation. It disrupts the performance path of the established firms. The disruptive innovation is used by some new entrants which provide lower cost of goods and services, introduce new designs and business models, and reshape the industry. In fact, these innovations are disruptive as these challenge the existing well established business models (Wan et al., 2015). The disruptive innovation also brings considerable improvement in the product, service, and process, along with new ideas or behavior (Kostoff et al., 2004).

Finally, disruptive technology is viewed in terms of its key characteristics (Christensen et al., 2015). Table 1 shows the key elements of disruptive technology as identified by scholars.

2.1.1 Disruptive Innovation and Technology

The concept of disruptive technology forms part of the theory of disruptive innovation. In line with the broader framework, the disruptive technology theory builds up around the same perspective but concentrates more on the technological aspect. As per the disruptive technology theory, the new firm introduces a superior technological aspect in the market, product, service, or process, and this action causes a disruption to the mainstream market. Normally, the technology change will initially generate a lower performance and address a niche market or a neglected part of the market. Eventually, this new technology will take over the existing market and become the leading and dominant technology (HRDQ, 2022).

Table 1. Key Elements of Disruptive Technology in the Literature.

Christensen et al. (2000)	Engaging customers to ensure long run commitment. Lower gains/profits. Divert from traditional pathways followed by mainstream customers. Introduce new pathways for performance and improved performance.
Christensen and Raynor (2003)	Disruptive business model which does not encourage existing firms to retaliate. Allow new business model to flourish and grow without threats.
Govindarajan and Kopalle (2006b)	New product, service, or process valued by new customers. Inferior performance which are valued by mainstream customers. Offering lower prices. Entering a niche market.
King and Baatartogtokh (2015)	Existing firms are improving as they are on the sustaining innovation pathways. Existing firms deal with disruptive threats. Existing firms over reach consumers' needs.
Husig, Hipp, and Dowling (2005)	Cheap and simple products. Initially low performing products, services, and processes eventually improve rapidly. Low profits. Emerging market success.
Nagy et al. (2016)	Alter performance metrics and shift customer expectations. New functions in the markets. Divert from established standards. New forms of ownership.

Source: Authors' compilation.

2.1.2 Disruptive Versus Sustaining Technology

While both disruptive and sustaining technology represent two different business models, they also interact with each other. Sustaining technology refers to situations where some firms innovate and improve faster than mass customers' demand. As a result, the products or services supplied end up being too sophisticated and expensive which ultimately represent a small market. Sustaining technology at the top end of the market can help in boosting profits. However, firms are providing for a smaller market and ignore mass customers' demand. In the quest of sustaining innovation and technology, disruptive innovation and technology enters the market, but at the lower end, whereby a niche market is targeted and profit margin is initially low. The disruptive innovators do not launch a new product or service but rather emerge with low prices and target a market which has been neglected by the mainstream producers.

Finally, it can be deduced that the disruptive innovation concept has made products and services more affordable and convenient for customers across many different sectors (Frizzo et al., 2020). Hwang and Christensen (2008) argued that this theory helps explain how complicated, expensive products and services become simple and affordable to customers.

2.2 Methodology

The literature review provides a foundation of existing knowledge, discusses important research gaps, and reviews new contributions. Various approaches are used to conduct a literature review (Rana et al., 2022). They range from systematic literature review (Dhiman et al., 2023; Rammal, 2023), critical literature review, content analysis, bibliometric review (Kaushal et al., 2023; Sahni & Kaurav, 2023), scoping review, meta-analysis, meta synthesis, framework-based literature review to umbrella review, to name a few.

This literature review followed a structured process. We conducted a comprehensive exploration across different databases. The initial screening phase involved a thorough search across PubMed, IEEE Xplore, and Google Scholar. Distinct inclusion and exclusion criteria were adopted for selection of papers. Papers which were peer-reviewed, or included systematic reviews and meta-analyses and papers adopting a multidisciplinary approach, were taken into consideration. In addition, we limited our search to articles published from 2000 to 2023. The exclusion criteria were strictly applied. Papers published outside the time range and not peer-reviewed as well as working papers and those papers not directly addressing the nexus of technological disruptions within the services sector or its subsectors were excluded. Conference proceedings, editorials, and opinion pieces were also excluded.

Across the different subsectors, an average of 30 articles were reviewed and analyzed. Specific keywords were used like "technological disruptions", the "services sector", along with subsector identifiers such as "tourism," "health," "education," "financial services," "communication," and "transport". The diverse subsectors, including health, tourism, financial services, education, transport, and communication, were systematically explored. The aim of adopting this particular method is to ensure a right balance between depth and breadth which enables a holistic analysis of each subsector and the evolution of technological disruptions over the last years. The approach ensures a better analysis of the dynamic evolution of technological disruptions.

This method ensured a thorough examination of the existing literature, facilitating a nuanced understanding of how technological disruptions manifest and impact various domains within the services sector. The aggregated findings contribute to a comprehensive overview of the state of knowledge on technological disruptions across diverse industries, shedding light on the multifaceted implications for each subsector.

3. REVIEW OF SUBSECTORS

Disruptive technologies encompass new technologies replacing existing ones (Buhalis et al., 2019; Rodriguez, 2016). The application of Robotics, AI, and IoT, biotechnology and nanotechnology are the most regular forms of disruptive technologies that drive business activities across varied sectors (Gupta & Saxena, 2012). Disruptive technologies in the services industry take the form of cloud computing, automation, and AI-driven solutions that have streamlined operations, induced efficiency, increased productivity, enhanced the quality of services and improved customer experiences (Manyika, 2017; Schwab, 2016). Technological disruptions have reshaped business models, customer interactions, and the competitive landscape.

3.1 Health Sector

The health sector has often been viewed as not responding to the changing environment and often failing to offer the appropriate services, especially in developing countries, which have inadequate infrastructure, constrained funding, and skills scarcity. On the demand side, asymmetric access to healthcare services and high medical cost further limit the efficiency of the healthcare system (Mwaza et al., 2022). With the COVID-19 pandemic, digital technologies have been brought to the forefront due to health restrictive measures like lockdowns and social distancing. There has been a heavy reliance on medical services, diagnosis, treatments, and advice through the internet (Kumar & Pumera, 2021). The rapid and extensive use of digital technologies during the health crisis has disrupted the traditional healthcare systems across many countries, and the whole health ecosystem has to adapt to this changing environment. The adoption of technologies is viewed as the most appropriate and cost-effective strategy which safeguards the lives and well-being of the population in the midst of crisis (Konstantinidis et al., 2021). Mishra and Sharma (2022) adopt a digital transformation evaluation model to evaluate telehealth and traditional care providers via three pillars namely convergence, maturity, and adoption, and their findings show improvements in telehealth providers.

Existing scholarly literature linking technological disruptions and the health system can be organized across five main axes namely: the different types and combination of digitized technologies adopted, second the benefits of digital technology in the health ecosystem, third the challenges encountered by new technologies, fourth the regulatory framework, and lastly the ethical and legal considerations of technological disruptions in the health sector. Cobianchi et al. (2022) support that digital technology in the health sector increases the overall efficiency and resilience of the sector during the COVID-19 pandemic. As per Susanto et al. (2020) and Zhang et al. (2020), technological tools like online applications, latest ICT tools among others provided the authorities with updated information and data on number of COVID-19 cases, deaths, and recoveries as well as the spread of the virus across regions. Such information was vital in containing the spread of the virus. Mustapha et al. (2021) focus both on medical care and administrative levels. They demonstrate that digital technologies improve healthcare standards measured by patient safety, patient satisfaction, and clinical effectiveness. However, the findings also indicate that the technologies can pose important challenges to patients and clinicians in terms of intellectual property, among others. Similarly, Dal Mas et al. (2023) analyze digital healthcare services enabled by digital technologies. They find that diverse digital technologies like smart health technologies and Industry 4.0 tools contribute significantly in enhancing the efficiency of day-to-day operations, facilitating the delivery of services and improving the overall performance of the healthcare sector.

On the patient side, telemedicine and other latest technologies have been very effective in distributing health care in a virtual form between the patient and the health care provider. Mosadeghi et al. (2016) further observe that virtual reality has proved to be an efficient and reliable treatment for pain management in inpatient settings. While digital technologies can be beneficial to the sector, they also present various challenges due to the complexity of their integration in the healthcare environment, a fact that the literature greatly overlooks. Studies like Sharma et al. (2021) and Talwar et al. (2020) note some of the risks associated with technological innovations such as patient privacy concerns and resistance from healthcare professionals to adopt new technologies due to concerns about job displacement of changes in workflows. Further, the complex regulatory landscape can be daunting for healthcare organizations, and this necessitates further analysis.

3.2 Education Sector

Education is an important sector in incorporating new technologies. Different models have been formulated to analyze technology acceptance and adoption in the education sector, namely Davis' (1989) model of technology acceptance, the decomposed theory of planned behavior (Taylor and Todd, 1995), and the combined model of technology acceptance. Technological disruptions are reshaping the way students learn, teachers instruct, and educational institutions operate. Some of these disruptive technologies adopted by learners and teachers range from augmented reality, the use of Big Data, mobile learning, blockchain technology, to name a few. These disruptions, driven by advancements in digital technology, have introduced both opportunities and challenges. Teachers, educational administrators, learners, parents, researchers, and policymakers need to be actively involved and support this technological innovation in the education sector (Serdyukov, 2017). Studies such as Lui et al. (2020) and Gamage and Tanwar (2018) have analyzed the acceptance and use of learning technologies among academics in the classroom, while others like Panigrahi et al. (2018) and Alghazi et al. (2020) have probed into the factors associated with students' intentions and adoption of technology. Moreover, Chang and Wills (2013) observe that e-learning services enable learning, training, and teaching at any time and in any location, hence reducing operational costs as well as logistic issues that often occur in person learning environment. They find that the use of a blended learning approach increases learners' satisfaction and performance relative to only classroom teaching approaches. Ng'ambi et al. (2016) show that the internet along with different types of new technologies improve competency-based and self-directed learning. Oke and Fernandes (2020) show that the 4th Industrial Revolution facilitates learning capabilities and experience of students and creates a dynamic workplace. However, for the education sector to benefit from such technological innovations, there is a need to improve the educational curricula as well as promote investment in the sector, especially in the African region. Other studies postulate that digital technologies have not been successful in improving the learning environment. Indeed, Ng'ambi et al. (2016) argue that mobile devices and social media have not been used in an efficient manner to transform education, and as such, teaching and learning have remained static. Another major challenge is that the design and use of educational technologies remain unregulated. Similarly, Rashid and Asghar (2017) show that although digital technologies enhance students' commitment, engagement, and self-learning, there is no evidence of a statistically significant effect on students' learning performance. While technological tools have altered the dynamics of teaching and learning over the past decades, there is inconclusive evidence on the consequences of this digital transformation on learning and teaching process, performance, and experience of students as well as teaching quality.

3.3 Tourism and Hospitality Sector

Technological disruptions play an important role in the tourism and hospitality industry. Indeed, the tourist experience has been transformed with technologies, leading to popular concepts like "smart tourism" and "smart hospitality" (Gretzel et al., 2015). The integration of technology has spread into various phases of the tourism ecosystem including travel organization, accommodation, transportation, destination management, and leisure activities. Digital transformation in the tourism and hospitality sector has led to a more connected, smooth, and personalized travel experience with emphasis on sustainable and responsible tourism practices. There is, however, scant evidence on digital transformation within the tourism and hospitality sector (Filimonau & Naumova, 2020). Recent work of Ruiz-Alba and Martín-Peña (2020) and Zhou et al. (2020) discuss the advantages of intelligent technologies in the sector through reduction in labor costs and improvement in service efficiency. These technologies range from IoT, big data analytics (Antonio et al., 2019), cloud computing, speech recognition, and facial recognition to social media (Gupta, 2019), mobile apps (Lee, 2018), virtual reality, and service robots (Liu & Hung, 2020). Recent empirical work of Ivanov et al. (2020) and Yadegaridehkordi et al. (2020) investigated the applications of digital technologies in the tourism sector, but as per Iranmanesh et al. (2023), there is a lack of a comprehensive review that provides a holistic and comprehensive overview of the transformative role of digital technologies in the tourism sector.

Within the tourism industry's management and administrative levels, the decision-making process has greatly improved as a result of technological advancement, but at very often, at the expense of jobs (Zhou et al., 2020). Leung (2019) postulates that smart systems enhance workers' efficiency and productivity, ease access to information on customer's preferences and demand, and at the same time decrease errors. For travelers, digital transformation has reduced the level of face-to-face contact and has reshaped service interactions thereby affecting customers' experiences and behaviors (Ivanov & Webster, 2019). Studies like Garrido-Moreno et al. (2020) and Kim and Chae (2018) observe that social media has a positive effect on the financial performance of hotels by reducing marketing costs, enhancing the brand reputation, and as such, influence customers' decisions. This is supported by the study of Halawani et al. (2020) whereby social media promotes customer experience by enabling better and easier communication between hotels and customers. Customer online comments are important in quality management, and hotels use these posted online reviews to improve the quality of services (Özgen & Kozak, 2015). Mobile devices characterize another form of disruptive digital technology which impacts positively on the efficiency of employees since they can undertake their work-related tasks remotely anywhere (Jeong et al., 2016). Mobile apps in particular reduce the waiting time through the provision of online check-in and check-out possibilities. They also provide in-room technology control, rapid bookings, and real-time personal services while simultaneously ensuring that the customers' needs and wants are effectively understood (Lei et al., 2019). In addition, robots and self-service technologies provide efficient service delivery (Mingotto et al., 2020), while virtual reality helps hotels enhance their service quality and provides the relevant information to consumers on the quality of service provided by hotels through virtual reality (Surovaya et al., 2020).

3.4 Financial Sector

Digital transformation has already spread its tentacles to the banking system, the insurance industry, and wealth management services. Gomber et al. (2018) argue that there are three key aspects for the current fintech revolution: technological innovation, process disruption, and services transformation. Indeed, the financial sector worldwide is not only rapidly investing in and adopting financial technology but also collaborating with fintech companies. Sibanda et al. (2020) find that UAE-domiciled banks and international banks from developed countries prefer the latter even if the most popular option remains a fintech collaboration. Nevertheless, they also find that shifting from the classical banking system is slower for low-income economies.

Subsequently, the adoption of the new technologies such as cloud computing, telematics, the IoT, blockchain, AI, predictive modeling, and robo-advisers is radically changing the insurance business model and the banking business model (Cappiello, 2020). Sibanda et al. (2020) find that the major implication of digitalization is the reduction in the number and size of the banks, as well as the number of employees. This is primarily due to the shrinking transaction volumes at physical branches and low cost of digital transactions (Liu et al., 2017). Similarly, Hodson (2021) also finds that the traditional banks in the United Kingdom and Germany are increasingly being replaced by digital or challenger banks, which offer the same services entirely online. Additionally, the adoption of financial technology within the financial services sector is reinventing the customer experience, with the physical client–bank interaction shifting toward a hybrid one, through digital technology platforms (Hodson, 2021; Sibanda et al., 2020). Interestingly, Liu et al. (2017) argue that the use of digital interfaces for banking services further increases the demand for other digital services. The insurance sector is also evolving similarly. They now offer chatbots and robo-advisors to provide an algorithm-driven service (Cappiello, 2020).

Furthermore, Big Data and AI are also being exploited via open digital inter- and intra-bank platforms (Sibanda et al., 2020). These enable the gathering of data on the clients, as well as risk profiling. Indeed, Gomber et al. (2018) illustrate how these are being used to build alternative credit scores and used to provide loans. Moreover, they also argue that technology has transformed the payment processes for consumers as we are moving toward a cashless society. Along the same vein, Sibanda et al. (2020) observed that the most disruptive impact of digital technology was on payment methods, mobile wallets, and loyalty and reward, while saving, lending, and wealth management will suffer the least disruption.

While customers, especially the younger generation, view the innovative digital channels positively, the banks are also able to reduce their transaction costs by using terminal or mobile-based channels (Wewege & Thomsett, 2020). A similar impact is detected in the insurance sector, whose efficiency is improved through cost reduction, that results from a fall in interaction time through the digitalization of the distribution channels (Cappiello, 2020; Coombs & Redman, 2018). In the insurance and wealth management sector, robo-advisors are also expected to reduce the costs and democratize access to the financial markets (Gurrea-Martínez & Wan, 2021). This also enables the companies to offer better pricing policies. Although the insurance sector has responded more slowly to the technological advancements, IsurTech is now picking up speed. Cappiello (2020) argues that Big Data analytics, IoT, and blockchain ledgers are becoming increasingly used for product design and development in the insurance sector. These technologies also ensure that the contracts are "smart", thereby enabling their execution without any human intervention (Cappiello, 2020).

3.5 Transport Sector

The transport sector has also been inevitably influenced by the recent technological revolutions. Buhalis et al. (2019) argue that in the current sharing economic era, with innovations such as Uber car renting/leasing and dockless scooters, individuals have been granted more flexibility, and the hold of the traditional transportation companies has loosened. This has drastically changed the market dynamics. Similarly, Wilson and Mason (2020) argue that the new transport services proposed (such as ride-hailing services, car- and bike-sharing services, ride-sharing/car-pooling services) along with the underlying technological platforms on which they are based are rapidly transforming the public transportation system. Consequently, new business models are now emerging. Indeed, Mobility as a Service or Transportation as a Service, which focuses on transport services provided by app-based platforms, is gaining momentum. The technology underpinning the apps is multifaceted: it can provide assistance to plan the journey, make bookings and payments, choose the travel mode, as well as save in terms of time and cost. Mouratidis et al. (2021) argue that ride-sharing and car-sharing can reduce emissions, the total distance traveled, parking space required, and congestion, if it is complementary with walking, cycling, or public transport. They also discuss the effects of evolving transportation technologies such as autonomous vehicles, drones, robots, and urban air mobility. These rely heavily on AI, sensors, and Big Data. Furthermore, they argue that automated driving could support public transport. In fact, autonomous buses could reduce operational costs (Pournader et al., 2020), alter the built environment (Fraedrich et al., 2019; Stead & Vaddadi, 2019), and relieve land previously used for parking for other purposes (Fagnant & Kockelman, 2015). While autonomous vehicles and urban air mobility are likely to encourage travel and reduce other public transport use, the other upcoming transportation technologies could possibly reduce and replace travel required to stores (Mouratidis et al., 2021). Nevertheless, the delivery drones and urban air mobility will require the introduction of air traffic, and the delivery robots will necessitate the relevant infrastructure that is adapted to them (Mouratidis et al., 2021). On another note, tele activities, which are activities that happen virtually, might also negatively influence the transportation system by lowering traveling needs (Mouratidis et al., 2021).

Additionally, blockchain technology and IoT are also reshaping transport monitoring process. In general, tracking vehicles can protect the drivers, passengers, and the vehicle itself. Indeed, tracking can allow rapid responses to unexpected events, especially if the vehicles are transporting dangerous cargoes. Interestingly, a study done by Valchanov and Aleksieva (2022) demonstrates how digital technologies can now chronologically record data captured through sensors fitted on the vehicles. These send timely signals to stakeholders if a certain threshold parameter is exceeded by the sensor. Additionally, the same system enables smart contracts to automatically release payments to suppliers once the tracking device confirms delivery to a specific destination (Pournader et al., 2020).

3.6 Communication Sector

The communications industry is no exception either: it has also been impacted by the ongoing digital disruptions. Wang et al. (2020) argue that AI technologies have the potential to solve seemingly intractable issues to optimize the fifth generation (5G) and Beyond 5G (B5G) wireless networks. They argue that adopting AI technologies in the wireless communications networks will allow the development and configuration of the network with minimum human interventions. Additionally, they believe that the system will have an improved performance, reliability, and adaptability (Wang et al., 2020). Additionally, Ferrari et al. (2021) argue that virtual network functions can be affected through the adoption of cloud virtual machines to maintain the pace with the big digital infrastructure expansion due to the development of the 5G network. On the other hand, machine learning, an aspect of AI, is also incorporated in communication systems. Wang et al. (2020) identify three benefits of machine learning: it learns from the massive historical communication data and knowledge and is able to better grasp channel and interference models; it can model nonlinear correlations while considering the increasing density of wireless access points in order to optimize the system's parameters; it enables a more proactive approach to unexpected events by adapting configurations of networks to behavioral patterns and responding quickly. While a better network is crucial for the customers, the latter are also expecting a digital customer experience. Indeed, Shrivastava (2017) points out that the customer demands real-time experiences 24/7 from the communication service providers, with interactions being seamless and effortless, stimulating, sensitive, synchronized, and smart.

4. CONCLUSION

The new wave of smart technologies is reengineering not only the product design and development but also the customer experiences, engagement, and requirements throughout the services sector. This entails the creation of smart, connected, and proactive services that have important implications on life, work, and travel. With the challenges posed by the COVID-19 pandemic, many digital services, especially in the education, financial, and communications sectors, have been propelled forward. Consequently, service management has been impacted. Buhalis et al. (2019) explain that the emerging digital platforms provided by service providers induce a "plug and play" system that ensures global accessibility. To capitalize on the recent technological innovation, government support is crucial (Sibanda et al., 2020). Incentives must be provided to companies to incorporate new digital technologies relevant to the services they provide, to remain competitive. Sibanda et al. (2020) maintain that proper telecommunications infrastructure must be put in place to ensure that digitally smart technologies have the desired impact.

While there are multiple benefits that emanate from the evolving technologies, there are also negative impacts that need to be minimized. Within the services sector, it is clear that the primary threat that accompanies technological development is the high likelihood that skill-intensive and knowledge-based jobs are at risk (Coombs & Redman, 2018). To limit the damage, there is a need to re-skill and re-educate the individuals who are most at risk (Sibanda et al., 2020). Nevertheless, when barriers to entry are high, incumbents can last longer. Sibanda et al. (2020) argue that the regulatory framework prevalent in the financial services sector is relatively burdensome, which makes the competition tough. Moreover, cybersecurity breaches are a serious threat to the service providers. Ironically, to circumvent the matter, AI and blockchain technologies will be used to specifically identify potential attacks, manage the attacks in real time, and protect sensitive customer information (Buhalis et al., 2019). Moreover, since the technologies are new and constantly evolving, it is important for rules and regulations to be formulated in a way that protects both the clients and the service providers while limiting the inherent ethical concerns (Gurrea-Martínez & Wan, 2021). However, overregulation might dampen the benefits of technological advancements.

5. SCOPE FOR FUTURE STUDIES

While most current studies have focused on the benefits of these technological disruptions on the diverse sectors, the challenges have often been ignored. Indeed, most studies have been addressing the positive impact of technological innovations in terms of efficiency, productivity, quality of service, and creation of jobs. However, technological disruptions in the services sector is a dynamic phenomenon with continuous opportunities for research. For the healthcare sector, it is crucial for more studies to probe the inherent challenges involved with the use of technology, especially in terms of the regulatory landscape and ethical considerations that need to be reformulated and readapted to cater for this evolving system. Similarly, for the education sector, there is currently a lack of studies assessing the impact of technology on the new ways in which students will need to be assessed or teachers will need to impart their knowledge and skills. On the other hand, technological disruptions in the tourism sector have major implications on the economy, especially in terms of job loss and income distribution. These need to be further explored and understood in order to ensure the ones most vulnerable to job losses in the tourism sector can survive this unstoppable transformation. Furthermore, studies assessing the regulatory challenges and policy responses with respect to data privacy, security, and consumer protection in the tourism sector need to be prioritized. Likewise, technological disruptions in the financial sector will also have serious regulatory and policy implications that will need to be reviewed. Future studies should also delve into the effects of how the new technology is reshaping financial intermediation and how it is also causing financial disintermediation. Additionally, studies assessing the impact of technological disruptions on market efficiency and volatility should also be favored in order to better understand the new mechanics of the market.

In general, there is a need to conduct in-depth impact assessments to measure the effects of technological disruptions on productivity, employment patterns, and customer experiences among other key indicators in each of the various subsectors. Existing work on the environmental implications of technological disruptions in the services sector is scant. It is important to explore sustainable practices and green technologies that can reduce the sector's carbon footprint. Exploring the long-term implications of technological disruptions on the services sector via economic, societal, environmental, and cultural changes is key and necessitates in-depth research. Future studies must provide an in-depth understanding of the evolving technological landscape and help stakeholders identify the challenges and opportunities of disruptive technologies.

REFERENCES

Al Ghazi, S. S., Wong, S. Y., Kamsin, A., Yadegaridehkordi, E., & Shuib, L. (2020). Towards sustainable mobile learning: A brief review of the factors influencing acceptance of the use of mobile phones as learning tools. *Sustainability*, *12*(24), 10527.

Ansari, S., Garud, R., & Kumaraswamy, A. (2016). The disruptor's dilemma: TiVo and the US television ecosystem. *Strategic Management Journal*, *37*(9), 1829–1853.

Antonio, N., de Almeida, A., & Nunes, L. (2019). Big data in hotel revenue management: Exploring cancellation drivers to gain insights into booking cancellation behavior. *Cornell Hospitality Quarterly*, *60*(4), 298–319.

Buhalis, D., Harwood, T., Bogicevic, V., Viglia, G., Beldona, S., & Hofacker, C. (2019). Technological disruptions in services: Lessons from tourism and hospitality. *Journal of Service Management*, *30*(4), 484–506.

Cappiello, A. (2020). The technological disruption of the insurance industry: A review. *International Journal of Business and Social Science*, *11*(1), 1–11.

Chang, V., & Wills, G. (2013). A university of Greenwich case study of cloud computing: Education as a service. In *E-logistics and E-supply chain management: Applications for evolving business* (pp. 232–253). IGI Global.

Christensen, C. M. (1997). *The innovator's dilemma: When new technologies cause great firms to fail*. Harvard Business School Press.

Christensen, C. M., Raynor, M. E., & McDonald, R. (2015). 17. Disruptive innovation. *Harvard Business Review*. *93*(12), 44–53.

Cobianchi, L., Verde, J. M., Loftus, T. J., Piccolo, D., Dal Mas, F., Mascagni, P., ... & Gallix, B. (2022). Artificial intelligence and surgery: Ethical dilemmas and open issues. *Journal of the American College of Surgeons*, *235*(2), 268–275.

Coombs, C., & Redman, A. (2018). *The impact of robo-advice on financial advisers: A qualitative case study*. UK Academy for Information Systems Conference Proceedings 2018. 17. https://aisel.aisnet.org/ukais2018/17

Dal Mas, F., Massaro, M., Rippa, P., & Secundo, G. (2023). The challenges of digital transformation in healthcare: An interdisciplinary literature review, framework, and future research agenda. *Technovation*, *123*, 102716.

Danneels, E. (2004). Disruptive technology reconsidered: A critique and research agenda. *Journal of Product Innovation Management*, *21*(4), 246–258.

Davis, W. E. (1989). The regular education initiative debate: Its promises and problems. *Exceptional Children*, *55*(5), 440–446.

Dhiman, R., Srivastava, V., Srivastava, A., Rajni, & Uppal, A. (2023). How to plan and write for systematic literature review papers in management domain. In S. Rana, J. Singh, & S. Kathuria (Eds.), *Advancing methodologies of conducting literature review in management domain. Review of management literature* (Vol. 2, pp. 37–55). Emerald Publishing Limited. https://doi.org/10.1108/S2754-586520230000002003

Fagnant, D. J., & Kockelman, K. (2015). Preparing a nation for autonomous vehicles: Opportunities, barriers and policy recommendations. *Transportation Research Part A: Policy and Practice*, *77*, 167–181.

Ferrari, C., Kovács, B., Tóth, M., Horváth, Z., & Reale, A. (2021, September). Edge computing for communication service providers: A review on the architecture, ownership and governing models. In *2021 international conference on software, telecommunications and computer networks (SoftCOM)* (pp. 1–6). IEEE.

Filimonau, V., & Naumova, E. (2020). The blockchain technology and the scope of its application in hospitality operations. *International Journal of Hospitality Management*, *87*, 102383.

Fraedrich, E., Heinrichs, D., Bahamonde-Birke, F. J., & Cyganski, R. (2019). Autonomous driving, the built environment and policy implications. *Transportation Research Part A: Policy and Practice*, *122*, 162–172.

Garrido-Moreno, A., García-Morales, V., King, S., & Lockett, N. (2020). Social Media use and value creation in the digital landscape: A dynamic-capabilities perspective. *Journal of Service Management*, *31*(3), 313–343.

Gilbert, C., & Bower, J. L. (2002). Disruptive change. Trying harder is part of the problem. *Harvard Business Review*, *80*(5), 94–101.

Gretzel, U., Sigala, M., Xiang, Z., & Koo, C. (2015). Smart tourism: Foundations and developments. *Electronic Markets*, *25*, 179–188.

Gupta, V. (2019). The influencing role of social media in the consumer's hotel decision-making process. *Worldwide Hospitality and Tourism Themes*, *11*(4), 378–391.

Gurrea-Martínez, A., & Wan, W. Y. (2021). The promises and perils of robo-advisers: Challenges and regulatory responses. *SMU Centre for AI & Data Governance Research Paper (2021/11)*.

Guttentag, D. A., & Smith, S. L. (2017). Assessing Airbnb as a disruptive innovation relative to hotels: Substitution and comparative performance expectations. *International Journal of Hospitality Management*, *64*, 1–10.

Hüsig, S., Hipp, C., & Dowling, M. (2005). Analysing disruptive potential: The case of wireless local area network and mobile communications network companies. *R&D Management*, *35*(1), 17–35.

Halawani, F. M., Soh, P. C., & Halawani, Y. M. (2020). Social media utilisation and business performance of hotels in Lebanon: Exploring the moderating effects of hotel classification. *Journal of Global Information Management (JGIM)*, *28*(3), 58–76.

Hodson, D. (2021). The politics of FinTech: Technology, regulation, and disruption in UK and German retail banking. *Public Administration*, *99*(4), 859–872.

HRDQ. (2022). *Disruptive innovation theory concepts*. https://hrdqstore.com/blogs/hrdq-blog/disruptive-innovation-theory-concepts#table-of-contents-0

Ivanov, S., Seyitoğlu, F., & Markova, M. (2020). Hotel managers' perceptions towards the use of robots: A mixed-methods approach. *Information Technology & Tourism*, *22*, 505–535.

Ivanov, S., & Webster, C. (Eds.). (2019). *Robots, artificial intelligence, and service automation in travel, tourism and hospitality*. Emerald Publishing Limited.

Jeong, M., Lee, M., & Nagesvaran, B. (2016). Employees' use of mobile devices and their perceived outcomes in the workplace: A case of luxury hotel. *International Journal of Hospitality Management*, *57*, 40–51.

Kaushal, N., Kaurav, R. P. S., Sivathanu, B., & Kaushik, N. (2023). Artificial Intelligence and HRM: Identifying future research Agenda using systematic literature review and bibliometric analysis. *Management Review Quarterly*, *73*(2), 455–493.

Kim, W. H., & Chae, B. (2018). Understanding the relationship among resources, social media use and hotel performance: The case of Twitter use by hotels. *International Journal of Contemporary Hospitality Management*, *30*(9), 2888–2907.

King, A. A., & Baatartogtokh, B. (2015). How useful is the theory of disruptive innovation? *MIT Sloan Management Review*, *57*(1), 77.

Konstantinidis, S. T., Bamidis, P. D., & Zary, N. (2021). Introduction to digital innovation in healthcare education and training. In *Digital innovations in healthcare education and training* (pp. 3–15). Academic Press.

Kostoff, R. N., Boylan, R., & Simons, G. R. (2004). Disruptive technology roadmaps. *Technological Forecasting and Social Change*, *71*(1–2), 141–159.

Kumar, K. P. A., & Pumera, M. (2021). 3D-printing to mitigate COVID-19 pandemic. *Advanced Functional Materials*, *31*(22), 2100450.

Lee, S. (2018). Enhancing customers' continued mobile app use in the service industry. *Journal of Services Marketing*, *32*(6), 680–691.

Lei, S. I., Wang, D., & Law, R. (2019). Hoteliers' service design for mobile-based value co-creation. *International Journal of Contemporary Hospitality Management*, *31*(11), 4338–4356.

Leung, R. (2019). Smart hospitality: Taiwan hotel stakeholder perspectives. *Tourism Review*, *74*(1), 50–62.

Liu, J., Abhishek, V., & Li, B. (2017). The impact of mobile channel adoption on customer omni-channel banking behaviour. SSRN 2912691.

Liu, S., Yang, L., Zhang, C., Xiang, Y. T., Liu, Z., Hu, S., & Zhang, B. (2020). Online mental health services in China during the COVID-19 outbreak. *The Lancet Psychiatry*, *7*(4), e17–e18.

Markides, C. (2006). Disruptive innovation: In need of better theory. *Journal of Product Innovation Management*, *23*(1), 19–25.

Mishra, V., & Sharma, M. G. (2022). Digital transformation evaluation of telehealth using convergence, maturity, and adoption. *Health Policy and Technology*, *11*(4), 100684.

Mosadeghi, S., Reid, M. W., Martinez, B., Rosen, B. T., & Spiegel, B. M. R. (2016). Feasibility of an immersive virtual reality intervention for hospitalized patients: An observational cohort study. *JMIR Mental Health*, *3*(2), e5801.

Mouratidis, K., Peters, S., & van Wee, B. (2021). Transportation technologies, sharing economy, and teleactivities: Implications for built environment and travel. *Transportation Research Part D: Transport and Environment*, *92*, 102716.

Mustapha, I., Khan, N., Qureshi, M. I., Harasis, A. A., & Van, N. T. (2021). *Impact of industry 4.0 on healthcare: A systematic literature review (SLR) from the last decade.*

Mwanza, J., Kawonga, M., Kumwenda, A., Gray, G. E., Mutale, W., & Doherty, T. (2022). Health system response to preventing mother-to-child transmission of HIV policy changes in Zambia: A health system dynamics analysis of primary health care facilities. *Global Health Action*, *15*(1), 2126269.

Nagy, D., Schuessler, J., & Dubinsky, A. (2016). Defining and identifying disruptive innovations. *Industrial Marketing Management*, *57*, 119–126.

Nair, A., & Ahlstrom, D. (2003). Delayed creative destruction and the coexistence of technologies. *Journal of Engineering and Technology Management*, *20*(4), 345–365.

Oke, A., & Fernandes, F. A. P. (2020). Innovations in teaching and learning: Exploring the perceptions of the education sector on the 4th industrial revolution (4IR). *Journal of Open Innovation: Technology, Market, and Complexity*, *6*(2), 31.

Panigrahi, R., Srivastava, P. R., & Sharma, D. (2018). Online learning: Adoption, continuance, and learning outcome – A review of literature. *International Journal of Information Management*, *43*, 1–14.

Pournader, M., Shi, Y., Seuring, S., & Koh, S. L. (2020). Blockchain applications in supply chains, transport and logistics: A systematic review of the literature. *International Journal of Production Research*, *58*(7), 2063–2081.

Rammal, H. G. (2023). Systematic literature reviews: Steps and practical tips. In S. Rana, J. Singh, & S. Kathuria (Eds.), *Advancing methodologies of conducting literature review in management domain* (pp. 27–35). Emerald Publishing Limited. https://doi.org/10.1108/S2754-586520230000002002

Rana, S., Sakshi, Singh, J., & Rana, S. (2022). Presenting the POWER framework of conducting literature review. In J. Singh (Ed.), *Exploring the latest trends in management literature* (pp. 1–13). Emerald Publishing Limited. https://doi.org/10.1108/S2754-586520220000001001

Reynolds, P., Primeaux, G., Spoth, C., Panicker, J., McNally, C., & Gupta, P. (2019). *Emerging technology, similar risks.* Deloitte Development LLC. [Online]. https://www2.deloitte.com/us/en/pages/financial-services/articles/disruptive-digital-technologies-in-the-financial-services-industry.html

Ruiz-Alba, J., & Martín-Peña, M. (2020). Sustainable business models: Integrating employees, customers and technology. *Journal of Business and Industrial Marketing*, *35*(3), 385–389.

Sahni, S., & Kaurav, R. P. S. (2023). What? Why? When? How? Where? of technology-based bibliometric review. In *Advancing methodologies of conducting literature review in management domain* (Vol. 2, pp. 79–101). Emerald Publishing Limited.

Schmidt, G. M., & Druehl, C. T. (2008). When is a disruptive innovation disruptive? *Journal of Product Innovation Management*, *25*(4), 347–369.

Serdyukov, P. (2017). Innovation in education: What works, what doesn't, and what to do about it? *Journal of Research in Innovative Teaching & Learning*, *10*(1), 4–33.

Sharma, G. D., Thomas, A., & Paul, J. (2021). Reviving tourism industry post-COVID-19: A resilience-based framework. *Tourism Management Perspectives*, *37*, 100786.

Shrivastava, S. (2017). Digital disruption is redefining the customer experience: The digital transformation approach of the communications service providers. *Telecom Business Review*, *10*(1), 41.

Sibanda, W., Ndiweni, E., Boulkeroua, M., Echchabi, A., & Ndlovu, T. (2020). Digital technology disruption on bank business models. *International Journal of Business Performance Management*, *21*(1–2), 184–213.

Stead, D., & Vaddadi, B. (2019). Automated vehicles and how they may affect urban form: A review of recent scenario studies. *Cities*, *92*, 125–133.

Surovaya, E., Prayag, G., Yung, R., & Khoo-Lattimore, C. (2020). Telepresent or not? Virtual reality, service perceptions, emotions and post-consumption behaviours. *Anatolia*, *31*(4), 620–635.

Susanto, H., Leu, F. Y., Caesarendra, W., Ibrahim, F., Haghi, P. K., Khusni, U., & Glowacz, A. (2020). Managing cloud intelligent systems over digital ecosystems: Revealing emerging app technology in the time of the COVID-19 pandemic. *Applied System Innovation*, *3*(3), 37.

Talwar, S., Talwar, M., Kaur, P., & Dhir, A. (2020). Consumers' resistance to digital innovations: A systematic review and framework development. *Australasian Marketing Journal (AMJ)*, *28*(4), 286–299.

Valchanov, H., & Aleksieva, V. (2022, September). Blockchain and IoT integration for smart transportation. In *Journal of physics: Conference series* (Vol. 2339(1), pp. 012012). IOP Publishing.

Wan, F., Williamson, P. J., & Yin, E. (2015). Antecedents and implications of disruptive innovation: Evidence from China. *Technovation*, *39*, 94–104.

Wang, C. X., Di Renzo, M., Stanczak, S., Wang, S., & Larsson, E. G. (2020). Artificial Intelligence enabled wireless networking for 5G and beyond: Recent advances and future challenges. *IEEE Wireless Communications*, *27*(1), 16–23.

Wilson, A., & Mason, B. (2020). The coming disruption – The rise of mobility as a service and the implications for government. *Research in Transportation Economics*, *83*, 100898.

Yadegaridehkordi, E., Nilashi, M., Shuib, L., Nasir, M. H. N. B. M., Asadi, S., Samad, S., & Awang, N. F. (2020). The impact of big data on firm performance in the hotel industry. *Electronic Commerce Research and Applications*, *40*, 100921.

Zhang, S. X., Sun, S., Jahanshahi, A. A., Alvarez-Risco, A., Ibarra, V. G., Li, J., & Patty-Tito, R. M. (2020). Developing and testing a measure of COVID-19 organizational support of healthcare workers – Results from Peru, Ecuador, and Bolivia. *Psychiatry Research*, *291*, 113174.

Zhohov, R., & Sharma, S. (2022). *Addressing disruptive technology trends in telecom market with business model innovation*.

Zhou, G., Chu, G., Li, L., & Meng, L. (2020). The effect of artificial intelligence on China's labour market. *China Economic Journal*, *13*(1), 24–41.

SECTION 4

STRATEGIC PERSPECTIVES IN BUSINESS AND TECHNOLOGY

NAVIGATING STRATEGIC LEADERSHIP: UNRAVELING THE DYNAMICS OF TECHNOLOGICAL INNOVATION IN ORGANIZATIONS

Anjali Singh and Sumi Jha

Indian Institute of Management Mumbai, India

ABSTRACT

This study explores the critical role of strategic leadership in driving organizational innovation amid rapid technological advancements. It delves into how strategic leaders, including top management teams and CEOs, capitalize on technological changes to foster innovation and sustain competitiveness. By employing bibliometric analysis, the research identifies pivotal themes within strategic leadership literature, highlighting the importance of adaptable leadership styles, executive influence, and the emergent role of social capital. The study underscores the necessity for strategic leaders to dynamically adjust their strategies to navigate the evolving technological landscape effectively. Through an extensive review, it offers insights into how leadership practices can drive organizational success in an era of technological disruption. This research not only extends the theoretical framework of strategic leadership in the context of technological innovation but also offers practical implications for leaders aiming to cultivate a culture of innovation within their organizations.

Keywords: Strategic leadership; change; technological innovation; technological advancements; bibliometric analysis; social capital; leadership practices

Review of Technologies and Disruptive Business Strategies
Review of Management Literature, Volume 3, 205–227

ISSN: 2754-5865/doi:10.1108/S2754-586520240000003011

1. INTRODUCTION

Strategic leadership, as defined by Ireland and Hitt (1999) as an individual's capability to anticipate, envision, maintain flexibility, think strategically, and collaborate for initiating changes toward a sustainable organizational future (p. 63), remains highly relevant in today's dynamic business environment. This study delves into the literature, examining pivotal themes and trends surrounding strategic leadership within the context of technological advancements. Recognizing the constantly evolving nature of strategic leadership is paramount for organizations aiming to adjust their business models and strategies, ensuring resilience amid rapid technological changes (Rader, 2019; Rindova & Courtney, 2020).

The dynamism of technological change is elucidated by the rapid evolution of technologies such as artificial intelligence (AI), blockchain, cloud computing, and the Internet of Things (IoT), which play a pivotal role in enhancing the survival and sustainability of organizations (Gill et al., 2019; Kaushal et al., 2021). The rapid pace of technological advancements presents a challenge for organizations as they grapple with adapting to the transformative impact of emerging technologies (George et al., 2021; Singh et al., 2021). To sustain the business, strategic leaders must guide the organization and businesses in implementing change (Garg et al., 2003; Pryor et al., 2017). Sustaining in the business alone is not enough in a business that changes every few years. A constant upgradation or innovation is necessary to advance technological innovation (Ahmed et al., 2020). Hence, the strategic leaders who are the power actors of the organization should explore opportunities for implementing new technologies and driving innovation by taking advantage of their competencies (Elenkov et al., 2005; Howell & Avolio, 1993; Singh et al., 2023). Strategic leaders are often referred to as "CxO," i.e., "Chief Executive Officer, Chief Marketing Officer, Chief Innovation Officer," "Top Management Team," and "Board of directors" (Georgakakis et al., 2017; Hambrick, 1989), and serve as the linchpins of organizations. They are responsible for steering the ship toward predefined objectives while navigating the unpredictable external and internal environment (Garg et al., 2003; Pryor et al., 2017).

In today's business environment, driven by an unstoppable pace of technological disruption, ever-changing governmental regulation, customer demand, environmental turbulence, and organizational goals focusing on long-term objectives, organizations constantly face challenges (Birkinshaw et al., 2016) questioning the already existing strategies of the organization. This turbulence demands the strategic alignment of business and IT/IS strategies (Shao, 2019), forcing organizations to adapt or risk falling behind. While some organizations are quick to adapt, others are unable to do so due to inertial solid forces caused by internal factors like standard structure, process, organization investment in plant or equipment, information available, political, and external constraints like legal, fiscal barriers, information, legitimacy, and collective rationality issue (Janssen & Ven der Voort, 2020; Yi et al., 2016).

Despite all this, it is well known that organizations and leaders face challenges while managing technological changes (Cohen & Tripsas, 2018). The decision regarding new technology adoption, transition, or implementation depends upon the CEO's attention to new technology (Guo et al., 2017; Kaplan, 2008) as they have a myriad of information, making it difficult to comprehend and make decisions (Cyert & March, 1963; Mintzberg, 1973; Ridge et al., 2017). Fortunately, emerging technologies like IoT, AI, machine learning (MI), and predictive algorithms can provide meaningful insights for making better decisions (George et al., 2014; Samba et al., 2022) by creating innovative ideas in the organization seeding creativity in the workforce which would ultimately help in gaining sustainable competitive advantage in the long run (Blomkvist et al., 2017; Bower & Christensen, 1995; O'Reilly & Tushman, 2013; Boone et al., 2018). For example, a new product development (NPD) decision requires innovative and creative ideas. The insights from advanced data analytics methods like AI and ML can help guide those ideas by providing insights from large amounts of customer/consumer data (Dwivedi et al., 2021).

Thus, decision-making, guided by real-time/past data, can drive innovation and creativity within the firm, which helps the organizations deal with the changing environmental complexities and technological change (Boone et al., 2018; Mishra et al., 2022). Hence, incorporating the appropriate technologies in the business process cannot be overlooked, especially in industries driven by high uncertainty and dynamism like banking (Samimi et al., 2020). Several studies deal with organizations' strategic change management process in different contexts like culture, policies, succession, and regulation (Quigley & Hambrick, 2012), but very few studies could explain the significance of strategic leadership in the context of technological change (Cortes & Herrmann, 2020). As strategic leaders have confidential access to the vast information of the organization, it is in their prerogative to utilize the information however and whenever they like (Cao et al., 2012; Samimi et al., 2020). With the tremendous growth in the studies dealing with strategic leadership in the context of technological changes (Qian et al., 2013; Westphal et al., 2006), e.g., further development and usage of new analytical methods like ML with Big Data and social media activity to understand the evolution of strategic leadership in the context of technological changes (Cortes & Herrmann, 2020).

In the following section, we discuss the conceptual background of the topic under study. Next, we explain the methodology for reviewing and selecting the papers for analysis. Next, we focus on the bibliometric analytical technique used. This is followed by the results section, which elaborates on the performance, network, and thematic analysis findings. Additionally, we delved on the discussion section with practical implications of our research, providing valuable insights for practitioners to sustain in the technological change era. We also discussed the study's limitations in terms of scope and sources of data, concluding with providing some future directions and a conclusion section.

2. CONCEPTUAL BACKGROUND: STRATEGIC LEADERSHIP

Until 1980, strategic leadership was not regarded as a unique field or different from general leadership. Till the 1970s, the majority of leadership studies were focused on low and middle-level managers (Covin & Slevin, 2017; House & Aditya, 1997). Finally, in 1996, the significance of "strategic leadership" increased with (Finkelstein & Hambrick, 1996; Hitt et al., 2003) and gained a new direction with the Upper Echelon theory (Hambrick & Mason, 1984) and top management team. Strategic leadership involves people who are responsible for the whole organization and not just some division or department. It is not just a titular head but comprises a top management team (Cyert & March, 1963). Strategic leaders are entrusted with responsibilities like strategic decision-making, creating and communicating a vision for the future, managing change, developing competencies and capabilities, and driving innovation in the organization (Boal & Hooijberg, 2000; Cortes & Herrmann, 2020). With the rise in environmental complexity and relentless technological disruption, the boundaries between firms have been diminished. Hence, organizations are now amenable to different external factors that impact their survival. The interdisciplinary nature of these advancements is evident in studies exploring the economic implications of technology-driven transformations in the tourism sector (Kaurav et al., 2020, pp. 469–486). This has been studied in a healthcare context, where the Digital Transformation Evaluation Model (DTEM) was introduced in the context of telehealth, offering insights relevant to healthcare administrators and policymakers (Mishra & Sharma, 2022). This complements our examination of strategic leadership amid rapid technological changes to understand the recent developments and trends in the field (Cortes & Herrmann, 2020; Samimi et al., 2020). Thus, the objective of this chapter is to understand the strategic leadership studies in the context of technological change in the past few years, to present a comprehensive overview of strategic leadership studies in response to the rising technological change.

3. REVIEW METHODOLOGY

The methodology involves state-of-the-art science mapping analysis tools like biblioshiny R studio (Aria & Cuccurullo, 2017). It is performed through R Studio as R is very flexible (Yen et al., 2019) in terms of usage. This approach aligns with Sahni and Singh Kaurav's (2023) and Anlesinya and Dadzie's (2023) recent work of further enhancing our understanding of bibliometric review methodologies. This methodology allows us to delve into the literature, uncover critical trends, map the growth of studies, discern the foundational knowledge in the field, and provide insights into the "what, why, when, how, and where" of bibliometric literature reviews (Aria & Cuccurullo, 2017). It further aids in identifying geographical distribution patterns and sheds light on the recent developments and trends in the field contributing to a comprehensive understanding of the study.

Additionally, our approach aligns with the framework introduced by Rana, Sakshi, and Singh (2022), emphasizing the importance of literature reviews in understanding the dynamics of strategic leadership within the technological landscape. Thus, bibliometric analysis is performed to analyze the literature in the study.

3.1 Defining the Search Terms

Data collection was carried out using two databases, "Web of Science" and "Scopus," using the keywords – "Strategic leadership," "technology," "change," "creativity," and "innovation." The focus of the search is to identify studies related to the role of strategic leadership in technology change, adoption, or innovation in the organization, particularly in the context of disruptive technologies and business strategies. The combinations of the search terms used in the two databases were: "Strategic leadership AND creativity," "Strategic leadership AND technology," "strategic leadership and change," and "strategic leadership and innovation" with the "All fields" tag. The results from the Web of Science were only 216 with duplications and 168 without duplication, whereas results from Scopus were 16,856 without duplication. The results from Scopus cover a wider range (Falagas et al., 2007) than the Web of Science. Thus, after comparison with both databases, Scopus was selected for analysis.

3.2 Inclusion Criteria: Initial Search Results and the Complete Process Overview

The results from the Scopus database had many duplicate entries for different combinations, which were excluded from the results of 16,855 documents. The remaining results stand at 7447. Further, the documents were restricted to the past 8 years, from 2015 to 2023. The database shows a tremendous increase in the number of documents from 2015. Considering the technologies that were there in the 2010s are not relevant today. Hence, data from only the past few years have been included with documents restricted to the English language, relevant subjects (business management, psychology, and social sciences), document type (articles and reviews), and source type (journal). The detailed process is mentioned in Fig. 1.

Initial findings reveal a significant focus on strategic leadership topics: 37.21% on change, 28.18% on innovation, 25.01% on technology, and 9.60% on creativity, with an analysis of 2,639 documents. Among these, 17% are from the top 10 journals, showcasing a widespread concentration. The primary journal is strategic management journal (15.79%), followed by the journal of management (14.04%) and the journal of business ethics (12.72%). journal of business research and leadership quarterly both contribute 9.43%. The interdisciplinary nature is evident in journals like the journal of cleaner production, reflecting a managerial focus in various disciplines, as seen in multidisciplinary studies by Kaurav and Gupta (2022).

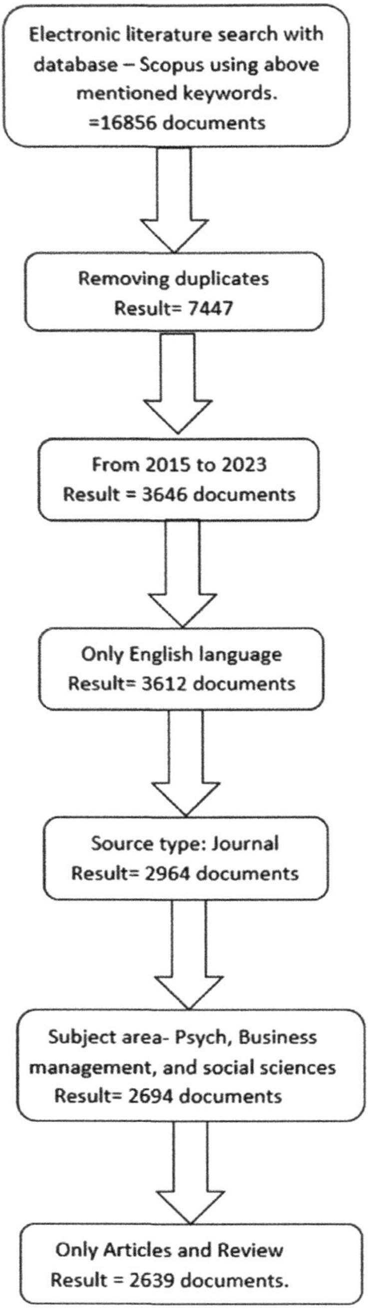

Fig. 1. Systematic Step-by-Step Process. *Source:* Author.

4. ANALYTICAL TECHNIQUE

R Studio with the biblioshiny package was selected for its flexibility, user-friendly interface, and diverse analytical capabilities. Unlike alternatives like HistCite and citNetExplorer, which are limited to Web of Science data, or Publish or Perish, which relies on Google Scholar, R Studio offers versatility. BibExcel, while flexible, involves complex data preparation. The analysis utilized R Studio with the Bibliometrix package, running the biblioshiny app through the biblioshiny command (Aria & Cuccurullo, 2017). Extracted from Scopus in BibTeX format, bibliographic data underwent analysis through R scripts and graph plotting.

5. RESULTS

5.1 Network Analysis

Network analysis provides three knowledge structures: conceptual, intellectual, and social. Conceptual knowledge uses co-word analysis with the help of authors' keywords to do network analysis between keywords of different authors. Social structure is about collaboration among authors, institutions, and journals. The intellectual structure uses co-citation and citation techniques on authors, references, and journals to do the network analysis on authors' co-citation, references, etc., as explained below.

5.1.1 Co-citation Analysis of Articles

Co-citation analysis, examining how authors influence the scientific community by citing each other, reveals relationships between nodes representing references (Aria & Cuccurullo, 2017). In a co-citation network, when two papers (A and B) are both cited in a third document (C), they have considered co-citation documents (Small, 1973). Fig. 2 illustrates a co-citation network with nodes and edges, using the Louvain algorithm and an automatic layout limited to 50 nodes and labels for better visibility. The network exhibits two clusters: a red cluster focusing on Upper Echelon theory and top management teams (Finkelstein & Hambrick, 1996; Hambrick & Mason, 1984) and a blue cluster addressing organizational resource utilization, learning (Vera & Crossan, 2004), and behavioral aspects (Podsakoff et al., 2003). Thus, the highly co-cited papers reflect two categories: top management teams (TMTs) and organizational capabilities/resources.

5.1.2 Thematic Analysis: Correspondence Analysis Method

It is a data reduction technique that helps in identifying the various subfields. There are many dimension reduction techniques within it, like "Correspondence analysis- CA," "Multiple correspondence analysis- MCA," and "Multidimensional scaling- MDS." The technique used here is correspondence analysis to understand the relationship between the keywords. Keywords are restricted to the top 50. The clusters are identified in the map by hierarchical clustering. In Fig. 3,

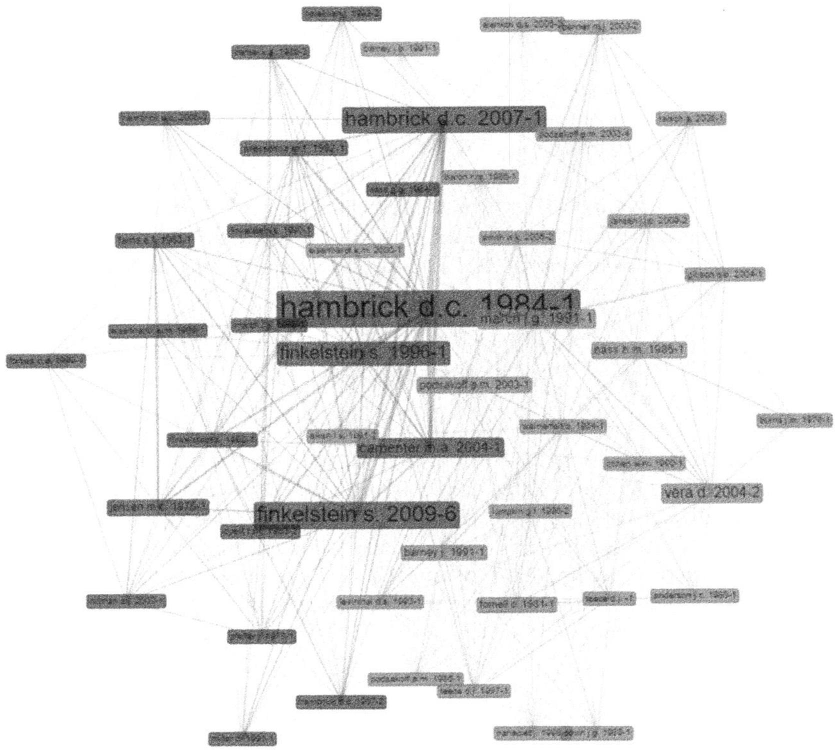

Fig. 2. Co-citation Network Among the Top 50 Articles. *Source:* Author and R software.

five clusters are developed with different colors: red, green, blue, purple, and orange.

Table 1 displays the most cited papers linked to the identified clusters, outlining connections between topics and highly cited documents.

5.2 Leadership Style and Adapting to Change

Cluster 1 in red color is about the leadership style/behavior in the context of changes that happen in the organization due to internal or external factors. Internal factors like change in technology or management and external factors like government policies or innovation due to the high dynamicity of the external environment. There are various ways in which organizations deal with the changes, first, by selecting an appropriate leadership style that might deal with the change effectively (Janssen & Van Der Voort, 2020). In other words, leaders adapt their styles to navigate technological disruptions. Studies emphasized understanding the role of different leadership styles, like transformational or transactional, in an entrepreneurial context,

Fig. 3. Correspondence Analysis. *Source:* Author and R software.

Table 1. Articles by Clusters: Top 5 Cited Documents in Each Cluster.

Cluster 1	Cluster 2	Cluster 3	Cluster 4	Cluster 5
Helfat and Peteraf (2015)	Petrenko et al. (2015)	Donate et al. (2015)	Masa'deh et al. (2016)	Cullen-Lester et al. (2017)
Engelen et al. (2012)	Van Essen et al. (2015)	Haynes et al. (2015)	Krause et al. (2015)	Smolović et al. (2015)
Mittal and Dhar (2015)	Tang et al. (2014)	Fischer et al. (2017)	Fitzsimmons and Callan (2016)	Mehrabani and Mohamad (2015)
Hughes et al. (2018)	Bergh et al. (2016)	Peng et al. (2015)	Yan and Guan (2018)	Megheirkouni (2016)
Osiyevskyy and Dewald (2015)	Jain et al. (2016)	Minichilli et al. (2015)	Gifford et al. (2017)	Elkington et al. (2017)

Source: Author.

where these technologies are catalysts for change (Engelen et al., 2012; Miller & Miller, 2020). As entrepreneurial-oriented leaders are proactive, creative, risk-taking, and aggressive, they align with the entrepreneurial context, focusing on a transformational leadership style. It also highlights the importance of this leadership style in improving employee creativity (Lee et al., 2020). As with the changing dynamics of the business with a highly complex and unpredictable environment, it is of utmost necessity to be creative and adaptive in how one works (Lee et al., 2020; Mittal & Dhar, 2015). With the transformational leadership style, the leaders can influence the employees to be supportive in the changing circumstances of management, technology change, or innovation, while with the transactional leadership style, leaders can focus on the current organizational goals and objectives. Thus, leadership, creativity, and innovation form important aspects in the current circumstances (Chamakiotis et al., 2021; Hughes et al., 2018), second by identifying existing methods/studies to deal with the change. Authors have identified different studies to understand the change and how to deal with it. Helfat and Peteraf (2015) talks about the specific cognitive capabilities that can identify the managerial capabilities for sensing, seizing, reconfiguring, and explaining the potential impact on strategic change. Finally, the third is understanding the appropriate response to change, which can be different, like explorative or exploitative. Findings emphasize the pivotal role of leadership in fostering employee creativity and innovation, which is essential in an environment characterized by rapid technological advancements (Chamakiotis et al., 2021; Mittal & Dhar, 2015).

5.3 Upper Echelons, Corporate Social Responsibility (CSR), and Influence of Technological Change

The second cluster is about the studies related to the upper echelons, CEOs, top executives, TMTs, the board of directors, corporate governance, and their CSR activities and their response to changing dynamics due to rapid technological changes (Li-Ming et al., 2022). The leaders are highly indulging in CSR activities to contribute to society. This cluster discusses the role of behavioral characteristics of top leaders in influencing CSR practices when there is a rising demand to channel the resources toward upgrading the technology and decisions leading to dilemmas on aligning resources to core activities and technology upgradation (Manning, 2022). Studies in this cluster explore the behavioral aspect of the CEOs or top leaders and their impact on CSR practices in the context of organizational technological changes (Li-Ming et al., 2022). The narcissistic CEO's effect on organizations' CSR practices by influencing decisions has also been examined (Petrenko et al., 2015).

Similarly, the CEO's hubris also affects decision-making processes, impacting the organization's CSR decisions and practices (Tang et al., 2014). The behavioral aspects and the different policies or corporate governance mechanisms also impact the CSR outcomes at the institution, firm, group, and individual levels (Jain & Jamali, 2016; Jain et al., 2016). Meta-analysis studies are conducted to understand that the Boards, rather than restricting, mediate the top management decisions (Bergh et al., 2016). The studies also discuss the relationship between CEO compensations and performance sensitivities. This cluster discusses the intricate relationship between disruptive technologies, leadership behavior, and CSR outcomes (Jain & Jamali, 2016; Jain et al., 2016).

5.4 Innovation/Organization Performance in the Age of Change

The third cluster is about achieving the desired organizational performance through disruptive technologies to seek innovation through a knowledge-oriented perspective, which utilizes knowledge management initiatives like human capital and social capital for innovation (Donate et al., 2015; Scuotto et al., 2022). The other way to achieve desired organizational success is by understanding the leaders' behavioral aspect on firms' social and human capital (Haynes et al., 2015; Kidron & Vinarski-Peretz, 2022). Some studies specify the leadership processes to achieve the desired performance through the networks of the employees and the collective processes of the groups at functional and higher levels in the hierarchy. Hence, this review paper explains the importance of different actions organizations undertake to innovate strategically to maintain sustainable competitive advantage in the context of rapid technological disruption (Fischer et al., 2017).

5.5 Social Capital's Role in Technological Disruption

The importance of human capital is explained in an earlier cluster. This cluster four talks about the emerging importance of social capital alongside human capital in organizations grappling with disruptive technologies (Kidron & Vinarski-Peretz, 2022). It is now considered par with human capital and plays an important role in CEO appointments (Fitzsimmons & Callan, 2016; Wang, 2021). Further, the Board's view of the chair as a valuable resource is highly dependent on the Board chair's human and social capital (Krause et al., 2015; Wang, 2021). There could also be an interaction between human and social capital, which might have positive and negative effects (Crane & Hartwell, 2019). Considering the dynamic environment faced by today's businesses, they need to be creative, innovative, and highly adaptable to situations. The innovations can be exploitative or explorative. Understanding how social capital affects these two types of innovation (Wang, 2021; Yan & Guan, 2018) is important.

5.6 Leadership Development Amid Technological Change

The fifth cluster is about leadership development and how leadership is developed, which identifies the high-quality leadership development program (Elkington et al., 2017). Other than the leadership development program, some conceptual models explain the different approaches for network-enhancing leadership development and help improve the leaders' capacity as individuals and as a collective (Cullen-Lester et al., 2017). Additionally, the paper includes a review of leadership development, presenting an instrument designed to evaluate preferred leader behavior factors within national cultural cognitive templates. This tool aims to enhance the training of managerial leaders in diverse organizations (Littrell et al., 2018). Different leadership skill development models are also developed (Mehrabani & Mohamad, 2015). These were the 5 clusters, and the details of the top 5 cited articles belonging to each of the 5 clusters are presented in Table 1.

Summarizing the findings of the above cluster provides us with a holistic understanding of strategic leadership studies in response to rising technological change. They discuss the critical role of strategic leaders in fostering innovation, adapting to change, and navigating the challenges posed by technological uncertainty. Notably, leadership styles, top executives' behavior, innovation strategies, and social and human capital influence all play crucial roles in shaping organizations' responses to technological disruption. The insights from these clusters collectively contribute to a deeper understanding of how strategic leadership drives organizational success in the digital age, offering valuable guidance for researchers and practitioners in this dynamic landscape.

6. DISCUSSION

The paper aimed to understand strategic leadership in the context of change in technology, innovation, or creativity in the organization by employing a bibliometric approach. The bibliometric analysis using R conducted above has provided meaningful insights about the key trends, themes, and relationships in strategic leadership and technological innovation, highlighting crucial areas for future research and practice in adapting to technological advancements. The review from the Scopus database resulted in 2,639 documents, showing the drastic increase in the rate of studies from 7% in 2015–2016 to 33% in 2023, and the major chunk of studies was related to the "change management" in the organization emphasizing the importance strategic leadership in navigating the complexities of organizational change, especially in response to technological disruptions. Further, only the top 17% of the documents were from the top 10 journals, indicating the widespread of the field. The top three journals in the field are Strategic Management Journal, Journal of Management, and Journal of Business Ethics. The co-citation analysis of the top 50 articles resulted in two clusters: red and blue. The red cluster discusses upper echelon theory, top executives, and Top management teams (Finkelstein & Hambrick, 1996; Hambrick & Mason, 1984), while the blue cluster discusses the better utilization of the resources of the organization, organization learning (Vera & Crossan, 2004). The thematic analysis has resulted in five clusters, of which most of the studies have been related to "leadership style and adapting to change," and an equal number of studies have been related to cluster "upper echelons, CSR, and influence of technological change." The other three clusters were related to "innovation/organization performance in the age of change," "social capital's role in technological disruption," and the least number of studies on "leadership development amidst technological change." As the area has primarily focused on change in the organizations, it has resulted in questioning the organizations' strategies and existing leadership style, advocating transformational leadership style, which has been found to initiate innovation in the organizations.

The presented conceptual model in Fig. 4 serves as a valuable framework for understanding the intricate dynamics of strategic leadership in the context of technological change, innovation, and organizational creativity

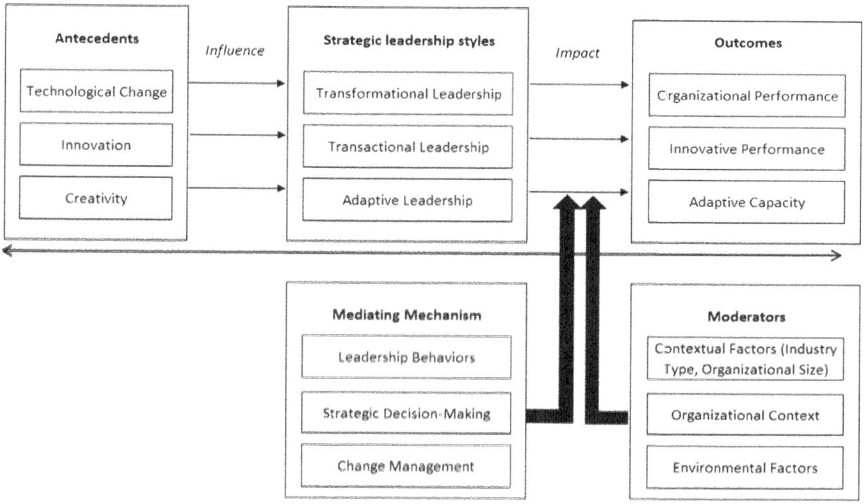

Fig. 4. Conceptual Model. *Source:* Author.

(Cortes & Herrmann, 2020). This model discusses the core elements identified through thematic analysis, providing a structured explanation of the antecedents, strategic leadership styles, moderators, and outcomes that underpin the strategic leadership process. Notably, technological change emerges as a critical antecedent, influencing the adoption of distinct leadership styles, including transformational, transactional, and adaptive approaches (Bunjak et al., 2022). These leadership styles, in turn, have a significant impact on various outcomes, such as organizational performance, innovative performance, and learning and adaptation. Moreover, the model recognizes the mediating role of leadership behaviors, strategic decision-making, change management, and further the moderating role played by factors like organizational context and environmental factors, acknowledging their capacity to influence the relationships within this framework. This conceptual model enhances our comprehension of the complex interplay between technological change, leadership styles, and organizational outcomes, offering a roadmap for future research endeavors to delve deeper into these relationships and their implications for strategic leadership practices in a rapidly evolving landscape. Following are the propositions.

Organizations undergoing rapid technological change significantly influence the choice of leadership styles adopted by strategic leaders. The study reveals that strategic leaders are aware of the evolving technological landscape and strategically tailor their leadership approaches to align with the specific demands posed by different types of technological changes. This adaptation ensures that leadership styles are not only responsive but also proactive in leveraging technological advancements to achieve organizational objectives. The empirical evidence underscores the critical importance of recognizing technological change as a fundamental antecedent shaping leadership behaviors and strategies in contemporary organizations.

P1. In organizations undergoing rapid technological change, the pace, nature, and extent of technological advancements significantly influence the choice of leadership styles adopted by strategic leaders.

Innovation has emerged as a critical driver of organizational success, especially in the age of rapid technological change. This proposition discusses the intricate relationship between knowledge management initiatives, social and human capital, and innovation performance. It states that technology-driven organizations that are able to capitalize on existing knowledge assets can significantly influence the organization's ability to innovate effectively. As organizations navigate the challenges posed by disruptive technologies, their capacity to tap into the collective knowledge of their workforce becomes increasingly vital. This suggests that organizations that prioritize the cultivation of social and human capital are better positioned to drive innovation and, in turn, achieve effective organizational performance in the dynamic environment of technological disruption.

P2. In technology-driven organizations, the strategic incorporation of knowledge management initiatives, utilizing existing social and human capital, positively influences innovation performance, which, in turn, enhances overall organizational performance.

7. LIMITATIONS AND FUTURE RESEARCH DIRECTIONS

This study, while contributing valuable insights into strategic leadership in the context of technological disruption and innovation, acknowledges certain limitations that present avenues for future research. The choice of keywords might have impacted the results, and a large set of keywords might have resulted in an exhaustive review. Further, the data from only the Scopus database was used data from other sources could also be used to identify the studies missed in the Scopus database. The other limitation is the scope, which was of 8 years. Hence, longitudinal analysis could be conducted in the future to match the findings presented here. The content analysis could be done to identify the research gaps. Studies in languages different from English are not considered. It would be advantageous to understand the studies in countries with different cultures publishing in their native language. The current analysis has not considered conference proceedings, trade journals, thesis, books, nonindexed journals, or any unpublished work with interesting findings. Future studies could explore using these sources to generate a broader perspective. Strategic leadership in the context of technology, change, innovation, and creativity is growing rapidly, the research directions from this study could further help in exploring the area in the context of different countries and the pattern followed, which could be compared and analyzed further by encompassing new analytical methods. The rapidly changing environment will further provide a lot of interest and opportunities to explore this field. The themes provide a roadmap for further investigation into these evolving dynamics.

7.1 Leadership Style and Adapting to Change

Exploring the nexus between leadership style and organizational adaptability, it is crucial to examine how leaders can foster environments that thrive on change. Hughes et al. (2018) and Pryor et al. (2017) have demonstrated that transformational leadership significantly enhances innovation and adaptability within organizations facing rapid technological changes. Future research should delve deeper into the mechanisms through which leadership styles can influence organizational performance and innovation orientation, with a particular focus on the mediating role of leadership behaviors and strategic decision-making (Elenkov et al., 2005; Samimi et al., 2020). Further, research scholars can investigate the association between various disruptive technologies like AI, blockchain, cloud computing, and leadership styles to understand how strategic leaders align their respective styles to leverage these technologies. The role of innovation orientation and creativity in influencing these leadership styles and fostering organizational creativity and innovation also presents a critical area for investigation.

7.2 Upper Echelons, CSR, and Influence of Technological Change

The impact of technological change on CSR initiatives and the strategic decision-making of upper echelons underscores its significance (Jain & Jamali, 2016; Tang et al., 2014). The evolving role of technology and senior executives' backgrounds, values, and experiences facilitating CSR activities, from enhancing stakeholder engagement to enabling more sustainable practices, presents a fertile area for future investigation. Research could further explore how the personal values and cognitive bases of top executives (Li-Ming et al., 2022) influence the integration of CSR in business strategies amid technological shifts.

7.3 Innovation/Organization Performance in the Age of Change

Innovation and organizational performance are intricately linked, particularly in the context of technological change. Innovation plays a critical role in driving organizational performance in the face of technological change (Donate et al., 2015; Scuotto et al., 2022). The link between digital transformation strategies and innovation ecosystems in fostering a competitive edge warrants further exploration. Future studies might examine the barriers to innovation adoption and the strategies that organizations can employ to overcome these challenges, thereby enhancing their innovation capacity and organizational agility.

7.4 Social Capital's Role in Technological Disruption

The importance of social capital in navigating technological disruptions is well-articulated by Kidron and Vinarski-Peretz (2022) and Crane and Hartwell (2019). The interplay between social networks, trust, and knowledge exchange in fostering innovation and adaptability to technological change suggests a need for more nuanced research. Future directions could include investigating the role of digital collaboration tools in enhancing social capital and the impact of social capital on innovation in technology-driven environments. Research could benefit from examining the interaction between human and social capital in CEO appointments and its impact on innovation and leadership development amid technological change (Crane & Hartwell, 2019; Fitzsimmons & Callan, 2016). Future research scholars can also investigate studies emphasizing the importance of human and social capital and their alignment with the organization's culture and structure. Future studies (see Table 2) can also focus on knowledge management activities in the context of change management in technology-driven organizations, as these activities drive the innovation needed in the organizations, further boosting creativity in the organizations in technological change-driven contexts. Furthermore, exploring the mediating influence of leadership behaviors and strategic decision-making in utilizing social capital during technological disruptions is needed.

7.5 Leadership Development Amid Technological Change

As technological advancements continue to reshape the business landscape, developing leaders who can effectively manage and leverage these changes become significant. Addressing leadership development in the context of technological change, studies by Fitzsimmons and Callan (2016) and Haynes et al. (2015) emphasized the evolving requirements for leadership competencies in the digital age. Investigating the design and effectiveness of leadership development programs that incorporate elements of technology management and digital literacy, identification of competencies and skills required for future leaders, is a critical area for future research. This includes exploring how organizations can cultivate a culture that supports ongoing leadership development in response to technological advancements.

Further, future researchers could also explore cross-culture studies to understand how strategic leadership differs across different countries, how practices differ, and the role of technology in such context. The lack of diversity in the leadership development cluster provides an arena for future scholars to explore the leadership development aspect in different contexts.

7.5.1 Implications for Practice

The findings from the study reveal valuable insights for practitioners in the field of strategic leadership in the context of technological change. Organizations and practitioners must build adaptive leadership styles with an innovation-centric approach among the strategic leaders in the technological-driven or digital era.

Table 2. Top 5 Cited Documents in Each Cluster.

Categories	Variables	Future Research Directions
Antecedents	Technological change	Explore the influence of emerging technology (e.g., AI, blockchain) on strategic leadership styles and organizational outcomes.
	Innovation orientation	Examine innovation orientation and its link with strategic leadership styles and technological innovation.
	Creativity	Investigate how creativity (creative mindset) influences strategic leadership styles and organizational creativity.
Strategic leadership styles	Transformational leadership	Explore transformational leadership's impact on organizational performance and adaptability in technological-driven contexts.
	Transactional leadership	Investigate how transactional leadership behaviors influence change management practices and outcomes.
	Adaptive leadership	Investigate adaptive leadership's role in driving innovation and organization agility during technological change.
Mediating mechanisms	Leadership behaviors	Examine specific leadership behaviors' effect on change management practices and organizational outcomes.
	Strategic decision-making	Investigate strategic decision-making's influence on aligning leadership styles with organizational goals in technological change.
	Change management	Investigate how change management strategies support the implementation of leadership styles during technology transitions.
Outcomes	Organizational performance	Examine relationships between antecedents, leadership styles, and various organizational performance dimensions in technology-driven contexts.
	Innovative performance	Investigate how innovation orientation, leadership styles, and change management practices influence innovative performance and competitiveness.
	Adaptive capacity	Examine the role of adaptive leadership behaviors and strategic decision-making in enhancing organizational agility and resilience during technological change.
Moderators	Organizational context	Explore how organizational size, industry, and culture influence relationships between antecedents, leadership styles, and outcomes.
	Environmental factors	Investigate how changes in regulatory environments and competitive landscapes affect relationships among antecedents, leadership styles, and outcomes.

Source: Author.

They can also align their hiring process to include leaders having this style. Further, organizations can also create training and development programs for leaders to inculcate the skills, knowledge, and mindset needed to sustain in the digital age. Next, considering the need for collaborative leadership practices emphasizing diverse perspectives across the globe, practitioners can focus on collaborating with leaders worldwide, providing varied insights and approaches.

Further, leaders and organizations must also be aware of the pitfalls of not upholding ethical standards when leveraging AI, IoT, and blockchain technologies.

Finally, organizations, leaders, and HR professionals need to acknowledge the value of both human and social capital. Harnessing this and fostering the social network within organizations can significantly enhance the adaptive capacity and further resilience of individuals and organizations in the context of technological disruption.

8. CONCLUSION

In conclusion, our study has provided a comprehensive view of strategic leadership literature within the context of technological change, innovation, and creativity. Through an extensive bibliometric analysis, we have unveiled valuable insights into the evolving role of strategic leadership in this age of technological disruption. Our research has resulted in key themes highlighting the importance of adaptable leadership styles, upper level executives' influence, innovation pursuit, social capital's emerging role, and the need for leadership development activities for strategic leaders. Collectively, these themes provide a comprehensive framework for comprehending the intricate relationship between strategic leadership and technological change. Our analysis highlights the need for strategic leaders to adapt their styles flexibly to navigate the constantly shifting technological landscape effectively. This adaptability is paramount for harnessing the potential of innovations such as AI, blockchain, cloud computing, and IoT.

Furthermore, our performance analysis findings emphasize the global dimension of leadership, with contributions emerging from diverse regions. This underscores the significance of collaborative leadership practices and ethical considerations, including CSR, in tech-driven environments. Our study points toward promising directions for future research, inviting deeper exploration into the uncharted territories of leadership amid technological disruption. We have presented a conceptual framework (see Table 2) that outlines pathways for scholars and practitioners to navigate this evolving landscape. In a world where technological change continually reshapes industries, our study tries to find direction for strategic leaders and researchers alike.

REFERENCES

Ahmed, W., Najmi, A., & Ikram, M. (2020). Steering firm performance through innovative capabilities: A contingency approach to innovation management. *Technology in Society*, *63*, 101385. https://doi.org/10.1016/j.techsoc.2020.101385

Anlesinya, A., & Dadzie, S. A. (2023). Technology and the conduct of bibliometric literature reviews in management: The software tools, benefits, and challenges. In S. Rana, J. Singh, & S. Kathuria (Eds.), *Advancing methodologies of conducting literature review in management domain, Review of management literature* (Vol. 2, pp. 57–78). Emerald Publishing Limited. https://doi.org/10.1108/S2754-586520230000002004

Aria, M., & Cuccurullo, C. (2017). Bibliometrix: An R-tool for comprehensive science mapping analysis. *Journal of Informetrics*, *11*(4), 959–975. https://doi.org/10.1016/j.joi.2017.08.007

Bergh, D. D., Aguinis, H., Heavey, C., Ketchen, D. J., Boyd, B., Su, P., Lau, C., & Joo, H. (2016). Using meta-analytic structural equation modeling to advance strategic management research:

Guidelines and an empirical illustration via the strategic leadership-performance relationship. *Strategic Management Journal*, *37*(3), 477–497. https://doi.org/10.1002/smj.2338

Birkinshaw, J., Zimmermann, A., & Raisch, S. (2016). How do firms adapt to discontinuous change? Bridging the dynamic capabilities and ambidexterity perspectives. *California Management Review*, *58*(4), 36–58. https://doi.org/10.1525/cmr.2016.58.4.36

Blomkvist, K., Kappen, P., & Zander, I. (2017). Gone are the creatures of yesteryear? On the diffusion of technological capabilities in the 'modern' MNC. *Journal of World Business*, *52*(1), 1–16. https://doi.org/10.1016/j.jwb.2016.10.003

Boal, K. B., & Hooijberg, R. (2000). Strategic leadership research. *The Leadership Quarterly*, *11*(4), 515–549. https://doi.org/10.1016/s1048-9843(00)00057-6

Boone, C., Lokshin, B., Guenter, H., & Belderbos, R. (2018). Top management team nationality diversity, corporate entrepreneurship, and innovation in multinational firms. *Strategic Management Journal*, *40*(2), 277–302. https://doi.org/10.1002/smj.2976

Bower, J. L., & Christensen, C. M. (1995). Disruptive technologies: Catching the wave. *Harvard Business Review*, *73*(1), 43–53. https://hbr.org/1995/01/disruptive-technologies-catching-the-wave

Bunjak, A., Bruch, H., & Černe, M. (2022). Context is key: The joint roles of transformational and shared leadership and management innovation in predicting employee IT innovation adoption. *International Journal of Information Management*, *66*, 102516. https://doi.org/10.1016/j.ijinfomgt.2022.102516

Cao, Q., Şimşek, Z., & Jansen, J. (2012). CEO Social capital and entrepreneurial orientation of the firm. *Journal of Management*, *41*(7), 1957–1981. https://doi.org/10.1177/0149206312469666

Chamakiotis, P., Panteli, N., & Davison, R. M. (2021). Reimagining e-leadership for reconfigured virtual teams due to COVID-19. *International Journal of Information Management*, *60*, 102381. https://doi.org/10.1016/j.ijinfomgt.2021.102381

Cohen, S. L., & Tripsas, M. (2018). Managing technological transitions by building bridges. *Academy of Management Journal*, *61*(6), 2319–2342. https://doi.org/10.5465/amj.2015.0690

Cortes, A. F., & Herrmann, P. (2020). Strategic Leadership of Innovation: A framework for future research. *International Journal of Management Reviews*, *23*(2), 224–243. https://doi.org/10.1111/ijmr.12246

Covin, J. G., & Slevin, D. P. (2017). The entrepreneurial imperatives of strategic leadership. In M. A. Hitt, R. D. Ireland, S. M. Camp, & D. L. Sexton (Eds.), *Strategic entrepreneurship*. https://doi.org/10.1002/9781405164085.ch14

Crane, B., & Hartwell, C. J. (2019). Global talent management: A life cycle view of the interaction between human and social capital. *Journal of World Business*, *54*(2), 82–92. https://doi.org/10.1016/j.jwb.2018.11.002

Cullen-Lester, K. L., Maupin, C. K., & Carter, D. R. (2017). Incorporating social networks into leadership development: A conceptual model and evaluation of research and practice. *The Leadership Quarterly*, *28*(1), 130–152. https://doi.org/10.1016/j.leaqua.2016.10.005

Cyert, R., & March, J. G. (1963). *A behavioral theory of the firm*. Prentice-Hall.

Donate, M. J., García-Pardo, I. P., & De Pablo, J. D. S. (2015). HRM practices for human and social capital development: Effects on innovation capabilities. *International Journal of Human Resource Management*, *27*(9), 928–953. https://doi.org/10.1080/09585192.2015.1047393

Dwivedi, Y. K., Hughes, L., Ismagilova, E., Aarts, G., Coombs, C., Crick, T., Duan, Y., Dwivedi, R., Edwards, J. S., Eirug, A., Galanos, V., Ilavarasan, P. V., Janssen, M., Jones, P., Kar, A. K., Kizgin, H., Kronemann, B., Lal, B., Lucini, B., …, & Williams, M. D. (2021). Artificial Intelligence (AI): Multidisciplinary perspectives on emerging challenges, opportunities, and agenda for research, practice, and policy. *International Journal of Information Management*, *57*, 101994. https://doi.org/10.1016/j.ijinfomgt.2019.08.002

Elenkov, D., Judge, W. Q., & Wright, P. (2005). Strategic leadership and executive innovation influence: An international multi-cluster comparative study. *Strategic Management Journal*, *26*(7), 665–682. https://doi.org/10.1002/smj.469

Elkington, R., Van Der Steege, M., Glick-Smith, J. L., & Breen, J. M. (2017). *Visionary leadership in a turbulent world*. Emerald Publishing Limited eBooks. https://doi.org/10.1108/9781787142428

Engelen, A., Gupta, V. K., Strenger, L. S., & Brettel, M. (2012). Entrepreneurial orientation, firm performance, and the moderating role of transformational leadership behaviors. *Journal of Management*, *41*(4), 1069–1097. https://doi.org/10.1177/0149206312455244

Falagas, M. E., Pitsouni, E., Malietzis, G., & Pappas, G. (2007). Comparison of PubMed, Scopus, Web of Science, and Google Scholar: Strengths and weaknesses. *The FASEB Journal*, *22*(2), 338–342. https://doi.org/10.1096/fj.07-9492lsf

Finkelstein, S., & Hambrick, D. C. (1996). *Strategic leadership: Top executives and their effects on Organizations*. Cengage Learning.

Fischer, T. M., Dietz, J., & Antonakis, J. (2017). Leadership process models: A review and synthesis. *Journal of Management*, *43*(6), 1726–1753. https://doi.org/10.1177/0149206316682830

Fitzsimmons, T. W., & Callan, V. J. (2016). CEO selection: A capital perspective. *The Leadership Quarterly*, *27*(5), 765–787. https://doi.org/10.1016/j.leaqua.2016.05.001

Garg, V. K., Walters, B. A., & Priem, R. L. (2003). Chief executive scanning emphases, environmental dynamism, and manufacturing firm performance. *Strategic Management Journal*, *24*(8), 725–744. https://doi.org/10.1002/smj.335

Georgakakis, D., Greve, P., & Ruigrok, W. (2017). Top management team faultlines and firm performance: Examining the CEO-TMT interface. *The Leadership Quarterly*, *28*(6), 741–758. https://doi.org/10.1016/j.leaqua.2017.03.004

George, G., Haas, M. R., & Pentland, A. (2014). Big data and management. *Academy of Management Journal*, *57*(2), 321–326. https://doi.org/10.5465/amj.2014.4002

George, G., Merrill, R. K., & Schillebeeckx, S. J. (2021). Digital sustainability and entrepreneurship: How digital innovations are helping tackle climate change and sustainable development. *Entrepreneurship Theory and Practice*, *45*(5), 999–1027. https://doi.org/10.1177/1042258719899425

Gifford, W., Graham, I., Ehrhart, M. G., Davies, B., & Aarons, G. (2017). Ottawa model of implementation leadership and implementation leadership scale: Mapping concepts for developing and evaluating theory-based leadership interventions. *Journal of Healthcare Leadership*, *9*, 15–23. https://doi.org/10.2147/jhl.s125558

Gill, S. S., Tuli, S., Xu, M., Singh, I., Singh, K. V., Lindsay, D., Smirnova, D., Singh, M., Jain, U., Pervaiz, H., Sehgal, B., Kaila, S. S., Misra, S., Aslanpour, M. S., Mehta, H., Stankovski, V., & Garraghan, P. (2019). Transformative effects of IoT, Blockchain and Artificial Intelligence on cloud computing: Evolution, vision, trends and open challenges. *Internet of Things*, *8*, 100118. https://doi.org/10.1016/j.iot.2019.100118

Guo, W., Katila, R., Maggitti, P. G., & Tesluk, P. E. (2017). Innovation at the top: Proactive CEO, top executive attention focus, and product innovation. *Proceedings – Academy of Management*, *2017*(1), 14562. https://doi.org/10.5465/ambpp.2017.14562abstract

Hambrick, D. C. (1989). Guest editor's introduction: Putting top managers back in the strategy picture. *Strategic Management Journal*, *10*(S1), 5–15. https://doi.org/10.1002/smj.4250100703

Hambrick, D., & Mason, P. (1984). Upper echelons: The organization as a reflection of its top managers. *Academy of Management Review*, *9*(2), 193-206. http://www.jstor.org/stable/258434. Accessed on September 23, 2020.

Haynes, K. T., Hitt, M. A., & Campbell, J. T. (2015). The dark side of leadership: Towards a mid-range theory of hubris and greed in entrepreneurial contexts. *Journal of Management Studies*, *52*(4), 479–505. https://doi.org/10.1111/joms.12127

Helfat, C. E., & Peteraf, M. A. (2015). Managerial cognitive capabilities and the microfoundations of dynamic capabilities. *Strategic Management Journal*, *36*(6), 831–850. https://doi.org/10.1002/smj.2247

Hitt, M. A., Ireland, R. D., & Hoskisson, R. E. (2003). *Strategic management: Competitiveness and globalization* (5th ed.). Southwestern College Publishing Company.

House, R. J., & Aditya, R. N. (1997). The social scientific study of leadership: Quo Vadis? *Journal of Management*, *23*(3), 409–473. https://doi.org/10.1177/014920639702300306

Howell, J. M., & Avolio, B. J. (1993). Transformational leadership, transactional leadership, locus of control, and support for innovation: Key predictors of consolidated-business-unit performance. *Journal of Applied Psychology*, *78*(6), 891–902. https://doi.org/10.1037/0021-9010.78.6.891

Hughes, D. J., Lee, A., Tian, A. W., Newman, A., & Legood, A. (2018). Leadership, creativity, and innovation: A critical review and practical recommendations. *The Leadership Quarterly*, *29*(5), 549–569. https://doi.org/10.1016/j.leaqua.2018.03.001

Ireland, R. D., & Hitt, M. A. (1999). Achieving and maintaining strategic competitiveness in the 21st century: The role of strategic leadership. *Academy of Management Perspectives*, *13*(1), 43–57. https://doi.org/10.5465/ame.1999.1567311

Jain, T., Aguilera, R. V., & Jamali, D. (2016). Corporate stakeholder orientation in an emerging country context: A longitudinal cross-industry analysis. *Journal of Business Ethics*, *143*(4), 701–719. https://doi.org/10.1007/s10551-016-3074-1

Jain, T., & Jamali, D. (2016). Looking inside the black box: The effect of corporate governance on corporate social responsibility. *Corporate Governance: An International Review*, *24*(3), 253–273. https://doi.org/10.1111/corg.12154

Janssen, M., & Van Der Voort, H. (2020). Agile and adaptive governance in crisis response: Lessons from the COVID-19 pandemic. *International Journal of Information Management*, *55*, 102180. https://doi.org/10.1016/j.ijinfomgt.2020.102180

Kaplan, S. (2008). Framing contests: Strategy making under uncertainty. *Organization Science*, *19*(5), 729–752. https://doi.org/10.1287/orsc.1070.0340

Kaurav, R. P. S., Baber, R., & Rajput, S. (2020). *Technology-driven tourism and hospitality industry as a tool for economic development: A bibliometric analysis*. Emerald Publishing Limited eBooks. https://doi.org/10.1108/978-1-83982-688-720201030

Kaurav, R. P. S., & Gupta, P. (2022). Trends in multidiscipline management research: Past, present and future of FIIB business review. *FIIB Business Review*, *11*(4), 382–404. https://doi.org/10.1177/23197145221136966

Kaushal, N., Kaurav, R. P. S., Sivathanu, B., & Kaushik, N. (2021). Artificial intelligence and HRM: Identifying future research agenda using systematic literature review and bibliometric analysis. *Management Review Quarterly*, *73*(2), 455–493. https://doi.org/10.1007/s11301-021-00249-2

Kidron, A., & Vinarski-Peretz, H. (2022). Linking psychological and social capital to organizational performance: A moderated mediation of organizational trust and proactive behavior. *European Management Journal*. https://doi.org/10.1016/j.emj.2022.11.008

Krause, R., Semadeni, M., & Withers, M. C. (2015). That special someone: When the board views its chair as a resource. *Strategic Management Journal*, *37*(9), 1990–2002. https://doi.org/10.1002/smj.2444

Lee, A., Legood, A., Hughes, D. J., Tian, A. W., Newman, A., & Knight, C. (2020). Leadership, creativity, and innovation: A meta-analytic review. *European Journal of Work & Organizational Psychology*, *29*(1), 1–35. https://doi.org/10.1080/1359432x.2019.1661837

Li-Ming, Z., Yang, M. M., Wang, Z., & Michelson, G. (2022). Trends in the dynamic evolution of corporate social responsibility and leadership: A literature review and bibliometric analysis. *Journal of Business Ethics*, *182*(1), 135–157. https://doi.org/10.1007/s10551-022-05035-y

Littrell, R. F., Warner-Søderholm, G., Minelgaitė, I., Ahmadi, Y., Dalati, S., Bertsch, A., & Kuskova, V. (2018). Explicit preferred leader behaviors across cultures. *The Journal of Management Development*, *37*(3), 243–257. https://doi.org/10.1108/jmd-09-2017-0294

Manning, S. (2022). From mainstream to niche: How value regimes shift in emerging economy upgrading. *Research Policy*, *51*(6), 104532. https://doi.org/10.1016/j.respol.2022.104532

Masa'deh, R., Obeidat, B.Y., & Tarhini, A. (2016). A Jordanian empirical study of the associations among transformational leadership, transactional leadership, knowledge sharing, job performance, and firm performance: A structural equation modelling approach. *Journal of Management Development*, *35*(5), 681–705. https://doi.org/10.1108/JMD-09-2015-0134

Megheirkouni, M. (2016). Leadership behaviours and capabilities in Syria: An exploratory qualitative approach. *Journal of Management Development*, *35*(5), 636–662. https://doi.org/10.1108/JMD-02-2015-0022

Mehrabani, S. E., & Mohamad, N. (2015). New approach to leadership skills development (developing a model and measure). *The Journal of Management Development*, *34*(7), 821–853. https://doi.org/10.1108/jmd-03-2013-0046

Miller, L., & Miller, A. F. (2020). Innovative work behavior through high-quality leadership. *International Journal of Innovation Science*, *12*(2), 219–236. https://doi.org/10.1108/ijis-04-2019-0042

Minichilli, A., Brogi, M., & Calabrò, A. (2015). Weathering the storm: Family ownership, governance, and performance through the financial and economic crisis. *Corporate Governance: An International Review*, *24*(6), 552–568. https://doi.org/10.1111/corg.12125

Mintzberg, H. (1973). *The nature of managerial work*. Harper & Row.

Mishra, V., & Sharma, M. G. (2022). Digital transformation evaluation of telehealth using convergence, maturity, and adoption. *Health Policy and Technology*, *11*(4), 100684. https://doi.org/10.1016/j.hlpt.2022.100684

Mishra, R., Singh, R., & Papadopoulos, T. (2022). Linking digital orientation and data-driven innovations: A SAP–LAP linkage framework and research propositions. *IEEE Transactions on Engineering Management*, *71*, 1346–1358. https://doi.org/10.1109/tem.2022.3153588

Mittal, S., & Dhar, R. L. (2015). Transformational leadership and employee creativity. *Management Decision*, *53*(5), 894–910. https://doi.org/10.1108/md-07-2014-0464

O'Reilly, C., & Tushman, M. (2013). Organizational ambidexterity: Past, present, and future. *Academy of Management Perspectives*, *27*(4), 324–338. http://www.jstor.org/stable/43822033. Accessed on September 23, 2020.

Osiyevskyy, O., & Dewald, J. (2015). Explorative versus exploitative business model change: The cognitive antecedents of firm-level responses to disruptive innovation. *Strategic Entrepreneurship Journal*, *9*(1), 58–78. https://doi.org/10.1002/sej.1192

Peng, M. W., Sun, S. L., & Markóczy, L. (2015). Human Capital and CEO Compensation during Institutional Transitions. *Journal of Management Studies*, *52*(1), 117–147. https://doi.org/10.1111/joms.12106

Petrenko, O. V., Aime, F., Ridge, J. W., & Hill, A. (2015). Corporate social responsibility or CEO narcissism? CSR motivations and organizational performance. *Strategic Management Journal*, *37*(2), 262–279. https://doi.org/10.1002/smj.2348

Podsakoff, P. M., MacKenzie, S. B., Lee, J. Y., & Podsakoff, N. P. (2003). Common method biases in behavioral research: A critical review of the literature and recommended remedies. *Journal of Applied Psychology*, *88*(5), 879–903. https://doi.org/10.1037/0021-9010.88.5.879

Pryor, C. G., Holmes, R. M., Webb, J. W., & Liguori, E. W. (2017). Top executive goal orientations' effects on environmental scanning and performance: Differences between founders and non-founders. *Journal of Management*, *45*(5), 1958–1986. https://doi.org/10.1177/0149206317737354

Qian, C., Cao, Q., & Takeuchi, R. (2013). Top management team functional diversity and organizational innovation in China: The moderating effects of environment. *Strategic Management Journal*, *34*(1), 110–120. https://doi.org/10.1002/smj.1993

Quigley, T. J., & Hambrick, D. C. (2012). When the former CEO stays on as board chair, effects on successor discretion, strategic change, and performance. *Strategic Management Journal*, *33*(7), 834–859. https://doi.org/10.1002/smj.1945

Rader, D. (2019). Digital maturity – The new competitive goal. *Strategy & Leadership*, *47*(5), 28–35. https://doi.org/10.1108/sl-06-2019-0084

Rana, S., Sakshi, & Singh, J. (2022). *Presenting the POWER framework of conducting literature review* (pp. 1–13). Emerald Publishing Limited eBooks. https://doi.org/10.1108/s2754-586520220000001001

Ridge, J. W., Johnson, S. G., Hill, A., & Bolton, J. F. (2017). The role of top management team attention in new product introductions. *Journal of Business Research*, *70*, 17–24. https://doi.org/10.1016/j.jbusres.2016.09.002

Rindova, V. P., & Courtney, H. (2020). To shape or adapt: Knowledge problems, epistemologies, and strategic postures under Knightian uncertainty. *Academy of Management Review*, *45*(4), 787–807. https://doi.org/10.5465/amr.2018.0291

Sahni, S., & Singh Kaurav, R. P. S. (2023). What? Why? When? How? Where? Of technology-based bibliometric review. In S. Rana, J. Singh, & S. Kathuria (Eds.), *Advancing methodologies of conducting literature review in management domain, Review of management literature* (Vol. 2, pp. 79–101). Emerald Publishing Limited. https://doi.org/10.1108/S2754-586520230000002005

Samba, C., Williams, D. W., & Fuller, R. M. (2022). The forms and use of intuition in top management teams. *The Leadership Quarterly*, *33*(3), 101349. https://doi.org/10.1016/j.leaqua.2019.101349

Samimi, M., Cortes, A. F., Anderson, M. H., & Herrmann, P. (2020). What is strategic leadership? Developing a framework for future research. *The Leadership Quarterly*, *33*(3), 101353. https://doi.org/10.1016/j.leaqua.2019.101353

Scuotto, V., Lemaire, S. L. L., Magni, D., & Maâlaoui, A. (2022). Extending knowledge-based view: Future trends of corporate social entrepreneurship to fight the gig economy challenges. *Journal of Business Research*, *139*, 1111–1122. https://doi.org/10.1016/j.jbusres.2021.10.060

Shao, Z. (2019). Interaction effect of strategic leadership behaviors and organizational culture on IS-Business strategic alignment and Enterprise Systems assimilation. *International Journal of Information Management*, *44*, 96–108. https://doi.org/10.1016/j.ijinfomgt.2018.09.010

Singh, A., Jha, S., Srivastava, D. K., & Somarajan, A. (2021). Future of work: A systematic literature review and evolution of themes. *Foresight*, *24*(1), 99–125. https://doi.org/10.1108/fs-09-2020-0093

Singh, A., Lim, W. M., Jha, S., Kumar, S., & Ciasullo, M. V. (2023). The state of the art of strategic leadership. *Journal of Business Research*, *158*, 113676. https://doi.org/10.1016/j.jbusres.2023.113676

Small, H. (1973). Co-citation in the scientific literature: A new measure of the relationship between two documents. *Journal of the American Society for Information Science*, *24*(4), 265–269. https://doi.org/10.1002/asi.4630240406

Smolović, J, O., Grint, K., & Cammock, P. (2015). Public leadership development facilitation and the crossroads blues. *Management Learning*, *46*(4), 391–411. https://doi.org/10.1177/1350507614537020

Tang, Y., Qian, C., Chen, G., & Shen, R. (2014). How CEO hubris affects corporate social (ir)responsibility. *Strategic Management Journal*, *36*(9), 1338–1357. https://doi.org/10.1002/smj.2286

Van Essen, M., Otten, J., & Carberry, E. J. (2015). Assessing Managerial Power Theory: A Meta-Analytic Approach to Understanding the Determinants of CEO Compensation. *Journal of Management*, *41*(1), 164–202. https://doi.org/10.1177/0149206311429378

Vera, D., & Crossan, M. (2004). Strategic Leadership and Organizational Learning. *Academy of Management Review*, *29*(2), 222–240. http://www.jstor.org/stable/20159030. Accessed on September 23, 2020.

Wang, T. (2021). Board human capital diversity and corporate innovation: A longitudinal study. *Corporate Governance*, *22*(4), 680–701. https://doi.org/10.1108/cg-03-2021-0126

Westphal, J. D., Boivie, S., & Chng, D. H. M. (2006). The strategic impetus for social network ties: Reconstituting broken ceo friendship ties. *Strategic Management Journal*, *27*(5), 425–445. https://doi.org/10.1002/smj.525

Yan, Y., & Guan, J. (2018). Social capital, exploitative and exploratory innovations: The mediating roles of ego-network dynamics. *Technological Forecasting and Social Change*, *126*, 244–258. https://doi.org/10.1016/j.techfore.2017.09.004

Yen, C.-Y., Chang, M. H., & Chan, C.-H. (2019). *A computational analysis of the dynamics of R style based on 94 million lines of code from All CRAN packages in the past 20 years*. https://doi.org/10.31235/osf.io/ts2wq

Yi, S., Knudsen, T., & Becker, M. C. (2016). Inertia in routines: A hidden source of organizational variation. *Organization Science*, *27*(3), 782–800. https://doi.org/10.1287/orsc.2016.1059

COLLABORATIVE ARRANGEMENTS IN DEVELOPING SUCCESSFUL BUSINESS STRATEGIES: LITERATURE REVIEW

Maria Prokofieva

Victoria University, Australia

ABSTRACT

Technology triggers business collaboration and partnership as well as becomes an essential part for disruptive business strategies. The literature on this topic is dispersed, and the chapter addresses this gap. This chapter aims to present a systematic literature review of academic studies in disruptive collaborative innovation frameworks and provide guidance for future research by identifying current research gaps. The study uses the PRISMA framework and collects literature from 2015 to 2023 from highly ranked academic venues with the final sample of 112 papers. The section is structured around the PRISMA framework, and results are reported accordingly. The analysis was conducted using a range of methods, including bibliometric analysis, multiple correspondence analysis (MCA), and text network analysis.

The analysis of the literature is presented to identify the main areas of research as well as to gauge the emerging streams. The overall results suggest that this area is starting to develop with limited research available to date. The study identified four theoretical foundations for existing research, aligned with behavioral, network, resource-based (RBV), and knowledge-based views (KBV). The identified theoretical views and themes are discussed, and examples of the studies are provided.

Keywords: Business collaboration; business partnership; business strategy; digital innovation; disruptive business strategy; digital strategy

Review of Technologies and Disruptive Business Strategies
Review of Management Literature, Volume 3, 229–252

ISSN: 2754-5865/doi:10.1108/S2754-586520240000003012

1. INTRODUCTION

With the enormous growth in technological advancement, globalization of the markets, and tightening competition, technological disruption is a topical area. Disruptive technology significantly changes the market and introduces some revolutionary products or services that disrupt existing industries and create new markets and new business players (Christensen, 2016). Disruption can relate to business models, unique market positioning, and competitive advantages that allow companies to create new value propositions, capture market share, and outperform competition (Hambrick, 2023).

Globalization, advances in technology, and tightening competition provide favorable conditions for the development of collaborative arrangements where businesses join efforts to resolve some mutual business problems, in some cases remaining competitors in their industry. With the scarcity of resources, innovation collaborative arrangements become critical to new incumbent firms as well as offer a way for more established companies to retain or improve their performance. Some recent cases of disruptive collaboration include the development of the edX platform as a disruption in the higher education (Corbo et al., 2023). The platform was launched in 2012 as a collaboration between Harvard and MIT universities which joined forces to develop the first platform to allow uniform online access to various educational courses. Another case is Apple and Amazon's partnership in 2017 which resulted in the disruption of the smart speaker and streaming music industries when Amazon Echo users started to access Apple's music streaming service on a competing platform. Another very recent example is the collaboration between Apple and Google during COVID-19: the companies developed jointly contact-tracing technology to monitor COVID-19 outbreak (Bouncken, Fredrich, Kraus, & Ritala, 2020).

Business collaboration can have many forms, including business collaboration in a broader sense and partnerships (Kaurav & Gupta, 2022). While both concepts refer to joint actions of multiple entities to achieve a common goal, business partnership is narrower in meaning and is different in its structural and organizational form. While both concepts relate to collaborative arrangements between two or more entities, partnerships require a more formal arrangement (e.g., a document with set goals and actions) and are usually governed by laws, such as the Uniform Partnership Act (UPA) in USA. The paper uses "collaborative arrangement" and "innovation collaboration" to refer to various forms of business collaboration.

Innovation collaborations are very common in business: they allow to pool resources, expertise, and capabilities and drive innovation in various domains, such as technology, business processes, product development, or research. The specific nature of an innovation can vary widely depending on the goals and objectives of the participating entities, but the overarching aim is to generate novel ideas, solutions, or products.

Disruptive collaborative arrangements are getting traction and can be seen across different industries, including electric vehicles, cybersecurity, fintech, pharmaceuticals, and others. Despite the effect of disruptive innovation on the lives of people, academic literature in this area is lagging, and research is limited and dispersed. While the literature on business collaborations and disruptive innovation is relatively established, research on disruptive collaborative arrangements is just starting to emerge. The current study addresses this gap by presenting a structured review of available resources regarding theoretical and methodological aspects as well as suggests a roadmap for future directions. This is the motivation and contribution of the study.

The current study focuses on collaborative innovation which is the case of multiple organizations or entities working together to create new products, services, or technologies that disrupt the current market or industry. Such innovation and disruption leverage complementary resources of the collaborators, shared knowledge, infrastructure, etc., as well as can lead to the development of platforms and ecosystems.

Based on this definition of collaborative disruptive innovation, the current study aims to present a comprehensive overview of the current literature in this area and addresses the research questions below:

- What are the common trends in academic research in business collaboration with a focus on disruptive innovation?
- What are the main themes that can be identified in the literature and gaps for future research?

The above research questions are addressed by developing a comprehensive literature review following the PRISMA framework (Page et al., 2021) and conducting a text analysis of the papers, using text network analysis techniques (as discussed in the relevant section).

The chapter is organized as follows. The next section provides an overview of business collaborations and partnerships and gauges the benefits and challenges of leveraging them in developing successful business strategies. The section also defines how to evaluate business strategies regarding their sustainability. Section 3 overviews the research design to select sources and papers for the systematic review and describes the procedures undertaken in the study. An overview of the PRISMA framework and applied procedures is provided. Section 4 discusses the findings, and the next section concludes the chapter.

2. BACKGROUND

Disruptive business strategy refers to a strategy used by companies to disrupt established markets and create innovative business models (Christensen, 2016). Disruptive business collaboration in this sense refers to collaboration or partnership between business entities with a common goal to disrupt traditional markets or industries. It usually involves two or more business parties working together on innovative ideas to leverage complementary strengths (Bouncken, Fredrich, Kraus, & Ritala, 2020). Collaborating business parties can come from the same or different industries, while they bring together diverse expertise and complementary resources to drive innovation (Bouncken, Fredrich, Ritala, &

Kraus, 2020). The existing industries are challenged by the introduction of more cost-effective solutions, customer experience, or creating an entirely new market (Eisenhardt & Martin, 2000).

Compared to sole performance, collaborative approaches are seen to amplify not only innovation performance, i.e., registered patents and inventions (Kim & Song, 2007), but also as usage of innovative products and solutions (Fang, 2011; Kang & Park, 2012; Lahiri & Narayanan, 2013). This can have a pronounced impact on the financial performance of the collaborating firms and increase their net income, sales, margins, and market share (Lahiri & Narayanan, 2013).

However, not all collaborations target disruption. The current paper adopts the definition of disruptive innovation as a set of key characteristics which include (Christensen & Overdorf, 2000; Christensen et al., 2015):

- The establishment of new customer engagement methods.
- Typically leading to reduced overall profits.
- Often diverging from the conventional track of enhancing performance expected by mainstream consumers.
- Introducing a fresh trajectory of performance and enhancing it in ways different from the traditional.

In summary, disruptive innovation results in a product or service that may be inferior as defined by the mainstream consumer as introduced but has new features that are valued by the low-end or new market customer (e.g., being cheaper, smaller, or easier to use). As an extent of this, disruptive business models have low margins, niche markets, and small scales (Govindarajan & Kopalle, 2006).

Collaborative arrangements may involve competing companies working together to develop novel approaches or products while sharing the responsibilities and expenses associated with R&D (e.g., Arranz & de Arroyabe, 2008). Very often, it is a blend of collaboration and competition with a trade-off between equity and opportunism, shared ownership, and control (Ricciardi et al., 2021). The literature refers to this as "coopetition" which is a coexistence of competitive and cooperative elements (Brandenburger & Nalebuff, 1996).

Collaborative innovation offers a new approach to disrupt the market. Collaboration and partnership open multiple opportunities for business, including accelerating growth, creating scale and learning economies, leveraging complementary resources, knowledge sharing, and risk management. While companies may lack the necessary resources and internal capabilities for innovation, seeking them from external sources, i.e., via collaborative agreements and partnerships, offers a solution (Feranita et al., 2017).

While some literature differentiates between "collaboration" and "partnership," the current study includes both and refers to them as "collaborative arrangements." The further sections investigate this phenomenon empirically.

3. RESEARCH DESIGN

The current paper conducts a comprehensive literature review (Rammal, 2023, pp. 27–35) following the PRISMA framework and addresses the following objectives:

- Identify the common in academic research in business collaboration with a focus on disruptive innovation.
- Identify and analyze the main themes in the academic literature and discuss the gaps to be addressed in future research.

The review of the literature intended to gauge the field from general management to disruptive innovation and develop a framework to align identified theoretical perspectives. The first assessment was done by analyzing papers at the bibliometrics level and then thematic mapping (Boyatzis, 1998) to identify emerging themes and patterns. The whole process was completed by a researcher and two research assistants.

3.1 Search Strategy

The study used the Lens platform to search literature (https://www.lens.org/) The Lens is an online aggregator of metadata that combines three repositories with scholarly literature metadata and citation indexing. The data sources include CrossRef, PubMed, OpenAlex, and Microsoft Academic (discontinued at the end of 2021) and supplementary data from additional data sources, including Unpaywall, OpenCitations, DOAJ, ORCID, ROR, PMC, and publishers such as Springer Nature. These sources cover a broad range of areas, including business studies, management, and technology and best fit with the focus of the study.

The study used structured search with the query "(Disruptive business strategy OR Disruptive strategy Or Disruption strategy) AND (Partnership OR Collaboration) AND Technology" in the Title/Abstract/Keywords. Inclusion criteria consisted of (a) journal and conference papers between 2015 and 2023; (b) papers matching the search query; (c) studies on business collaboration and/or partnership for technological disruption. Given the heterogeneity of methodological approaches both quantitively, qualitative and mixed methods studies were considered.

Fig. 1 panel A shows the PRISMA flowchart selection process (Kaurav et al., 2020; Rana et al., 2022). The search strategy produced 308 relevant records. The use of the aggregator platform allowed avoiding duplicate records. After initial screening and exclusion of irrelevant records, 172 papers remained. Further screening was undertaken by two researchers using full-text assessment of the remaining papers. Overall, 112 studies providing empirical evidence met the outlined criteria.

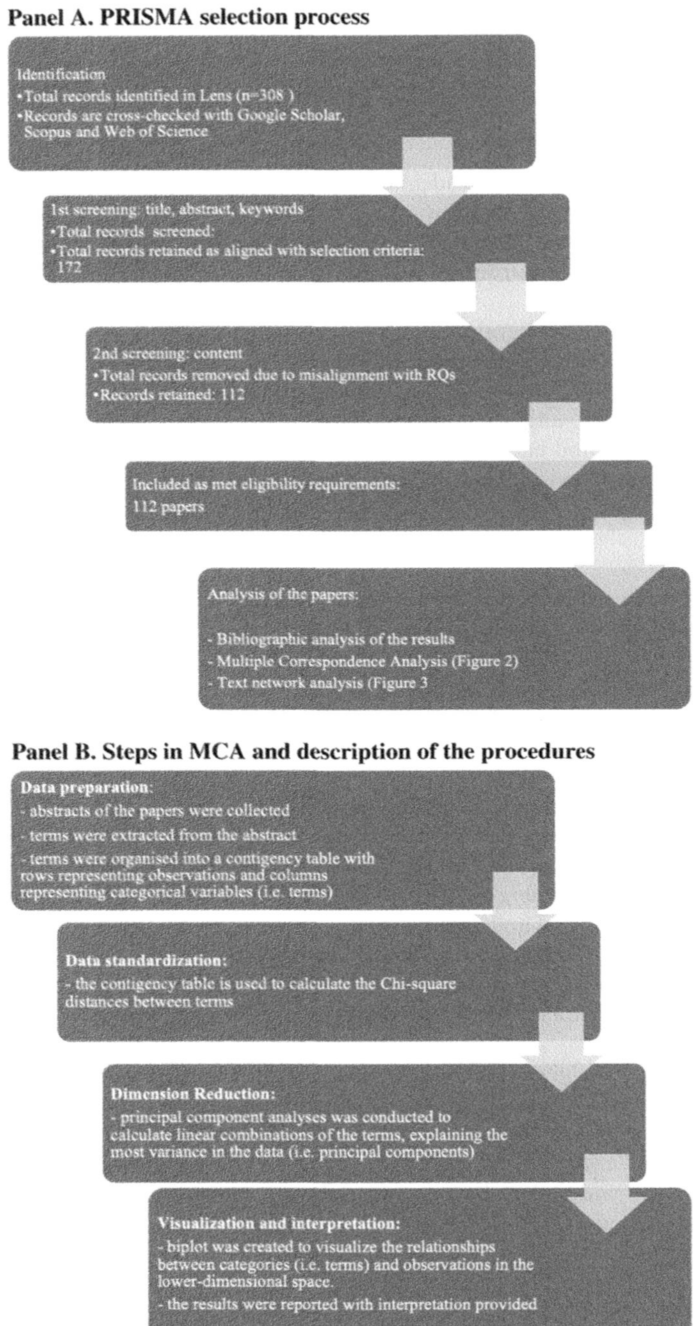

Fig. 1. Research Design. Panel A. PRISMA selection process. Panel B. Steps in MCA and description of the procedures. *Source:* Authors.

3.2 Methods

To address the RQ1, the study conducted bibliometric analysis (Sahni & Kaurav, 2023) using R package "bibliometrix" (Aria & Cuccurullo, 2017). All collected literature was exported from Lens and imported into RStudio where it was analyzed with the following findings. Bibliometric analysis is an emerging area of research (Srivastava, 2021; Wang et al., 2020) that aims to classify and identify relationships between publications (Anlesinya & Dadzie, 2023, pp. 57–78). It identifies main sources of academic content (Gauthier 1998) while quantifying and visually representing the results (Dagnino et al., 2015). This method uses quantitative indicators to identify possible main themes through mapping of the studies and cluster analysis (Srivastava, 2021).

The analysis started with cluster analysis using association strength of the keywords (Ali & Anwar, 2021), which was assessed using equation (1):

$$AS_{ij} = \frac{C_{ij}}{w_i w_j}, \tag{1}$$

where,

C_{ij} is the co-occurrences of items i and j.
w_i and w_j are the total occurrences of items i and j.

With independence of co-occurrences of i and j, the similarity is proportional to the ratio between the observed number of co-occurrences of i and j and the expected number of co-occurrences of i and j (van Eck & Waltman 2010). The similarity was used to allocate collected papers into clusters as presented in Fig. 1 and different clusters are highlighted in different colors. These clusters form the basis for discussion to address RQ2 further.

Further analysis was done using multiple correspondence analysis (MCA). MCA is commonly used in literature reviews (Le Roux & Rouanet, 2010) because it allows exploration of relationships and patterns in multidimensional categorical data. Fig. 1 Panel B shows the steps in MCA in relation to the analysis conducted:

Further analysis was done using two-mode (i.e., Bipartite) network analysis with R/Python packages "igraph" (Horvát et al., 2023) and "textnets" (Boy, 2020) and conducted using the following steps:

Step 1. Preparation and preprocessing of the text.
Step 2. Creating a text network.
Step 3. Visualizing the text network.
Step 4. Detecting themes within the text network.

During step 1, the papers were preprocessed for networks based on word co-occurrence and then preprocessed further using word co-occurrence and sentiment analysis of sentences containing the words (i.e., tokens).

In step 2, the generated data frame was used to create a weighted adjacency matrix, where the rows and columns were grouping variables, i.e., papers, and tokenized words. This step is described in more details in Bail (2016).

In the next step, the weighted adjacency matrix was used to visualize the network structure with colored nodes identifying clusters (i.e., modularity classes). The density of the created network was leveraged using the network backbone technique where selected edges were removed using the disparity filter algorithm to make the network presentation more informative. The default tuning parameter for alpha of 0.25 was used. Additional visualization was created as an interactive JavaScript component and is available under supplementary material.

4. RESULTS AND DISCUSSION

4.1 What Are Common Trends in Academic Research in Business Collaboration and Partnerships to Develop a Disruptive Business Strategy?

The results indicate the evolution of research on collaborative disruptive innovation from 2015 to 2021. Fig. 2 (Panel A) illustrates the rapid development of the studies in this topic, but the growth pattern in the volume of research was inconsistent in the earlier years. This inconsistency reflects technological advancements and demonstrates the increasing traction of the concept. Fig. 2 (Panels B) shows the distribution of papers across research areas and confirms the emerging, but widespread applicability of collaborative arrangements.

The growth in the number of papers as well as increasing recognition of this field shows the development in different industries, such as pharma, biotech (Mishra & Sharma, 2022), and AI (Kaushal et al., 2023).

The results of MCA are presented in Fig. 3 where higher interdependences are shown as closer descriptor positioning. A closer proximity around the center indicates a larger proportion of papers on a topic (Bendixen, 1995). This allowed further analysis for RQ2 which revealed four theoretical foundations (i.e., views) and three themes (i.e., focus views), mapped in Fig. 4.

The generated network and modularity classes were used to identify latent. The Louvain community detection approach was applied to edge weights to identify the number of clusters (i.e., latent themes) within the network. The results showed assignment of each document and modularity class to the identified cluster. The identified theoretical views and themes in the research are discussed below.

4.2 What Are Theoretical and Methodological Approaches Used in the Studies?

Disruptive business collaboration, though a relatively new concept, has a substantial academic foundation in disruptive innovation literature. Introduced by Christensen in 1997, disruptive innovation is rooted in the S-curve and technology life cycle, illustrating typical technology development phases (Christensen, 2016). These innovations often arise from a mix of factors, including technological enablers, business model innovation potential, and evolving customer

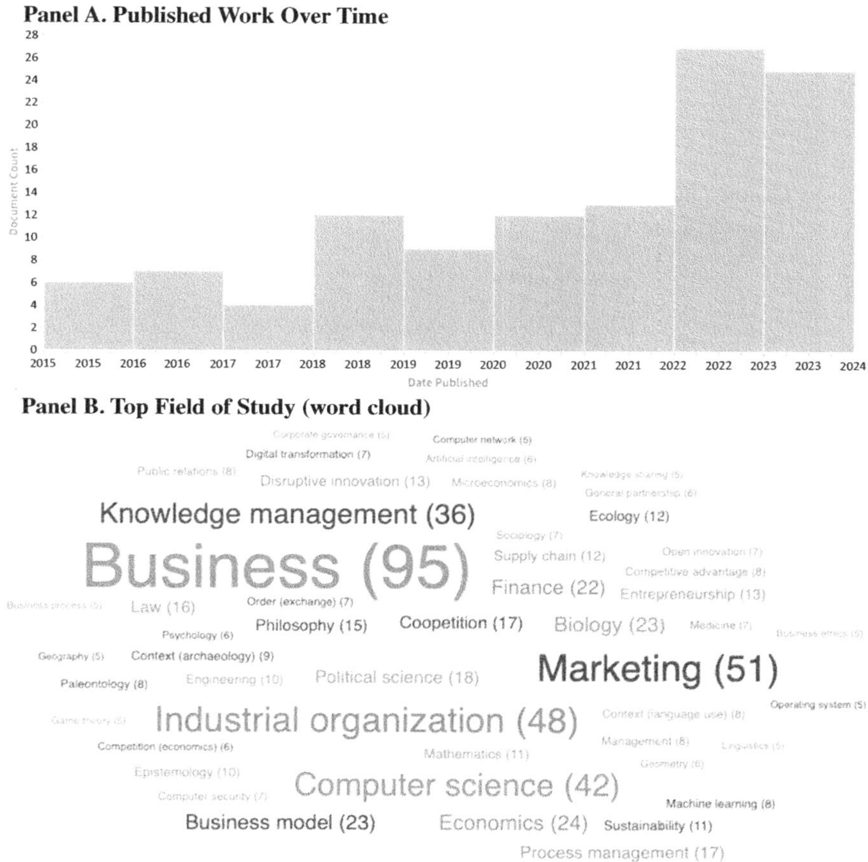

Fig. 2. Evolution of Research Between 2015 and 2023. Panel A. Published work over time. Panel B. Top fields of study (word cloud). *Source:* Authors.

preferences, often originating from niche markets. The value network and modularity are crucial, fostering conditions for disruptive innovations to integrate into existing markets and facilitating market entry. Networks, encompassing ecosystems of customers, suppliers, and complementors, are essential for promoting technology adoption and disruption. Complementors, in particular, play a pivotal role by enhancing and complementing disruptive technology offerings, contributing to the development of platforms and ecosystems (Brandenburger, 1996).

The theoretical foundations of business collaboration stem from diverse fields, including management, economics, and sociology, and offer insights into the motivations, processes, and outcomes of collaboration across various industries. For instance, Transaction Cost Economics (TCE), as proposed by Oliver

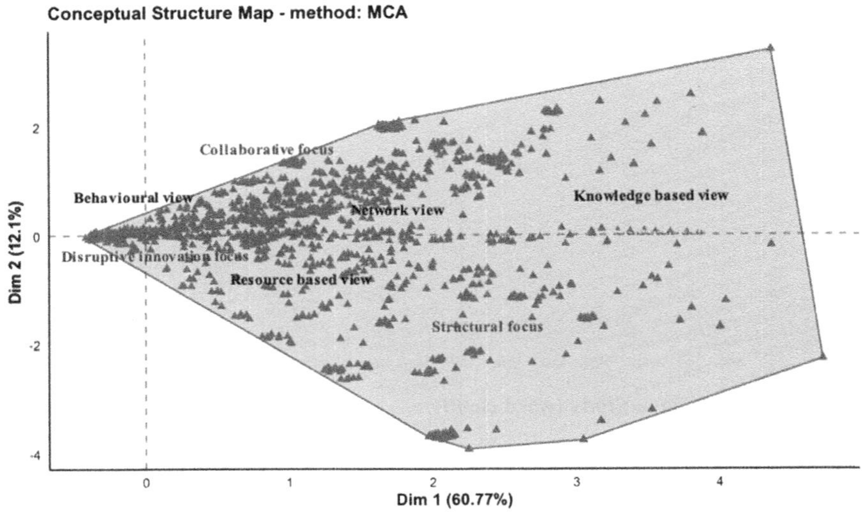

Fig. 3. The Results of MCA on the Collected Literature. *Source:* Authors.

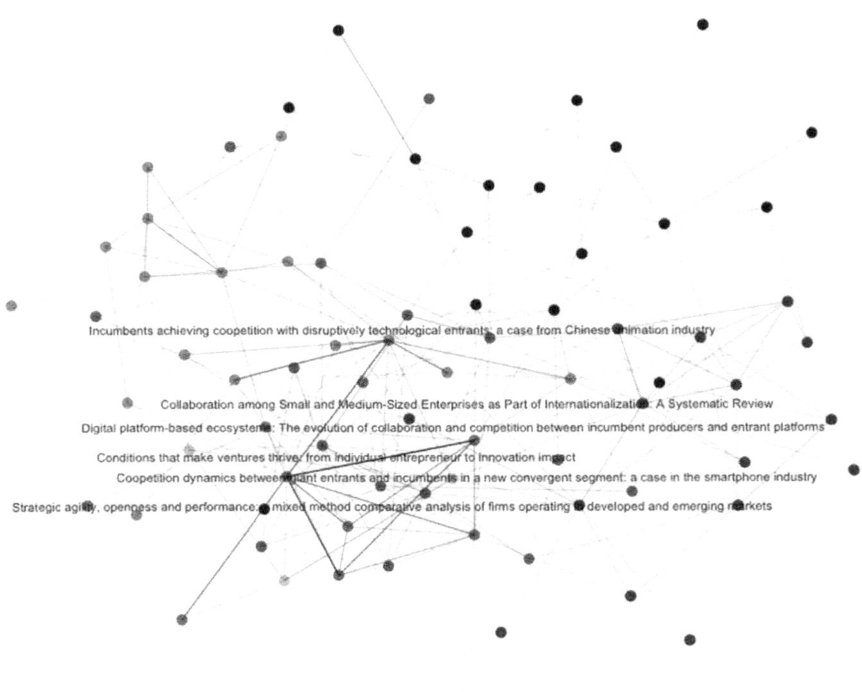

Fig. 4. Visualized Text Network (Based on Abstracts). *Source:* Authors.

Williamson, examines how firms operate under different economic conditions (Williamson, 1987). TCE posits that collaboration is chosen over market transactions when it reduces inefficiencies and uncertainties, influencing the governance structure of collaborations such as alliances or partnerships, crucial for innovation and potentially leading to disruptive innovation. Additionally, Gulati (1999) shifts the focus from viewing firms as autonomous entities to analyzing strategic business networks. This study outlines five key strategic research areas, including industry structure, firm positioning, unique resources, costs (coordination and contracting), dynamic constraints, and network benefits.

During the past few years, academic research has started to emerge and look closely at the intersection of collaboration and disruptive innovation streams: which particular collaborations can lead to disruptive innovation and how collaboration governance structure can promote or hinder critical innovation.

The analysis of the studies conducted in the previous section shows four main theoretical foundations, including behavioral, network, resource, and knowledge-based views.

The behavioral view in business research, rooted in the bounded rationality concept (Simon, 1972) and behavioral theory of the firm (Cyert & March 1963), focuses on the limitations of rational choices due to cognitive constraints, information availability, and time. This perspective forms the basis for understanding internal decision-making and behaviors within organizations, emphasizing the complex nature of business decisions influenced by individual rationality limits. Recent studies in this area, such as Czakon et al. (2020) and Zheng et al. (2023), explore these concepts further. Czakon et al. (2020) investigated the behavioral aspects of coopetition antecedents from managers' viewpoints, highlighting strategic rationale and coopetition mindset as key drivers of intentional coopetition strategy. Zheng et al. (2023) focused on top managers' mindsets and behaviors in collaborative innovation, revealing that CEOs with coopetitive mindsets are more inclined toward alliance-based innovation, influenced by factors like innovation challenges, technological uncertainty, and regional intellectual property dynamics. These studies underscore the reciprocal nature of disruptive innovation collaboration and the moderating role of executive job demands on CEOs' mindsets in the context of firms' innovation coopetition.

The behavioral view in disruptive collaboration suggests that bounded rationality makes it challenging for entities to navigate the inherent ambiguity in diverse collaborative relationships. Formalized collaborations, like partnerships, often result in more defined business outcomes, but evaluating the action-outcome nexus becomes complex in developing disruptive strategies. Dorn et al. (2016) highlighted the difficulty in assessing outcomes against key indicators, especially with delayed results in collaborative innovation. Chai et al. (2020) explored innovation in coopetition (simultaneous cooperation and competition) within B2B relationships, emphasizing the mediating role of conflicts (affective and cognitive) on the innovation process. Raza-Ullah and Kostis (2020) found that collaborative innovation leads to superior performance, significantly influenced by the balance of trust and distrust. Trust enhances relationships, while distrust positively impacts coopetition intensity and performance. Sellitto et al. (2018) demonstrated that failing to meet customer requirements can initiate coopetition, supported by sustainability, knowledge and resource sharing, risk mitigation, and increased sales through price reduction as reinforcing feedback factors.

A different aspect on collaborative disruptive innovation is presented using the network perspective, initially introduced in Gulati (1999). This perspective reviews disruptive collaboration through examining the structure and dynamics of relationships among businesses. The disruptive innovation and business models emerge from the connection and interaction in the business network. As information, knowledge, and resources flow through networks between nodes (i.e., business) and ties (i.e., business connections), collaboration stimulates generation and diffusion of innovations. For example, technological networking was identified among the best predictor of technological innovation (Arranz et al., 2020; Lafuente et al., 2023; Poorkavoos et al., 2016).

Additional references within this perspective pertain to relational capital and Open Innovation (Lenart-Gansiniec, 2016). The relational capital concept highlights the value of relationships and social capital as embedded in business networks. It becomes particularly important in developing a sustainable strategy with disruptive innovation, development of trust, and positive attitude toward the change.

Disruptive innovation via networks allows firms to be more flexible. However, Hynes and Elwell (2016) showed that business networks can either enable or delay disruptive technologies. The effect largely depends on collaborative and collective actions of the network participants. Global network coopetition increases firm performance and boosts innovation through structural features, such as network size, position, and diversity. The key concept in this network perspective is the strategic network with a focus on specialization in value chain to develop a sustainable competitive advantage. Such network is orchestrated with formal or informal arrangements with the ultimate goal of disruptive innovation.

Networks foster collaborative arrangements with flexible setup. Xie et al. (2016) identified four factors of collaborative innovation network. They include the network size, heterogeneity, tie-strength, and centrality. The study showed that the network size, network centrality, and network tie strength were critical for knowledge transfer performance, while network heterogeneity was less significant on these arrangements. In line with these findings, Hani and Dagnino (2021) demonstrated that globally driven network structures improve firm innovation and performance. Global network coopetition (GNC) structural characteristics, e.g., network size, position, and diversity, affect innovation significantly: with positive effects of GNC on firm performance and firm innovation indicators.

Research shows that network and prior ties are particularly important with smaller companies and start-ups and become critical in less formal business arrangements (Bouncken, Fredrich, Kraus, & Ritala, 2020; Bouncken, Fredrich, Ritala, & Kraus, 2020; Corbo et al., 2023). More formalized arrangement provides more focus to the collaboration, and the parties are more motivated and strategic about developing strategic goals and innovative outcomes.

An interesting view for further research is in comparing the horizontal versus vertical collaborations. While horizontal collaborative arrangements have been studied in Estrada et al. (2016), Park et al. (2014), and others, vertical collaborations, e.g., vertical coopetition, is an emerging area of research. Some early references to this can be found in Mariani (2007) and its implications for innovation were referenced in Chai et al. (2020). Lafuente et al. (2023) further show that firms with the highest innovation rating are more likely to have vertical co-innovation strategies.

Another interesting finding that is suggested for future research is to relate disruptive innovation to networks structure, e.g., structural deficiencies. Since there are some evidences that innovation success is more likely in less developed innovation systems (Lafuente et al., 2023), the effect of the network structure may be more pronounced, but it is yet to be researched.

Further research was highlighted on the classification of collaborative arrangements into direct and indirect coopetition (Klimas & Czakon, 2018), where indirect coopetition is viewed as collaboration with entities offering different products or services, but targeting the same customer and the same demand/need (Kraus et al., 2018). As it is seen, coopetition studies have been growing extensively, and further consideration was to analyze the composition of coopetition as the balance of collaboration and competition for disruptive innovation. Some references can be found in Park et al. (2014) where the concept of balanced coopetition for effective innovation is introduced as a balance between cooperation and competition.

The third theoretical perspective on disruptive collaborative arrangements is based on the resource-based view (RBV) of the firm (Barney et al., 2011). This approach posits that competitive advantage is developed over time as firms have resources that are valuable, nonsubstitutable, inimitable, and rare. The assumption is the conceptualization of complimentary shared resources distributed across firms. The underlying foundation stems from Resource Dependence Theory (RDT) (Pfeffer, 2003) which stipulates that organizations and institutions do not live in vacuum and depend on external resources to survive and thrive. To get access to external resources, organizations engage with external environment by building a relationship with external organizations to secure resources required for operations and growth. The nature of the resources can be diverse (e.g., raw materials, labor, technology, political support, etc.) as well as the developed relationship with external firms (e.g., alliances, partnerships, or business networks). While RDT does not directly explain disruptive innovation, it provides a necessary ground for explanation of development and maintenance of collaborative arrangements that can lead to it. Interesting aspect is highlighted that relational view is critical for family firms and community-based engagement where family firms are shown to be more sensitive to social capital and long-lasting relationships building (Miller & Le Breton-Miller, 2005).

With application to collaborative arrangements and disruptive business strategy, RBV perspective enhances the importance of unique resources and capabilities, such as technological expertise, proprietary knowledge, or specialized skills that a company brings to the collaborative arrangement, as well as selection of collaboration partners that complement resource gaps. Markovic and Bagherzadeh (2018) demonstrated that seeking appropriate external collaborations for innovation for resources sharing generated many advantages, including better innovation performance.

RBV highlights that resource bundling and knowledge sharing are prone to create circumstances for value creation through innovative solutions (products, services, or business models) to disrupt. Studies showed that capabilities are needed to integrate, reconfigure, gain, and release resources, consisting of identifiable and specific routines that put these resources into use (Eisenhardt & Martin, 2000). Some examples of the studies, based on RBV, include Fredrich et al. (2019) who looked at configurations of strong and weak interfirm learning in coopetition alliances. Interorganizational co-innovation was analyzed in Zhong and Nieminen (2015) who showed it as a successful strategy for mobile payment service innovation.

Related to RBV is the knowledge-based view (KBV) which focuses on how companies use their knowledge and capabilities to gain competitive advantage. This view assumes that knowledge and intellectual assets are crucial factors that allow businesses to innovate to establish their competitive position (Grant, 2002). In the context of collaborative innovation and disruptive technologies, how companies collaborate with other businesses becomes essential with knowledge being the most critical strategic asset. Knowledge transfer mediates technology exchange in collaborative arrangements and networks and allows access to novel expertise and breakthroughs. This is shown in Bouncken and Kraus (2013): collaborative arrangements trigger radical innovation. However, they can also be detrimental, especially in the case of small and medium-sized enterprises (SMEs) and knowledge sharing. The optimal balance of knowledge sharing and information ownership arrangement is an important area of future research. Evidence provided in Markovic and Bagherzadeh (2018) shows that knowledge-sharing mechanisms impact the breadth of external stakeholder cocreation and affect innovation performance.

This highlights an important point for future research: the role and impact of social capital in developing collaborative arrangements leading to disruptive business strategy. The results show a lack of research on how community ties affect collaboration with an interesting special case of crowdfunding in business collaboration and disruption. Further attention can be directed to the effect of disruption and collaboration on the community. Such an effect can be reviewed through the lens of other theories, such as institutional theory and social contract theory.

The identified theoretical foundations allow identification three thematic areas of research as a cross-section of disruptive innovation studies (Theme 1), collaborative arrangements research (Theme 2), and implementational side, i.e., structural focus (Theme 3).

4.2.1 Theme 1: The Disruptive Innovation Focus

The focus of this theme is more on innovation itself, such as product innovation or service innovation. The collaborative aspect is review as orchestration of the arrangement that provides favorable conditions for critical innovation development. Some studies in this area include Bouncken, Fredrich, Kraus, and Ritala (2020). Bouncken et al. (2016) investigated the influence of collaborative arrangements and governance mechanisms in particular on product innovation. Analyzing the European medical device industry, the study showed that a higher degree of collaboration or coopetition related to the use of transactional governance, i.e., explicit and formal contracts, actually hampers product innovation. Interestingly, relational governance, i.e., higher degree of trust and commitment in inter-entity exchanges, had positive effects on product innovativeness and development of critical innovation.

Another example is Chai et al.'s (2020) study on vertical B2B collaboration and its impact on innovative processes, process innovation in particular. The study showed that critical innovation is contingent on factors, such as interfirm characteristics, conflict, and trust. The study revealed a positive link between collaboration (i.e., coopetition in this case) and efficiency process innovations. However, this association was influenced by affective conflict, which had a negative indirect effect despite interfirm trust. Additionally, cognitive conflict exerted a negative indirect effect when interfirm trust is high.

In a broader exploration involving a cross-industry sample of over 16,000 firms, Markovic et al. (2020) sought to determine whether firms could enhance service innovation through coopetition and whether product innovation played a role in this dynamic. Their findings demonstrated that when firms engage in cooperative endeavors with competitors, service innovation becomes 1.38 times more likely compared to situations where such cooperation does not occur. Interestingly, the presence or absence of product innovation did not alter this relationship.

4.2.2 Theme 2: The Collaborative Focus

The studies in this theme focus on the structure of the collaborative arrangements. For example, Park and Kim (2020) investigated coopetition as a strategy to enter newly convergent segments dominated by giant entrants. Cozzolino et al. (2021) supported this study and provided analysis of how incumbent producers were challenged by digital entrant platforms with a focus on disruptive innovation. The study identified three sequential phases in the industry dynamics, including allied competition, selective cooperation, and coopetition. The results showed how changes using multilevel strategies were effective for incumbent companies as growing producer and market segments and technological components.

Coopetition is a prominent category of research in this stream: as companies operate in the same industry, they are more likely to target disruptive innovation due to shared industry knowledge and united resources. Xie et al. (2022) developed a conceptual framework explaining SMEs' business model innovation mediated via digital platforms through capability reconfiguration. The results of the evaluation with a sample of SMEs in China showed that digital platforms enhance both capability reconfiguration and SMEs' business model innovation. The study also reviewed the effect of evolutionary and substitutional capability reconfiguration during collaboration.

Apart from collaboration and partnership, another type of collaborative arrangement is coopetition. The concept of "coopetition" originates from Brandenburger and Nalebuff in "Co-Opetition: A Revolution Mindset" (1996). Coopetition is referred to an arrangement where there is a simultaneous cooperation and competition between business with a target to achieve mutually beneficial outcomes while remaining competitors. It becomes one of the widely recognized business strategies and is showcased across different industries. One of the most common examples of coopetition for disruptive innovation is collaboration with competitors to develop new technologies or enter emerging markets, however, while collaborating, companies maintain their rivalry in other areas. A good example of such a case is coopetition between Apple and Samsung, where Apple uses Samsung to supply components (e.g., semiconductors) as well as they collaborated to develop some wireless standards, while they still remained competitors in the smartphone market segment (Park & Kim, 2021).

GNC is another good example where joint actions of multinational enterprises aim to improve performance: companies share complementary resources with competitors (i.e., cooperating), but at the same time take independent actions to improve performance (i.e., competition part) (Hani & Dagnino, 2020). GNC is usually common in areas where companies need to collaborate to address complex global challenges, e.g., climate change mitigation, pandemic response, supply chain resilience, global education access, etc.). For example, in the electrical vehicle market, the electric vehicle charging infrastructure (e.g., Tesla Supercharger Network) is a collaborative effort of rival automakers who built a robust charging infrastructure to encourage the adoption of electric vehicles (Czakon et al., 2020).

4.2.3 Theme 3: The Structural Focus

This theme includes studies that relate to cases of disruptive innovation resulting from collaborative arrangements. The case study method is employed to relate to the theoretical foundation, understand success factors, analyze business strategy, or provide guidance and policy advice.

Disruptive technology may emerge because of collaboration within the same industry as well as across different industries. Table 1 shows examples of research in this theme and a brief description.

The understanding of the common trends supported with the analysis of the theoretical and methodological themes allows identifying future research directions, discussed in the next section.

Table 1. Examples of Papers in Theme 3.

Area	Sampled Papers	Brief Description
Interindustry (i.e., industry specific) collaboration		
	Jin and Shin (2020)	The paper is focused on the fashion retail industry and provides an analysis of disruptive business model innovations and how they disrupt the industry. The paper presents a case of three disruptor–collaborators in the industry: Born-digital brands, AI-based forecasting and product design, and collaborative consumption.
	Park and Kim (2021)	This study explores the evolving dynamics of coopetition between major new entrants from various sectors and established industry leaders, particularly examining its impact on battles for industry leadership within converging segments. It includes a case study of coopetition between Apple and Samsung in the smartphone market, adopting both a wide-ranging and a detailed perspective.
Cross-industry collaboration		
	Galvin et al. (2020)	This research explores the role of DIY laboratories in fostering the development of new technologies, products, and services, particularly through the utilization of cost-effective facilities by enterprising individuals. The focus of the study is on the widespread use, functioning, and various contextual elements influencing DIY laboratories within the bicycle industry, specifically for creating innovations at the component level. Central to the study is the concept of leveraging knowledge spillovers across industries, where DIY laboratories act as incubators for transferring and repurposing specialized knowledge from high-tech sectors to less technologically advanced sectors, thereby facilitating incremental innovation.
Platform ecosystem		
	Peters et al. (2015)	The paper analyses the case of telemedicine which is a disruptive collaborative innovation. The paper reviews the topic from the complex services perspective and uses a design research approach to develop and evaluate a framework for a successful business model and suggests three business model patterns for implementation.
	Cozzolino et al. (2021)	This study delves into the global digital advertising landscape, exploring how established producers navigate between competitive and cooperative tactics in reaction to emerging digital platforms. The research uncovers various layered strategies that enhance impact across market segments, products, and technological aspects, focusing on how incumbent producers adjust to the challenges posed by new entrant platforms.

Source: Authors.

5. FUTURE RESEARCH DIRECTIONS

The conducted analysis suggests four main directions for further research, including behavioral, structural, resource-based, and knowledge creation directions.

5.1 Direction 1: Behavioral Direction

The behavioral direction emphasizes the complexities of decision-making within organizations and focuses on mindset, psychological aspects, and behavioral dynamics in collaborative arrangements. While some work in this direction is already present in the research of Chai et al. (2020), Czakon et al. (2020) and

Zheng et al. (2023), this direction becomes more complex and topical with globalization, remote environments, and cross-country opportunities. The identified further direction is suggested in the application of sociocultural theories addressing social dynamics, cultural context, and psychological aspects of disruptive innovation. Some suggested topics may investigate how social and cultural contexts influence the behaviors, interactions, and decision-making processes of individuals and groups within collaborative settings.

The examples of research questions are:

- What are the effects of cultural norms, values, and social structures on collaboration dynamics, innovation process, and outcomes across different contexts?
- How does cross-cultural and intersocietal collaboration impact community development, social capital, and local innovation ecosystems?
- In what ways do cultural differences affect the trust-building process and knowledge sharing in international innovation teams?
- How can sociocultural theories be applied to understand the resistance or adoption of disruptive technologies in diverse cultural settings?
- What role do societal values play in shaping the policies and regulatory frameworks for collaborative disruptive innovation?
- How do social structures influence the distribution of benefits and credit in collaborative innovation across different cultures?

These questions aim to explore the multifaceted impact of sociocultural factors on the process and success of collaborative innovations, particularly when these collaborations cross cultural and societal boundaries.

5.2 Direction 2: Structural Direction

The structural direction focuses on the organizational structure and its dynamics in relationships among businesses during collaboration. The focus is on how these elements can foster or hinder the emergence of disruptive innovation and business models. This perspective is based on Gulati (1999) and subsequent studies and extends understanding of relational capital, open innovation, and network coopetition in enhancing firm performance and innovation. Apart from the use of the business networks, further research is suggested to look into Structural Holes Theory (Burt, 2004) and Strength of Weak Ties (Granovetter, 2003).

The application of Structural Holes Theory could provide more insights on how gaps within a network can be exploited to facilitate innovative interactions and ideas. On the other hand, the use of the Strength of Weak Ties theory could provide more insights on how peripheral connections may lead to unexpected insights and opportunities, essential for disruptive collaborations.

Research questions suggested for further exploration include:

- What is the impact of structural holes within industry networks on collaborative arrangements and disruptive business models?
- What role do structural holes play in the dissemination of disruptive technologies across different sectors?

- What is the impact of weak ties on the spread of collaborative disruptive innovations beyond the originating industry or sector?
- What is the impact of density and centrality in business networks on collaboration and spread of disruptive innovations?
- How does the structure of a social network affect the resilience and adaptability of businesses during disruptive shifts?

These questions are focused on the role of networks in innovation, providing valuable insights to understand the power of relationships for disruptive innovation.

5.3 Direction 3: Resource-Based Direction

The resource-based direction focuses on building competitive advantage through unique resources, including digital assets, dynamic capabilities, and access to emerging markets. Examining the synergy between RBV and game theories will help to understand changing environments and the orchestration of collaboration to maximize dynamic capabilities and reconfigure resources for agile development.

Suggested research questions may include:

- What are the applications of RBV to digital assets and dynamic capabilities?
- With rapidly changing environments, how collaboration for disruption can be orchestrated with a view of dynamic capabilities and reconfiguration of resources to address agile developments?
- What are the applications of RBV in emerging markets with resource constraints and institutional factors?
- What is a possible symbiosis of the RBV and game theories to address agility?

5.4 Direction 4: Knowledge Creation Direction

The knowledge creation direction aims to extend current research into knowledge ecosystems and dynamics of knowledge creation and sharing. With recent advances in ML/AI domains, generative AI, and data-driven decision-making, this direction aims to understand the effect of accessible AI on global knowledge markets and the overall innovation process.

Some possible research questions may include:

- What are the effects of knowledge ecosystems on collaborative arrangements and disruptive innovation?
- How do the dynamics of knowledge creation, sharing, and exchange affect collaboration and disruptive innovation?
- What strategies can facilitate or hinder disruptive collaboration with digital knowledge and ML/AI, such as data-driven decision-making, big data implications?
- What is the effect of Knowledge-Based Networking (KBN) on global knowledge markets and global collaborative arrangements?

The focus of this direction is on accelerated knowledge discovery, enhanced knowledge sharing, customized knowledge creation, and transformative knowledge ecosystems. Further research in this direction can shed light on global changes that fundamentally alter how knowledge is generated, disseminated, and utilized, leading to new products, services, and business models.

6. CONCLUSION

Innovation collaboration is a crucial strategy for developing disruptive ideas and technologies that significantly impact industries and markets and offer innovative solutions to existing challenges. Collaborative efforts foster disruptive innovation and create new competitive advantages via diverse expertise, sharing resources, developing ecosystems, facilitating market access, and mitigating risks. However, research in this area is limited due to the emerging nature of the phenomenon.

This study bridges this gap by evaluating existing literature on disruptive collaboration using the PRISMA framework and a range of approaches, including bibliometric analysis, MCA, and text network analysis. The analysis of academic literature from 2015 to 2023 indicates that this research area is nascent, with only 112 studies identified, showing rapid growth and cross-disciplinary interest in management, entrepreneurship, and information systems. Most studies are exploratory with methodological weaknesses, predominantly qualitative, reflecting the emerging nature of the field and challenges like data availability, rapid business changes, and complex stakeholder interactions.

The analysis revealed the structural composition of the field, key concepts, and themes at various granularity levels, presented dynamically. Clusters within the corpus were analyzed to identify four theoretical foundations (behavioral view, network view, RBV, and KBV) and three main themes (disruptive innovation-specific, collaboration-specific, and process-specific), highlighting research gaps for future studies.

The study contributes to the existing literature by providing a structured framework of the studies in innovative disruptive collaboration and suggesting four distinct directions for future research. It also has a practical contribution as it identifies growth areas and suggestions for future research. The results also benefit policymakers and regulators in informing policy changes and development to promote and support innovation and business growth.

The study is subject to limitations: disruptive innovation is an emerging area of research, and while the current study focuses on academic papers, given the time lag in publication of the studies, some emerging trends are yet to be captured in the literature. Further, given the diverse and widespread nature of the phenomenon, the selection of papers may not be exhaustive due to limitations of the literature search and focus on the collaborative aspect of disruptive innovation as well as the complexity of the field and its ontological emergence.

REFERENCES

Ali, B. J., & Anwar, G. (2021). An empirical study of employees' motivation and its influence job satisfaction. *International Journal of Engineering, Business and Management*, *5*(2), 21–30.

Anlesinya, A., & Dadzie, S. A. (2023). *Technology and the conduct of bibliometric literature reviews in management: The software tools, benefits, and challenges*. https://doi.org/10.1108/S2754-586520230000002004

Aria, M., & Cuccurullo, C. (2017). bibliometrix: An R-tool for comprehensive science mapping analysis. *Journal of Informetrics*, *11*(4), 959–975. https://doi.org/10.1016/j.joi.2017.08.007

Arranz, N., Arroyabe, M. F., & Fernandez de Arroyabe, J. C. (2020). Network embeddedness in exploration and exploitation of joint R&D projects: A structural approach. *British Journal of Management*, *31*(2), 421–437. https://doi.org/10.1111/1467-8551.12338

Arranz, N., & de Arroyabe, J. C. F. (2008). The choice of governance structure in R&D alliances: An empirical analysis. *Technovation*, *28*(4), 211–225.

Bail, C. A. (2016). Emotional feedback and the viral spread of social media messages about autism spectrum disorders. *American Journal of Public Health*, *106*(7), 1173–1180.

Barney, J. B., Ketchen, D. J., & Wright, M. (2011). The future of resource-based theory. *Journal of Management*, *37*(5), 1299–1315. https://doi.org/10.1177/0149206310391805

Bendixen, M. (1995). Compositional perceptual mapping using chi-squared trees analysis and correspondence analysis. *Journal of Marketing Management*, *11*(6), 571–581.

Bouncken, R. B., Clauß, T., & Fredrich, V. (2016). Product innovation through coopetition in alliances: Singular or plural governance? *Industrial Marketing Management*, *53*, 77–90. https://doi.org/10.1016/j.indmarman.2015.11.011

Bouncken, R. B., Fredrich, V., Kraus, S., & Ritala, P. (2020). Innovation alliances: Balancing value creation dynamics, competitive intensity and market overlap. *Journal of Business Research*, *112*, 240–247. https://doi.org/10.1016/j.jbusres.2019.10.004

Bouncken, R. B., Fredrich, V., Ritala, P., & Kraus, S. (2020). Value-creation-capture-equilibrium in new product development alliances: A matter of coopetition, expert power, and alliance importance. *Industrial Marketing Management*, *90*, 648–662. https://doi.org/10.1016/j.indmarman.2020.03.019

Boy, J. D. (2020). *From news to political opinions: The role of social media*. Routledge.

Boyatzis, R. E. (1998). *Transforming qualitative information: Thematic analysis and code development*. SAGE Publications, Inc.

Brandenburger, A. (1996). *Co-opetition/Adam M. Brandenburger and Barry J. Nalebuff* (1st ed.). Doubleday.

Brandenburger, A. M., & Nalebuff, B. J. (1996). *Co-opetition*. Currency Doubleday.

Burt, R. S. (2004). Structural holes and good ideas. *American Journal of Sociology*, *110*(2), 349–399. https://doi.org/10.1086/421787

Chai, L., Li, J., Tangpong, C., & Clauss, T. (2020). The interplays of coopetition, conflicts, trust, and efficiency process innovation in vertical B2B relationships. *Industrial Marketing Management*, *85*, 269–280. https://doi.org/10.1016/j.indmarman.2019.11.004

Christensen, C. M. (2016). *The innovator's dilemma: When new technologies cause great firms to fail/ Clayton M. Christensen* (3rd ed). Harvard Business Review Press.

Christensen, C. M., & Overdorf, M. (2000). Meeting the challenge of disruptive change. *Harvard Business Review*, *78*(2), 66–76.

Christensen, C. M., Raynor, M. E., & McDonald, R. (2015). What is disruptive innovation? *Harvard Business Review*, *93*(12), 44–53.

Corbo, L., Kraus, S., Vlačić, B., Dabić, M., Caputo, A., & Pellegrini, M. M. (2023). Coopetition and innovation: A review and research agenda. *Technovation*, *122*, 102624. https://doi.org/10.1016/j.technovation.2022.102624

Cozzolino, A., Corbo, L., & Aversa, P. (2021). Digital platform-based ecosystems: The evolution of collaboration and competition between incumbent producers and entrant platforms. *Journal of Business Research*, *126*, 385–400. https://doi.org/10.1016/j.jbusres.2020.12.058

Cyert, R. M., & March, J. G. (1963). *A behavioral theory of the firm*. Prentice-Hall.

Czakon, W., Klimas, P., & Mariani, M. (2020). Behavioral antecedents of coopetition: A synthesis and measurement scale. *Long Range Planning*, *53*(1), 101867.

Dagnino, G. B., Di Guardo, M. C., & Battista, D. (2015). Coopetition and business models: A new approach to business model innovation. *Management*, *18*(1), 10–26.

Dorn, S., Schweiger, B., & Albers, S. (2016). Levels, phases and themes of coopetition: A systematic literature review and research agenda. *European Management Journal*, *34*(5), 484–500. https://doi.org/10.1016/j.emj.2016.02.009

Eisenhardt, K. M., & Martin, J. A. (2000). Dynamic capabilities: What are they? *Strategic Management Journal*, *21*(10–11), 1105–1121. https://doi.org/10.1002/1097-0266(200010/11)21:10/11<1105::AID-SMJ133>3.0.CO;2-E

Estrada, I., Faems, D., & de Faria, P. (2016). Coopetition and product innovation performance: The role of internal knowledge sharing mechanisms and formal knowledge protection mechanisms. *Industrial Marketing Management*, *53*, 56–65. https://doi.org/10.1016/j.indmarman.2015.11.013

Fang, E. (2011). The effect of strategic alliance knowledge complementarity on new product innovativeness in the high-tech industry. *Journal of Marketing*, *75*(2), 1–18.

Feranita, F., Kotlar, J., & De Massis, A. (2017). Collaborative innovation in family firms: Past research, current debates and agenda for future research. *Journal of Family Business Strategy*, *8*(3), 137–156.

Fredrich, V., Bouncken, R. B., & Kraus, S. (2019). The race is on: Configurations of absorptive capacity, interdependence and slack resources for interorganizational learning in coopetition alliances. *Journal of Business Research*, *101*, 862–868. https://doi.org/10.1016/j.jbusres.2018.11.038

Galvin, P., Burton, N., & Nyuur, R. (2020). Leveraging inter-industry spillovers through DIY laboratories: Entrepreneurship and innovation in the global bicycle industry. *Technological Forecasting and Social Change*, *160*, 120235. https://doi.org/10.1016/j.techfore.2020.120235

Gauthier, J. (1998). The dialectics of post-modernity in the film theories of Christian Metz. *Semiotica*, *121*(3/4), 263–289.

Govindarajan, V., & Kopalle, P. K. (2006). The usefulness of measuring disruptiveness of innovations ex post in making ex ante predictions. *Journal of Product Innovation Management*, *23*(1), 12–18.

Granovetter, M. S. (2003). The strength of weak ties. In *Networks in the knowledge economy*. Oxford University Press. https://doi.org/10.1093/oso/9780195159509.003.0010

Grant, R. M. (2002). *Contemporary strategy analysis: Concepts, techniques, applications*. Blackwell.

Gulati, R. (1999). Network location and learning: The influence of network resources and firm capabilities on alliance formation. *Strategic Management Journal*, *20*(5), 397–420.

Hambrick, M. E. (2023). *Disruptive innovation/Marion Hambrick*. SAGE Publications, Inc.

Hani, U., & Dagnino, G. B. (2020). Coopetition capability: How to create and appropriate value. *Strategic Management Journal*, *41*(12), 2488–2518.

Hani, M., & Dagnino, G.-B. (2021). Global network coopetition, firm innovation and value creation. *Journal of Business & Industrial Marketing*, *36*(11), 1962–1974. https://doi.org/10.1108/JBIM-05-2019-0268

Horvát, E.-Á., Wu, A., & Uzzi, B. (2023). Network bridging ties in creative problem solving. *Proceedings of the National Academy of Sciences*, *120*(2), e2214798120.

Hynes, N., & Elwell, A. D. (2016). The role of inter-organizational networks in enabling or delaying disruptive innovation: A case study of mVoIP. *Journal of Business & Industrial Marketing*, *31*(6), 722–731. https://doi.org/10.1108/JBIM-10-2012-0168

Jin, B. E., & Shin, D. C. (2020). Changing the game to compete: Innovations in the fashion retail industry from the disruptive business model. *Business Horizons*, *63*(3), 301–311. https://doi.org/10.1016/j.bushor.2020.01.004

Kang, J., & Park, Y. (2012). Influence of government R&D support and inter-firm collaborations on innovation in Korean biotechnology SMEs. *Technovation*, *32*(1), 68–78.

Kaurav, R. P. S., Baber, R., & Rajput, S. (2020). Technology-driven tourism and hospitality industry as a tool for economic development: A bibliometric analysis. *The Emerald Handbook of ICT in Tourism and Hospitality*, 469–486. https://doi.org/10.1108/978-1-83982-688-720201030

Kaurav, R. P. S., & Gupta, P. (2022). Trends in multidiscipline management research: Past, present and future of FIIB business review. *FIIB Business Review*, *11*(4), 382–404. https://doi.org/10.1177/23197145221136966/ASSET/IMAGES/LARGE/10.1177_23197145221136966-FIG11.JPEG

Kaushal, N., Kaurav, R. P. S., Sivathanu, B., & Kaushik, N. (2023). Artificial intelligence and HRM: Identifying future research Agenda using systematic literature review and bibliometric analysis. *Management Review Quarterly*, *73*(2), 455–493. https://doi.org/10.1007/S11301-021-00249-2

Kim, J., & Song, Y. I. (2007). Creating new technology through alliances: An empirical investigation of joint patents. *Technovation*, *27*(9), 461–470.

Klimas, P., & Czakon, W. (2018). Organizational innovativeness and coopetition: A study of video game developers. *Review of Managerial Science*, *12*(2), 469–497. https://doi.org/10.1007/s11846-017-0269-5

Kraus, S., Meier, F., Niemand, T., Bouncken, R. B., & Ritala, P. (2018). In search for the ideal coopetition partner: An experimental study. *Review of Managerial Science*, *12*(4), 1025–1053. https://doi.org/10.1007/s11846-017-0237-0

Lafuente, E., Vaillant, Y., & Rabetino, R. (2023). Digital disruption of optimal co-innovation configurations. *Technovation*, *125*, 102772. https://doi.org/10.1016/j.technovation.2023.102772

Lahiri, N., & Narayanan, S. (2013). Vertical integration, innovation, and alliance portfolio size: Implications for firm performance. *Strategic Management Journal*, *34*(9), 1042–1064.

Le Roux, B., & Rouanet, H. (2010). *Multiple correspondence analysis*. SAGE Publications, Inc. https://doi.org/10.4135/9781412993906

Lenart-Gansiniec, R. (2016). Relational capital and open innovation – In search of interdependencies. *Procedia – Social and Behavioral Sciences*, *220*, 236–242. https://doi.org/10.1016/j.sbspro.2016.05.495

Mariani, M. M. (2007). Coopetition as an emergent strategy: Empirical evidence from an Italian consortium of opera houses. *International Studies of Management & Organization*, *37*(2), 97–126. https://doi.org/10.2753/IMO0020-8825370205

Markovic, S., Bagherzadeh, M., & Stevanovic, M. (2020). Sustainability performance in a dynamic business environment: The role of organizational resilience, adaptability culture, and organizational learning. *Business Strategy and the Environment*, *29*(1), 241–251.

Markovic, S., & Bagherzadeh, M. (2018). How does breadth of external stakeholder co-creation influence innovation performance? Analyzing the mediating roles of knowledge sharing and product innovation. *Journal of Business Research*, *88*, 173–186. https://doi.org/10.1016/j.jbusres.2018.03.028

Miller, D., & Le Breton-Miller, I. (2005). Management insights from great and struggling Family businesses. *Long Range Planning*, *38*(6), 517–530. https://doi.org/10.1016/j.lrp.2005.09.001

Mishra, V., & Sharma, M. G. (2022). Digital transformation evaluation of telehealth using convergence, maturity, and adoption. *Health Policy and Technology*, *11*(4), 100684. https://doi.org/10.1016/J.HLPT.2022.100684

Page, M. J., Moher, D., Bossuyt, P. M., Boutron, I., Hoffmann, T. C., Mulrow, C. D., Shamseer, L., Tetzlaff, J. M., Akl, E. A., Brennan, S. E., Chou, R., Glanville, J., Grimshaw, J. M., Hróbjartsson, A., Lalu, M. M., Li, T., Loder, E. W., Mayo-Wilson, E., Mcdonald, S., … Mckenzie, J. E. (2021). PRISMA 2020 explanation and elaboration: Updated guidance and exemplars for reporting systematic reviews. *The BMJ*, *372*. https://doi.org/10.1136/BMJ.N160

Park, B.-J., & Kim, D. (2021). Coopetition dynamics between giant entrants and incumbents in a new convergent segment: A case in the smartphone industry. *Asian Journal of Technology Innovation*, *29*(3), 455–476. https://doi.org/10.1080/19761597.2020.1818109

Park, B.-J., Srivastava, M. K., & Gnyawali, D. R. (2014). Walking the tight rope of coopetition: Impact of competition and cooperation intensities and balance on firm innovation performance. *Industrial Marketing Management*, *43*(2), 210–221. https://doi.org/10.1016/j.indmarman.2013.11.003Robert).

Peters, C., Blohm, I., & Leimeister, J. M. (2015). Anatomy of successful business models for complex services: Insights from the telemedicine field. *Journal of Management Information Systems*, *32*(3), 75–104. https://doi.org/10.1080/07421222.2015.1095034

Pfeffer, J. (2003). *The external control of organizations: A resource dependence perspective/Jeffrey Pfeffer and Gerald R. Salancik*. Stanford Business Books.

Poorkavoos, M., Duan, Y., Edwards, J. S., & Ramanathan, R. (2016). Identifying the configurational paths to innovation in SMEs: A fuzzy-set qualitative comparative analysis. *Journal of Business Research*, *69*(12), 5843–5854. https://doi.org/10.1016/j.jbusres.2016.04.067

Rammal, H. G. (2023). *Systematic literature reviews: Steps and practical tips*. https://doi.org/10.1108/S2754-586520230000002002

Rana, N., Chams-Anturi, O., & Mendoza, E. (2022). The impact of digital technologies on sustainable development: Evidence from the United Nations Conference on Trade and Development. *Journal of Business Research*, *137*, 415–428.

Raza-Ullah, T., & Kostis, A. (2020). How and when does coopetition lead to negative outcomes? A multilevel framework. *Industrial Marketing Management*, *90*, 200–213.

Ricciardi, F., Zollo, L., & Bruno, G. B. (2021). Strategic alignment and information systems integration: Key drivers of operational performance in M&A. *Journal of Business Research*, *132*, 637–651.

Sahni, S., & Kaurav, S. P. R. (2023). *What? Why? When? How? Where? Of Technology-Based Bibliometric Review*, *2*, 79–101. https://doi.org/10.1108/S2754-586520230000002005

Sellitto, M. A., Pereira, G. S., Marques, R., & Lacerda, D. P. (2018). Systemic understanding of coopetitive behaviour in a Latin American technological park. *Systemic Practice and Action Research*, *31*(5), 479–494. https://doi.org/10.1007/s11213-017-9439-2

Simon, H. A. (1972). Theories of bounded rationality. In C. B. McGuire & R. Radner (Eds.), *Decision and organization* (pp. 161–176). North-Holland.

Srivastava, P. (2021). Impact of social media on mental health of youth. *Journal of Psychology and Clinical Psychiatry*, *8*(2), 100–109.

van Eck, N. J., & Waltman, L. (2010). Software survey: VOSviewer, a computer program for bibliometric mapping. *Scientometrics*, *84*(2), 523–538.

Wang, Y., Park, S., & Fan, W. (2020). The adoption of digital technologies in healthcare: A cross-country analysis. *Journal of Medical Internet Research*, *22*(3), e17423.

Williamson, O. E. (1987). *The economic institutions of capitalism: Firms, markets, relational contracting/Oliver E.* Free Press.

Xie, J., Huo, B., & Zhao, X. (2022). Green supply chain management practices and firm performance: The mediating effect of innovation capabilities. *International Journal of Logistics Management*, *33*(1), 121–142.

Xie, K., Wu, Y., Xiao, J., & Hu, Q. (2016). Value co-creation between firms and customers: The role of big data-based cooperative assets. *Information and Management*, *53*(8), 1034–1048. https://doi.org/10.1016/j.im.2016.06.003

Zheng, J., Zhao, S., & Lee, K. (2023). Strategic responses to environmental regulation in the Chinese manufacturing industry. *Journal of Cleaner Production*, *268*, 121728.

Zhong, J., & Nieminen, M. (2015). Resource-based co-innovation through platform ecosystem: Experiences of mobile payment innovation in China. *Journal of Strategy and Management*, *8*(3), 283–298. https://doi.org/10.1108/JSMA-03-2015-0026

SECTION 5

OVERVIEW OF SMART TECHNOLOGIES AND SERVICES

A LITERATURE REVIEW ON SMART TECHNOLOGIES IN SERVICE SYSTEMS: HOW SHOULD WE WORK IN FUTURE?

Goknur Arzu Akyuz and Dursun Balkan

University of Turkish Aeronautical Association, Turkey

ABSTRACT

Smart technologies in today's Internet of Things (IoT) era cover a wide spectrum, including smart identification technologies, robotics, virtual reality (VR), augmented reality (AR), wearable technologies, cloud, artificial intelligence (AI), machine learning (ML), and blockchain. This study aims at revealing the role and importance of smart technologies in service systems which encompass a wide spectrum of sectors. The scope of this study covers the main applications in transportation and logistics, retail, health care, hospitality, and financial services sectors. A broad overview is provided for the potentials and benefits of smart technology utilization in these service areas, and future research agenda is suggested. Findings reveal that simultaneous use of smart technologies bring tremendous opportunities in terms of efficiencies and automation, reshaping and transforming operations and business processes of the service enterprises. The study highlights that although core proven applications of smart technologies are in manufacturing, generally lagging service sector applications promise radical productivity improvements, performance enhancements, and increased service quality. By radically upgrading the customer satisfaction to entirely new levels and providing unique customer experiences, smart technologies lead to bottom line profitability improvements as well competitiveness.

Keywords: Service systems; smart technologies; disruptive technologies; technological transformation; Internet of Things (IoT); artificial intelligence (AI)

Review of Technologies and Disruptive Business Strategies
Review of Management Literature, Volume 3, 255–273

ISSN: 2754-5865/doi:10.1108/S2754-586520240000003013

1. INTRODUCTION

The service sector has unique characteristics which differentiate it from the manufacturing industry. Customer participation, intangibility, heterogeneity, simultaneity, perishability, nontransferrable ownership, and perishability are the main issues that distinguish the service sector (Bordoloi et al., 2019; Mercan et al., 2021). Within the economical context, we witness a transformation following the steps of agrarian, industrial, service, and experience-based economic activities (Bordoloi et al., 2019). In this evolution, a shift from product-oriented to service-oriented logic is experienced. Along with digitalization, virtualization, e-commerce integration (B2B, B2C), and utilization of IT tools and advances, technology is well-proven as a game changer in the service sector and has gained increasing importance to provide seamless omnichannel service delivery (Drezgić et al., 2020; Gonçalves et al., 2020; Ostrom et al., 2015).

In this context, recent dramatic IT advances started to reshape the entire service systems, restructuring and automating the processes, minimizing the human intervention, and bringing standardization, efficiency, productivity, and performance improvements (Drezgić et al., 2020) for superior customized service and customer experience (Gonçalves et al., 2020). Starting with 2000s which focus on radio-frequency identification (RFID)-based logistics perspective, the transformation continued with the diffusion of management information systems. With the ongoing technological advancements, we have evolved into a physical world web utilizing sensor-based smart technologies within Internet of Things (IoT) context (Behera et al., 2023), providing real-time information and analytics, and leading to virtual value chains. By the simultaneous use of various disruptive technologies and techniques (such as robotics, additive manufacturing, augmented reality (AR), virtual reality (VR), big data, artificial intelligence (AI), machine learning (ML), simulation and cloud), it became possible to obtain descriptive, diagnostic, prescriptive, and predictive analytics for different service processes (Al-Rawashdeh et al., 2022; Behera et al., 2023). This provided managerial decision support at operational, tactical, and strategic levels (Laudon & Laudon, 2015). Key activities such as demand management, pricing and revenue optimization, sales management, portfolio management, and risk assessment as well as the management of the overall service supply chain (SC) are supported.

This technology-based transformation brought us to a new era of service concept, emphasizing the use of the smart technologies (Drezgić et al., 2020). It is well-supported that IoT-related smart technologies have sound and proven applications in manufacturing industry. However, service sector enterprises significantly lag manufacturing sector companies in utilizing and assimilating these technologies (Rehse et al., 2016). In this context, applications of IoT technologies in service sector are continuously evolving, and the topic deserves further attention.

The purpose of this study is to provide an overview of smart technology utilization in service sector to suggest future research agenda. Frequently seen applications are elaborated on a sectoral basis for the most fundamental service sectors.

This study is beneficial to practitioners, researchers as well as service sector managers and valuable for:

- Providing a multi-sector overview under services concept.
- Creating an awareness and knowledge of potential benefits and improvements that smart technologies can bring for the service sector.
- Highlighting the need for re-engineering service processes based on IT availabilities and reorganizing service enterprises based on current smart technologies to obtain swift, smooth, agile, and customer-centric services.
- Highlighting the need that service sector companies should adapt smart technologies for their survival and competitiveness, utilizing the lessons learned from manufacturing companies.

Section structure for the remainder of the study is as follows: Section 2 offers the methodology. Section 3 puts forward the role and importance of smart technologies as the enabler of the service sector. Section 4 elaborates on the sector-based applications. Section 5 provides a comprehensive overview of challenges for implementing smart service systems. Section 6 offers discussion, Section 7 provides further research agenda, and Section 8 contains conclusion.

2. METHODOLOGY

This study follows a literature review methodology at the intersection of "smart technologies" and "service systems". Review studies assist summarizing a research field and synthesizing the previous knowledge to reveal the gaps to shed light on future research agenda (Farrukh & Sajjad, 2023; Rammal, 2023). They can come in various types such as narrative, scoping, integrative, meta-analysis, hybrid, and systematic reviews (Farrukh & Sajjad, 2023; Rammal, 2023).

Since service concept covers an extremely wide spectrum, scoping was crucial in this study. Scope of our review is limited to the following five major service sectors: transportation and logistics, retail, health care, hospitality, and financial services. We reckoned that other service applications (such as smart government or smart education applications) will deserve special attention and treatment. In order to keep the scope reasonable and manageable, such applications are considered beyond the scope of this study. Therefore, our literature review can be classified as a scoping review.

In our study, synthesis is performed for the technologies involved, applications, and benefits on a sectoral basis using the taxonomy table developed (Table 1). Identified implementation challenges are synthesized and treated under a separate section. Our resource set includes the key items from a date range of 2008–2023 which covers the most dramatic advancements in technological aspects.

Table 1. Technologies Involved, Applications, and Benefits for the Major Service Sectors.

	Transportation and logistics	Retail	Health Care	Hospitality	Financial Services
Technologies involved	• RFID, sensors, nano-sensors, actuators, 5G mobile, integration with smart stores, wearable devices, vehicle tracking systems • Big data, data mining, ML, and AI	• RFID, QR codes, smart shelves, smart shopping carts, smart stores (including robotics, automated material handling, wearable devices), smart mirrors integrated with VR and AR • Big data, data mining, ML and AI	• Sensor-based smart equipment (smart watches, smart beds…), call centers • Blockchain and smart contracts • Big data mining, ML, and AI	• Mobile applications, kiosks, robotics, chatbots, voice activation systems, biometric identification systems, call centers • Big data, data mining, ML, and AI	• Chatbots, robo-advisors, virtual assistants, call centers, wearable devices, smart ATMs • Blockchain and smart contracts • Big data, data mining, ML, and AI
Applications and benefits for the major service sectors	• Automated processes and efficiencies • Integration with fully automated smart stores and smart inventory management systems • End-to-end vehicle, load, shipment traceability • Smart fleet management • Tracking and controlling key product and transportation attributes • Full visibility • Real-time monitoring and analytics	• Automated processes and efficiencies • Integration with fully automated smart stores and smart inventory management systems • Accurate, integrated material management • Full visibility • Analyzing shopping habits, preferences, interests, and demand patterns • Unmanned, technology-driven shopping experiences	• Automated processes and efficiencies • Online real-time patient follow-up • Assisted living and elderly care • Real-time tracking of emergency fleets • Secure and private medical records • Advanced analysis of medical data/accurate health analytics • Traceability of pharmaceutical items • Medical asset traceability	• Automated processes and efficiencies • Online self-service • Personalized guest experience • Advanced analysis of visitor patterns and accurate demand forecasts • Real-time customer feedback and measuring customer satisfaction	• Digitizing and streamlining traditional financial services • Automated payments with e-commerce and e-procurement applications • AI-supported credit risk management • AI-supported stock exchange transactions and investment advices • Stock market predictive and behavioral analytics • Blockchain-based
References	Loebbecke et al. (2008) Ren (2015) Barge et al. (2013) Draskovic et al. (2016) Hussain et al. (2020) Penna et al. (2017) Akyuz and Gursoy (2019) Akyuz and Tunc (2023) Lampropoulos et al. (2018)	Chen and Chang (2023) Kaur et al. (2022) Shankar et al. (2021) Dacko (2017) Isharyani et al. (2021) Chen et al. (2018)	Lampropoulos et al. (2018) Akkaş et al. (2020) Hussein et al. (2022) Amendola et al. (2014) Agbo et al. (2019) Akyuz and Gursoy (2020) Mishra and Sharma (2022)	Pillai and Sivathanu (2020), Berman (2023) Tussyadiah and Park (2018) Mercan et al. (2021) Berezina et al. (2019) Ivanov et al. (2017) Blöcher and Alt (2021) Ivanov (2019) Kaurav et al. (2020)	Bringas et al. (2020) Wang et al. (2020) Walden (2022)

3. SMART TECHNOLOGIES AS THE ENABLER OF THE SERVICE SECTOR

Smart technologies offer totally new ways of doing business and restructure the entire business scene. IoT technologies leading to smart systems typically encompass the following components: controllers, sensors, network infrastructure, actuators, processors, robotic components, cloud platform, AI, and ML algorithms (Holnicki-Szulc et al., 2008; Kusiak, 2023). They typically possess the capabilities of self-control, self-configuration, self-awareness, self-organizing, self-optimizing as well as working independently and initiating actions (Akyüz & Balkan, 2023; Gajo, 2021). They can communicate with each other to guarantee online, real-time data collection and analysis, leading to multidimensional business analytics. In manufacturing context, benefits obtained are quite well supported with increased automation, efficiencies and productivity, improved inventory management, improved predictive maintenance, increased transparency, real-time monitoring, enhanced quality control, better asset tracking, and improved logistics network management (Behera et al., 2023; Boyes et al., 2018; Dalenogare et al., 2018; Gupta et al., 2021).

Smart technologies hold significant potential in service context. With advances in robotics, huge improvements in increased process automation, increased efficiencies, and minimized manual operations are made possible for services. Blöcher and Alt (2021) highlight the opportunities for augmenting the existing workforce as well as total replacement of manual service operations with the technology. Replacing human tasks by robotics and support of AI offer dramatic process innovation and re-engineering prospects. Therefore, AI and robotics became highly important enablers of automated processes and innovation in service organizations (Bughin et al., 2018, pp. 1–64; Ishengoma et al., 2022; Willcocks et al., 2015; Zebec, 2019). It is well-proven that process automation brings radical improvements in productivity, speed and operations, ensuring overall standardization and improvements in performance along with the substitution of technology for labor. Gonçalves et al. (2020) put forward that smart services bring visibility, controllability, self-configuration, sustainability, autonomy, and accessibility. This radically simplifies the workflows and re-engineers the processes, resulting in leaner service systems and structures. Hence, technology becomes the greater enabler for triggering the re-engineering in service processes, radically transforming the way processes are handled.

Another key issue by which smart technologies transform the service sector is that they change the interface between the customer and the service provider. Customer touchpoints are changed, and face-to-face contacts are being transformed into screen-to-face contacts. This enables technology-mediated and technology-generated (self-service) operations. Technology-supported self-service empowers the customers, leaving the service control to the customer, increasing the opportunities for service customization, and minimizing the need for the service labor requirements. This is especially valuable for the essential service reservation process in various sectors (airlines, hotels, tourism agencies, restaurants, and hospitals). Hence, service delivery and service encounter concepts are significantly changed.

Simultaneous use and integration of various smart technologies (mobile devices, sensors, and robotic systems) enable online, real-time data, information, and reports from all the service processes. Real-time dashboards and decision support for service managers are provided. Real-time data coming from the IoT systems leverage big data to assist in forecasting customer preferences and needs, service experience personalization, and faster service recovery to offer a holistic and improved customer experience (Antons & Breidbach, 2018). Real-time data serve for service differentiation via real-time customer feedback. Online customer and personnel satisfaction surveys, as well as feedback from social media are also made possible. Claim and complaint management processes are automated and standardized for the cases of unavailable service, slow service performance or unacceptable service. It is also important to highlight that call center management assumes a critical role in these processes, offering huge and continuous streams of data. Therefore, instant reporting and analysis for the claim and complaint management process becomes possible for better service recovery in integration with the call center data.

With smart technologies, online real-time feedback on customer service preferences and service purchase records can be analyzed, and their satisfaction levels can be tracked continuously. As such, from Customer Relationship Management (CRM) perspective, smart technologies provide the foundation for analytical CRM, serving for analytical customer segmentation based on facts. In this way, individualized, differentiated, and targeted service offerings can be provided. Frequent users, premium customer policies and related discounts, special offerings, and differentiated pricing options can easily be developed. Customer satisfaction, customer retention, and loyalty parameters can be instantly analyzed to guide future customer-related decisions. Such fact-based analyses bring systematic customer coding, classification, and clustering the customers. Faster service recovery, improved service guarantee processes in case of service failures, and improved perceived service quality can be assured. Therefore, advanced big data analysis techniques enable analytical CRM and support the key CRM concepts of customer satisfaction, retention, and loyalty. Hence, customer-centric processes are affected, and improvements in this regard result in radically enhanced customer experiences. Better CRM management with smart technology-based advanced managerial reporting undoubtedly supports the development of more agile and dynamic service strategies with more appropriate service concepts.

It is also well-supported that smart technologies assume a significant role in the management of human resources (HR) activities (Kaushal et al., 2023; Pillai & Srivastava, 2022). Embedding technologies such as chatbots, AI, and ML into HRM subprocesses (such as selection, recruitment, onboarding and training) assist and accelerate these processes (Kaushal et al., 2023; Pillai & Srivastava, 2022). HR analytics obtained by smart technologies support performance monitoring, feedback, and managing human capital. Since service sector is more dependent on the workforce when compared with manufacturing, potential of the smart technologies for the service sector is higher from HR perspective. Hence, HRM processes are also radically affected.

The following diagram (Fig. 1) offers a generic representation of the smart technology-based service system to summarize the enabler role of smart technologies.

The diagram indicates that all the steps of the service management are handled with the integration of smart technologies, managerial, organizational, and human components. Based on the above-discussed potentials of the smart systems, it can be argued that smart technologies totally reshape all these stages. Radical re-engineering is experienced in the service process designs to obtain highly automated, transparent, and traceable processes with instant managerial reporting. Along with the operational transformation, CRM-centric and HRM-centric processes are radically changed. Service delivery modes and service encounters are highly affected. All these issues result in improved customer experience and overall performance improvements. This integration undoubtedly leads to improved managerial reporting and supports the development of more appropriate service strategies and service concepts.

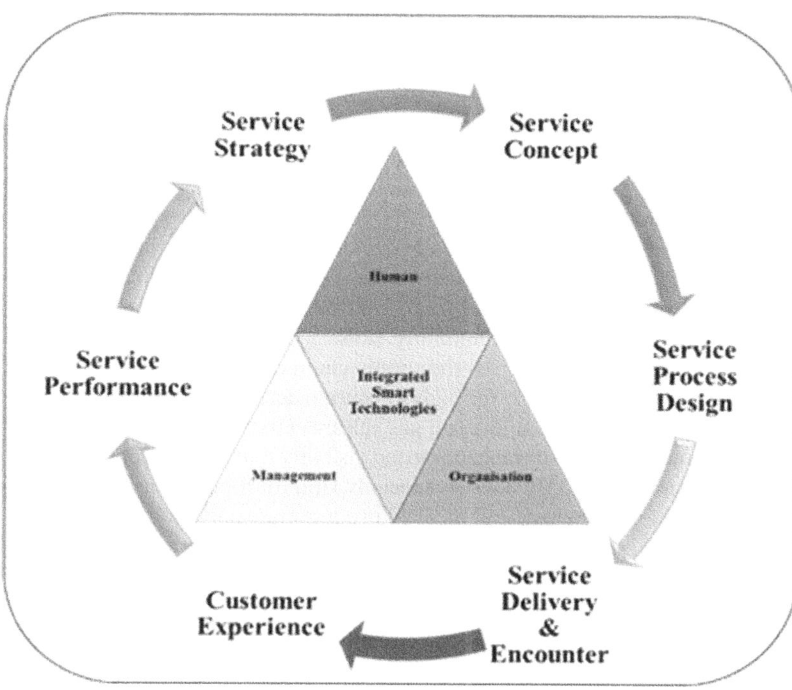

Fig. 1. Smart Service Systems. *Source:* Developed by the authors.

4. SECTOR-BASED APPLICATIONS

Section 1 already described the enabler role of smart technologies for service systems. A variety of smart technologies mentioned are gaining more and more applications in service sector. This section identifies and elaborates on the potential applications of these technologies on a sectoral basis.

4.1 Transportation and Logistics

One of the most critical areas of application of these technologies is transportation and logistics, which assumes a vital importance for the continuity of manufacturing as well as service sector.

Smart logistics understanding involves advanced vehicles, transported goods, and roads equipped with technological devices (such as sensors, RFID tags, actuators, etc.) to connect and communicate with each other. Working in combination with 5G mobile networks, sensors, and vehicle tracking systems, their hybrid usage enables exchanging mission-critical data and information in an accurate and timely manner (Barge et al., 2013; Draskovic et al., 2016; Loebbecke et al., 2008; Ren, 2015). End-to-end visibility and traceability of goods, information, vehicles, and drivers are ensured, leading to smart fleet management systems (Hussain et al., 2020; Penna et al., 2017). In this context, entire transportation cycle can be tracked and traced along with the shipments and mobile assets.

With these recent technologies, tracking and controlling various product attributes and transportation parameters (such as temperature, humidity, shelf-life, cold chain conditions, product origin, organic character of the items) become real time and accurate. In this regard, blockchain technology holds significant potential with the capability of ensuring permanent and immutable records about the product origins, ingredients, and shelf lives (Akyuz & Gursoy, 2020). The technology ensures that these information pieces are accurately preserved during the entire transportation and logistics cycle, and that product is send to the customer in desired conditions. With sensor-based technologies, environmental sensing, tracking and tracing of various parameters (such as temperature, humidity, noise, light intensity, radiation, pollution [CO, CO_2, etc.]) are enabled across the supply chain (SC). In this connection, nanosensors also come into the scene for highly accurate detection of sensitive parameters for controlling deterioration and toxic gas release. Hence, a combination of smart technologies enables levels of traceability and visibility that have never been imagined before (Akyuz & Tunc, 2023). This is especially vital for food chains (e.g., cold chain applications), pharmaceutical, and medical product transportation networks.

It is evident that smart technologies accelerate productivity, profitability, and operations. Efficient and cost-effective end-to-end transportation management and control is established with full visibility (Lampropoulos et al., 2018). Downtimes are reduced, and effective route planning and optimization is enabled. Increased visibility, tracking, and real-time monitoring across the SC are ensured. Real-time data across the entire transportation cycle enabled instant analytics and more intelligent reporting across the value chain via advanced data capturing and analysis techniques.

All these issues are positively related with the efficiencies of inbound and outbound material flow of the SC's. This is directly relevant with the performance and risk management, as well as adaptiveness and responsiveness of the SCs.

4.2 Retail

Retail is an enormous sector inherently having a service-based and direct interface with the customers. It requires handling huge number of inventory items, high inventory turnovers, and successful completion of the order fulfillment cycle of multiple customers. It also requires direct intertwining of inventory management and e-commerce systems.

Therefore, smart technologies provide significant benefits for end-to-end automated and accurate order processing. Applications like QR codes, electronic shelf labels, smart shelves, smart shopping carts, mobile shopping carts, and automated checkout applications integrate with fully automated smart stores and smart inventory management systems (Chen & Chang, 2023; Kaur et al., 2022; Shankar et al., 2021). Self-service is also enabled (Chen et al., 2018). Such applications significantly change the service encounter and customer experience with accurate integration of material management activities.

Since retail is directly customer-centric, understanding the demand patterns in multi-item context is also a very critical issue. In this regard, big data and data mining tools play an especially important role. This allows retailers to collect data on customers' shopping habits, preferences, and interests. Instant and real-time analysis enables customized product recommendations/offers, leading to increased sales as well as improved customer experience and loyalty (Isharyani et al., 2021; Kaur et al., 2022).

Smart technologies also provide unmanned and technology-driven shopping environments. Smart mirrors integrated with VR and AR applications create 3D interfaces that facilitate personalized and unique shopping experiences (Dacko, 2017). This is especially relevant to women's wear and cosmetics items. Such applications allow buyers to try on the product in a smart environment, resulting in totally redefined service encounters and customer experience.

Consequently, new technologies enable full traceability and visibility as well as new shopping experiences across the retail SCs.

4.3 Health Care

We witness a wide range of applications of various smart technologies in healthcare sector (Lampropoulos et al., 2018). Smart technologies simplify, automate, and accelerate the basic processes such as patient check-in and checkout and tracking the patient across all stages of their personalized treatment services in medical systems.

Smart beds equipped with sensors which can gather data on vital signs of the patients is one of the most critical and recent applications. They enable online real-time monitoring and allow the development of remote patient state and health monitoring services (Akkaş et al., 2020). This is especially suitable for assisted living and elderly care (Hussein et al., 2022). By sensor-based instant signaling, smart devices such as smart watches facilitate remote follow-ups and alerts for the elderly people. By this way, instant interventions are made possible in case of accidents and medical emergency conditions.

Smart traceability systems also offer online, real-time monitoring of equipment and personnel. This leads to better asset management (e.g., condition monitoring and preventive management of the equipment). Personnel allocation and scheduling are made flexible, fast, automated, and easy to update. Via integrating vehicle tracking systems and geographical information systems (GIS), real-time tracking and managing medical vehicle fleets can perform more efficiently, directly serving for improved emergency service performance.

With big data and data mining techniques, effectively keeping and analyzing the electronic health records is made possible (Amendola et al., 2014). Combined with AI and advanced statistical analysis, these techniques offer intelligent and speedy expert decision support, increasingly mimicking an expert doctor. This results in better identification and management of chronic diseases, better diagnosis and treatment, as well as enhanced drug management and personalized medication. Thus, advanced decision support is provided to doctors.

Advanced statistical analysis of medical data can also lead to further decision support to the medical managers. Data can be reported and consolidated at different breakdowns (e.g., by hospitals, cities, regions, and countries). Advanced reporting in the form of online analytical processing (OLAP) cubes and drill-down reports can be obtained and systematically utilized. This can provide strategic feedback for health systems planning. Regional and city-based dynamic decisions are made possible in case of serious conditions like pandemics.

Blockchain technology also deserves specific attention with its significant potential in healthcare applications. Blockchain is used for keeping secure and immutable medical records, serving for preserving privacy and accuracy of patient data, remote patient monitoring, and obtaining accurate health data analytics (Agbo et al., 2019). Blockchain also contributes to drug/pharmaceutical SCs by ensuring the traceability of pharmaceutical items including shelf-life and expiration date control and guaranteeing that cold-chain conditions are controlled and maintained across the entire transportation cycle (Akyuz & Gursoy, 2020). Smart packaging applications which can sense and alert according to the environmental conditions also play role in the traceability of medical items. Hence, combined use of a variety of technologies is directly relevant to drug safety and security, and especially critical for the items such as vaccines.

Therefore, all these smart technologies created an ongoing transformation of the way health services are provided, and in this context, we increasingly witness various terms such as e-health, telehealth, telecare, and mobile care, referring to the internet-based, distant, and continuous character of health services and monitoring (Al-Atawi et al., 2022; Mishra & Sharma, 2022). New service experiences and ways of doing business are offered for the patients, elderly people, and medical sector people.

4.4 Hospitality

Hospitality services concept is a broad term involving various industries such as food, beverage, travel, accommodation, and event management. It basically covers hotels, airlines, restaurants/cafes, and cruise ships.

Key issue in hospitality is to offer the guests or passengers a customized unique experience according to the customer preferences. Technologies such as mobile applications, kiosks, robotics, AI, chatbots, voice activation systems, and biometric identification systems dramatically changed the guest experience (Berman, 2023; Pillai & Sivathanu, 2020; Tussyadiah & Park, 2018). Online reservation systems already minimized the travel agency's role and turned the operation into self-service by which the guest can handle the reservations and purchasing tickets in airlines, hotels, and restaurants. With real-time data capture, advanced analysis of visitor patterns, more accurate demand forecasts, and advanced decision support are enabled. Measuring customer satisfaction is also a critical issue in service sector. Recent technologies enable real-time feedback and online surveys to capture the customer feedback and satisfaction levels.

When different sectors under hospitality are concerned, the following summarizes the key aspects that are brought about by the smart technologies:

- In airlines, automation capabilities such as smart check-in and baggage control, and instant gate displays and announcements showing the flight and plane status dramatically change the passenger experience.
- In hotels, smart technologies are used for offering personalized guest experience. This includes a variety of applications such as sending location data to guests for a smoother arrival, express check-in and check-out, and greeting the guest by their name when they enter the room. Smart applications enable room customization, including smart lighting/curtains, controlling heating, ventilation, air conditioning, and beds. Smart applications also assist the guest during in-resort navigation (Mercan et al., 2021). It is also supported that IoT devices reduce operational costs, save energy, and provide preventive maintenance opportunities in service facilities for service continuity.
- In restaurants and cafes, mobile devices integrity in order processing (QR codes, tablets, smart watches) already became part of the operation. This enables easy menu selection and remote ordering, improves the order accuracy, and reduces the customer waiting times. Customized offerings (specialized reservations, menu options, and waiter assignments) are possible. Depending on the health condition of the guest, suggesting specialized menus (such as gluten-free, sugar-free, and alcohol-free) can be arranged. Increasing AI and robotics utilization in restaurants is another key transformation that is witnessed (Berezina et al., 2019; Blöcher & Alt, 2021; Ivanov et al., 2017) as a main value driver. Robotic waiter systems and robots employed for serving are increasingly in use and continue to reform the operations (Ivanov, 2019).

Above issues mentioned for the hotel and restaurants are also valid for event management. Events such as cruise tours, cultural tours, and foreign tours all have even more specialized and unique customer requests. In this regard, they can be considered as the combination of traveling, hotel, and restaurant services. Hence, IoT technologies help the overall planning and execution of such events for more exclusive guest experience.

In essence, all of these hospitality services are integral parts of tourism activities. In this regard, Kaurav et al. (2020) offer a comprehensive discussion of technology, tourism, and economic development. Consequently, smart technologies contribute to the tourism sector via each one of these hospitality services.

4.5 Financial Services

One of the early integrations of smart technologies is for financial services, and technological components are increasingly being used for customer service in financial institutions. Fintech concept became part of our lives, referring to the integration of multiple technologies to streamline and digitize traditional financial services (Walden, 2022).

In this technological evolution, automation of payment processing matured along with the evolving e-commerce and e-procurement applications, and became an inevitable part of our daily life.

Call center integration, prompt customer assistance, and chatbots with expanding AI capabilities and AI-fueled virtual assistants are increasingly becoming integral part of financial services. For financial institutions, credit risk management is one of the key processes in which ML and AI algorithms started to play a highly critical role, since the process involves a series of sequential and rigorous controls. Stock market applications are also increasingly supported by AI and mobile chatbots, enabling instant stock exchange transactions based on learned rules and conditions. Robo-advisors automate investment advices. Big data and data mining algorithms offer instant and advanced trend analysis in the context of stock markets, enabling predictive behavioral analytics.

Wearable devices (rings, bracelets) and smart phones are gradually replacing the traditional credit cards. Classical ATMs are being replaced by smart ATMs, which are IoT-enabled machines capable of performing basic maintenance tasks and restocking cash automatically. In relation to ATM's, IoT sensors are also being used to track traffic and monitoring queues near ATMs.

Blockchain technology is a major disruptive technology from financial services perspective. Recent innovations of cryptocurrencies (bitcoin, etherium, etc.), non-fungible tokens (NFT), and digital cash all rely on blockchain infrastructure, and these financial services are one of the earliest applications on the blockchain platforms. Fundamentally, blockchain is applied via distributed networks, consensus mechanisms, and smart contracts (Bringas et al., 2020). Blockchain ensures immutable, untemperable, and permanent proof of transactions and bring a trusted environment across different stakeholders. The technology is critical for the trade of marketable securities and exchange of assets as well as detecting financial frauds. Furthermore, internet payments, credit investigations, P2P lending, equity finance, crowdfunding, anti-money laundering, cross-border remittance, and supply chain finance are highlighted as the main applications of blockchain and smart contracts (Wang et al., 2020).

To sum up, financial services stand out as one of the key service sector applications.

Main findings under these five service sectors are summarized in Table 1 below, with the main technologies involved, main applications, benefits, and the supporting references.

Table 1 is not meant to be fully exhaustive but to highlight the key issues. It can be seen that a multiplicity of technologies are relevant to transportation and logistics and retail sectors in relation to end-to-end traceability and visibility. Enabling self-service and customization capabilities appear to be more predominant in almost all services. Applications like chatbots, call centers are relevant to almost all of these service sectors. Healthcare systems seem to benefit especially from remote follow-up and advanced patient-based analysis. Blockchain applications are more advanced and applicable in health care and financial services in relation to ensuring the immutability and security of the records. Advanced reporting and analytics is essential in all of these sectors. Hence, big data algorithms, AI, and ML are again relevant and beneficial in all of these major sectors.

5. CHALLENGES FOR IMPLEMENTING SMART SERVICE SYSTEMS

In compatibility with the existing literature on manufacturing sector implementations and company-wide Enterprise Resources Planning (ERP) system implementations across partners, challenges of implementing smart systems are multifold. In this regard, major challenges can be summarized and classified as given in Fig. 2 below.

As can be seen in the figure, technological issues pose significant challenges despite the availability of a variety of options and configurations. Ensuring

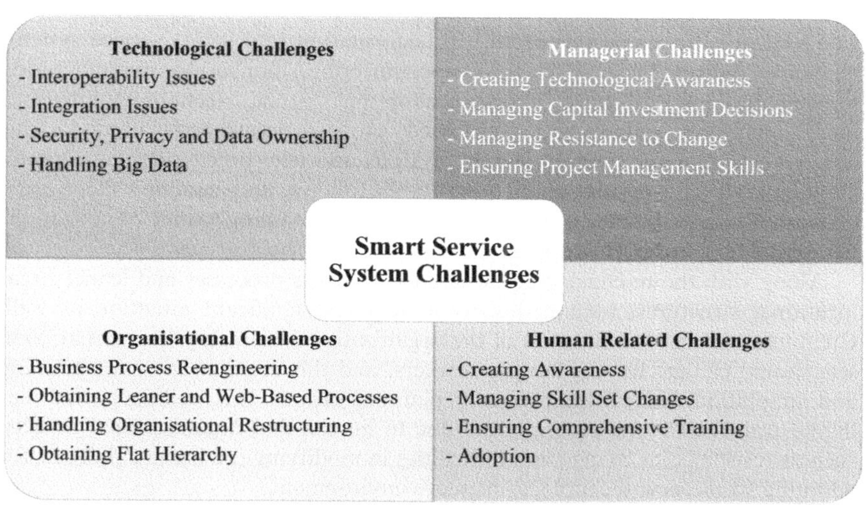

Fig. 2. Multi-Dimensional Challenges of Smart Service Systems *Source:* Developed by the authors.

interoperability and integrity of multiple systems is still one of the major challenges under the technology dimension (Al-Atawi et al., 2022; Khorasani et al., 2022; Mohamad Jawad et al., 2022; Ngu et al., 2016). Applications of middleware (Ngu et al., 2016), web services and Application Programming Interfaces (API's), utilizing proven application solutions from the cloud providers, and ensuring the compatibility of the new technological components with the new ones during the investments are the major solution options in this regard. Security, privacy, and data ownership challenges still prevail for the service network (Mercan et al., 2021; Mohamad Jawad et al., 2022). Handling these challenges is critical, especially for the financial and medical sectors. Proper cloud utilization by deciding on the right service provider and imposing comprehensive service level agreements (SLAs) between companies and service providers can minimize the problems regarding these issues (Zhong et al., 2017). Handling the big data obtained and converting it to the maximum business intelligence is another challenge (Al-Atawi et al., 2022; Mohamad Jawad et al., 2022), and the solution is directly related with the business intelligence (BI) maturity and the utilization of advanced AI, data mining, and algorithmic techniques.

Undoubtedly, smart service systems involve more than technological components as depicted in Fig. 1. Therefore, transformation into smart systems requires more than implementing the technological aspects.

From managerial perspective, creating technological awareness and managing capital investment decisions are major challenges (Mohamad Jawad et al., 2022). Since the issue involves an enterprise-wide transformation, managing resistance to change is crucial for a successful transformation. It is critical that a systematic project management approach is followed, and necessary project management skills are present in the company. Along with the investment on the technological components, implementing a systematic project plan and an appropriate transition strategy are essentials (Laudon & Laudon, 2015).

From organizational perspective, transformation into smart service systems demands radical business process re-engineering, similar to manufacturing implementations. Business models adopting leaner, technology-intensive, increasingly automated, and web-based process designs are needed. This requires a systematic existing system analysis and new process design. Organizational restructuring and change inevitably follows, and handling these organizational issues assumes a vital importance for obtaining leaner organizations with flatter hierarchy (Laudon & Laudon, 2015).

Along with the re-engineered automated business processes and leaner organizational structures, human dimension requires significant attention as well. Creating awareness at all levels of the organizational hierarchy is essential. Skill sets should change for the human workers, and this requires extensive training and adaptation with all the necessary planning efforts. It is well-supported that digital transformations generally fail due to human and organizational aspects, such as resistance to change and difficulties in modifying the human skill sets for adopting to the new technology-intensive environment.

Consequently, it is evident that transition into smart service systems requires an overall project management to guide the transformation, considering technological, organizational, managerial, and human aspects.

6. DISCUSSION

This study puts forward that smartness built up via IoT-based technologies promises significant opportunities for the service sector. Various applications and potentials are revealed for the five main service sectors covered in this study, namely transportation and logistics, retail, health care, hospitality, and financial services.

It became evident that application of the smart technologies elevates tracking and monitoring capabilities to entirely new levels. More efficient, automated, and accurate operations as well as real-time managerial support for service planning, execution, and control activities are provided. Analytical CRM processes are supported to obtain advanced fact-based reports and analysis, leading to improved customer clustering and segmentation, as well as totally new strategies and customized service offerings. It can easily be argued that these results show significant parallelism with their manufacturing sector counterparts.

Competitiveness and winning customers in the service marketplace depends on the dimensions of personalization, speed, quality, availability, dependability, convenience, price, safety, and reputation. It is put forward that simultaneous use of smart technologies serves for the improvement of these parameters, elevating the competitiveness of the enterprise to entirely new levels. Therefore, IoT technologies appear as the strategic weapon in harsh volatile, uncertain, complex, and ambiguous (VUCA) business conditions for the service enterprises. Widespread assimilation of IoT technologies and improvement of the key service dimensions directly serve for the socio-environmentally and socioeconomically stable and sustainable services. Consequently, adoption of these smart technologies offers a strategic competitive advantage to enterprises and countries.

7. FUTURE RESEARCH AGENDA

Based on the previous sections, the authors reckon that our study topic promises a rich future research agenda. In this regard, the following can be mentioned as the main future research suggestions:

- Case-based as well as comparative studies on smart service applications will continue to deserve attention in further research efforts. Studies containing multiple case companies from a specific sector can be conducted to compare the technological components utilized, integration issues, business process re-engineering efforts involved, as well as managerial and organizational changes addressed. Cross-sectoral studies can also be developed for such comparisons.

- Investigations on the sample cases using particular hybrids of smart technologies in different service settings can contribute to the literature of best practices and lessons learned to guide the companies toward world-class service delivery.
- Big data and data mining applications in specific contexts are still hot topics. Their applications in different service sectors deserve further attention.
- Blockchain integration into the smart service ecosystems containing different technological hybrids in different service sectors can be another key research item in the agenda. Since blockchain is a relatively immature technology with significant challenges of application and rules of the game not fully defined, this search avenue is also worthwhile.
- Performance and risk measurement in smart service context can be suggested as another avenue of research. Since smart technologies enable online, real-time capturing and processing of data, composite KPI's, and managerial dashboards can be developed specific to different sectoral needs. Complexities of metrics and difficulties of standardization in this domain are already proven, especially in the multi-partner setting. Combining them further with the smart technologies will also be a challenging and attractive area of research.
- Customer satisfaction measurement in different service sectors in smart context is also vital. With smart technologies, real-time data capturing capabilities from the customer side open up new opportunities in this direction. With the instant feedback from the customer side, assessing the impact of different smart hybrids on customer satisfaction can be a subject of further research.
- Focusing on strategic alignment of the smart ecosystem partners is vital. Therefore, studies at the intersection of "strategic management" and "smart service systems" will also be valuable contributions.

The main limitation of this study was that smart education systems, smart government, smart homes, and smart city applications are not included. This was necessary for narrowing down the extremely wide service scope. Therefore, service applications such as smart education or smart government services can be subject to different further research topics.

8. CONCLUSION

Technological transformation is disruptive in the IoT age, along with ever-changing transformation in the business processes, business models, man–machine interfaces, and changing roles of humans. This study overviewed the applications of smart technologies from service sector perspective and showed that smart technologies are changing the scene for the service enterprises.

The major takeaway from this study is that smart systems based on IoT technologies are not for manufacturing only. Service sector companies should be aware of the improvement opportunities coming from the combined use of smart technologies. It became evident that leaner and more efficient service system designs are possible for meeting ever-increasing customer expectations and creating completely new customer experiences with innovative service encounters.

In this regard, systemic thinking with an overall transformational approach is needed for the service enterprises in their smartness journey. The authors believe that lessons learned from the IoT and smart system implementations in the manufacturing sector should guide the service sector companies.

To sum up, it is put forward that future research agenda at the intersection of "smart systems" and "service sector" is quite promising and fruitful in different service settings.

REFERENCES

Agbo, C. C., Mahmoud, Q. H., & Eklund, J. M. (2019). Blockchain technology in healthcare: A systematic review. *Healthcare*, *7*(2), 56–86.

Akkaş, M. A., Sokullu, R., & Çetin, H. E. (2020). Healthcare and patient monitoring using IoT. *Internet of Things*, *11*, 1–12, 100173.

Akyüz, G. A., & Balkan, D. (2023). Smart manufacturing maturity assessment: A Turkish case study in glass balcony manufacturing enterprise. *Smart Science*, *12*(1), 13–26.

Akyuz, G. A., & Gursoy, G. (2020). Transformation of supply chain activities in blockchain environment. In *Digital business strategies in blockchain ecosystems: Transformational design and future of global business* (pp. 153–175).

Akyuz, G. A., & Tunc, I. (2023). Nanosensor-based smart and innovative packaging in food supply chains. In *2. International conference on innovative academic studies, Konya, Turkey* (p. 200).

Al-Atawi, A. A., Khan, F., & Kim, C. G. (2022). Application and challenges of IoT healthcare system in COVID-19. *Sensors*, *22*(19), 7304.

Al-Rawashdeh, M., Keikhosrokiani, P., Belaton, B., Alawida, M., & Zwiri, A. (2022). IoT adoption and application for smart healthcare: A systematic review. *Sensors*, *22*(14), 5377.

Amendola, S., Lodato, R., Manzari, S., Occhiuzzi, C., & Marrocco, G. (2014). RFID technology for IoT-based personal healthcare in smart spaces. *IEEE Internet of Things Journal*, *1*(2), 144–152.

Antons, D., & Breidbach, C. F. (2018). Big data, big insights? Advancing service innovation and design with machine learning. *Journal of Service Research*, *21*(1), 17–39.

Barge, P., Gay, P., Merlino, V., & Tortia, C. (2013). Radio frequency identification technologies for livestock management and meat supply chain traceability. *Canadian Journal of Animal Science*, *93*(1), 23–33.

Behera, B. C., Moharana, B. R., Muduli, K., & Islam, S. M. (Eds.). (2023). *Smart technologies for improved performance of manufacturing systems and services*. CRC Press.

Berezina, K., Ciftci, O., & Cobanoglu, C. (2019). Robots, artificial intelligence, and service automation in restaurants. In *Robots, artificial intelligence, and service automation in travel, tourism and hospitality* (pp. 185–219). Emerald Publishing Limited.

Berman, D., (2023). Revolutionazing the hospitality industry with artificial intelligence. https://www.forbes.com/sites/forbesbusinesscouncil/2023/09/11/revolutionizing-the-hospitality-industry-with-artificial-intelligence/?sh=5892136d23d1. Accessed on October 7, 2023.

Blöcher, K., & Alt, R. (2021). AI and robotics in the European restaurant sector: Assessing potentials for process innovation in a high-contact service industry. *Electronic Markets*, *31*(3), 529–551.

Bordoloi, S., Fitzsimmons, J. A., & Fitzsimmons, M. J. (2019). *Service management: Operations, strategy, information technology*. McGraw-Hill.

Boyes, H., Hallaq, B., Cunningham, J., & Watson, T. (2018). The industrial internet of things (IIoT): An analysis framework. *Computers in Industry*, *101*, 1–12.

Bringas, G. P., Pastor-López, I., & Psaila, G. (2020). BlockChain platforms in financial services: Current perspective. *Business Systems Research: International Journal of the Society for Advancing Innovation and Research in Economy*, *11*(3), 110–126.

Bughin, J., Seong, J., Manyika, J., Chui, M., & Joshi, R. (2018). *Notes from the AI frontier: Modeling the impact of AI on the world economy*. McKinsey Global Institute. https://www.mckinsey.com/

~/media/McKinsey/Featured%20Insights/Artificial%20Intelligence/Notes%20from%20the%20frontier%20Modeling%20the%20impact%20of%20AI%20on%20the%20world%20economy/MGI-Notes-from-the-AI-frontier-Modeling-the-impact-of-AI-on-the-world-economy-September-2018.ashx. Accessed on October 7, 2023.

Chen, J., & Chang, Y. W. (2023). How smart technology empowers consumers in smart retail stores? The perspective of technology readiness and situational factors. *Electronic Markets*, *33*(1), 1–24.

Chen, Y., Yu, J., Yang, S., & Wei, J. (2018). Consumer's intention to use self-service parcel delivery service in online retailing: An empirical study. *Internet Research*, *28*(2), 500–519.

Dacko, S. G. (2017). Enabling smart retail settings via mobile augmented reality shopping apps. *Technological Forecasting and Social Change*, *124*, 243–256.

Dalenogare, L. S., Benitez, G. B., Ayala, N. F., & Frank, A. G. (2018). The expected contribution of industry 4.0 technologies for industrial performance. *International Journal of Production Economics*, *204*, 383–394.

Draskovic, M., Bauk, S., & Dzankic, R. (2016). Concerning the increasing SCM integration with a reference to some RFID challenges. *Transformations in Business and Economics*, *15*(1), 77–93.

Drezgić, S., Žiković, S., & Tomljanović, M. (2020). *Smart governments, regions and cities*. University of Rijeka, Faculty of Economics and Business.

Farrukh, A., & Sajjad, A. (2023). A critical review of literature review methodologies. *Advancing Methodologies of Conducting Literature Review in Management Domain*, *2*, 103–123.

Gajo, A. H. A. (2021). *A managerial roadmap development for industry 4.0-based smart manufacturing enterprise: A study in Turkish Automotive Sector*. PhD thesis. University of Turkish Aeronautical Association.

Gonçalves, L., Patrício, L., Grenha Teixeira, J., & Wuenderlich, N. V. (2020). Understanding the customer experience with smart services. *Journal of Service Management*, *31*(4), 723–744.

Gupta, A., Singh, R., & Mangla, S. (2021). Evaluation of logistics providers for sustainable service quality: Analytics based decision making framework. *Annals of Operations Research*, *315*(3), 1617–1664.

Holnicki-Szulc, J., Motylewski, J., & Kołakowski, P. (2008). Introduction to smart technologies. In *Smart technologies for safety engineering* (pp. 1–9).

Hussain, S., Mahmud, U., & Yang, S. (2020). Car e-talk: An IoT-enabled cloud-assisted smart fleet maintenance system. *IEEE Internet of Things Journal*, *8*(12), 9484–9494.

Hussein, W. N., Hussain, H. N., & Humod, I. M. (2022). A proposed framework for healthcare based on cloud computing and IoT applications. *Materials Today: Proceedings*, *60*, 1835–1839.

Isharyani, M. E., Sopha, B. M., Wibisono, M. A., & Tjahjono, B. (2021). Smart retail adaptation framework for traditional retailers: A systematical review of literature IEEE. *International Conference on Industrial Engineering and Engineering Management*, *2021*, 143–147.

Ishengoma, F. R., Shao, D., Alexopoulos, C., Saxena, S., & Nikiforova, A. (2022). Integration of artificial intelligence of things (AIoT) in the public sector: Drivers, barriers and future research agenda. *Digital Policy, Regulation and Governance*, *24*(5), 449–462.

Ivanov, S. (2019). Ultimate transformation: How will automation technologies disrupt the travel, tourism and hospitality industries? *Zeitschrift für Tourismuswissenschaft*, *11*(1), 25–43.

Ivanov, S. H., Webster, C., & Berezina, K. (2017). Adoption of robots and service automation by tourism and hospitality companies. *Revista Turismo & Desenvolvimento*, *27*(28), 1501–1517.

Kaur, J., Santhoshkumar, N., Nomani, M. Z. M., Sharma, D. K., Maroor, J. P., & Dhiman, V. (2022). Impact of Internets of Things (IOT) in retail sector. *Materials Today: Proceedings*, *51*, 26–30.

Kaurav, R. P. S., Baber, R., & Rajput, S. (2020). Technology-driven tourism and hospitality industry as a tool for economic development: A bibliometric analysis. In *The Emerald handbook of ICT in tourism and hospitality* (pp. 469–486). Emerald Publishing Limited.

Kaushal, N., Kaurav, R. P. S., Sivathanu, B., & Kaushik, N. (2023). Artificial intelligence and HRM: Identifying future research agenda using systematic literature review and bibliometric analysis. *Management Review Quarterly*, *73*(2), 455–493.

Khorasani, M., Loy, J., Ghasemi, A. H., Sharabian, E., Leary, M., Mirafzal, H., ..., & Gibson, I. (2022). A review of industry 4.0 and additive manufacturing synergy. *Rapid Prototyping Journal*, *28*(8), 1462–1475.

Kusiak, A. (2023). Smart manufacturing. In *Springer handbook of automation* (pp. 973–985). Springer International Publishing.

Lampropoulos, G., Siakas, K., & Anastasiadis, T. (2018). Internet of Things (IoT) in Industry: Contemporary application domains, innovative technologies and intelligent manufacturing. *People*, *6*(7), 109–118.

Laudon, K. C., & Laudon, J. P. (2015). *Management information system*. Pearson Education India.

Loebbecke, C., Huyskens, C., & Gogan, J. (2008, August 10–13). Emerging technologies in the service sector: An early exploration of item-level RFID on the fashion sales floor. In *Information technology in the service economy: Challenges and possibilities for the 21st century: IFIP TC8 WG8. 2 international working conference* (pp. 189–198). Springer US.

Mercan, S., Cain, L., Akkaya, K., Cebe, M., Uluagac, S., Alonso, M., & Cobanoglu, C. (2021). Improving the service industry with hyper-connectivity: IoT in hospitality. *International Journal of Contemporary Hospitality Management*, *33*(1), 243–262.

Mishra, V., & Sharma, M. G. (2022). Digital transformation evaluation of telehealth using convergence, maturity, and adoption. *Health Policy and Technology*, *11*(4), 100684.

Mohamad Jawad, H. H., Bin Hassan, Z., Zaidan, B. B., Mohammed Jawad, F. H., Mohamed Jawad, D. H., & Alredany, W. H. D. (2022). A systematic literature review of enabling IoT in healthcare: Motivations, challenges, and recommendations. *Electronics*, *11*(19), 3223.

Ngu, A. H., Gutierrez, M., Metsis, V., Nepal, S., & Sheng, Q. Z. (2016). IoT middleware: A survey on issues and enabling technologies. *IEEE Internet of Things Journal*, *4*(1), 1–20.

Ostrom, A. L., Parasuraman, A., Bowen, D. E., Patrício, L., & Voss, C. A. (2015). Service research priorities in a rapidly changing context. *Journal of Service Research*, *18*(2), 127–159.

Penna, M., Arjun, B., Goutham, K. R., Madhaw, L. N., & Sanjay, K. G. (2017, May). Smart fleet monitoring system using Internet of Things (IoT). In *2017 2nd IEEE international conference on recent trends in electronics, information and communication technology* (pp. 1232–1236).

Pillai, R., & Sivathanu, B. (2020). Adoption of AI-based chatbots for hospitality and tourism. *International Journal of Contemporary Hospitality Management*, *32*(10), 3199–3226.

Pillai, R., & Srivastava, K. B. (2022). Smart HRM 4.0 for achieving organizational performance: A dynamic capability view perspective. *International Journal of Productivity and Performance Management*, *73*(2), 476–496.

Rammal, H. G. (2023). Systematic literature reviews: Steps and practical tips. In *Advancing methodologies of conducting literature review in management domain* (Vol. 2, pp. 27–35). Emerald Publishing Limited.

Rehse, O., Hoffmann, S., & Kosanke, C. (2016). *Tapping into the transformative power of Service 4.0*. BCG.

Ren, J. (2015, July). RFID enable food supply chain traceability and safety. In *2015 international conference on Logistics, Informatics and Service Sciences (LISS)* (pp. 1–5).

Shankar, V., Kalyanam, K., Setia, P., Golmohammadi, A., Tirunillai, S., Douglass, T., ..., Waddoups, R. (2021). How technology is changing retail. *Journal of Retailing*, *97*(1), 13–27.

Tussyadiah, I. P., & Park, S. (2018, January 24–26). Consumer evaluation of hotel service robots. In *Information and communication technologies in tourism 2018: Proceedings of the international conference in Jönköping* (pp. 308–320). Springer International Publishing.

Walden, S. (2022). What is fintech? *Forbes Advisor*. https://www.forbes.com/advisor/banking/what-is-fintech/. Accessed on October 9, 2023.

Wang, Y., Kim, D. K., & Jeong, D. (2020). A survey of the application of blockchain in multiple fields of financial services. *Journal of Information Processing Systems*, *16*(4), 935–958.

Willcocks, L. P., Lacity, M., & Craig, A. (2015). *The IT function and robotic process automation. The London school of economics and political science*. Outsourcing unit working research paper series, Paper: 15/5, 1–39.

Zebec, A. (2019). Cognitive BPM: Business process automation and innovation with artificial intelligence. In *BPM (PhD/Demos)* (pp. 51–59).

Zhong, R. Y., Xu, X., Klotz, E., & Newman, S. T. (2017). Intelligent manufacturing in the context of industry 4.0: A review. *Engineering*, *3*(5), 616–630.

EXPLORING THE INTERNET OF THINGS-MARKETING CONNECTION: A BIBLIOMETRIC REVIEW AND DIRECTIONS FOR FUTURE RESEARCH

Mohammad Zaid and Rahela Farooqi

Jamia Millia Islamia, India

ABSTRACT

Internet of Things (IoT) has seen rapid penetration with widespread applications at individual user level and organizational level. Marketing is among the critical areas where IoT has brought significant transformation for businesses. This bibliometric analysis aims to understand the present IoT-marketing trends and inform the future research agenda accordingly. This chapter also seeks to identify some common threads explored across the studies. This bibliometric analysis uses research papers from Scopus database. Preliminary analysis showed a growth in the number of articles published over the past decade, indicating increased interest among researchers. This growth is spread across geographies, including developed and developing countries. The findings indicate that the research on IoT in the marketing, being an enticing area for researchers, is growing and will further escalate in future. This study makes novel contributions to the literature around the topic as it reviews IoT research trends in marketing. The analysis further helps to establish the collective viewpoint of many researchers who agree that IoT has enormous potential in marketing. Lastly, the study discusses limitations and future avenues for research related to the topic.

Keywords: Internet of Things; IoT; marketing; bibliometric analysis; PRISMA; IoT applications

Review of Technologies and Disruptive Business Strategies
Review of Management Literature, Volume 3, 275–292

Published under exclusive licence by Emerald Publishing Limited
ISSN: 2754-5865/doi:10.1108/S2754-586520240000003014

1. INTRODUCTION

In 1999, Kevin Ashton propounded the term "Internet of Things" (IoT). Still, the technology concept can be traced back to 1982 when an internet-connected Coke machine could report the drinks left in the machine and the temperature for keeping the drinks cold (Farooq et al., 2015). The IoT is a new wrinkle in technology that has disrupted diverse industries. Researchers, as well as industry experts, are betting high on the potential of IoT with its characteristics that make it a widely applicable technology, further paving the way for new business models and offerings. A unique aspect of IoT is that it enables interaction between intelligent objects/things by integrating heterogeneous technologies. Based on this interactive nature, IoT is expected to bring the next wave of evolution of the internet (Mathur & en Ghai, 2020). This interaction further leads to the collection of unprecedented data, which can additionally be used for developing novel applications across business processes. This data collection phenomenon is a crucial characteristic of IoT technology.

IoT being ubiquitous, coupled with the fast-paced enhancement of enabling technologies like big data, machine learning, and artificial intelligence (AI), suggests the enormous potential impact of the technology (Jia et al., 2019). There is significant optimism surrounding the prospective potent ways the IoT can help transform and enhance interaction patterns between customers and companies, people and products, and the internet (Lo & Campos, 2018). They added that IoT-enabled developments necessitate various digital services and capabilities, delivering innovative interaction between customers and businesses. Fast-forwarding to today, it is estimated that there will be 30 billion connected devices by 2023, including 20 billion IoT-related devices (Ericsson, 2017). Moreover, rapid advancements in sensor and communication technologies have been seen in recent years, transforming the vision for networked IoT systems and their probable deployment (Australian Council of Learned Academies, 2020). IoT has rapidly become one of the most promising expressions across business and technology, researchers, and policymakers.

The basic idea behind IoT is to embed physical objects with sensors, software, and technologies to allow interaction between these distinctively recognizable objects and deliver autonomously exchanged useful information (Farooq et al., 2015). The information-gathering phenomenon of IoT has been an essential characteristic for attracting scholars and researchers to explore and establish IoT's potential in enhancing business models for developing and delivering novel, innovative offerings (Rymaszewska et al., 2017). IoT has gained significant attention recently due to its ability to link physical objects and facilitate communication and information sharing between these devices (Sula et al., 2013). IoT is a technological innovation that shapes consumers' lives through novel, connected, smart products (Christensen, 1997). The ultimate vision of IoT is a smart world made up of sensing technologies and intelligent mechanisms featuring Web 3.0, which includes deeper involvement of users with the technology (Lu et al., 2018). With the worldwide expansion of novel technologies, the ways through which consumer–retailer interaction takes place will also significantly change (Sorescu et al., 2011). Various objects like smartphones, surveillance cameras, home appliances, monitoring sensors, etc., can be connected through the internet to collect a massive amount of data from users. The collected data can further help develop innovative applications and services for customers and society (Bellavista et al., 2013). IoT is considered a vital element of the Fourth Industrial Revolution, and the expected growth in the number of IoT devices reflects its popularity (Lu et al., 2018). The Fourth Industrial Revolution started in the year 2000 and is characterized by product design generated through computers and 3D printing, which can create solid objects by building up sequential layers of materials (Xu et al., 2018).

IoT offers a range of benefits for businesses, including developing competitiveness by using the technology and integrating the same into business models and products (Suppatvech et al., 2019). According to Greenough and Camhi (2016), the most significant adoption of IoT will be across businesses as IoT-based business solutions can improve productivity and profitability of the business while bringing in operating efficiency and facilitating the expansion across new markets and even developing new offerings/solutions for customers (Greenough & Camhi, 2016). The data collected on product usage and performance can help businesses develop a solid competitive advantage for delivering services tailored toward improved profitability and enhanced satisfaction of customers (Rymaszewska et al., 2017). The past decade has been vital for advancing IoT by developing new internet-based business models. For marketers, one of the most prosperous areas benefitting from such business models is online advertising and marketing, as it utilizes internet capabilities to generate promotional content for end users (Aksu et al., 2018).

Therefore, this chapter aims to conduct a bibliometric analysis to understand how IoT has been researched in the past decade in the area of marketing. Bibliometric analysis is a method for systematically evaluating scholarly literature using various techniques to present publication patterns of a journal within a defined timeframe, offering insights into prevalent topics of interest and outlining potential directions for future research while serving as a valuable resource for contributors (Rana & Singh, 2022; Rojas-Sánchez et al., 2023). Further, the current study discusses various research gaps and the potential scope for impending research from the research articles published in the marketing domain.

Given the backdrop of the IoT research trends, the current study aims to answer the following questions:

- What are the most influential studies among IoT research in marketing?
- What is the thematic structure of IoT research literature?
- What is the intellectual structure of the knowledge base on the IoT in marketing?
- What are the recent trends in IoT research in marketing?
- What can be the future direction of IoT research in marketing?

2. RESEARCH METHODOLOGY

The current study involves a bibliometric analysis to understand the current IoT research trends in marketing and investigate the structure of the available literature. For these purposes, the authors took into account the most relevant publications. Scopus database, which contains millions of entries from around 5000 publishers (De Mauro et al., 2016), was searched to find the relevant publications. The search request included keywords "Internet of Things OR IoT" AND "Marketing" OR "e-marketing" OR "Advertising" OR "e-advertising". The results so obtained showed 1,123 documents that included these keywords in the title, abstract, or keywords of the articles.

Further, the resultant documents for further research were refined using various criteria. In the first stage, the article had to be written in English (Cardella et al., 2020); then, it ought to be a scientific paper published in a peer-reviewed journal since this increases the reliability of the article as the source of information (Podsakoff et al., 2005). Another criterion to further refine the search was to limit the article to subjects of interest, i.e., "Business, Management, and Accounting", "Social Science", "Psychology", "Decision Science", "Arts and Humanities", and "Multidisciplinary". Lastly, the research article must not have been published in a conference proceeding or as a chapter in a book and must be from "Journal" sources only.

Applying such filters returned 132 final documents, which the researchers read to identify and exclude articles unrelated to IoT research in marketing. This step follows the exclusion criteria followed by Gümüş et al. (2020) and Soriano et al. (2018), wherein the studies that were not related to the scope of their research (not related to organizational studies) were not considered for further analysis.

After applying this exclusion criterion to all 132 articles, 76 articles were excluded from the dataset due to their lack of relevance to the topic of study. For instance, articles with keywords not discussing IoT research in the marketing context were excluded. Consequently, there were 56 articles arrived to be more deeply examined. This significant decline in the number of articles seems unusual when conducting a bibliometric analysis; however, it has occurred in a variety of other studies as well, including, Galvagno and Giaccone (2019), Gümüş et al. (2020), Keathley-Herring et al. (2016), and Tigre et al. (2023).

This practice of filtering the documents is in line with the guidelines of the PRISMA method (Liberati et al., 2009; Moher et al., 2009; Urrútia & Bonfill, 2010), as shown in Fig. 1. This method has been used by Cardella et al. (2020) and can be replicated. The authors used numerous bibliometric indicators to analyze the progression of scientific research over time, identify the most impactful authors on the subject, the scientific journals that have published the most articles, and the countries that host the most significant scientific contributions.

The analysis was conducted using VOSviewer software version 1.6.19.0, as it uses bibliometric techniques that provide graphical representation, identification, and categorization of research groups based on similarities and differences. VOSviewer software is open-source software that helps in analysis by generating,

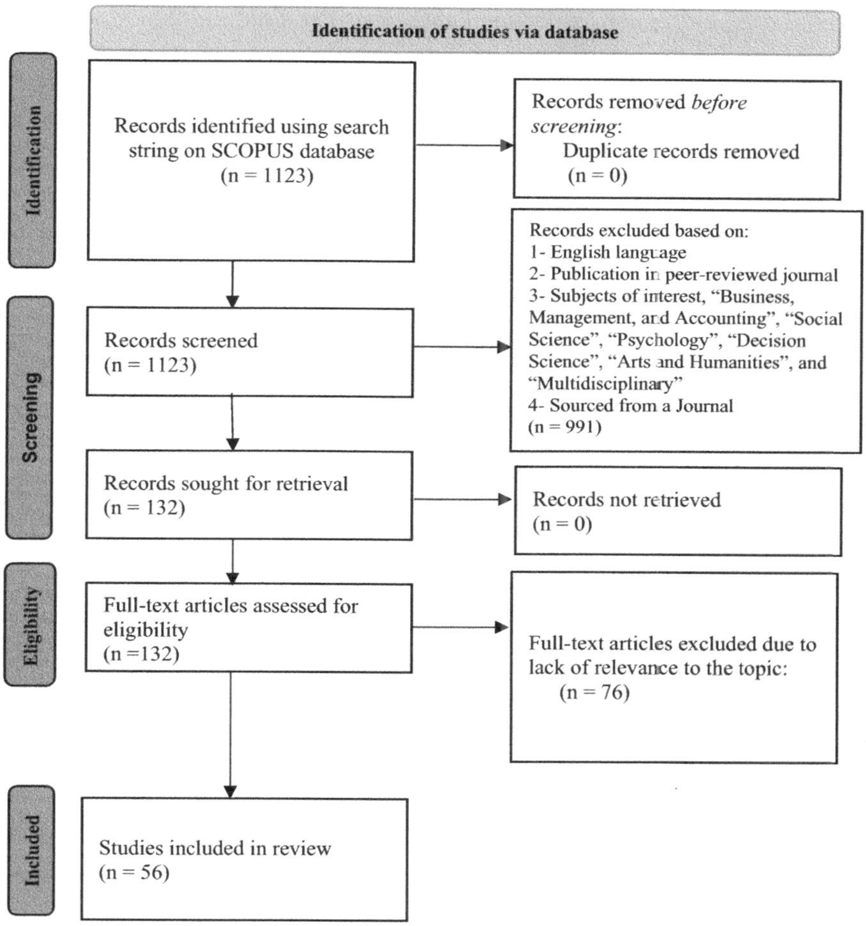

Fig. 1. PRISMA Method. *Source:* Page et al. (2021).

visualizing, and analyzing term maps and generating a keyword co-occurrence network and graphical illustrations of research groups based on commonalities and distinctions.

3. ANALYSIS AND RESULTS

The research on IoT revolves around several aspects of marketing, wherein numerous researchers assessed the association between IoT and various marketing aspects. Here, we discuss the various research trends identified through the current research.

3.1 Scientific Publications Per Year

Fig. 2 shows the number of scientific papers published yearly, which showed an increasing trend until 2023. Although the term IoT was first coined by Kevin Ashton in 1990 (Chin et al., 2019), the first scientific paper talking about IoT and its role in marketing was published only recently. In the early phase of IoT research in marketing, Jara et al. (2013) stated that the potential of the IoT and big data across sectors is nascent. Moreover, the study discusses participative marketing that enables novel interaction and participation models based on ubiquitous identification. The research focuses on participative marketing as the evolution from social media marketing and utilizing IoT's identification and interaction capabilities. Social media is a powerful tool for data collection as it uses various identification mechanisms for participative marketing using new technologies in smartphones. According to Zolkepli and Kamarulzaman (2015), participative marketing is facilitated through the increasing penetration of social networking and the convenient participation for interaction with users through smartphones and other smart devices.

Moreover, the IoT is a growing phenomenon and is increasingly used along with big data by business decision-makers and information professionals (Abu Ghazaleh & Zabadi, 2020). The expanding horizon of IoT applications and the subsequent increase in the number of IoT-enabled devices shall lead to increased interactions between the users and the devices, further enabling the sellers to develop and offer a wide range of innovative services (Zaid et al., 2019). With a significant increase in research over the last few years, there lies substantial optimism for growth in this area as researchers, scholars, and policymakers continue to pay more attention to IoT's marketing aspect.

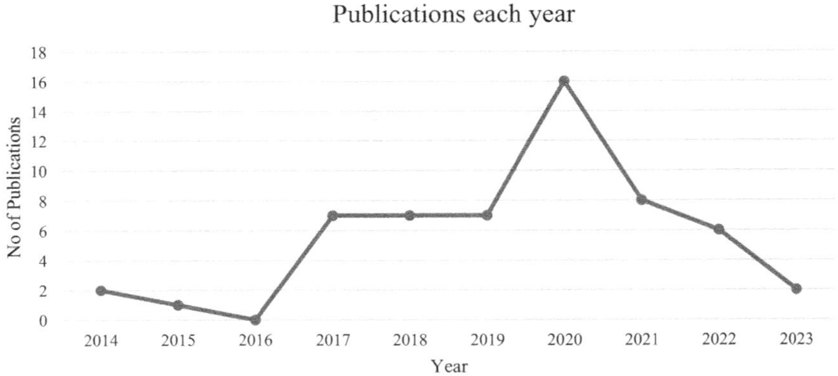

Fig. 2. Cumulative Growth in the Number of Source Documents. *Source:* Author.

3.2 Country-Wise Publication

The analysis based on the country of origin suggests that the research is not limited to developed nations or a specific region. Fig. 3 shows the scientific output concerning IoT research in marketing from respective countries as published in Scopus. Notably, most papers come from the United States, followed by the United Kingdom, India, Indonesia, China, France, Germany, etc. Such dispersion across more countries for IoT research within the marketing field shows that research has been conducted worldwide.

The top four contributing countries, including the United States, United Kingdom, India, and Indonesia, account for nearly half (50%) of the scientific research output related to IoT research in marketing. Notably, these four countries include two developed and two developing nations. Although the scientific research output in the domain may seem highly concentrated among the developed nations, it also extends to include research from developing countries. This calls for the solidification of scientific collaboration across borders, albeit this study only includes publications in the English language (Rejeb et al., 2020).

The research related to IoT in marketing was produced across 24 nations globally. Therefore, the growth in research related to the topic over the years comes from various countries spread across distinct regions, suggesting that the IoT is an area of interest for researchers globally.

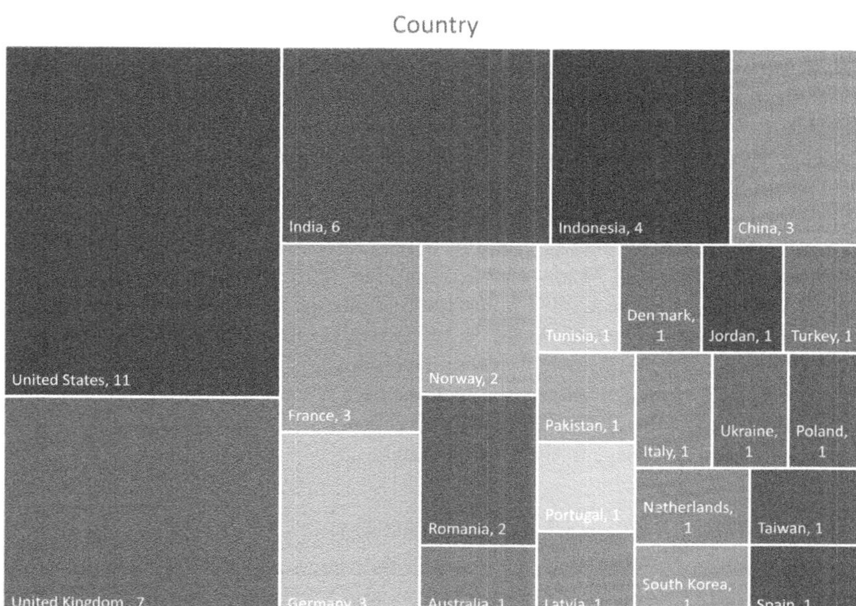

Fig. 3. Contributing Countries. *Source:* Author.

3.3 Leading Publishing Journals

The final 56 papers considered in this research were published across 44 journals, meaning the number of articles published per journal is low. The most number of articles (5) were published in the "Sustainability (Switzerland)" journal. "Industrial Marketing Management" and "Journal of Interactive Marketing" have three articles each. Similarly, four journals ("Business Process Management Journal", "International Journal of Research in Marketing", "Journal of Business and Industrial Marketing," and "Journal of Cases on Information Technology") published two articles each, and the remaining journals published one article each. These top seven publishing journals contribute roughly 33% of the research papers. Notably, the most published studies are in journals related to business marketing, technology topics, and business function management.

3.4 Influential Authors and Affiliation Statistics

Looking at the top 10 most cited articles, the most influential authors come from the United States, with around 40% of the citations spread over 50% of the research articles. This is followed by the United Kingdom, with approximately 35% of the citations distributed among 30% of the research papers. Other most influential authors come from Italy and Portugal, with 253 citations and 122 citations, respectively, for 10% of the articles each. The research contributing to IoT in marketing originates from 4 countries only when looking at the top 10 most cited research articles; however, there are 24 countries in totality contributing to the research base.

A closer look at the list of most influential authors reveals names like Ng and Wakenshaw; Ardito, Petruzzelli, Panniello, Garavelli; and Hoyer, Kroschke, Schmitt, Kraume, and Shankar (Hoyer et al., 2020). These authors are the top most cited authors and have been impactful in studies related to IoT and its marketing aspects. It is worth noting that the 10 most cited articles come from American and European countries. None of the Asian countries constitute the 10 most cited articles. The University of Warwick is the leading university for IoT research in marketing. The second highest number of citations is Bari Polytechnic Department of Mathematical Mechanics and Management, Italy. The third and fourth most influential institutions are from the United States and include the University of Texas and the University of Massachusetts Amherst, respectively. Other universities contributing to the IoT research literature in marketing include the University of Porto, Portugal; University of Groningen, Netherlands; Lancaster University Management School, UK; Iowa State University; Center for Excellence in Brand and Customer Management, Babson College in the United States.

3.5 Co-occurrence Keywords

Zhang et al. (2019) suggest that the top author keywords can give a sense of the research priorities and interests of scientists and researchers in a particular field. This makes it significant to conduct a co-occurrence analysis of author keywords in the publications selected for this bibliometric study.

The sample comprising 56 documents was considered for analysis, wherein a keywords co-occurrence network map was created. This network map is a bibliometric indicator that shows clusters and allows a broader view of distinct research agendas in a specific scientific field. VOSviewer software tool was used to generate the keywords co-occurrence map by selecting: (1) type of analysis – co-occurrence; (2) counting method – full counting; (3) unit of analysis – author keywords; (4) the minimal number of keyword occurrences in the names, keywords, and abstracts of the chosen documents = 2. Besides, keywords that were synonymous or unrelated were deleted; as a result, 24 keywords out of 242 met the threshold.

Table 1 shows the fundamental concepts embedded in the selected publications that are classified into seven broad clusters. These are based on the co-occurrence network of the most frequently used keywords as shown in Fig. 4.

These clusters show that the most important keywords were "Internet of Things", "Big Data", "Artificial Intelligence", "Social Media", "Marketing", "Business Models", and "Smart Cities". Subsequently, the keywords "Big Data", "Artificial Intelligence", and "Social Media" have the highest link strength. This may be because big data, AI, and social media are collectively studied in association with IoT across the selected studies. Big corporations have been using social media marketing campaigns as tools to engage consumers in cocreation (Misra et al., 2020). Moreover, when the user-related metadata (age, profession, geolocation, etc.) is analyzed with the data collected from social campaigns, it helps gather insights and market segmentation of the brands.

The analysis further reveals that the term "Internet of Things" was highly associated with "purchase intention" and "IoT adoption", forming another cluster. Besides this, the IoT also extends its links to terms like "marketing", "mobile marketing", "marketing analytics", "business models", etc., from different clusters. The literature reveals that researchers have shown interest in studying the relationship between these highly associated terms together with IoT

Table 1. Clusters and Various Key Concepts.

Cluster 1	Cluster 2	Cluster 3	Cluster 4	Cluster 5	Cluster 6	Cluster 7
Business Models	Marketing Strategies	Internet of Things	Big Data	Marketing	Artificial Intelligence	Blockchain
Circular Economy	Privacy	IoT Adoption	Marketing Analytics	New Product Development	Mobile Marketing	Smart Cities
Consumer Experience	SME	Purchase Intention	Retailing	Supply Chain Management		
E-commerce	Social Media					
Innovation						
Service						
Technology						

Source: Author.

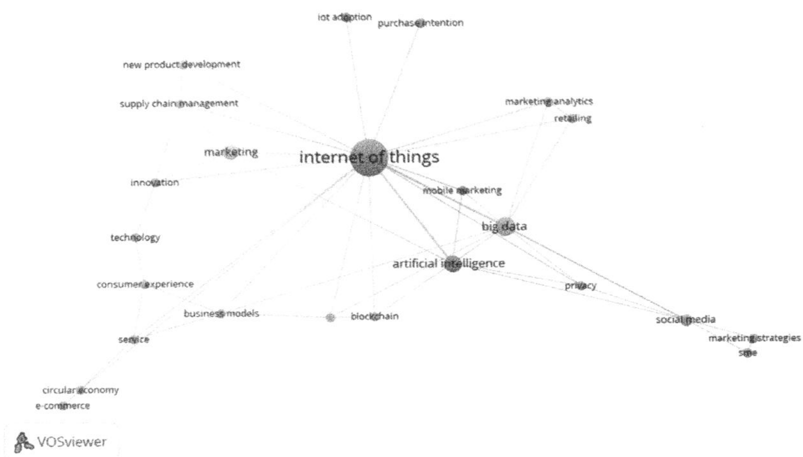

Fig. 4. Network Map on Co-occurrences of Keywords. *Source:* Author.

(see Aggarwal et al., 2020; Das, 2019; Donner & Steep, 2021; Ng & Wakenshaw, 2017; Pillai & Sivathanu, 2020; Princes et al., 2020; Sivathanu, 2018; etc.).

Big Data is the keyword with the second highest link and has a link strength of 9, including the Internet of Things. The concepts related to big data included marketing analytics and retailing within the same cluster and artificial intelligence, social media, mobile marketing, smart cities, and privacy from different groups. The existing literature provides evidence that research around big data explores and explains its role in marketing analytics for businesses, especially retailing. Moreover, big data research has also focused on challenges like privacy and its potency in developing new business models, smart cities, mobile marketing opportunities, and social media integration. One of the key reasons that these concepts have been combined would be the individual interest of researchers in studying the role of big data concerning these concepts. The applications of big data are enormous, and it is becoming more significant than ever to learn since it can deliver opportunities for enterprises in B2B domains with their marketing functions, enhance their service proposition, enable a more focused and targeted collaboration with customers, and ultimately help the enterprises become profitable (Sivarajah et al., 2020).

The keyword "Artificial Intelligence" forms another cluster with its link to mobile marketing. However, AI is also related to keywords in other clusters, including marketing, privacy, social media, blockchain, and big data. The linkage of terminologies from different clusters to AI can be supported by recent research that studies these areas combined. One of the reasons for researchers to integrate these terminologies is to explore and apply the various facets of the technology to ascertain the opportunities and challenges for businesses.

Another cluster comprises keywords "marketing", "new product development", and "supply chain management". The term marketing has an occurrence of 5, and the terms new product development and supply chain management have an equal occurrence of 2 each. Of the three keywords, marketing has the highest link strength of 7, followed by supply chain management which has five links, and new product development has the least link strength of 3. Besides being linked to supply chain management, marketing is directly related to keywords like innovation, artificial intelligence, and the Internet of Things from other clusters. The data gathered from the operational use of IoT devices and their analysis can deliver marketing outcomes like new product development (Tariq et al., 2020). There is a considerable need to implement the IoT landscape in new product development (Yerpude & Singhal, 2018). The real-time data can be frequently analyzed, and organizations can thus develop and deliver value propositions in the new product development (NPD) process (Lee et al., 2022).

The market and operational data gathered through IoT and cloud solutions throughout the supply chain can be used across supply chain management and marketing functions (Ardito et al., 2019). Since concepts like "new product development" and "supply chain management" are discussed in conjunction with IoT and their implications on related business functions, the authors believe that researchers intended to understand these concepts about marketing.

The keyword "social media" had the fourth highest link strength of 8 and formed a new cluster that included "privacy", "SME," and "marketing strategies" as keywords. The three keywords in the cluster had a link strength of 5, 3, and 2, respectively. Privacy has been a significant concern (Huang & Kieffer, 2019) as the user data generated from social media can be used to curate marketing strategies and campaigns that are more customer-centric and on a personal level (Castronovo & Huang, 2012). It is believed that the researchers were interested in understanding the challenge related to privacy in the era of social media and the implications for small and medium enterprises (SMEs)/businesses, especially in shaping marketing strategies.

The most significant cluster with seven keywords along with their link strength includes "Business Models" (5), "Circular Economy" (4), "Consumer Experience" (4), "E-commerce" (2), "Innovation" (4), "Service" (4), and "Technology" (3). Moreover, all the keywords in this cluster have an occurrence of 2. Compared to other keywords across different clusters, it can be noted that most of these keywords focus on enhancement aspects of business or industry. This can make sense in understanding why this set of keywords appeared farthest from other clusters with technology and marketing-related concepts. Therefore, in the 56 selected papers, the researchers have not only studied the IoT and its implications for marketing but also focused on other essential aspects closely associated with technology integration.

The last cluster includes only two keywords, namely "Block Chain" and "Smart Cities" with occurrence of 2 each and link strength of 4 and 3, respectively. Besides smart cities, the keyword blockchain is also linked with the IoT and artificial intelligence. Similarly, smart cities are most closely linked with "business models" and also linked with "big data" and "internet of things". This may suggest that the researchers have explored the role of various technologies in developing smart cities and evolving business models.

4. FINDINGS AND DISCUSSION

The analysis reveals that the marketing aspect of IoT is still an emerging field for research. A thorough analysis of the identified documents asserts that conceptual or literature papers constitute a significant part of this research area. This could mean that there is a lack of empirical evidence from the organizational and user perspective in IoT research related to marketing.

Several common themes can be noted, including marketing analytics, innovation, supply chain, new product development, consumer experience, business models, retailing, etc. The findings are of great significance for industry and academia as they relate to the contemporary concerns, research themes, and theoretical perspectives on the potential of IoT in business, especially marketing.

4.1 Common Threads Explored Across Studies

The analysis identifies that a common idea where the application of IoT across multiple facets of business converges is that it will significantly impact marketing practices and outcomes for firms as well as customers. Several researchers further suggest that IoT can also have a significant impact on other aspects of the business and the overall ecosystem when coupled with disruptive technologies like AI, big data, machine learning, etc. Although the umbrella of IoT application is still expanding to include more and more aspects of business, we find that only a few studies have been conducted to date that empirically establish the potential of IoT in marketing. Other than business, IoT is believed to influence various aspects of society. Therefore, many studies have focused on the adoption of IoT, especially for wearable products. The analysis shows that the studies related to the adoption and acceptance of IoT are not limited to a single country and are spread across countries. The applications employing emerging technologies are being developed in the United States and across several European and Asian countries (Shah & Chircu, 2018).

The existing studies focus on highlighting the benefits and challenges in the adoption of IoT for businesses and individuals. Numerous studies of IoT from the user perspective have primarily focused on factors influencing the acceptance and use of a specific service or application, especially the wearables and hospitality domain. Privacy and security issues have been a critical area for exploring the challenges related to the adoption of IoT. Some researchers also offer implications of its policy and a legal framework for crucial issues like trust among users. Furthermore, some studies highlight the significance of considering the effects of IoT solutions on businesses, particularly on user behavior aspects and the incubation of targeted strategies (Lo & Campos, 2018). Some researchers also discuss the real-time interactivity nature of the IoT technology and the usage of real-time data to enhance the effectiveness of new product development and improve efficiency in marketing through analytics, mobile marketing, personalized marketing, etc.

A key finding of the analysis is that the ecosystem comprising IoT-based solutions like smart devices, smart homes, and smart cities will significantly impact the outcomes for firms. Some key aspects already discussed by researchers from the organizational perspective include circular economy (Alves et al., 2022; Rejeb et al., 2022; Voulgaridis et al., 2022; etc.), business models (Paiola et al., 2021; Palmaccio et al., 2021; Suppatvech et al., 2019; etc.), supply chain management (Abdel-Basset et al., 2018; Aryal et al., 2018; Ben-Daya et al., 2019; etc.), marketing strategies (Lo & Campos, 2018; Maiorescu et al., 2020; Nguyen & Simkin, 2017; etc.), retailing (Caro & Sadr, 2019; Hossain et al., 2021; Kalange et al., 2017; etc.), and new product development (Thongprasert & Jiamsanguanwong, 2021; Yerpude & Singhal, 2018; etc.).

5. IMPLICATIONS AND CONCLUSION

The current research summarizes the existing literature on IoT in marketing into various clusters. The keywords analysis helps in identifying various themes across the IoT research landscape, and the research clusters provide insights into various subdomains and the interconnectedness of research topics. This will help researchers and practitioners understand the current focus of the academic community and provide them with direction for undertaking qualitative and quantitative research based on specific themes. The bibliometric analysis also recognizes influential research and contributors and areas with limited research attention. This will help in identifying potential research gaps for further exploration and also promote future research collaboration opportunities among researchers.

Since this research informs about the current state of the art in IoT in the marketing domain, it can guide practitioners in developing IoT-based marketing strategies and applications. Business entities and institutions can enhance and shift their focus on research and development (R&D) and investment based on the research trends identified. Moreover, the identification of influential authors and institutions can be useful for seeking future collaboration opportunities as well as expert insights or comments. This bibliometric analysis has delivered key findings regarding the most prominent authors, journals, publications, citations, institutions, and countries. Overall, the insights related to significant keywords, relevant publications, and key authors should help future researchers and practitioners interested in a similar research domain take a head start for their research work.

The analysis shows that the maximum number of publications was in 2020, and the papers from 2017 are the most cited. Distinct institutions have contributed significantly toward the scholarly work undertaken with IoT in marketing. Besides this, the United States alone has contributed substantially to the research base, with approximately 20% of the publications coming from the country. The study notices a growth trend, although inconsistent, in the number of publications and citations over the years, indicating increasing interest of the researchers. However, more empirical studies relevant to the research domain are needed to build a knowledge base supported by empirical evidence. Such research would further help in assessing and improving the quality of products, services, or processes for businesses while helping in informed policy development and strategic planning for policymakers and relevant associations. The accumulated knowledge base related to IoT in marketing indicates that IoT can have significant implications for the marketing aspect of the business. This makes it a more exciting area of research for scholars as they can focus on testing the existing literature by assessing the practical implications of IoT in marketing activities. Taking a step further, several researchers suggest that IoT can have a far more significant impact on other aspects of the business and the overall business ecosystem when coupled with disruptive technologies like AI, big data, machine learning, etc. Therefore, the authors encourage researchers to develop empirical works for future research in this domain, showing practical relevance from the managerial point of view, along with theoretical studies, to incentivize researchers' interest in the domain.

6. LIMITATIONS AND FUTURE RESEARCH

The current research analyses the growth and adoption trends of IoT technologies in marketing along with examining the scholarly discourse on the keywords, citations, authors, and journals associated with IoT in marketing. A challenge to studies like ours is to match the pace of innovations in technologies and their expanding applications. Besides this, the changes in research topics and methodologies can challenge the relevance of bibliometric indicators over time. Therefore, this would require extensive bibliometric and literature work from time to time to cover the gaps in this research area.

The current research, like any other research, is not free from certain limitations and offers scope for future research. The current study includes articles retrieved from a single database, i.e., Scopus. Future research can include publication data from alternate research databases or a combination of more than one databased. The current research also provides scope for similar research over extended timelines for a longitudinal study. Moreover, the sample for the research was restricted to peer-reviewed research articles published in English-language journals, limiting a part of the overall knowledge base related to the topic. The citation analysis involves assigning weight to a paper's citation, which may be biased toward older articles as they have more citations than recent publications. While doing the citation analysis, future researchers can restrict the search results to the number of citations; this would highlight more recent articles.

Future research can also focus on the practical applications of IoT in shaping the marketing landscape. The bibliometric analysis shows that IoT studies related to marketing themes like consumer behavior, customer decision-making processes, as well as psychological aspects of consumer interaction with IoT-enabled marketing strategies are not highlighted through the bibliometric analysis. Exploring these key areas is very significant to establish the effectiveness and applications of IoT-based marketing in contemporary times. Besides this, the themes associated with the potential of IoT in personalized marketing, the opportunities for IoT in marketing in emerging markets, as well as the importance of IoT in promoting sustainable and environmentally friendly marketing practice, could not be identified through the analysis. Future research should focus on these key areas to fill the major gap and provide a foundation for exploring uncharted areas within the intersection of IoT and marketing.

More attention is needed to investigate the real-life application of IoT in facilitating seamless integration across various marketing channels and the strategies for leveraging IoT data to create cohesive and consistent marketing campaigns across online and offline channels. On a deeper level, research should also focus on exploring and establishing the impact of cultural, economic, and regulatory factors on the implementation of IoT-driven marketing strategies across different countries and regions.

REFERENCES

Abdel-Basset, M., Manogaran, G., & Mohamed, M. (2018). Internet of things (IoT) and its impact on supply chain: A framework for building smart, secure and efficient systems. *Future Generation Computer Systems*, *86*(9), 614–628. https://doi.org/10.1016/j.future.2018.04.051

Abu Ghazaleh, M., & Zabadi, A. M. (2020). Promoting a revamped CRM through Internet of Things and Big Data: An AHP-based evaluation. *International Journal of Organizational Analysis*, *28*(1), 66–91. https://doi.org/10.1108/IJOA-12-2018-1602

Aggarwal, N., Albert, L. J., Hill, T. R., & Rodan, S. A. (2020). Risk knowledge and concern as influences of purchase intention for internet of things devices. *Technology in Society*, *62*, 101311. https://doi.org/10.1016/j.techsoc.2020.101311

Aksu, H., Babun, L., Conti, M., Tolomei, G., & Uluagac, A. S. (2018). Advertising in the IoT era: Vision and challenges. *IEEE Communications Magazine*, *56*(11), 138–144. https://doi.org/10.1002/smj.454

Alves, L., Ferreira Cruz, E., Lopes, S. I., Faria, P. M., & Rosado da Cruz, A M. (2022). Towards circular economy in the textiles and clothing value chain through blockchain technology and IoT: A review. *Waste Management & Research*, *40*(1), 3–23. https://doi.org/10.1177/0734242X211052858

Ardito, L., Petruzzelli, A. M., Panniello, U., & Garavelli, A. C. (2019). Towards industry 4.0: Mapping digital technologies for supply chain management-marketing integration. *Business Process Management Journal*, *25*(2), 323–346. https://doi.org/10.1108/BPMJ-04-2017-0088

Aryal, A., Liao, Y., Nattuthurai, P., & Li, B. (2018). The emerging big data analytics and IoT in supply chain management: A systematic review. *Supply Chain Management*, *25*(2), 141–156. https://doi.org/10.1108/SCM-03-2018-0149

Australian Council of Learned Academies. (2020). A year of rapid digital change- How the Internet of Things builds on this momentum to support safer, healthier and more connected lives. https://acola.org/media-release-nov-2020-iot-rapid-digital-change/. Accessed on January 5, 2022.

Bellavista, P., Cardone, G., Corradi, A., & Foschini, L. (2013). Convergence of MANET and WSN in IoT urban scenarios. *IEEE Sensors Journal*, *13*(10), 3558–3567. https://doi.org/10.1109/JSEN.2013.2272099

Ben-Daya, M., Hassini, E., & Bahroun, Z. (2019). Internet of things and supply chain management: A literature review. *International Journal of Production Research*, *57*(15–16), 4719–4742. https://doi.org/10.1080/00207543.2017.1402140

Cardella, G. M., Hernández-Sánchez, B. R., & Sánchez-García, J. C. (2020). Women entrepreneurship: A systematic review to outline the boundaries of scientific literature. *Frontiers in Psychology*, *11*, 1557. https://doi.org/10.3389/fpsyg.2020.01557

Caro, F., & Sadr, R. (2019). The Internet of things (IoT) in retail: Bridging supply and demand. *Business Horizons*, *62*(1), 47–54. https://doi.org/10.1016/j.bushor.2018.08.002

Castronovo, C., & Huang, L. (2012). Social media in an alternative marketing communication model. *Journal of Marketing Development and Competitiveness*, *6*(1), 117–134.

Chin, J., Callaghan, V., & Allouch, S. B. (2019). The Internet-of-Things: Reflections on the past, present and future from a user-centered and smart environment perspective. *Journal of Ambient Intelligence and Smart Environments*, *11*(1), 45–69. https://doi.org/10.3233/AIS-180506

Christensen, C. M. (1997). *The Innovator's Dilemma*. Harvard Business School Press.

Das, S. (2019). The early bird catches the worm-first mover advantage through IoT adoption for Indian public sector retail oil outlets. *Journal of Global Information Technology Management*, *22*(4), 280–308. https://doi.org/10.1080/1097198X.2019.1679588

De Mauro, A., Greco, M., & Grimaldi, M. (2016). A formal definition of Big Data based on its essential features. *Library Review*, *65*, 122–135. https://doi.org/10.1108/LR-06-2015-0061

Donner, H., & Steep, M. (2021). Monetizing the IoT revolution. *Sustainability*, *13*(4), 2195. https://doi.org/10.3390/su13042195

Ericsson. (2017). Ericsson mobility report November 2017. https://www.ericsson.com/en/reports-and-papers/mobility-report/reports. Accessed on December 20, 2021.

Farooq, M. U., Waseem, M., Mazhar, S., Khairi, A., & Kamal, T. (2015). A review on internet of things (IoT). *International Journal of Computer Applications*, *113*(1), 1–7. https://doi.org/10.5120/19787-1571

Galvagno, M., & Giaccone, S. C. (2019). Mapping creative tourism research: Reviewing the field and outlining future directions. *Journal of Hospitality & Tourism Research*, *43*(8), 1256–1280. https://doi.org/10.1177/1096348019862030

Greenough, J., & Camhi, J. (2016). Business insider. In *Here are IoT trends that will change the way businesses, government, and consumers interact with the world*. http://uk.businessinsider.com/top-internet-of-things-trends-2016-1. Accessed on January 15, 2022.

Gümüş, S., Bellibaş, M. Ş., Gümüş, E., & Hallinger, P. (2020). Science mapping research on Educational leadership and management in Turkey: A bibliometric review of international publications. *School Leadership & Management*, *40*(1), 23–44. https://doi.org/10.1080/13632434.2019.1578737

Hossain, M. S., Chisty, N. M. A., Hargrove, D. L., & Amin, R. (2021). Role of Internet of things (IoT) in retail business and enabling smart retailing experiences. *Asian Business Review*, *11*(2), 75–80. https://doi.org/10.18034/abr.v11i2.579

Hoyer, W. D., Kroschke, M., Schmitt, B., Kraume, K., & Shankar, V. (2020). Transforming the customer experience through new technologies. *Journal of Interactive Marketing*, *51*(1), 57–71. https://doi.org/10.1016/j.intmar.2020.04.001

Huang, Q., & Kieffer, K. (2019). An intelligent internet of things (IoT) sensor system for Building environmental monitoring. *Journal of Mobile Multimedia*, 29–50. https://doi.org/10.13052/1550-4646.15122

Jara, A. J., Varakliotis, S., Skarmeta, A. F., & Kirstein, P. (2013). Extending the Internet of Things to the future internet through IPv6 support. *Mobile Information Systems*. IOS Press. https://doi.org/10.3233/MIS-130169.

Jia, M., Komeily, A., Wang, Y., & Srinivasan, R. S. (2019). Adopting Internet of Things for the development of smart buildings: A review of enabling technologies and applications. *Automation in Construction*, *101*, 111–126. https://doi.org/10.1016/j.autcon.2019.01.023

Kalange, S. H., Kadam, D. A., Mokal, A. B., & Patil, A. A. (2017). Smart retailing using IOT. *International Research Journal of Engineering and Technology (IRJET)*, *4*(11), 263–268.

Keathley-Herring, H., Van Aken, E., Gonzalez-Aleu, F., Deschamps, F., Letens, G., & Orlandini, P. C. (2016). Assessing the maturity of a research area: Bibliometric review and proposed framework. *Scientometrics*, *109*(2), 927–951. https://doi.org/10.1007/s11192-016-2096-x

Lee, B., Hands, D., Cooper, R., & Coulton, P. (2022). Emergent NPD process and development risks for IoT: An exploratory case study in agri-tech. *International Journal of Business and Systems Research*, *16*(2), 183–198. https://doi.org/10.1504/IJBSR.2022.121141

Liberati, A., Altman, D. G., Tetzlaff, J., Mulrow, C., Gøtzsche, P. C., Ioannidis, J. P., . . ., Moher, D. (2009). The PRISMA statement for reporting systematic reviews and meta-analyses of studies that evaluate health care interventions: Explanation and elaboration. *Annals of Internal Medicine*, *151*(4), W–65. https://doi.org/10.7326/0003-4819-151-4-200908180-00136

Lo, F. Y., & Campos, N. (2018). Blending Internet-of-things (IoT) solutions into relationship marketing strategies. *Technological Forecasting and Social Change*, *137*, 10–18. https://doi.org/10.1016/j.techfore.2018.09.029

Lu, Y., Papagiannidis, S., & Alamanos, E. (2018). Internet of Things: A systematic review of the business literature from the user and organisational perspectives. *Technological Forecasting and Social Change*, *136*, 285–297. https://doi.org/10.1016/j.techfore.2018.01.022

Maiorescu, I., Bucur, M., Georgescu, B., Moise, D., Strat, V. A., & Zgură, I. D. (2020). Social media and IOT wearables in developing marketing strategies. Do SMEs differ from large enterprises?. *Sustainability*, *12*(18), 7292. https://doi.org/10.3390/su12187292

Mathur, G., & en Ghai, W. (2020). A totalitarian technique for wormhole detection using big data analytics in IoT network. *International Journal of Scientific & Technology Research*, *9*, 1672–1678.

Misra, N. N., Dixit, Y., Al-Mallahi, A., Bhullar, M. S., Upadhyay, R., & Martynenko, A. (2020). IoT, big data, and artificial intelligence in agriculture and food industry. *IEEE Internet of Things Journal*, *9*(9), 6305–6324. https://doi.org/10.1109/JIOT.2020.2998584

Moher, D., Liberati, A., Tetzlaff, J., & Altman, D. G., & PRISMA Group. (2009). Preferred reporting items for systematic reviews and meta-analyses: The PRISMA statement. *Annals of Internal Medicine*, *151*(4), 264–269. https://doi.org/10.7326/0003-4819-151-4-200908180-00135

Ng, I. C. L., & Wakenshaw, S. Y. L. (2017). The Internet-of-Things: Review and research directions. *International Journal of Research in Marketing*, *34*(1), 3–21. https://doi.org/10.1016/j.ijresmar.2016.11.003

Nguyen, B., & Simkin, L. (2017). The Internet of things (IoT) and marketing: The state of play, future trends and the implications for marketing. *Journal of Marketing Management*, *33*(1–2), 1–6. https://doi.org/10.1080/0267257X.2016.1257542

Page, M. J., McKenzie, J. E., Bossuyt, P. M., Boutron, I., Hoffmann, T. C., Mulrow, C. D., Shamseer, L., Tetzlaff, J. M., Akl, E. A., Brennan, S. E., Chou, R., Glanville, J., Grimshaw, J. M., Hróbjartsson, A., Lalu, M. M., Li, T., Loder, E. W., Mayo-Wilson, E., McDonald, S., & Moher, D. (2021). The PRISMA 2020 statement: An updated guideline for reporting systematic reviews. *International Journal of Surgery*, *88*, 105906. https://doi.org/10.1016/j.ijsu.2021.105906

Paiola, M., Schiavone, F., Grandinetti, R., & Chen, J. (2021). Digital servitization and sustainability through networking: Some evidences from IoT-based business models. *Journal of Business Research*, *132*, 507–516. https://doi.org/10.1016/j.jbusres.2021.04.047

Palmaccio, M., Dicuonzo, G., & Belyaeva, Z. S. (2021). The internet of things and corporate business models: A systematic literature review. *Journal of Business Research*, *131*, 610–618. https://doi.org/10.1016/j.jbusres.2020.09.069

Pillai, R., & Sivathanu, B. (2020). Adoption of internet of things (IoT) in the agriculture industry deploying the BRT framework. *Benchmarking: An International Journal*, *27*(4), 1341–1368. https://doi.org/10.1108/BIJ-08-2019-0361

Podsakoff, P. M., MacKenzie, S. B., Bachrach, D. G., & Podsakoff, N. P. (2005). The influence of management journals in the 1980s and 1990s. *Strategic Management Journal*, *26*(5), 473–488. https://doi.org/10.1002/smj.454

Princes, E., Manurung, A. H., So, I. G., & Abdinagoro, S. B. (2020). A closer look at the consumer conformity in industry 4.0: Purchase intention redefined. *Polish Journal of Management Studies*, *22*(1), 401–417. https://doi.org/10.17512/pjms.2020.22.1.26

Rana, S., Sakshi, & Singh, J. (2022). Presenting the POWER framework of conducting literature review. In *Exploring the latest trends in management literature* (pp. 1–13). https://doi.org/10.1108/S2754-586520220000001001

Rejeb, A., Simske, S., Rejeb, K., Treiblmaier, H., & Zailani, S. (2020). Internet of Things research in supply chain management and logistics: A bibliometric analysis. *Internet of Things*, *12*, 100318. https://doi.org/10.1016/j.iot.2020.100318

Rejeb, A., Suhaiza, Z., Rejeb, K., Seuring, S., & Treiblmaier, H. (2022). The Internet of Things and the circular economy: A systematic literature review and research agenda. *Journal of Cleaner Production*, *350*, 131439. https://doi.org/10.1016/j.jclepro.2022.131439

Rojas-Sánchez, M. A., Palos-Sánchez, P. R., & Folgado-Fernández, J. A. (2023). Systematic literature review and bibliometric analysis on virtual reality and education. *Education and Information Technologies*, *28*(1), 155–192. https://doi.org/10.1007/s10639-022-11167-5

Rymaszewska, A., Helo, P., & Gunasekaran, A. (2017). IoT powered servitization of manufacturing–an exploratory case study. *International Journal of Production Economics*, *192*, 92–105. https://doi.org/10.1016/j.ijpe.2017.02.016

Shah, R., & Chircu, A. (2018). IoT and AI in healthcare: A systematic literature review. *Issues in Information Systems*, *19*(3). https://doi.org/10.48009/3_iis_2018_33-41

Sivarajah, U., Irani, Z., Gupta, S., & Mahroof, K. (2020). Role of big data and social media analytics for business to business sustainability: A participatory web context. *Industrial Marketing Management*, *86*, 163–179. https://doi.org/10.1016/j.indmarman.2019.04.005

Sivathanu, B. (2018). Adoption of internet of things (IOT) based wearables for healthcare of older adults–a behavioural reasoning theory (BRT) approach. *Journal of Enabling Technologies*, *12*(4), 169–185. https://doi.org/10.1108/JET-12-2017-0048

Soriano, A. S., Álvares, C. L., & Valdés, R. M. T. (2018). Bibliometric analysis to identify an emerging area: Public relations intelligence—A challenge to strengthen technological observatories in the network society. *Scientometrics*, *115*(3), 1591–1614. https://doi.org/10.1007/s11192-018-2651-8

Sorescu, A., Frambach, R. T., Singh, J., Rangaswamy, A., & Bridges, C. (2011). Innovations in retail business models. *Journal of Retailing*, *87*, S3–S16. https://doi.org/10.1016/j.jretai.2011.04.005

Sula, A., Spaho, E., Matsuo, K., Barolli, L., Miho, R., & Xhafa, F. (2013, October). An IoT-based system for supporting children with autism spectrum disorder. In *2013 eighth international conference on broadband and wireless computing, communication and applications* (pp. 282–289). IEEE. https://doi.org/10.1109/BWCCA.2013.51

Suppatvech, C., Godsell, J., & Day, S. (2019). The roles of internet of things technology in enabling servitized business models: A systematic literature review. *Industrial Marketing Management*, *82*, 70–86. https://doi.org/10.1016/j.indmarman.2019.02.016

Tariq, B., Taimoor, S., Najam, H., Law, R., Hassan, W., & Han, H. (2020). Generating marketing outcomes through Internet of things (Iot) technologies. *Sustainability*, *12*(22), 9670. https://doi.org/10.3390/su12229670

Thongprasert, A., & Jiamsanguanwong, A. (2021). New product development processes for IoT enabled home use medical devices: A systematic review. *Engineering Journal*, *25*(2), 15–48. https://doi.org/10.4186/ej.2021.25.2.15

Tigre, F. B., Curado, C., & Henriques, P. L. (2023). Digital leadership: A bibliometric analysis. *Journal of Leadership & Organizational Studies*, *30*(1), 40–70. https://doi.org/10.1177/15480518221123132

Urrútia, G., & Bonfill, X. (2010). Declaración PRISMA: Una propuesta para mejorar la publicación de revisiones sistemáticas y metaanálisis. *Medicina Clínica*, *135*(11), 507–511. https://doi.org/10.1016/j.medcli.2010.01.015

Voulgaridis, K., Lagkas, T., Angelopoulos, C. M., & Nikoletseas, S. E. (2022). IoT and digital Circular economy: Principles, applications, and challenges. *Computer Networks*, *219*, 109456. https://doi.org/10.1016/j.comnet.2022.109456

Xu, M., David, J. M., & Kim, S. H. (2018). The fourth industrial revolution: Opportunities and challenges. *International Journal of Financial Research*, *9*(2), 90–95. https://doi.org/10.5430/ijfr.v9n2p90

Yerpude, S., & Singhal, T. K. (2018). Enhancing new product development effectiveness with internet of things origin real time data. *Journal of Cases on Information Technology*, *20*(3), 21–35. https://doi.org/10.4018/JCIT.2018070102

Zaid, M., Farooqi, R., & Garg, P. (2019). Understanding the influence of IoT advertising on The Customer choice: A conceptual framework. *CASS Studies*, *3*(1), 410. Addendum 7 (Special Issue).

Zhang, X., Estoque, R. C., Xie, H., Murayama, Y., & Ranagalage, M. (2019). Bibliometric analysis of highly cited articles on ecosystem services. *PLoS One*, *14*(2), e0210707. https://doi.org/10.1371/journal.pone.0210707

Zolkepli, I. A., & Kamarulzaman, Y. (2015). Social media adoption: The role of media needs and innovation characteristics. *Computers in Human Behavior*, *43*, 189–209. https://doi.org/10.1016/j.chb.2014.10.050

INDEX